GREEN WING

THE COMPLETE FIRST SERIES SCRIPTS

Dr. Alan Statham
Consultant Radiologist

GREEN WING
THE COMPLETE FIRST SERIES SCRIPTS

ISBN 1 84576 421 8
ISBN-13 9781845764210

Published by Titan Books, a division of
Titan Publishing Group Ltd.
144 Southwark Street
London
SE1 0UP

First edition October 2006
2 4 6 8 10 9 7 5 3 1

All photographs courtesy of FremantleMedia Limited/Channel 4, except those which appear on the front cover and pages: 8, 20, 30-31, 42, 67, 72-73, 76, 92, 98-99, 108, 138, 142, 156-157, 180, 196-197, 204, 209, 212, 226, 244-245, 248, 263, 268-269, 284, 296-297, 311 which are courtesy of Paul Rider (paulriderphotos.com).
Lines from 'All That She Wants' Words & Music by Buddha & Joke © Copyright 1992 Megasong Publishing, Sweden. Universal Music Publishing Limited. Used by permission of Music Sales Limited. All Rights Reserved. International Copyright Secured.
Lines from '(They Long To Be) Close To You' Words by Hal David. Music by Burt Bacharach. © Copyright 1963 Casa David Music Incorporated/New Hidden Valley Music Company, USA. Universal/MCA Music Limited (50%). Used by permission of Music Sales Limited. All Rights Reserved. International Copyright Secured.
Lines from '(They Long To Be) Close To You' Burt Bacharach & Hal David © 1963 New Hidden Valley Music. Used by kind permission from P & P Songs Ltd.
Lines from 'All By Myself ' Words & Music by Eric Carmen © Copyright 1975 & 1976 Eric Carmen Music, USA. Universal/Island Music Limited. Used by permission of Music Sales Limited. All Rights Reserved. International Copyright Secured.
Lines from 'The Greatest Love Of All' Words by Linda Creed. Music by Michael Masser. © 1977 EMI Gold Horizon Music Corp and EMI Golden Torch Music Corp, EMI Music Publishing Ltd, London WC2H 0QY (Publishing) and Alfred Publishing Co, USA (Print). Administered in Europe by Faber Music Ltd. Reproduced by permission. All Rights Reserved.
Lines from 'Chirpy Chirpy Cheep Cheep' Words by Giuseppe Cassia and Claudio Fabi. Music by Harold Stott © 1971 Gruppo Intersong S.r.l. and Warner/Chappell Italiana S.p.A., Italy. All rights administered by Warner/Chappell Music Ltd, London W6 8BS. Reproduced by permission.
Lines from 'Up Where We Belong' from the Paramount picture An Officer and a Gentleman. Words by Will Jennings. Music by Buffy Sainte-Marie and Jack Nitzsche. Copyright © 1982 by Famous Music LLC and Ensign Music LLC. International Copyright secured. All Rights Reserved.

Acknowledgments
Victoria Pile and Robert Harley would like to thank the following people: Gary's brother for info on the NHS. Gina and all at Basingstoke for letting us do everything we needed to. Cat Ledger for chasing us. Alison Denyer and Karen Clayton. Steve Rosier at Channel 4 press office. Special thanks to Caroline Leddy for massive support, understanding and contributions to writing process (as well as the rest). Also thanks to Katy Wild, Marcus Scudamore, Cath Trechman, Adam Newell and Bob Kelly at Titan Books.

The publishers would like to thank Victoria Pile and Robert Harley for their invaluable contribution to this book. Thanks also to Cat Ledger, Cathy McLoughlin, Karla Berry, Nick Irving, Ben Willis and Claire Fox for all their help, and to Ned Hartley for his kind donation.

What did you think of this book? We love to hear from our readers. Please email us at:
readerfeedback@titanemail.com or write to us at the above address.
You can also visit us at **www.titanbooks.com**

A CIP catalogue record for this title is available from the British Library.

Printed and bound by Butler & Tanner, Frome, Somerset, UK.

500 mL

GREEN WING
The Complete First Series Scripts

Created, produced and devised by
VICTORIA PILE

Written by

**Robert Harley, James Henry,
Gary Howe, Stuart Kenworthy,
Oriane Messina, Victoria Pile,
Richard Preddy, Fay Rusling**

Baxter

THE WRITING TEAM

VICTORIA PILE
(PRODUCER/WRITER)

In The Beginning...

Channel 4 asked if I could develop a comedy show that retained the comic sensibilities of *Smack the Pony* (observational, non-gender-aware jokes about hair, biscuits and shoes largely) but was altogether more mature as a format, with proper stories and characters that could sustain for longer than sixty seconds. So obviously I said no. In the end, however, I was persuaded to recruit a handful of the most depraved writers I could find – I shut them into quite a small room, and occasionally threw in a bag of Maltesers. I pretended they would all get a diamond or a jet-ski each, and a bushel of fresh stationery if they tried really hard to spin the Maltesers into gold. After several months we had a stack of paper with some cracking words on, albeit mostly rude ones. Lovely Patrick put them into red files, and we got cocky enough to invite some actors in to read it out loud. We threw most of it away, went back into 'the room' and finally after about ninety-two years we ended up with a sketch slash sitcom slash drama slash soap slash porn thing.

How I Write My Bits:

Coffee. Wine. Day dreaming. Pacing about. Imitating characters. Visualisation. Chair spinning. Ranting. Worrying. More wine. On the train. In my sleep. Beta-blockers. Banging head on door. Meetings. Listening to the voices. Always the voices...

STUART KENWORTHY

How Green Was My Wing

When I look back through the mists of time at the genesis of the *Green Wing* project, sitting as I am now on the sun-kissed island of Koorakiki in the South Pacific, I am filled with a certain fondness for a more innocent age-gone-by. As I recall, the brief was audaciously simple: to write a hospital-based comedy with a narrative structure, but which had scope for sketch-like material within. The process itself turned out to be equally simple: draw some carefully-plotted story arcs, ignore them, and spend the next two years writing 850,000 random scenes. They were marvellous days in the *Green Wing* writers' room; it was one big happy gang – we were like a family, always willing to help out a fellow scribe with a *bon mot* here, a witty stage direction there, a tip on the use of apostrophes or a friendly suggestion on the correct spelling of the word 'rabbit'. I forget the names of the other writers now, but I feel sure that they will have found happiness in whatever alternative career paths they have chosen, and who knows, if it hadn't been for the unpleasantness with the DVD contracts, some of us may even have been in touch with each other to this very day. I have to go now as Wayan is going to treat me to one of her incomparable massage therapies. See you in Zurich, perhaps.

ROBERT HARLEY

JAMES HENRY

How To Write An Episode Of *Green Wing*

– A game for around seven players, or 'writers'.

1. Sit around.
2. Sit around a bit more.
3. Drink coffee.
4. Say "Wouldn't it be funny if... oh, I've forgotten."
5. Wonder if you have any old *Smack the Pony* sketches you could recycle.
6. Realise you've already sent them to *Man Stroke Woman*.
7. Sigh.
8. Fret when one of the other writers suddenly starts typing with furious intensity.
9. Relax when you realise they're just bidding for a new sofa on eBay.
10. Another writer suggests a new detective series called *Wanking and Crying*, about Detective Sergeant John Wanking and his sidekick, Trevor Crying.
11. Start writing episodes of *Wanking and Crying* instead.
12. Producer comes in, everyone quickly changes the character names to 'Statham' and 'Martin', this seems to work.
13. Wonder which superhero ability would be better: flight or invisibility.
14. Decide on invisibility.
15. No wait, flight.
16. Producer announces they desperately need a scene in which Caroline has some emotional resolution with Mac in a way that satisfies the audience, but keeps them wanting more.
17. Instead, write a scene where Statham has a duel with Guy and accidentally cuts his hand off with a metal ruler.
18. Wonder why it sounds like things are being broken in Producer's office.
19. Remember something vaguely amusing that happened to self in 1997, change names so it happens to Caroline and Boyce instead.
20. Print out, double spaced so it takes up two pages.
21. Sigh again.
22. Go home.

Oriane's Top Tips

Base all characters on ex-lovers – reveal to your fellow writers all the weird things they did in bed... Steal funny lines you hear your mates saying down the pub... End every scene with a swear word... Write drunk – it makes everything funnier... Stalk an actor claiming it's research... Sleep with all the other writers to give yourself a sense of self-loathing and create an awkward atmosphere in the room which generates creativity... Put your name on other people's work... Write in the nude.

ORIANE MESSINA

RICHARD PREDDY

Richard's *Green Wing* Guide
– A typical writing day

10.00   James Henry arrives in *Green Wing* writing office, puts on headphones and does something complicated with emails and technology.

10.04   Fay Rusling and Oriane Messina arrive and search for leftover sweets from the day before.

10.06   Stuart Kenworthy arrives then instantly leaves again in search of breakfast that won't make his ears swell through allergies.

10.07   Victoria Pile and Rob Harley arrive, already on two phones and variously arranging casting, car services, contract wrangles and the removal of small whistle from child's nose.

10.09   Richard Preddy arrives. Lays hungover head on desk and quietly says "Mmm, nice and cool."

10.11   Stuart returns. Team lightly bicker and bitch. Small competition develops around trying to drive remote-controlled tractor into joke pair of pants.

10.20   Victoria rallies the writing team. They really do have to crack that tricky episode today otherwise — phone rings with props request for clarification re: prosthetic shoes.

10.21   Rob sits at computer with script document open. Underneath a website detailing arcane Scottish football statistics.

10.33   Various members sneak into other office to see which of their own material has been put in the 'OK' pile and which rejected.

10.35-11.29   Light to moderate bickering and bitching.

11.30   Various trips to loo, newsagent, fag breaks etc.

11.35   Richard says "I think I feel a bit better now" but is then forced to put head back on desk.

11.39   James tries to interest team in American TV show he saw about snowboarding Victorian elves.

11.41   Fay tells anecdote about the time she was on a theatrical tour with the man who has recently advertised pressure washers on Bid Up TV.

11.42   Victoria emerges with script for discussion. There is only one copy. Someone sent to photocopier.

FAY RUSLING

Fay's Random Memories

"Where are all the great scenes? What happened to Statham having an eighty-year-old wife? Or Martin selling his lungs?"

"In the pilot days the actors would come in and workshop the scripts. Steve and Julian (Guy and Mac) would spend most of their time trying to outdo each other – and the writers would shout out helpful suggestions, like 'do funnier impro'."

"Certain behaviour would define a character – we did a lot of work on each character's 'given' – or as Oriane thought at first, 'gibbon'..."

GARY HOWE

Photocopier broken. Someone sent out to photo-copy shop.

11.49 The musing about lunch begins.

11.59 Stuart draws a picture of a duck stabbing a weasel.

12.03 Rob leaves office, wearing reflective yellow bike gear. No-one knows why.

12.09 Oriane relates latest tale of insane neighbour. Stuart had a similar thing happen in Australia. Richard hasn't been listening. James pops out to buy comics.

12.28 Photocopied scripts return. They are not stapled. Slippery pile of paper inexorably collapses onto floor.

12.29 Someone incredibly important in the comp-any comes into office to find entire team scrabbling on floor with loose scripts. They leave again.

12.31 Member of cast turns up and says they'll wait on balcony.

12.32 Team realises no-one knows why cast member is there.

12.35 More diplomatic members of writing team sent to gently interrogate cast member who is unfor-tunately more interested in telling angry stories about agent.

13.00 Lunch. Team disperses and reconvenes with food. Emails checked and phone calls made.

13.40 Stuart's ears swell up.

14.00 Victoria gathers team. They really need to crack that episode. Someone suggests a white board would be useful. Someone sent out for white board.

14.01 The deafening drilling somewhere else in the building starts.

14.21 White board arrives. Victoria tests it by draw-ing obscene picture. Realises pen was perma-nent marker. Entire team starts giggling. James says "I came all the way from Cornwall for this."

14.22- 17.00 Team variously try to remember which episode this is, argue, bicker, fag breaks, toilet breaks, remote-controlled tractor breaks, realis-ing the cast member is still on the balcony breaks.

17.01 Team takes to computers.

17.04 Power cut.

17.11 Giggling about obscene drawing on whiteboard restarts.

17.25 Someone suggests opening some wine might help the process.

17.50 Meeting fragments in chaos.

17.55 Someone stands on remote-controlled tractor.

18.18 Team disperses.

EPISODE 1

WE CAN SEE A MAN'S LEGS — HE IS STANDING HIGH UP ON A LADDER WHICH IS LEANING AGAINST THE FRONT OF A HOUSE. ON THE SECOND BOTTOM RUNG OF THE LADDER SITS A TIRED AND FRUSTRATED CAROLINE TODD, BRUSHING HER TEETH. HER CAR IS PARKED WITH THE BOOT OPEN — BLACK BAGS AND HOUSEHOLD PARAPHERNALIA ARE SCATTERED AROUND.

CAROLINE: (ON MOBILE PHONE) Hello, it's Caroline Todd, again, it's now 7.09 am, so that's what, eight and a half hours since you claimed you were on your way home from the Pink Lagoon, and I'd have the keys to my brother's house before midnight.

SHE RINSES HER MOUTH WITH SOME TAKE-AWAY COFFEE AND SPITS IT OUT.

CAROLINE: (INTO PHONE) He said you were a bit of an unreliable neighbour, but luckily for me the man from number thirty-seven has a big heart and his own ladder.

▸▸ GARAGE FORECOURT

JOANNA CLORE IS TALKING TO A YAWNING SALESMAN. HE HAS A POLYSTYRENE COFFEE CUP IN HIS HAND. THEY ARE ASSESSING TWO SPORTS CARS.

CAR SALESMAN: Yeah, so as I was saying, the fuel consumption on both models is fairly similar, but the variable valve timing on the XK8 really helps acceleration at low speeds. Gives you that extra bit of wallop. In terms of litres, you can really do what you want, three point eight, three point nine, it's your call.

JOANNA: Yeah, yeah, yeah, yeah, but, you know, which one's going to make me look young?

CAR SALESMAN: Well... neither. They are both just cars.

JOANNA DOESN'T LOOK PLEASED.

▸▸ OUTSIDE THE HOUSE

CAROLINE SMELLS HER ARMPITS. SHE PULLS SOME DEODORANT FROM HER BAG — BUT IT'S EMPTY.

CAROLINE: (STILL ON MOBILE) I am starting a new job at 8.30 in a hospital. I am dirty and exhausted. People will possibly die as a result and you will be responsible.

▸▸ GARAGE FORECOURT

JOANNA: You know I could damage you quite badly for wasting my time?

CAR SALESMAN: Yeah.

SHE MESSES UP HIS HAIR, KNOCKS HIS GLASSES ONTO THE GROUND AND STORMS OFF.

▸▸ OUTSIDE THE HOUSE

CAROLINE: (TO MAN ON LADDER) Listen, thanks, thanks anyway, it was really kind of you for trying. (INTO MOBILE) And you'll be paying for a locksmith, all right?

CAROLINE STANDS UP AND TRIES TO PICK HER BAG UP BUT THE STRAP IS CAUGHT UNDER THE FOOT OF THE LADDER. SHE TUGS AND MANAGES TO FREE IT, BUT THE LADDER TOPPLES OVER AND THE NEIGHBOUR FALLS OFF.

CAROLINE: Oh, sorry! Er, don't try and move your neck. You'll be... you'll be fine. I'm a doctor.

SHE RUBS A CAR AIR-FRESHENER UNDER HER ARMPITS.

CAROLINE: Ah ah ah, I said don't move.

▸▸ GARAGE FORECOURT

JOANNA: In the meantime, I don't know if you ever go to the Winners Gym, but I'm there most Thursdays after six.

CAR SALESMAN: Right.

SHE DRIVES OFF.

▸▸ KIM AND ANGELA'S KITCHEN

DR ANGELA HUNTER IS EATING A GRAPEFRUIT, GASPING AT THE SOURNESS WITH EACH MOUTHFUL. HER FLATMATE, KIM ALABASTER, COMES IN WITH AN EYE PATCH OVER ONE EYE.

KIM: Morning.

ANGELA: What happened to you?

KIM: Don't say anything. I got sperm in my eye.

THEY BOTH EAT GRAPEFRUIT AND TAKE IT IN TURNS TO WINCE AT THE SOURNESS.

ANGELA: It's time to be off.

KIM BLOWS HER CIGARETTE SMOKE OUT AND ANGELA SUCKS IT IN.

▸▸ OUTSIDE THE HOSPITAL

AN AMBULANCE WITH LIGHTS FLASHING IS TRYING TO GET

PAST MARTIN DEAR ON HIS SCOOTER. MARTIN PANICS AND AS HE DESPERATELY TRIES TO GET HIS HAND SIGNALS RIGHT, THE ENGINE STALLS AND HE PULLS THE SCOOTER ONTO THE VERGE.

JOANNA'S CAR SCREECHES UP. SHE GETS STUCK BEHIND THE AMBULANCE BUT THEN DRIVES AROUND THE BARRIER AND INTO THE CAR PARK.

JOANNA: (OUT OF CAR WINDOW) Get out of my way, you great big piece of white shit!

CAR PARK SECURITY: (TO MARTIN) No, I'm sorry, you can't.

MARTIN: (ON SCOOTER) No, I have got to go through.

SECURITY: No, I'm sorry, we've gone over this many, many times.

MARTIN: Exactly.

SECURITY: You cannot go through.

MARTIN: Just open the barrier.

JOANNA PARKS HER CAR AND SENSUALLY RUNS HER FINGERS OVER THE BONNET AS SHE WALKS AWAY FROM IT.

CAROLINE: Can you just raise the barrier, because I'm working at the hospital and this is my first day...

SECURITY: Look, I'm sorry.

AS SHE GOES INTO THE HOSPITAL, JOANNA AUTOMATICALLY HANDS HER LIT CIGARETTE TO BOYCE, WHO IS COMING OUT.

JOANNA: Sorry to hear about your shower breaking, maybe you'd like me to come and test it some time.

BOYCE: I didn't know you could plumb.

JOANNA: Yeah...

AS SHE WALKS INTO THE BUILDING, RACHEL WALKS ALONG BEHIND HER WIGGLING HER BACKSIDE IN A SIMILAR — IF SLIGHTLY EXAGGERATED — WAY.

JOANNA: I know what you're doing Rachel.

RACHEL HEADS OFF DOWN A DIFFERENT CORRIDOR.

▶▶ CORRIDOR

MAC: Good morning.

ANGELA: Hello.

MAC: So, new doctor arriving today?

ANGELA: So?

MAC: Worried?

ANGELA: Why?

MAC: Female, apparently.

ANGELA: It was a fifty fifty chance.

MAC: She might be very good.

ANGELA: Let's hope so.

MAC: She might be stunningly attractive. And she could be tall, incredibly tall. Willowy. She may be intelligent, but humble. Men, women and small children will fall in love with her instantly. She might be Latin, olive skin, husky voice.

ANGELA: That'll be nice for everyone.

MAC: You put all these elements together, what have we got? We've got potentially, today in this hospital, a very tall, genius, woman-of-the-people, über-babe, Latino-chick coming to work here.

ANGELA: Will she be too tall to get through the doors?

MAC: Oh no, no. She'll be the perfect height.

ANGELA: Good. Well that's all tickety boo by me.

MAC: So, not even a flicker?

ANGELA: No.

MAC: Not even the tiniest bit?

ANGELA: No no no no no no, because jealousy is an ugly emotion and only for the weak.

MAC: Okay, what I want you to do, for me, just once, try it, pretend.

ANGELA: Why? Because it turns you on?

MAC: Yes. Please. For me.

CAROLINE ENTERS UNSEEN BEHIND THEM AS ANGELA GRABS A RATHER STARTLED MARTIN.

ANGELA: If you see the new bitch, snap off her fingers, burn her hair and pluck out her nipples!

MARTIN: Okay.

MAC: Yes! Fantastic. How did you feel? How did you feel? Dangerous? Liberating, yeah? Orgasmic?

ANGELA: Exhilarating in a dirty sort of way.

MAC: Hmmm.

ANGELA AND MAC GO.

A WORRIED-LOOKING CAROLINE COMES OVER TO MARTIN.

CAROLINE: Are you all right?

MARTIN: Oh yeah, yeah, there's a new female doctor coming today, that's all...

HE WALKS OFF, DROPPING HIS BELONGINGS REPEATEDLY ON THE FLOOR AS HE GOES.

▸▸ **OFFICE**

KAREN BALL IS GOING ROUND THE OFFICE WITH A BIRTH-DAY CARD AND PEN. SHE APPROACHES OLIVER.

KAREN: Do you want to sign Kerry's birthday card?

Kim,

Zoo contacted me about the hospital sponsoring an animal. Find out if we can sponsor the Ebola virus.

Joanna

OLIVER: No, not really.

KAREN: Do you want to make a contribution to the present?

OLIVER: No, not really.

SHE GOES UP TO KIM.

KAREN: Do you want to sign Kerry's birthday card?

KIM: Yeah, all right.

KAREN: Do you want to make a contribution to the present?

KIM: Who is Kerry?

KAREN POINTS OUT KERRY.

KIM: No.

JOANNA COMES FROM HER OFFICE INTO THE OUTER OFFICE.

JOANNA: Kim, Kim, Kimmy Kimmy Kim Kim Kim. Right, Wednesday's admissions list sooner rather than later please. I'd like to see an updated meetings diary.

KIM: Oh —

JOANNA: (CUTS HER OFF) Still talking Kim. Inform me when the new surgical registrar arrives, I'd like a chicken bhuna for one, can you book the car in for wheel alignment, can you please call the Aztec Centre and tell them it does not reduce puffiness — and coffee please. (NOTICING KIM'S EYE

PATCH) Have you gone blind?

KIM: It's conjunctivitis.

JOANNA GOES BACK INTO HER OWN OFFICE AS HARRIET SCHULENBURG ENTERS IN A RUSH.

HARRIET: I am so sorry I'm late, the traffic was awful this morning and I left in bags of time as well.

KIM: Oh well, don't worry. If I had to do a school run, I'd never get to work on time.

A LOOK OF HORROR SPREADS ACROSS HARRIET'S FACE AND SHE RUSHES OUT. THE OTHERS WATCH FROM THE WINDOW. THE THREE CHILDREN ARE PLAYING IN THE CAR PARK.

HARRIET: Come on now, back in the car, off to school, here we come, no time to chase you.

BOY: (HIT BY A SIBLING) Ow!

THEY ALL GET IN THE CAR AND DRIVE OFF, BUT HARRIET HAS LEFT HER BAG ON THE ROOF.

DR ALAN STATHAM ADJUSTS HIS CROTCH AND GOES INTO SUE WHITE'S ROOM.

SUE WHITE: Well, what can I do for you this time, Doctor Statham?

STATHAM: I'd like a new badge please.

SUE: May I ask what happened to the old one?

STATHAM: I've still got it. I'm sorry to report it's been vandalised by some bloody bastards!

SUE: In what way?

STATHAM: I'd rather not talk about it.

SUE: Well if you don't, I can't order you a new one.

STATHAM: And where does it say that in the regulations?

SHE GETS OUT A LARGE BOOK, THUMBS QUICKLY TO A PAGE AND POINTS, WITHOUT LOOKING AT THE PAGE.

SUE: There.

STATHAM: All right. Um... somebody has used a marker pen to make some alterations. The badge should read Dr Alan Statham, next line: Consultant Radiologist. And on the word 'Consultant', they've blacked out the letters O N S and L T A.

SUE: I see. So that would in fact leave... a C, a U, an N...

STATHAM: Yes, yes, yes, exactly. Yes.

SUE: And an, oh I see. So your badge now reads Alan Statham, Cu—

STATHAM: — Yes, thank you. That's what it's, that's what it's been changed to.

SUE: Again?

STATHAM: Yes, again.

SUE: Well, all right, I'll see what I can do. It's going to take a couple of weeks to order you a new one though.

STATHAM: Well, what — what am I going to do in the meantime?

SUE: Well, I suggest you black out the bits you don't want.

STATHAM: Well, then right, I will.

SUE: I'd lose the second line, rather than the first.

STATHAM: What?

SUE: Just trying to help.

STATHAM LEAVES AND THROWS THINGS AT HER OFFICE WINDOW IN THE CORRIDOR. HE STRIDES OFF, PULLS A DOOR, THEN REALISES HE HAS TO PUSH IT.

MARTIN IS WALKING DOWN THE HOSPITAL CORRIDOR. HIS WHITE COAT IS BUTTONED UP ON THE WRONG BUTTONS. HE ADJUSTS HIS COAT AND SEES A SMALL BOY IN BED IN A WARD. THE BOY HOLDS OUT SOMETHING TOWARDS MARTIN.

MARTIN: Is that for me? Oh thanks very much there, thank you. (HE LOOKS AT IT) Sweet. (HE PUTS IT IN HIS MOUTH AND SUCKS IT) Hmmm. Oh that's um, that's quite interesting. What is that? (THE BOY SHRUGS) You don't know?

CHILD: I found it in my bed.

MARTIN: Urrgh!

MARTIN SPITS OUT THE 'SWEET', DRINKS SOME OF THE BOY'S SQUASH AND LOOKS THREATENINGLY AT HIM AS HE LEAVES THE WARD.

JOANNA IS TAKING CAROLINE ON A TOUR OF THE HOSPITAL. THEY ARE IN A LIFT. JOANNA PULLS AT CAROLINE'S HAIR.

JOANNA: Could you say you were Asian? It would really help my end of year quotas, it's a bit hard to tell in this light, but no, I think we might get away with it. (SHE BANGS ON THE LIFT BUTTON) Come on, come on, come on, come on! Staff Liaison really ought to be here to sort out your bits and bobs...

CAROLINE: Oh yeah, talking about bits and bobs, I do have a bit of an accommodation problem...

JOANNA CUTS HER OFF AND SNIFFS.

JOANNA: Ah ah ah! Curious smell. Sort of... toiletty. Have you been to a festival?

CAROLINE: No, it's just I had to spend the night in my car, so —

JOANNA: (CUTTING HER OFF AGAIN) Ah! Walk and talk!

THEY GET OUT OF THE LIFT.

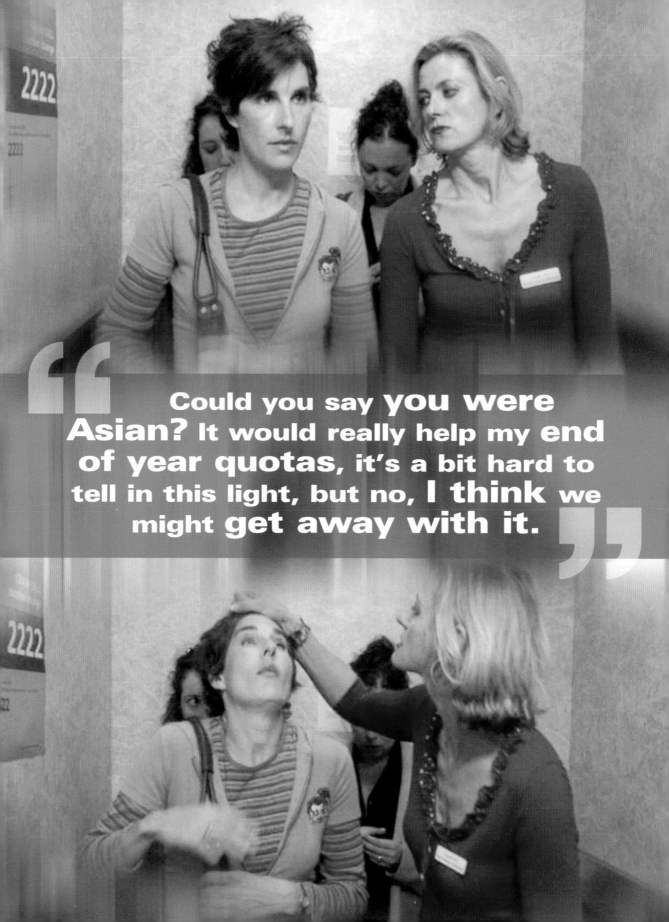

Could you say **you were Asian?** It would really help my **end of year quotas,** it's a bit hard to tell in this light, but no, **I think** we might **get away with it.**

DR STATHAM IS LECTURING TO SOME STUDENTS.

STATHAM: ...This is the same gall bladder and here we can see the small object has become dislodged and is now down here. This is what I like to call the Mick Jagger effect, because it is essentially... a rolling stone. Which is a joke, you may laugh.

SOME POLITE SMILING FROM EVERYONE EXCEPT BOYCE.

STATHAM: You're not laughing Mr Boyce.

BOYCE: That's because it wasn't funny.

STATHAM: Yes it was.

BOYCE: Not really.

STATHAM: I'll be the judge of that.

BOYCE: You can't be the judge.

STATHAM: Look, you only don't find it funny because you know very little about imaging techniques. When you've had as much experience as I have, you will find it funny.

BOYCE: I doubt it.

STATHAM POKES BOYCE AROUND THE FACE WITH HIS EXTENDABLE POINTER.

STATHAM: Hmm? Hmm? Ah ha.

BOYCE: You can't make me laugh by poking me.

STATHAM: Well just... Heed me. Hmm?

THEY ARE JOINED BY JOANNA AND CAROLINE, WHO ARE STILL ON THEIR TOUR.

JOANNA: And Radiology... (TO STATHAM) Sorry to interrupt you, I just wanted to introduce the new surgical registrar, Doctor um... Caroline...

CAROLINE: Caroline Todd.

JOANNA: Todd.

STATHAM: Doctor Alan Statham...

JOANNA: Doctor Alan Statham, yes.

STATHAM: Consultant Radiologist. Welcome to the lunatic asylum.

CAROLINE: "You don't have to be mad to work here, but it helps"?

STATHAM: Well no, come on, hang on now. The doctors

aren't mad here. I mean, that — that certainly wouldn't be allowed, not at my level. There again, we are an equal opportunities employer, so I dare say there might be one or two of the ancillary workers, or even some of the clerical staff who might be considered a little bit...

JOANNA: Oh dear God... Sorry, we're going to have to be moving along. So sorry to have disturbed...

STATHAM CARESSES JOANNA AS SHE LEAVES. JOANNA IS AROUSED.

STATHAM: I'm like a loaded catapult.

JOANNA: I can't talk right now.

STATHAM STROKES HER BUM — SHE SHIVERS WITH PLEASURE.

JOANNA: Ooooh...

GUY AND MAC COME ROUND A CORNER.

GUY: Have you seen them?

MAC: What?

GUY: The juniors, the students, Martin, Boyce, all of them?

MAC: Yeah, what about them?

GUY: Well a new woman turns up, right, a frankly pretty ordinary woman and they're all like bees round a honey pot.

MAC: No. No, bees make honey, don't they?

GUY: Yeah, so?

MAC: Yeah, so, so why are bees bothering with a pot of honey, yeah? Why not stay back at the hive, where there's as much honey as they could have, yeah? Yeah? Why flap all the way down to the supermarket, or somebody else's house, or wherever this honey pot is, when there's plenty of honey at home?

GUY: Yeah, all right, well flies round a honey pot then.

MAC: No, flies prefer shit.

GUY: Well wasps. The fact is, it makes men look like a sad, desperate species.

MAC: Right, so — what? You probably think that it would be better if everybody was a little bit more like you?

GUY: Well yeah.

MAC: Yeah, well no, because then of course there would be a great surge in lesbianism.

GUY: Bet you can't head-butt that sign.

MAC JUMPS UP AND HEAD-BUTTS ONE OF THE SIGNS HANGING FROM THE CEILING AS THEY WALK ALONG.

GUY: Yeah, well, that was actually quite an easy one.

GUY GOES TO HEAD-BUTT A SIGN AND MISSES. HE WHACKS ANOTHER HANGING SIGN WITH HIS HAND — IT FALLS TO THE FLOOR.

MAC: Nice.

MAC STRIDES OFF IN TRIUMPH AS GUY SHEEPISHLY PICKS UP THE SIGN AND STUFFS IT UNDER HIS WHITE COAT.

▸▸ **RADIOLOGY CORRIDOR**

STATHAM: No no no, but it is funny, you do see that, don't you?

ANGELA: Well it makes sense, a rolling stone.

STATHAM: Yes, thank you. I thought I was going mad for a minute there. (HE SPOTS MAC) Ah, you see Doctor MacCartney, some people do have a sense of humour.

MAC: Yeah, sorry, I'm with Boycie on this one. And Angela was just being polite.

STATHAM: Yes, well, who asked you anyway?

MAC: I think you did actually, about two minutes ago. Oh — any news on the other thing?

STATHAM: What other thing?

MAC: Whether or not moustaches are back in fashion yet? No, no news? You'll keep me posted, yeah?

STATHAM: Yes, and I'll let you know when they find a blonde who's got more than two brain cells to rub together.

A BLONDE NURSE WALKS PAST.

STATHAM: Not, not you...

HE SEES ANGELA HAS BLONDE HAIR.

STATHAM: Or you, obviously you've got lots. Well done. But you, Doctor MacCartney, are about as intelligent as a gracilis myocutaneous flap on a perineal hernia repair. (TO ANGELA) Banter.

MAC: Sorry, sorry — was that a come-back? It's not that I heard it, I was about twenty yards down the corridor, but Emma said something about you were talking to a light box?

STATHAM: Do you want me to report you for that earring?

MAC: Only if I can report you for the moustache.

STATHAM: Most women find male body-piercing repugnant. I, thankfully, am completely intact.

MAC: Well, even I draw the line at piercing arseholes.

STATHAM: Exactly.

DR MACCARTNEY GOES. STATHAM TURNS ANGRILY AS HE REALISES HE'S BEEN INSULTED AGAIN — TOO LATE.

ANGELA: Banter?

STATHAM: Yes.

▸▸ **STAFF LIAISON OFFICE**

MARTIN AND SUE WHITE PLAY IMAGINARY PING-PONG ACROSS THE DESK. THE IMAGINARY BALL HITS MARTIN ON THE FOREHEAD.

MARTIN: Ow.

SUE: When you're ready Martin.

MARTIN: Well... the patients don't like me.

SUE: Really? Anything else?

MARTIN: No.

SUE: Good. Well, don't hesitate to pop in again if there are any other worries.

MARTIN: What, is that it?

SUE NODS.

MARTIN: Will you go out with me?

SUE: No. Get out.

MARTIN GOES. SUE PLAYS ONE LAST IMAGINARY PING-PONG SHOT.

⏵ CORRIDOR

JOANNA AND CAROLINE ARE STILL ON THEIR TOUR OF THE HOSPITAL.

JOANNA: Oh, I love the smell of formaldehyde. I must say, you're not as young as I thought you'd be.

THEY COME ACROSS A CHILD-FRIENDLY MURAL, WHICH INVOLVES FURRY ANIMALS, A RAINBOW AND A POT OF GOLD.

JOANNA: Oh, my sainted lord in heaven, what is this bollocks?! (INTO HER WALKIE-TALKIE) Channel two? Yeah, I thought I said no more fucking rainbows! Yeah, over my rotting cadaver, I'd rather stick pins in my eyes, frankly. Can you deal with it?

⏵ STAFF LIAISON OFFICE

SUE IS ON THE OTHER END OF THE WALKIE-TALKIE. SHE MAKES DISTRESSED DOG YELPS, SHUTS THE WALKIE-TALKIE INTO A DESK DRAWER AND POINTS AT IT THREATENINGLY.

SUE: Sit!

⏵ BACK IN THE CORRIDOR

CAROLINE: I didn't think walkie-talkies were allowed in hospitals.

JOANNA: No, it's a talking pager.

CAROLINE: No no, it's a walkie-talkie. They're really dangerous, what with their potential interference with vital equipment.

JOANNA: Dangerous? Right, and I suppose a flood, or a patient on fire, or an outbreak of AIDS isn't dangerous, hmm?

JOANNA HITS CAROLINE OVER THE HEAD AS THEY WALK OFF DOWN THE CORRIDOR.

CAROLINE: Ow!

JOANNA: Just seeing how you deal with stress.

⏵ OFFICE

HARRIET: (ON PHONE) Yeah, um... give him some Calpol. Calpol. Yeah, it's in the cupboard next to the Bob The Builder pasta. Okay. Yeah. Paula, put him on to me... (CHILD-SPEAK) "Hello little man. Oh hello, have you got a hurty tummy? Have you? Where does it hurt? Oh poor little poot."

JOANNA WALKS PAST AND GRABS THE PHONE.

JOANNA: Nah nah nah nah nah nah! Me me me me me me. Oh just grow up!

SHE SLAMS THE PHONE DOWN AND GOES INTO HER OFFICE. HARRIET IS SHOCKED. SHE PICKS THE RECEIVER UP.

HARRIET: Hello? Paula?

KAREN: (ON PHONE) Can you send someone to fix the printer? It's jammed.

WE SEE HER HAIR IS STUCK IN THE PRINTER.

KAREN: It is quite urgent, yes. Thanks. Bye. (SHE PUTS THE PHONE DOWN) Ow...

▶▶ SECURITY

SUE IS SITTING BEHIND A SECURITY GUARD, AIMING A LARGE RUBBER BAND AT THE BACK OF HIS HEAD. CAROLINE COMES IN.

CAROLINE: Is this right for ID tags?

SUE: (JUMPING UP) Oh one sec, I'll do it myself, Security always chops heads off. Any chance you brought a photo?

CAROLINE: Oh no, no — should I have?

SUE: No, no, no problem, we can work with this. Just pop yourself up against the white wall for me would you?

CAROLINE POSES.

SUE: Gosh, aren't we a pale Janet? And — smile...

CAROLINE: Wait, no, wait. No, sorry, I haven't got the right face on.

CAROLINE SPENDS SOME TIME ADJUSTING HER HAIR. SUE GETS IMPATIENT.

CAROLINE: No wait, hold on. Um, sorry... can we do a kind of three-quarter profile? My hair's not really enjoying a full frontal approach.

SUE: Three, two, one.

SHE TAKES THE PICTURE.

SUE: I think that's a winner.

▶▶ COFFEE AREA

GUY IS HOLDING OUT A SPOONFUL OF GROUND COFFEE TOWARDS MAC.

GUY: I bet you can't eat the coffee.

MAC: I don't want to eat the coffee.

GUY: I bet you can't eat the coffee.

MAC: Why should I want to eat the coffee?

GUY: Eat the coffee!

MAC: No!

GUY: You can't eat it can you?

MAC: No, I probably could.

GUY: So eat it.

MAC: No, no, you eat the coffee.

GUY: All right, I'll eat it.

MAC: Yeah, go on then.

GUY: I will.

MAC: Yeah, go on, go on, eat the coffee. Eat it, go on.

GUY: Yeah, all right, well I'm going to eat, I'm going to eat the coffee.

MAC: Let's see you then, let's see you.

GUY PUTS THE SPOONFUL OF DRY COFFEE IN HIS MOUTH. HE PUTS ON A BRAVE FACE, BUT IT IS CLEARLY AN EXTREMELY UNPLEASANT EXPERIENCE.

MAC: Jesus!

GUY: I'm eating the coffee.

MAC: You are. You are, aren't you.

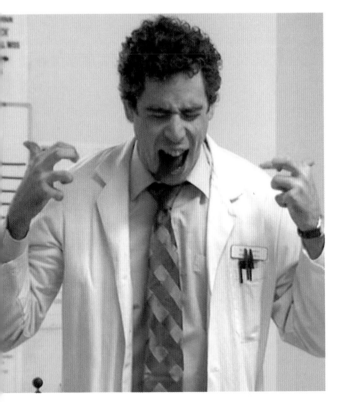

GUY: Hmm, I'm eating the coffee.

MAC: You are eating the coffee.

GUY: Hmm.

MAC: You are eating the coffee. You ate the expensive coffee.

GUY: I have.

MAC: Yeah, well done. Yeah. Do you know what that means? Do you know what the whole of that means?

GUY: Uh uh.

MAC: That means — that means that you won.

MAC WALKS OFF. GUY PULLS FACES AT THE DISGUSTING TASTE IN HIS MOUTH.

GUY: Hmmm... eurgh....

▸▸ **SECURITY**

SUE AND CAROLINE ARE LOOKING AT LOTS OF PHOTOS OF CAROLINE.

CAROLINE: I think I look like a moose in that. So I mean, well, that's a security risk, so... Do you think we could just have one more go?

SUE SIGHS.

▸▸ **COFFEE AREA**

GUY IS TRYING TO GET THE TASTE OF COFFEE OUT OF HIS MOUTH.

GUY: Right. Tea.

HE BREAKS OPEN A TEABAG AND POURS THE TEA LEAVES INTO HIS MOUTH. HE FINDS IT DISGUSTING AND SPITS.

GUY: Tea is horrible!

▸▸ **JOANNA'S OFFICE/STATHAM'S OFFICE**

STATHAM AND JOANNA ARE TALKING TO EACH OTHER ON THE PHONE.

STATHAM: Please, please, please!

JOANNA: Well, I may not be in the mood tonight. Perhaps if your girlfriend hadn't cocked up the mural.

STATHAM: But I'm a firework, I'm primed and ready to go off.

JOANNA: Well, then I shall retire to a safe distance, and possibly wear protective clothing.

STATHAM: I'm not wearing any pants...

BOYCE WALKS PAST IN EARSHOT.

STATHAM: ...So there it is, when, no, thank you sir. Yes. Goodbye to you.

HE PUTS THE PHONE DOWN.

JOANNA TAKES OFF HER BOOT AND SUCKS THE HEEL.

▸▸ CORRIDOR

GUY: It's forty-one feet of freedom, I guarantee it will change your life. It gives you the chance to breathe. It's moored on the Hamble.

NURSE: I get travel-sick, sorry.

THE NURSE GOES AND MARTIN JOINS GUY.

GUY: Ugly.

MARTIN: What? She was gorgeous.

GUY: Ugly. Deep down inside, ugly.

MARTIN: You know, I've never really even touched anyone that attractive.

GUY: Well, I don't mind you touching my arm if you want.

MARTIN: It's not quite the same is it? Oh — Path Lab alert!

THREE MEMBERS OF THE PATH LAB STAFF WALK PAST. MARTIN

AND GUY HOLD THEIR NOSES.

▸▸ OFFICE

JOANNA: Rachel, where's the hand-out for the meeting?

RACHEL: I haven't photocopied it yet.

JOANNA: Why not?

RACHEL: Because Oliver's using the photocopier. He's doing 500 fliers for some party he's organised.

JOANNA: He's using office equipment for his own personal use?

RACHEL: Yeah.

JOANNA: Go and kick him.

▸▸ WARD

GUY: Okay, I'll pretend I'm a woman and you come up to me, give me your best line, right.

MARTIN: Right, okay, best line. Hi, what's your name?

GUY: Rubbish.

MARTIN: Right. No. More adventurous... um, right. (PAUSE) Do you like swimming?

GUY: Pathetic. Get over there, get — Look, two things women want, okay? Money and protection.

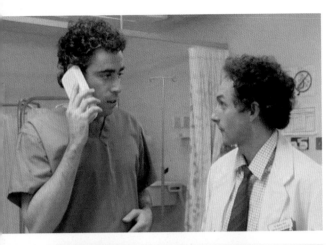

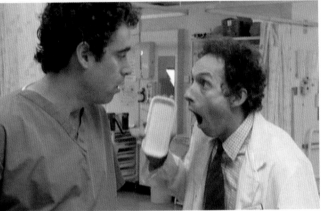

MARTIN: Well, I've got a helmet and a credit card.

GUY: Right.

MARTIN: So the two...

GUY: Why don't you shut up for a second and watch what I... You be the woman and I'm... Okay, ready?

GUY MIMES BEING ON A MOBILE PHONE.

GUY: "Er yeah, I'll see you in Zurich." (HE LOOKS AT MARTIN, AS IF STUNNED) No, and I've seen you, I'm so astonished by your beauty, I can't speak — you see?

MARTIN: Oh, okay. Why Zurich?

GUY: Because it sounds jet-setty, you know.

MARTIN: Oh right, because I've actually been to Katlic, so... It's in Holland.

GUY: Get on with it.

MARTIN: (INTO IMAGINARY PHONE) "Yeah, hello Mum, I'm

in Zurich..."

GUY: You're not, you're not in Zurich.

MARTIN DOES STUNNED FACE.

GUY: What is that?

MARTIN: That's — I'm looking — you're beautiful! You've caught me!

GUY: Well, all I caught from you is that you've got a coated tongue. What? That — what are you doing now? You look like you...

MARTIN: I'm just trying some looks.

GUY: Well, that's a look, you look like you've had your head beaten against a rock fifteen times.

▸▸ OFFICE

JOANNA COMES OUT OF HER OFFICE.

JOANNA: Now, please.

RACHEL: What?

JOANNA: Kick him, kick him, kick him.

RACHEL GOES OVER TO OLIVER AT THE PHOTOCOPIER. SHE KICKS HIM.

OLIVER: Argh! Fuck! That really hurt! What did you do that for?!

RACHEL: Um... Joanna told me to, sorry.

OLIVER: Hmm, it's all right, I guess you're just following orders then. Um — I just, um... wondered if you'd like to come out for a drink with me some time?

RACHEL: Um, okay.

OLIVER: Okay.

RACHEL: Oh, and just so you know, I always fuck on the first date.

OLIVER: Oh, okay.

RACHEL WALKS AWAY.

▸▸ CORRIDOR

GUY: You're a doctor, for God's sake!

MARTIN: So what?

GUY: So, you don't have to be good-looking, or charismatic. And, you know, women love it. Especially foreign girls.

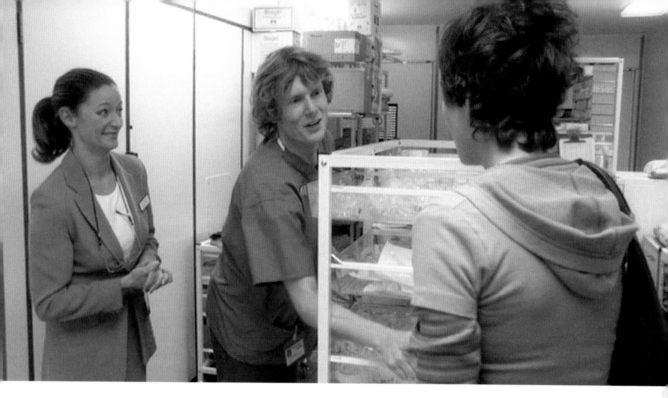

MARTIN: Oh, foreign ladies.

GUY: Yeah, especially Eastern Europeans, and they always look quite sad, don't they? Which gives it a certain something.

MARTIN: Oh, next you'll be telling me they're queuing up for threesomes.

GUY: Yeah, well actually threesomes are totally overrated.

MARTIN: Yeah, sure.

GUY: No, they are, think about it. When you've done the deed, it's just one more hairy Mary prattling on in your ear. Who can be arsed with that? Not me, for one. Go and have a wank in the cupboard, go on. I won't tell anyone, have a hand-shandy. Go on. Go on.

MARTIN STANDS IN THE CORRIDOR, AS GUY WALKS ON.

GUY: (SHOUTING) Martin's having a wank in the cupboard!

MARTIN: I'm not! (TO PASSERS-BY) I'm not.

▶▶ CORRIDOR OUTSIDE THEATRE

SUE ESCORTS CAROLINE UP THE CORRIDOR — SHE WIPES HER HAND ON CAROLINE'S BUM.

SUE: Sorry, it's just chocolate, chocolaty fingers. (THEY MEET MAC) Ah, Doctor MacCartney, listen, sorry to intrude, I know you're busy, but this is Henry's new surgical registrar, Caroline Todd. This is Doctor MacCartney.

MAC: Hi, Mac, call me Mac, hi.

CAROLINE: Hi. Any relation to — ?

MAC: Ringo Starr? No actually, but impeccable timing, because we're a pair of hands down on a routine hernia operation.

SUE: Woah dear, no! She hasn't had her pager yet.

MAC: Well then, that's good, because you won't be paged halfway through the operation.

SUE: What about her ID tags, thought about that?

MAC: Yeah, I can vouch for her ID. You definitely look like a doctor, yeah, dilated pupils, no sense of humour and what do you smell of? Is that minicabs?

SUE: (ADORINGLY) He's terrible!

MAC: Okay, let's go.

SUE: Go on, go on.

MAC: Come on.

DR MACCARTNEY THROWS A GOWN AT CAROLINE AND SHE FOLLOWS HIM INTO THE OPERATING THEATRE.

▶▶ OPERATING THEATRE, LATER

MAC: Okay, let's sew this mother up.

CAROLINE: Sorry if I seem a bit stressed out, I didn't sleep very well last night. (PAUSE) Mind you, I did have a rather disturbing lesbian dream.

GUY: Bingo.

MAC: (SYMPATHETIC) Aaah. Would you like to talk about it...?

CAROLINE: I don't really remember it.

MAC: Well — make it up?

GUY: Positions, numbers?

MAC: Numbers, positions.

GUY: Were they shaved?

MAC: Yeah, were they shaved?

CAROLINE: Perhaps I could try and have another one tonight, take a few notes, bring them in for you tomorrow.

GUY: Can you draw?

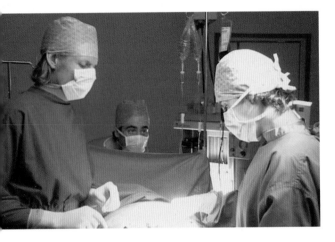

MOBILE PHONE RINGS.

GUY: (TO CAROLINE) Your shoes are ringing.

MAC: (TO GUY) It might be a lesbian.

CAROLINE — VERY EMBARRASSED — RETRIEVES HER PHONE AND CREEPS OFF INTO A CORNER.

CAROLINE: (WHISPERING) Hello?

GUY: Or the mother ship.

CAROLINE: Mum, you're going to have to stop phoning me at work.

GUY: Right, for a tenner, name me five famous lesbians.

MAC: Joan of Arc, Boadicea...

GUY: Boudicca.

MAC: Boudicca and the Brontë sisters.

GUY: You can't have the Brontë sisters.

MAC: Okay. Um, Martina Navratilova, K. D. Lang and...

CAROLINE: (ON PHONE) Yes, I'll have him put down.

MAC: The Queen of Lesbos.

GUY: Yeah, well — a name would be good.

MAC: Cassandra.

GUY: Cassandra.

MAC: Cassandra, yeah. Yeah.

GUY: Right, top-up time, how long do you need?

MAC: I think five minutes, thank you very much.

GUY: I bet you can't do it in three.

▸▸ **HOSPITAL GROUNDS**

THREE OF THE OFFICE GIRLS ARE EATING THEIR PACKED LUNCHES OUTSIDE.

KIM: God, how much do you need for lunch?

RACHEL: Well, I'm food combining. Crispy duck, shredded lettuce, rich plum sauce wrap and banana milkshake.

KAREN: Right.

KIM: How can you eat duck? That's so mean.

RACHEL: Why? I spent half my childhood feeding them.

KIM: What have you got Karen?

KAREN: Luncheon meat.

RACHEL: Eurgh, God!

KAREN: My friend made them.

KIM: Friend? Male or female?

KAREN: Male.

KIM: So what you're saying is, a man made your sandwiches this morning?

Guy's To Do List

1. THE NEW NURSE IN OBSTETRICS.
2. TELL EVERYONE ABOUT IT.

THAT'S IT.

KIM: God! Karen and sex.

KAREN: Not sex.

KIM: (CONFUSED) Not sex.

KAREN: No. He thinks we're not sexually compatible. We just lie together, naked.

▸▸ CANTEEN

MAC AND GUY ARE QUEUING AT THE HOT FOOD COUNTER.

GUY: I am starving. And they never give you decent portions here.

MAC: No, they do, you just have to be nice. If you flatter them, you'll have more food on your plate than you can ever deal with, it's very simple.

GUY: Yeah, and how do you flatter a woman like that? Nice overall. Ooh, what an alluring scent of fat. I've always admired career women such as yourself.

MAC: Yeah, that'll do, yeah.

CANTEEN WOMAN: What can I get you, love?

MAC: Hello. Hello. Um, well, oh crikey, the chilli looks fantastic, as ever. So does the steak and kidney pie also look tremendous. You're spoiling us today, as ever.

CANTEEN WOMAN: I could do you a bit of both if you want.

KAREN: Yeah.

RACHEL: Well? What's his name?

KAREN: Tim.

KIM: Tim? God! So is he your boyfriend?

KAREN: Don't know.

KIM: Don't know? Well have you slept with him?

KAREN: Slept, yes.

MAC: Could you? Could you? That would be brilliant, thank you.

CANTEEN WOMAN: Chips and peas?

MAC: Yes please. Brilliant. These are the best chips in the whole country. Superb chips. And always nice to have a little bit of glamour while you're dining. So...

CANTEEN WOMAN: There you go.

MAC: Great, thank you very much, thank you. You have a fantastic day now.

CANTEEN WOMAN: I will, same to you my love. Tara.

SMILES ALL ROUND. NOW IT'S GUY'S TURN.

GUY: I'll have the same as him please... my darling.

CANTEEN WOMAN: We're out of chilli.

GUY: You're joking? You only started serving about twenty minutes ago, you're out of chilli already? That is unbelievable! Never mind, I'll have some of that scrumptious looking pie and some chips and peas. Please. Great chips he said, and er... I love chips. Hmm.

THE WOMAN DOESN'T GIVE HIM MANY CHIPS.

GUY: You're looking very... fit.

SHE TAKES A COUPLE OF CHIPS OFF HIS PLATE.

GUY: Is that it? Pikey! The earrings are a dead giveaway. And I was going to say "see you around", but I don't hang out in gutters.

MAC USHERS GUY AWAY FROM THE COUNTER.

GUY: Oh, and when I said you were looking fit, I meant fat!

MAC: Yeah, I think you should bring packed lunches from now on.

▸▸ ADMIN OFFICE

MARTIN IS AT A COMPUTER, WITH BOYCE LOOKING OVER HIS SHOULDER AT THE SCREEN.

MARTIN: Oh yes!!

BOYCE: What?

MARTIN: Thank you!

BOYCE: What?

MARTIN: Mark Burgess sells fridges! Yes!

BOYCE: Who? Who's Mark Burgess?

MARTIN: Mark Burgess? Mark Burgess? Mark Burgess is like, school captain of everything — and now he sells fridges. Um — what does it say... (READS FROM THE SCREEN) "I'm a regional deputy director of a leading refrigerating manufacturer, I still have time for Sunday football and the occasional round of golf." Tosser! I win that one.

BOYCE: You win, how do you win, exactly?

MARTIN: Er, well, I think doctors are better than regional deputy directors. Er, you know, "Hello Mark, what do you do?" "Oh, well I sell fridges. What do you do Martin?" "I'm a doctor. Thank you, captain that you flidoid."

BOYCE: I think you've got a few unresolved conflict issues there, mate.

MARTIN: (STARING AT THE SCREEN) Oh you're joking!

BOYCE: What? What?

MARTIN: Adam Ross is a pilot.

BOYCE: Bastard!

MARTIN: I can't believe that.

BOYCE: Who's Adam Ross?

MARTIN: He was my best friend at school, now he's a pilot!

BOYCE: Shit!

MARTIN: Pilots are better than doctors, aren't they? They are, aren't they?

BOYCE: Yeah.

MARTIN: They're better than...

BOYCE: No, no, they're not. And, anyway, for all you know... People exaggerate — he could be a lonely alcoholic with diseases. People exaggerate, don't they?

MARTIN: Well that's true, yeah.

BOYCE: Yeah.

MARTIN: Yeah, he could, he could.

▸▸ CAR PARK

GUY: (ON MOBILE PHONE) Nobody buys a jet-ski, you hire them, you tosser. How are you going to get it there? (PAUSE) No, trust me. No airline in the world will let you take a jet-ski.

HE SPOTS CAROLINE RUMMAGING IN THE BOOT OF A CAR WHICH IS CRAMMED WITH ALL HER WORLDLY POSSESSIONS.

GUY: Um, look, I'm going to call you back. See you in Zurich. (HE PUTS THE PHONE AWAY AND GOES UP TO CAROLINE) How are you doing? Are you all right there?

CAROLINE: I'm fine, I'm just getting a change of clothing.

GUY: Need a hand?

CAROLINE: I think I can manage to get dressed by myself, thank you.

GUY: No, I meant with the bike.

HE POINTS TO AN EXERCISE BIKE THAT SHE HAS UNLOADED.

CAROLINE: Yeah, I know you did.

GUY: Impulse buy was it?

CAROLINE: Well, I will use it, it's just that...

GUY: Do you always carry so much stuff with you?

CAROLINE: Oh look, Mr Questions, I can't get into my house until tomorrow! My life is in this car.

GUY: I haven't got anything to honk with.

CAROLINE: What?

GUY: Your sticker. "Honk me to bonk me."

CAROLINE: Oh God no, that's not my sticker. Um, it's not my car, you know, I borrowed it from a friend, you know, because, you know, it takes more stuff. I'm — I'm Caroline by the way.

GUY: I know. (HE SINGS THE RING TONE FROM CAROLINE'S MOBILE PHONE)

CAROLINE: Oh God, you weren't there, were you? Anaesthetist?

GUY: Guy Secretan. It's Swiss.

CAROLINE: Ah, cuckoo clocks, no beaches. Theft of Jewish gold after the fall of Nazi Germany. Sorry, I expect everyone says that.

GUY: No. So, where are you going to sleep tonight? (LOOKS IN THE BOOT OF THE CAR) In between the wine rack and the lava lamp?

CAROLINE: I'm still working on it. I expect there'll be a hotel somewhere.

GUY HOLDS OUT SOME KEYS.

CAROLINE: What — you own a hotel? Bloody hell!

GUY: No no no, it's a flat, it's my flat, you can stay there.

CAROLINE: At your flat?

GUY: No, I know what you're thinking, don't worry, I'm on nights. I won't be there. It's a spare room, clean sheets.

CAROLINE: Oh no, I can't do that.

GUY: I use Bounce.

CAROLINE: I bet you do.

GUY: Toblerone in the fridge.

CAROLINE: I couldn't, I couldn't do that.

GUY: Barry White.

CAROLINE: In the fridge?

GUY: He's very sweaty otherwise. Yes?

CAROLINE: I am quite tempted.

GUY: How tempted out of ten?

CAROLINE: Well I said...

GUY: Out of twelve?

CAROLINE LAUGHS.

GUY: Yeah, you see, you've got a lovely smile when you do that.

CAROLINE: When I what?

GUY: When you smile.

CAROLINE: I've got a lovely smile when I smile?

GUY: Yes.

▶▶ ADMIN OFFICE

MARTIN IS STILL AT THE COMPUTER WITH BOYCE.

MARTIN: Oh, Sally Dalton works for Asda, thank you God!

BOYCE: Yes!

MARTIN: Oh fucking brilliant, she wouldn't kiss me at school and now she works for Asda.

BOYCE: Good!

MARTIN: That is poetic justice.

BOYCE: Yes.

MARTIN: (RAPPING) So you want a career, you've got to get with Martin Dear, but only if you're a lady, because I'm not queer. That's a rap. My name is — oh! My name is — oh! My name is — Martin! ...I've got to go.

AS MARTIN GOES, BOYCE READS THE COMPUTER SCREEN.

BOYCE: "Martin Dear... I am a senior doctor at a large teaching hospital, but I still find time to spend with my young Brazilian wife and two beautiful children; not to mention my collection of classic British sports cars." You twat! Go...

THE RIGHTFUL COMPUTER OPERATOR RETURNS TO HIS DESK — HE LOOKS DISAPPROVINGLY AT BOYCE.

BOYCE: I'm going. Yeah, I just came to get this bit of paper. (GETS UP AND CALLS AFTER MARTIN) Oi, twat!

▶▶ LIFT

HARRIET AND KAREN COME OUT OF THE LIFT — HARRIET IS CRYING.

KAREN: What? What's the matter?

HARRIET: I haven't had sex since Oscar was born and then last night Ian touched my boob during *Frost* and then his mother phoned in the middle of it and interrupted.

KAREN: Oh, I'm sorry.

HARRIET: Oh no, don't be. I had a twinge down there, it was wonderful!

▸▸ **STAFF LIAISON OFFICE**

GUY: Fucking Mac! I know he fucking gets to the fucking canteen before me and he takes all the fucking jelly and hides it because he knows I fucking like it! What are you going to fucking do about it?!

SUE: Well you can have mine.

SHE PRODUCES A JELLY FROM HER DRAWER.

GUY: This doesn't mean that it's over.

HE SHOVELS THE JELLY INTO HIS MOUTH.

GUY: The fucker's going to get it!

SUE: Get out.

GUY: What?

SUE: Out.

HE GOES.

SUE: Wanker.

▸▸ **POST ROOM**

RACHEL IS WEIGHING HER BREASTS ONE AT A TIME ON SOME SCALES. MARTIN ENTERS.

MARTIN: I wasn't prying — I didn't — you were... It's just, I wasn't, I'm not even — I don't know what you're doing, so...

RACHEL: Okay. I'm just weighing my breast.

MARTIN: Right.

RACHEL: That's one point two kilos, so if I was going to post it in the UK, that would be £4.56, or to Europe, £6.12. Have you got anything you want to weigh?

MARTIN: No, no, no. Just... What, you mean my penis?

RACHEL: Well, you could do, I suppose. See how much it would be to post. I'd say 28p UK, or 68p Australia.

MARTIN: 28p?

RACHEL: That's light.

MARTIN: Right.

RACHEL: But I mean, if you want to just pop it on the scales, I'd be happy to...

MARTIN: Hmm, no, because I'm going to, well I've got scales at home, I'll weigh it on them, so I'll just...

RACHEL: What are you doing anyway?

MARTIN: I'm lurking about, yeah. I'm not... Hey, maybe you and your one point two kilograms would like to come out for a drink with me?

RACHEL: No.

MARTIN: No. Right.

▸▸ **CORRIDOR**

STATHAM AND SUE WHITE ARE WALKING QUICKLY, WITH

STATHAM TRYING VARIOUS WAYS TO PREVENT HER GOING ANY FURTHER.

STATHAM: No, no, no, no!

SUE: But the bottom line is, she asked me to deal with it!

STATHAM: Yeah, well, if you'll just wait!

SUE: I haven't got time for this, Doctor Statham.

STATHAM: Yes, well, it will free up more of your time if you just leave it to me to deal with it.

SUE: Yes, well, as I say, I was only following Joanna's instructions.

STATHAM: Yes, and I am only trying to help!

SUE: Yes, well, let me handle it!

STATHAM: Well look, patient welfare is my responsibility...

SUE: Exactly, and this is a wall, not a patient!

STATHAM: Yes, but the wall affects the patient, psychologically.

SUE: No, I haven't got time for this, I'm afraid.

STATHAM: I'll deal with it.

STATHAM PUSHES HER SHOULDER.

SUE: Did you just push me?

STATHAM: No, no. It wasn't a push.

SUE: You did, you pushed me.

STATHAM: No no, it wasn't a push, it was just a, just a...

HE PUSHES HER AGAIN AND TOUCHES HER BREASTS.

SUE: Oh!

STATHAM: Sorry, that...

ANGELA AND BOYCE COME OUT OF A WARD AND INTO THE CORRIDOR.

ANGELA: Are you all right Suse?

SUE: He just pushed me.

STATHAM: No, Doctor Hunter, it wasn't a push.

ANGELA: Did you just push her?

STATHAM: No, no, it wasn't a push, she was just trying to squeeze past there.

ANGELA: But did you actually push her?

STATHAM: No, as I say, as I say, it, it, well, it wasn't, it wasn't so much a push, it was, it was actually self-defence.

ANGELA: Self-defence?

STATHAM: Yes.

SUE: He pushed me twice.

BOYCE: He does hit people.

STATHAM: You — you can go away!

ANGELA: Did you just push her twice?!

STATHAM: No, no, that, that was just merely, merely a demonstration...

ANGELA: Of what?

STATHAM: Of, well, of the first p— u—, pu, p— pat.

ANGELA: Pat?!

BOYCE: By "pat" — you mean push?

STATHAM: No.

SUE: Yes.

BOYCE: Well you do find when people are bullied, it often creates a cycle of violence.

STATHAM: I don't think I have to remind everybody here that I have seniority!

SUE: (TO THE OTHERS) Yeah, well, why do you behave like

a five-year-old then...

STATHAM: I heard that!

STATHAM HITS HER PONY TAIL.

SUE: Did you just touch my squirrel?

STATHAM: No.

SHE WALKS OFF DOWN THE CORRIDOR. STATHAM REMEMBERS HE IS SUPPOSED TO BE TALKING ABOUT THE MURAL AND RUNS AFTER HER.

STATHAM: But the point is, the point is...

▸▸ WARD

THE MAN WHO FELL OFF THE LADDER IS ON A HOSPITAL TROLLEY, BADLY INJURED. CAROLINE HAS A BALLOON FOR HIM.

CAROLINE: Hi. I am so sorry, I hear they're keeping you in for mild observation. It's probably only concussion, but if there's anything I can do. Sorry.

MAC COMES OVER TO HER WHEN SHE HAS LEFT THE PATIENT.

MAC: Hi, listen — just so as you're not out of step with everybody else, yeah — in this hospital very few of us actually give presents to the patients at the end of the day. I mean, obviously it is your decision, but apart from anything else, it will cost you a fortune. So you know, I mean God knows, I know, it's so easy to get involved.

CAROLINE: Get off me, I know this man. He tried to break into my brother's house.

MAC: Right, thank you, yeah, cool, that makes everything a lot clearer, thanks.

BOYCE: Martin! Consuela called, left a message, urgent.

MARTIN: Who?

BOYCE: Consuela? Your young Brazilian wife? Something about your 1957 Jaguar being delivered?

MAC: Martin, Martin, see this? (HE HOLDS OUT A FILE) Is that your — is that your signature?

MARTIN: Yeah, it is, yeah.

MAC: Yeah, can't really do smiley faces on death certificates, it does look a little bit insensitive, okay?

MARTIN: All right.

MAC: Do you want to just sort that? Thanks mate.

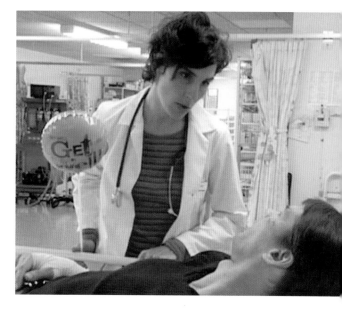

▸▸ JOANNA'S OFFICE

JOANNA: (ON THE PHONE) Well, I think we'll have time to sort that out at the meeting, don't you? Yeah. Yeah. Yeah, I'll fix that, bye.

STATHAM COMES TO JOANNA'S OFFICE ON THE PRETEXT OF RETURNING A PEN.

STATHAM: Um, is Aphrodite in for her Apollo?

JOANNA: Well I'm up to my neck in vacancy factors at the moment.

STATHAM: (FOR THE BENEFIT OF THE OFFICE GIRLS) Yes, yes, well there's the pen.

STATHAM DELIBERATELY DROPS THE PEN, AND HE AND JOANNA GROPE EACH OTHER AS THEY PRETEND TO LOOK FOR IT.

STATHAM: I do beg your pardon.

THEY CARRY ON FUMBLING.

STATHAM: So, um...

JOANNA: Er yeah, sort it yourself. If you could...

STATHAM: Good. That's more or less...

JOANNA: I think you've covered it really.

STATHAM: Yes, I think, and perhaps further...

JOANNA: Fine, that's fine.

STATHAM: As it t'were.

▸▸ **STAFF LIAISON OFFICE**

STATHAM: Well, a friend of mine is... is having a relationship with another friend of mine, and... the er... the second friend... doesn't want anybody to know. And the first friend... wants to shout from the rooftops, you know, "I love you! I need you! Purr!" But obviously, the first friend would, I think, prefer something a little more reciprocal, and... so this leads to...

HE PAUSES FOR QUITE SOME TIME.

STATHAM: ...a great deal of frustration.

SUE: Yes. Well. Have you discussed it with Joanna?

STATHAM: Oh! (SUDDENLY LOOKING OUT OF THE WINDOW) Is that —? Good heavens! There's a grebe, is it? No, no, tufted duck, I think, perhaps. Redshank. Um. Hmm.

HE SIDLES OUT.

SUE: Fuck off!

▸▸ **CORRIDOR**

JOANNA WALKS PAST A BED — SHE STOPS AND GOES UP TO IT. SHE TURNS ON A SWITCH AND THE BED STARTS TO VIBRATE.

LIAM: I had a very good day. Did you?

ANGELA: Yeah, I had a good day, yeah. I missed you.

LIAM: I missed you.

ANGELA: I missed you. I missed you. I missed you and your nose.

LIAM: Yeah, my nose misses you.

ANGELA: I love your little nose.

LIAM: Yeah, my little nose.

ANGELA: Your little button nose.

LIAM: It's not that little though.

ANGELA: A little button nose, a little bit on the end. A little ping pong ball on the end. Look, boing, boing, boing, boing, boing, boing...

LIAM: Yes. Hmm.

THEY MAKE MORE "NOSE" NOISES.

LIAM: Ah, that's better.

ANGELA: Lovely little nose.

SHE RUBS HERSELF AGAINST IT AND THEN LIES FACE DOWN ON IT. HER BODY TREMBLES AND JUST AS THE PLEASURE STARTS TO GET INTENSE, A NURSE COMES PAST, SO SHE QUICKLY JUMPS UP, SWITCHES IT OFF AND PRETENDS SHE WAS MERELY TESTING IT.

JOANNA: Oh yes, that seems to be working very well.

▸▸ **CAR**

ANGELA GETS INTO HER BOYFRIEND LIAM'S CAR.

ANGELA: Hello Liam.

LIAM: Hello Angel.

ANGELA: Did you have a good day?

> Harriet,
>
> One of your children called (no idea which one), he's trapped in something. Down a well? Hard to tell – poor signal, screaming etc. You can call them at lunchtime but NOT before.
>
> Joanna

LIAM: Yeah, more kisses. Hmm.

ANGELA: Hmm. Sweetie little nose.

LIAM: Yeah, but quite manly as well.

ANGELA: Little nose.

LIAM: Quite manly.

ANGELA: Little nose.

LIAM: Oh yes.

ANGELA: You should get the kink taken out of that. Then it would be perfect. Only cost you about a grand. Come on, let's go.

THEY DRIVE OFF.

▸▸ GUY'S FLAT

CAROLINE COMES INTO GUY'S FLAT AND LOOKS AT SOME OF HIS THINGS.

SHE IMAGINES HIS VOICE:

GUY V/O: No no no, it's a flat, my flat, you can stay there...
Guy Secretan, it's Swiss...
Clean sheets...
There's Toblerone in the fridge...

SHE GOES TO THE TOILET.

▸▸ BAR

GUY IS BY THE BAR, PLAYING WITH HIS PHONE. MARTIN COMES IN.

GUY: Smacka-ma-bitchup, I smacka... Oh! Hello? Hi. Hey...

MARTIN: Hi Guy.

GUY: Hi.

MARTIN: You don't often honour us with your presence in here.

GUY: Yeah, that's because it's full of people like you. I'm killing time.

MARTIN: Right. (TO THE BARMAN) Um, can I have my usual please? Er, my usual pint of Guinness that I usually have, because I love Guinness. So that's um... Why are you killing time?

GUY: If I go back too early, then my prey will have a chance to make another plan and escape. I go back too late and she'll be asleep. Timing is crucial.

MAC JOINS THEM.

MARTIN: That's fantastic. I haven't a clue what you're on about, but that is... (TO MAC) He's got prey.

MAC: Really? Has he? Great.

MARTIN: 'King great, mate.

MARTIN TRIES TO HIGH-FIVE GUY.

GUY: Don't.

▸▸ GUY'S FLAT

CAROLINE FLUSHES THE TOILET — WITHOUT SUCCESS.

CAROLINE: Go down will you!

SHE SPRAYS AIR FRESHENER.

SHE STABS AT THE BOWL WITH A COAT HANGER AND THEN A SKI.

CUT TO:

▸▸ BAR

MAC: So tell me, why are you wearing a blouse?

GUY: What?

MAC: It's a blouse, isn't it?

GUY: Fuck off! It's designer.

MAC: What, Laura Ashley? Are those roses?

GUY: No. (TURNING TO MARTIN) Well?

MARTIN: Blouse.

MAC: Blouse.

GUY: Fuck!

MAC: A blouson.

GUY: You are a ginger.

MAC: I am a fraise blonde.

GUY GOES. MARTIN SIPS HIS GUINNESS, AND IT CLEARLY CAUSES HIM CONSIDERABLE DISCOMFORT.

MARTIN: Ooh... oh that's lovely.

MAC: You get used to it.

MARTIN: Yeah, one of my favourite drinks. (TO BARMAN) Can I have a Britvic chaser then, with that please?

▶▶ GUY'S FLAT

CAROLINE IS TRYING A FOOD WHISK, SCISSORS AND SKI POLE IN THE TOILET. NOTHING WORKS.

CAROLINE: Aaargh!

▶▶ BAR

JOANNA AND STATHAM ARE SITTING AT A TABLE, HAVING A DRINK.

STATHAM: I mean, you've got a super vagina.

JOANNA: Yeah, thanks.

STATHAM: You're supposed to say something.

JOANNA: Why?

STATHAM: Well, you know, it's... it's always me, you know, saying the nice things about you.

HE GIVES HER A QUICK GROPE.

STATHAM: It might be nice if you, you know... reciprocated.

JOANNA: All right. Um... You're — er...

STATHAM: Ah ha.

JOANNA: No, sorry, I can't think of anything.

STATHAM: No, that's a joke, yes, I can see the funny side of that, that's er... no but seriously, it might be nice to get a bit of feedback. The same goes for our physical relationship, it's er... I never get serviced, you know, it's always me, you know, servicing you.

JOANNA: Ooh, servicing?! Oh God, you make me sound like a Ford Mondeo. Do you think I need my exhaust checking then?

STATHAM: Well yes, it might be nice if I had my exhaust pipe checked every now and again.

JOANNA: Yeah, well, that wouldn't take long would it? That would be a job for Very-Kwik-Fit.

STATHAM: There's — that's a joke of size isn't it?

JOANNA: I don't know, you tell me, you're the joke expert.

STATHAM: Yes, yes I know. I know. Though obviously I am not concerned, I have seen many a cock... cocky... I am a doctor.

JOANNA: Well yeah, radiologist.

STATHAM: Well, I've seen quite a few.

JOANNA: What, x-rays? Sort of — pictures of cockies?

STATHAM: How does it compare?

JOANNA: To what? A gherkin? Baseball bat? Twiglet?

STATHAM: Other people's?

JOANNA: Oh for heaven's sake!

STATHAM: Well, come on, I'm a grown-up, I can take the truth.

JOANNA: All right. I'd say you're um... slightly below average.

STATHAM CONSIDERS THIS FOR A MOMENT.

STATHAM: And you've got shit tits!

SHE PUTS HER CIGARETTE IN HIS COCKTAIL, THEN CHECKS OUT HER TITS.

▸ GUY'S FLAT

CAROLINE, WEARING A TEA TOWEL OVER HER NOSE AND MOUTH, IS HOLDING A SKI POLE. GUY BREEZES IN.

GUY: Hi, I'm back! You won't believe the day I've had.

CAROLINE: (SHOCKED) I thought you were going to be on nights!

GUY: (INSPECTING HER FACE MASK) Oh, spotty chin skin, or Ramadan? Spotty chin skin. Fancy a drink? I know I do.

CAROLINE: (PULLING DOWN THE TOWEL) I said, I thought you were going to be on nights.

GUY: Yeah, so did I, it's such a boring story, I won't bore you with it. Now, a little white wine, or some Bollinger? You look like a Bolly dolly. Oh — my ski pole, now that's...

CAROLINE: Don't touch that end.

GUY: Are you telling me how to hold a ski pole?

CAROLINE: No, no no no. I'm just a little bit confused. Partly because you said you were going to be on nights, and partly because you said you had a spare room.

GUY: The spare room has gone? Phone, phone the police, I'll... We're looking for a man with a spare room and a bottle of Bollinger.

CAROLINE: Look, you said you had a spare room and you don't. That was a lie!

GUY: No, I've got a spore room. I keep, I collect spores from all over the world, I keep them in a, in a drawer actually, in a spore drawer.

CAROLINE: I'm going.

Handwritten note:

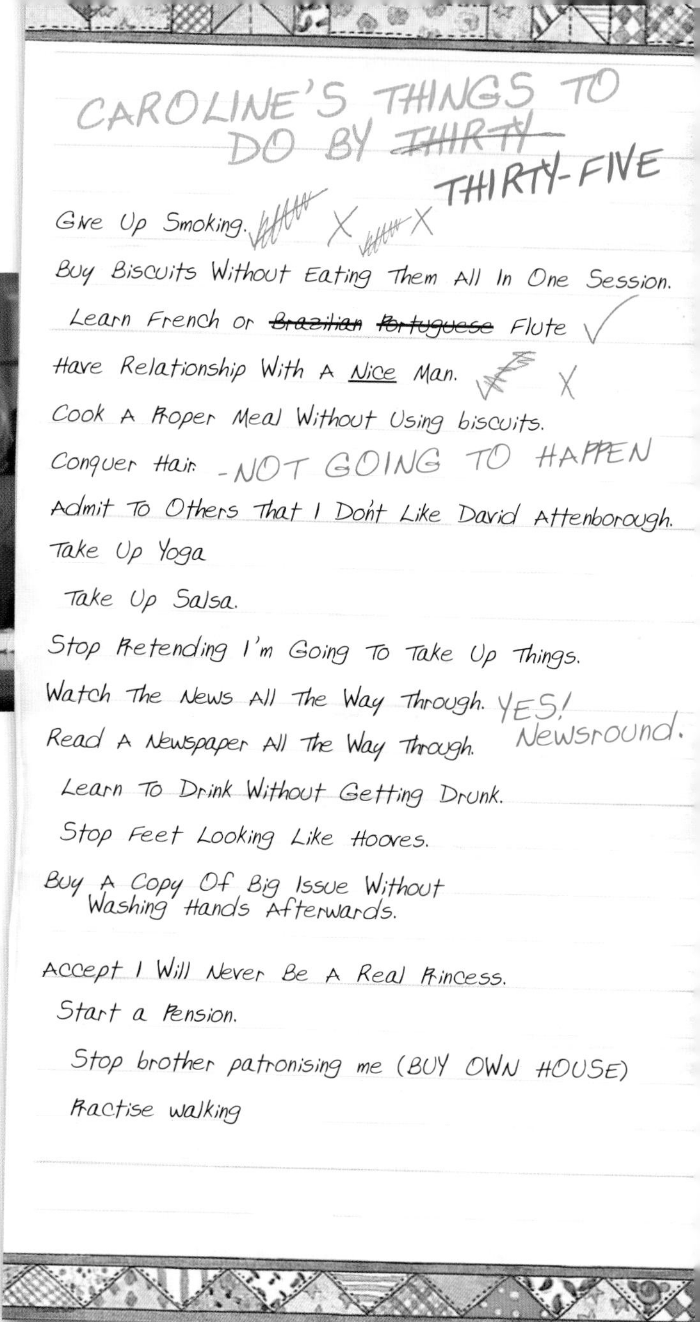

CAROLINE'S THINGS TO DO BY ~~THIRTY~~ THIRTY-FIVE

Give Up Smoking. ✓✓✓✓✓ X ✓✓✓ X

Buy Biscuits Without Eating Them All In One Session.

Learn French or ~~Brazilian Portuguese~~ Flute ✓

Have Relationship With A Nice Man. ✗ X

Cook A Proper Meal Without Using biscuits.

Conquer Hair. - NOT GOING TO HAPPEN

Admit To Others That I Don't Like David Attenborough.

Take Up Yoga

Take Up Salsa.

Stop Pretending I'm Going To Take Up Things.

Watch The News All The Way Through. YES! Newsround.

Read A Newspaper All The Way Through.

Learn To Drink Without Getting Drunk.

Stop Feet Looking Like Hooves.

Buy A Copy Of Big Issue Without Washing Hands Afterwards.

Accept I Will Never Be A Real Princess.

Start a Pension.

Stop brother patronising me (BUY OWN HOUSE)

Practise walking

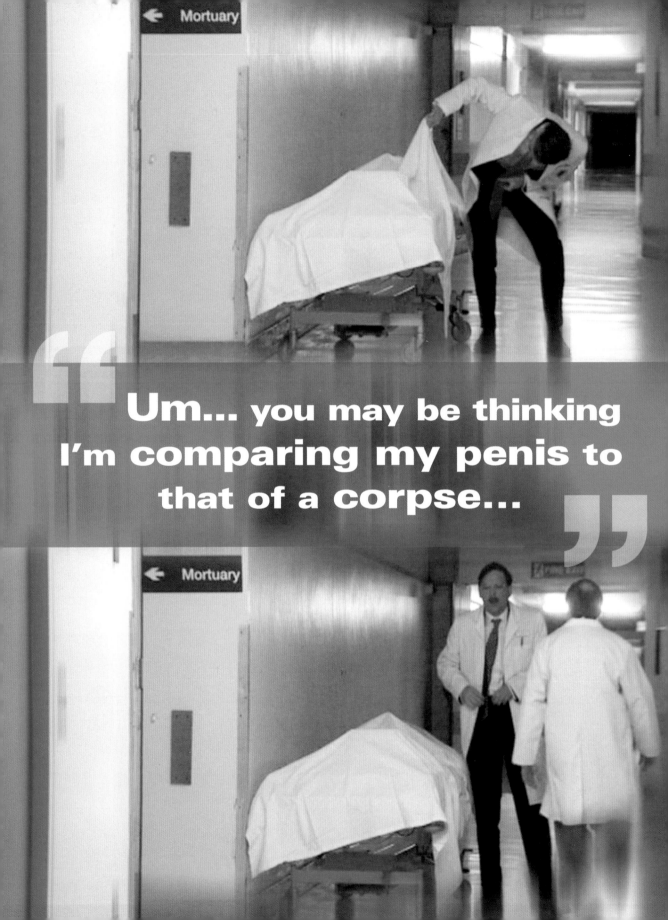

GUY: No no, wait. Wait, no no wait, because look, I'll tell you what, let's have something to eat and then we can talk. You've got a...

CAROLINE: Get off!

GUY: No, because — how about some quails eggs with a little raspberry jus?

CAROLINE: Look, just stop it! Okay? I have slept in my car, I don't have a home, I smell, I have had a traumatic first day at work, someone pulled my hair, I have come to a strange man's flat who is probably a psychopath, and to top it all, I have just done the biggest monster that won't go down!

GUY: It won't go any further.

CAROLINE: I think I'm going to have to kill you. I'm going.

GUY: No no, no no, tell you what, I'll tell you what, I'll go.

CAROLINE: But it's your flat.

GUY: No, no but but buts, I'll go. And if you need anything, just yell, because I — Well, you could actually whisper under the door, because I'll just be there, okay? And that smell, is that a good smell or a bad smell?

CAROLINE: Oh God!

GUY: Yeah. Goodnight.

HE GOES OUT AND SHUTS THE DOOR.

CAROLINE: Shit!

▶ MORTUARY

STATHAM IS LOOKING DOWN HIS TROUSERS AND LIFTING UP THE COVER ON A CORPSE, WHICH IS LYING ON A TROLLEY IN THE CORRIDOR. AN ORDERLY COMES TO TAKE THE TROLLEY.

STATHAM: Um... you may be thinking I'm comparing my penis to that of a corpse...

▶ STAFF LIAISON OFFICE

SUE WHITE IS PLAYING WITH HER COMPUTER MOUSE, ROLLING IT AROUND IN A VERY SENSUAL WAY.

▶ OPERATING THEATRE

THEATRE STAFF ARE RUSHING FROM ONE SIDE OF THE ROOM TO THE OTHER.

MAC: Hey, come on guys, come on. You know we don't play British Bulldogs in theatre, yeah? If you want to mess around, bugger off back to A & E.

▶ STAFF LIAISON OFFICE

SUE RUBS THE MOUSE AGAINST HERSELF, GETTING MORE AND MORE AROUSED.

▶ OPERATING THEATRE

THE STAFF ARE ALL STILL RUNNING UP AND DOWN IN THE THEATRE.

MAC: Can we just try and be a little bit more professional?

NURSE: There's a wasp!

MAC: Jesus!

HE RUNS OUT.

EPISODE 2

▶▶ JOANNA'S CAR — OPEN ROAD

JOANNA IS DRIVING, WITH STATHAM IN THE PASSENGER SEAT.

STATHAM: Joanna?

JOANNA: No.

STATHAM: Joanna...

JOANNA: No.

STATHAM: Joanna, will you — Why? Why? Why do we have to go through this rigmarole every time? It's ludicrous.

JOANNA: Because they're the rules Alan. I can't possibly be seen with you. Now get out.

JOANNA MAKES STATHAM GET OUT OF THE CAR – THEY ARE STILL QUITE SOME WAY SHORT OF THE HOSPITAL.

STATHAM: It's ridiculous.

JOANNA: Come on, get out. Out, out!

STATHAM: All right, all right, I'm getting out.

STATHAM IS WEARING A LARGE, RATHER OBVIOUS WIG.

JOANNA: Cut through the East Block and come in through the Nurse's Wing, And for Christ's sake, try to look normal!

STATHAM SETS OFF ACROSS THE GRASS VERGE, BUT FALLS INTO A DITCH.

▶▶ GUY'S CAR — HOSPITAL CAR PARK

INCREDIBLY LOUD RAP MUSIC IS PLAYING ON THE STEREO. GUY IS BANGING THE STEERING WHEEL WITH THE PALMS OF HIS HANDS IN TIME TO THE MUSIC. CAROLINE IS SITTING VERY LOW IN THE PASSENGER SEAT, LOOKING UNEASY. GUY HAS HIS EYES SHUT AS HE ENJOYS THE MUSIC'S SENTIMENTS — SEX, VIOLENCE AND CONSPICUOUS CONSUMPTION: "I TOOK THE BITCH HOME, I TOOK THE BITCH HOME, I TOOK THE BITCH HOME — LAST NIGHT."

▶▶ OPEN ROAD

JOANNA REVERSES HER CAR TO SHOUT AT STATHAM AS HE CLAMBERS OUT OF THE DITCH.

JOANNA: Alan! Wig!

STATHAM: Yes, I know.

JOANNA: Christ!

SHE ROARS OFF IN HER CAR.

▶▶ GUY'S CAR — HOSPITAL CAR PARK

THE LOUD MUSIC CONTINUES, WITH GUY MIMING, "BITCH, BITCH, BITCH." CAROLINE LOOKS ACROSS AT HIM NERVOUSLY. HE EVENTUALLY TURNS THE MUSIC OFF.

GUY: What?

CAROLINE: I wasn't at your flat last night, okay.

GUY: Okay. (CONSPIRATORIALLY) And nothing happened.

CAROLINE: No, nothing did happen.

GUY: Well you say that, but —

CAROLINE: Yeah, I do say that, I say that because it is in fact a statement of fact.

GUY: Hey, I may be many things, but not being indiscreet isn't one of them.

HE GOES TO GET OUT. SOME MEMBERS OF STAFF ARE STANDING AROUND THE ENTRANCE.

CAROLINE: Oh shit! We can't possibly get out here.

GUY: Why not?

CAROLINE: Well — because they... you... I, um — I don't know what any of these buttons do.

GUY: Oh right, well this is the...

CAROLINE: No, you go on in, I'll just check it out. Oh shit!

SHE PUSHES THE WRONG BUTTONS AND THE WINDSCREEN WIPERS START UP. SHE SETS OFF THE ALARM. BY NOW EVERYONE IS LOOKING.

CAROLINE: Oh, shit!

THE CD STARTS UP AGAIN.

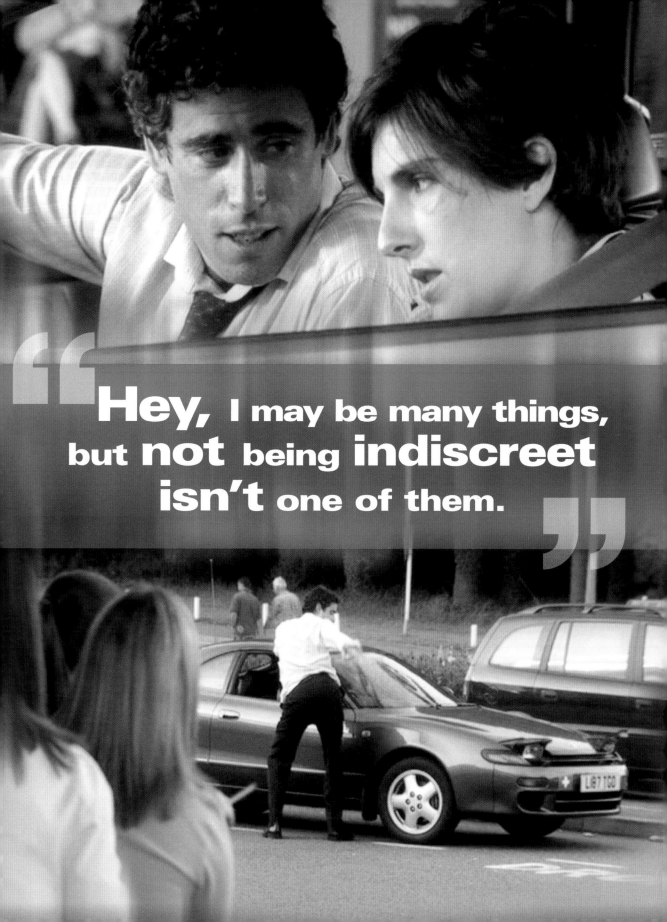

"Hey, I may be many things, but not being indiscreet isn't one of them."

CAROLINE: Oh shut up! Shut up!

▶▶ CAR PARK BARRIER

JOANNA PULLS UP AT THE CAR PARK BARRIER AND BLOWS THE HORN.

JOANNA: Yeah, when you're quite ready love...

STATHAM ARRIVES AT THE BARRIER ON FOOT AT THE SAME TIME.

JOANNA: Go back. Slow down.

STATHAM: Yes.

JOANNA: And fuck off. Right?

STATHAM: Right.

JOANNA DRIVES ON.

STATHAM: (TO ATTENDANT) She's my secret lover, the lady, over there.

▶▶ GUY'S CAR — NEAR ENTRANCE

LOUD MUSIC IS STILL PLAYING IN THE CAR. GUY HAS GOT OUT AND IS MOVING TO THE MUSIC, WIGGLING HIS BUM IN A SUPPOSEDLY AROUSING FASHION.

CAROLINE: (TO THE CAR) Shut up! Shut up!

▶▶ CAR PARK

HARRIET GETS OUT OF HER CAR THINKING SHE HAS FORGOTTEN SOMETHING. SHE REALISES SHE'S FORGOTTEN HER SKIRT AND TRIES TO COVER HERSELF UP WITH HER BAGS. SHE GETS BACK IN THE CAR AND DRIVES OFF.

▶▶ OUTSIDE HOSPITAL ENTRANCE

CAROLINE HAS GOT OUT OF THE CAR AND TRIES TO SNEAK INTO THE BUILDING BY HIDING BEHIND A LAUNDRY TROLLEY, BUT ENDS UP IN FRONT OF THE WATCHING STAFF.

CAROLINE: Yes, I stayed at Doctor Secretan's flat on my very first night here, but no we did not have sex. All right?

SHE WALKS INTO THE HOSPITAL. AS SOON AS SHE HAS GONE, THE GIRLS ALL GRAB THEIR MOBILES AND START TEXTING.

GUY STRUTS UP TO THEM.

GUY: Good morning ladies. Wow! "Oh what a night!"

HE SWAGGERS INTO THE BUILDING.

▶▶ HOSPITAL DOORWAY

JOANNA AND STATHAM ARRIVE AT THE DOOR AT THE SAME TIME. MARTIN COMES PAST.

MARTIN: Hiya. You two come together?

JOANNA: Are you mad?

JOANNA PUSHES MARTIN'S HEAD.

▶▶ CORRIDOR

MARTIN WALKS ALONG, DOING KARATE CHOPS AT A NURSE.

GUY IS HITTING THE VENDING MACHINE HE'S LOST MONEY IN. HE NOTICES SOMEONE GIVING HIM A DISAPPROVING LOOK.

GUY: I'm a doctor.

MARTIN: So, did you catch your prey?

GUY: Can't say.

MARTIN: Why not?

GUY: She told me not to divulge any details.

MARTIN: Ah, so you did catch her?

GUY: I've been sworn to secrecy.

MARTIN: By whom?

GUY: By Caroline Todd. Oh damn!

MARTIN: No!

GUY: You bastard!

MARTIN: Oh you...

GUY: You're just too smart for me.

MARTIN: You didn't?

GUY: Oh no, now you'll tell everyone.

MARTIN: No, I promise I won't.

GUY: (DISAPPOINTED) Why not?

MARTIN: Well, because Caroline wouldn't want me to.

GUY: So?

MARTIN: So... you've got to respect her feelings.

GUY: Why?

MARTIN: Well because, Caroline... well, because you have.

GUY: Oh, I see. You think she's lovely, don't you?

MARTIN: No I don't.

GUY: She's only been here a day, she's the woman of your dreams!

MARTIN: Shut up.

GUY: Yeah, well dream on mate, because she's hooked. Hooked, played and safely in the landing net. She's only human after all.

CAROLINE COMES UP TO THEM ON THE STAIRS.

CAROLINE: Oh — um... morning Doctor — ? Secretan, isn't it?

GUY: Yes. Good morning Doctor — ? Plodd?

MARTIN: Todd.

CAROLINE: Todd.

GUY: Todd. Yes, how are you since I last saw you, *yesterday after-noon?*

CAROLINE: Er, I'm fine. Yes, thank you very much for asking.

MARTIN: Um — did you sleep well?

CAROLINE: Yes, like a log.

GUY: Oh — the loo's completely clear now, by the way.

CAROLINE: What? What loo?

MARTIN: Yeah, what loo?

GUY: The... disabled toilet next to the — was that you? Or was that somebody else?

CAROLINE: It wasn't me.

SHE WALKS OFF.

GUY DOES A 'REELING IN A FISH' MIME TO MARTIN.

▸▸ LADIES' TOILETS

JOANNA IS CHECKING HER MAKE-UP IN THE MIRROR. SUE WHITE COMES IN.

JOANNA: How's the liaising going?

SUE: Hmm, it's all right, yeah.

JOANNA: Anything I should know about?

SUE: Um... no.

JOANNA REARRANGES HER TITS.

SUE DOES THE SAME, LIFTING UP HER T-SHIRT AND JIGGLING THEM ABOUT. THEY CONTINUE TO TRY TO OUTDO EACH OTHER, PUSHING THEM OUT AND PLUMPING THEM UP.

▸▸ MESS

MARTIN SITS AT A TABLE, PEN IN HAND, LOOKING STUDIOUS.

BOYCE: Ah, revision.

MARTIN: No, it's a note and it's actually quite hard.

GUY: Suicide note?

MARTIN: No.

GUY: Shame.

MARTIN: It's a note to the cleaners, it's about my yoghurt.

GUY: Oh really? Oh tell me about it.

MARTIN: Well, I always put the yoghurt in the...

GUY SNORES ON MARTIN'S SHOULDER.

BOYCE: So what's the problem with the yoghurt?

MARTIN: Well, I always hide the yoghurt in the Perspex drawer at the bottom of the fridge. They come in, they move it to the top drawer where the milk and ordinary yoghurt is.

GUY: The bastards!

BOYCE: So yours isn't ordinary yoghurt?

GUY GOES TO THE FRIDGE AND TAKES OUT MARTIN'S YOGHURT AND EATS IT PROVOCATIVELY. MARTIN DOESN'T NOTICE.

MARTIN: No, it's soya, Oakwood Farm fruits of the forest natural live yoghurt.

BOYCE: Well, what's wrong with the note?

MARTIN: Do you think it's too friendly? I mean, do you think they're going to think I'm taking the piss with "Dear Cleaners"?

BOYCE: Do you actually speak to them?

MARTIN: Well not really, I just kind of go "urh", and they sort of go "urh".

BOYCE: Well that's pretty relaxed. What about "Hi there"?

GUY: What about "To the useless bunch of shit-heads that move my yoghurt"?

MARTIN: No, God, you've got to keep them on your side!

GUY: Jesus Christ! Just put "Dear Cleaners" and hope they don't take it as some sort of sexual advance.

MARTIN: Okay.

▸▸ LADIES' TOILETS

JOANNA AND SUE WHITE ARE STILL TRYING TO OUT-FLAUNT EACH OTHER. JOANNA HITCHES UP HER SKIRT TO SHOW HER SUSPENDERS. SUE TAKES HER SKIRT OFF COMPLETELY, THROWS IT OVER HER SHOULDER, TOSSES HER HAIR BACK AND WALKS OUT IN KNICKERS AND STOCKINGS.

▸▸ MESS

MARTIN: Oh shit!

BOYCE: What?

MARTIN: Well now I've underlined the word "please".

BOYCE & GUY: Oh no.

BOYCE: "Please leave", ah, you sound really angry now.

GUY: Hmm.

MARTIN: So what are they going to do to my yoghurt now? They'll probably piss in it, like they did in that restaurant.

GUY: Which restaurant?

MARTIN: Um... there was no restaurant.

GUY: They won't piss in your yoghurt Martin.

MARTIN: Are you sure?

GUY IS STILL EATING MARTIN'S YOGHURT.

GUY: Hmm, it's too obvious. Much easier to hide little bits of shit and glue the top back on.

MARTIN: Thanks Guy!

GUY GOES. CAROLINE COMES OVER TO THEM.

BOYCE: You wouldn't guess he was really sweet deep down, would you?

MARTIN: No he's not.

BOYCE: Well he must be in touch with his feminine side, considering his middle name is Valery.

MARTIN: His middle name's not Valery!

BOYCE: Oh yes it is, Mac told me and he's seen his passport.

MARTIN: Oh brilliant! Oh yes, roll on lunchtime. Girls' names gags-a-gogo. Valery! Brilliant!

▸▸ **STATHAM'S OFFICE**

THERE IS A KNOCK AT THE DOOR.

STATHAM: In tray!

STATHAM SMILES TO HIMSELF, PLEASED WITH HIS LITTLE JOKE. MAC ENTERS.

MAC: Funny.

STATHAM: Ah, Doctor MacCartney, take a seat.

MAC: I'd rather stand, if it's all the same.

STATHAM: I'd rather you sat.

MAC: Surely it's my choice if I sit or stand.

STATHAM: Not on this occasion, no. Please be seated.

MAC: No thank you. Er — what did you want to see me about?

STATHAM: This is my office, please be seated for our discussion,

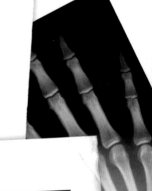

Subject: I know it was you!
From: Astatham@ehtrust.gov.uk
To: BoycieBoyceBoyce@hotmail.com

Dear Mr Boyce,

Don't try and pretend you didn't do it, because I know you did.

Yours, Dr Statham.

Subject: Re: I know it was you!
From: BoycieBoyceBoyce@hotmail.com
To: Astatham@ehtrust.gov.uk

Dear Alan,

Yes, I did do it and to be honest I'll do it again. If I don't, I find that my bladder gets stretched by the pressure of the urine inside it and causes me great discomfort. I call it "Going to the Gents'". Is this what you meant? I do hope I haven't deliberately misunderstood you.

Cheers,

Boyce

I'd like us to be at the same eye-level, it creates easy flowing conversation.

MAC: Hmm, you could stand if you want.

STATHAM: You sit.

MAC: You stand.

STATHAM: You sit!

MAC: You stand.

STATHAM: I will not be...

MAC SITS.

STATHAM: Thank... Right, now... Er, I wanted to have a discussion with you about your review with the board next week.

MAC STANDS UP. STATHAM STANDS, SO MAC SITS. THEY BOB UP AND DOWN BETWEEN SITTING AND STANDING.

STATHAM: This isn't... This is, this is the kind of behaviour that they will not tolerate. Now will you be — sit!

MAC: No.

STATHAM: Look, this kind of insubordination is precisely the reason you were overlooked for promotion last Wednesday.

STATHAM ENDS UP BENT HALFWAY BETWEEN SITTING AND STANDING.

MAC: Right.

STATHAM: And as a result... Get out! I'll discuss this with you later, when you're less...

MAC: Handsome?

STATHAM: No, no, less, less...

MAC: Charming?

STATHAM: Less sitting. Get out!

MAC: Thank you.

MAC GOES TO LEAVE.

MAC: You can sit now if you want.

STATHAM: I will not!

MAC: Okay.

STATHAM STAYS HALFWAY BETWEEN STANDING AND SITTING.

MAC GOES.

▶▶ OFFICE

KIM: Shred these before Joanna sees them. How are things going with Tim?

KAREN: Well, it's just I was with him last night. The thing is, he said I had a furry face.

KIM AND RACHEL ARE TRYING NOT TO SMIRK.

KAREN: That can't be a good thing, can it?

KIM: No, I guess not.

KIM AND RACHEL EXCHANGE LOOKS.

KAREN: (BURSTING INTO TEARS) Damn my furry face!

KIM: Oh, don't worry, you'll find someone else. Besides, your face isn't that furry. I can't see it.

KAREN: Touch it.

KIM: No.

KAREN: I need another perspective.

KIM FEELS KAREN'S FACE.

KIM: I'd have said downy. Never furry.

KAREN: Thanks.

KIM AND RACHEL FIND FURRY OBJECTS TO HOLD UP TO THEIR FACES AND GIGGLE.

KAREN: Downy.

HARRIET COMES IN AND IS SPOTTED BY JOANNA.

JOANNA: Late again Harriet.

▶▶ **STATHAM'S OFFICE**

MAC COMES BACK IN. STATHAM IS EXACTLY AS HE WAS BEFORE, REFUSING TO SIT.

▶▶ **STAFF LIAISON OFFICE**

SUE WHITE IS AT HER DESK, STUFFING HER FACE WITH SNACKS. MARTIN ENTERS.

MARTIN: Is the lost property box here?

SUE: Looking for your wee tinkle?

MARTIN: What's a tinkle?

SUE: All in good time little man, all in good time.

MARTIN: Oh. Um — has anybody handed in any yoghurt?

SUE: In a pot?

MARTIN: Yeah.

SUE: No.

MARTIN: It's just that I've had trouble with my yoghurt, because it does keep getting moved around and it's now gone missing — stolen.

SUE: Woah, back up there Columbo! Calling me a thief?

MARTIN: No. No.

SUE: Well I hope not — careful, careful, careful, careful.

MARTIN: No. Just, has anyone handed in any food at all?

SUE: Satsuma. Two Curly Wurlys and some kind of Bombay Mix, which is far spicier than I really like it, you know, much too er, "hot..."

MARTIN: Hmm. Could you have um... maybe eaten it by mistake?

SUE LOOKS AT MARTIN.

MARTIN: Well, I'll let myself out.

HE GOES.

▶▶ **THEATRE CORRIDOR**

GUY AND MAC MEET.

GUY: Oh God, what a night!

MAC: Are you all right?

GUY: Yeah, I'm fine, just a bit stiff. A few aching... probably a little bit of a groin strain.

MAC: Ah, yeah.

GUY: Oh, and ah — an aching tongue.

MAC: I can't have my staff working with aching tongues.

GUY: Your staff?

MAC: Yeah, my staff. I am the surgeon, you are my anaesthetist.

GUY: I'm not your anaesthetist. You're my surgeon, you're my surgeon bitch.

MAC: No, you create the environment in which I can do my job.

GUY: Cut her open, bitch!

MAC: Gas her, fucker!

GUY: Sew it up, gimp!

MAC: You are essentially part of my team.

GUY: What? I'm not part of your team.

MAC: You are part of my fucking team!

GUY: What the fuck are you talking about?! I am not part of your team!

MAC: You are part of my team.

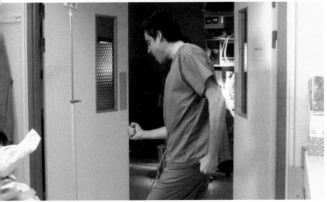

GUY: You're part of my anus!

MAC: You are like the unprofessional co-pilot that causes a massive aeroplane disaster, because he has no real sense of his true position — how you owe me respect by being part of my team. I am the captain, you are effectively the first officer.

GUY: No, I am the captain, you're the trolley dolly.

MAC: I bet you I'm the captain.

GUY: I bet you I am.

MAC: I bet you I am.

GUY: Bet you I am!

MAC: Bet you I am!

GUY: Bet you I am!

MAC: I bet you don't even know where the cockpit is.

GUY: All right, here we go, let's make it fair. Whoever gets the newest member of the surgical team to spend the night at their place first gets to be captain.

MAC: Why?

GUY: You're too late, I win!

MAC: Why?

GUY: You're the baby, I'm the placenta.

MAC: Sorry, sorry...

GUY: What?

MAC: (POINTS TO A TROLLEY) Can I get some more nuts please?

GUY: Yeah, well you can't use mine, because they're all...

MAC: I'm trying to fly my plane.

GUY: They're squeezed out, they're juiced out, you know what I'm saying?

MAC: I'm trying to fly my plane. You go and clean the toilet.

GUY: They've been... (HE SUCKS IN HIS CHEEKS AND SQUEEZES HIS HANDS)

MAC: Yeah?

GUY: I've been using my nuts.

MAC: Get in! Have you?

GUY: Yeah. All night!

THEY GO INTO THEATRE.

▶▶ **THEATRE, LATER**

AN OPERATION IS ABOUT TO BEGIN. MAC, GUY AND CAROLINE ARE ALL PRESENT.

MAC: Good day ladies and gentlemen.

GUY: We're all part of his team, apparently.

MAC: Thank you very much. Everything should be pretty straightforward this morning, except for the bits that are pretty straight backward. What can I tell you? A few ground rules: no bombing, no running, no petting, no diving, no inflatables. In fact, probably best to leave all swimming related activities until later, because this is an operating theatre after all.

GUY: Yeah, perhaps we should all have badges made up, "Mac's Team".

MAC: I forgot to tell you, we have of course one non-swimmer joining us today, Doctor Secretan. Welcome to him. Okay, let's go. See if we can find this...

GUY: I'm an excellent swimmer, if you must know.

MAC: Yep. Do you know what Guy? We have moved on.

GUY: Yeah. I can swim two miles, easy. No problemo. I can do the butterfly — which is the hardest style — and I can do a surface dive in my pyjamas.

MAC: That's probably very handy for a bed-wetter.

GUY: Yeah, all I'm saying is that I am a first class swimmer, superb, and on a scale of one to ten, I'd be an eight, probably shading a nine.

MAC: I think you should calm down, because I was only playing, my insecure little friend.

GUY MIMES FRONT CRAWL. HE COMES UP FROM 'UNDERWATER'.

GUY: Yeah, actually I'm not insecure, I'm very secure, very very secure. The Man From Atlantis, that's what they used to call me at my swimming club.

GUY HOLDS HIS NOSE AND SINKS 'UNDER' AGAIN.

▸▸ CORRIDOR

CAROLINE AND ANGELA ARE WALKING SIDE BY SIDE. ANGELA IS HOLDING AN ORANGE, CAROLINE IS STUFFING CHOCOLATE INTO HER MOUTH.

ANGELA: Are you finding your way okay? It's hard being new isn't it?

CAROLINE: Oh God yes, isn't it awful? Did you feel like you were walking around with a big neon sign saying "clueless twat"?

ANGELA: No. No, I meant finding your way around, it's a big building, it's hard to get your bearings. Oh poor you.

CAROLINE: Yeah, well it hasn't helped half the hospital assuming I've jumped into bed with the first man I set eyes on...

ANGELA: I know, hideous.

CAROLINE: Which I didn't. As it happens.

ANGELA: Quite right so.

CAROLINE: And I think that's quite good for me, because I haven't had any in quite some time now, and I could easily have been persuaded to enter into a spot of rough and dirty sex up against a wall, or in fact any hard surface, between you and me.

ANGELA: Grief!

CAROLINE: No, oh no, not with you. No, I didn't mean between you and me like in a literal sense; I meant between me and men. Man. One man.

ANGELA: Yeah, I know.

▸▸ THEATRE

GUY IS MIMING UNDERWATER SWIMMING.

MAC: Let's see if we can save this young lady's life, despite Johnny Weissmuller.

GUY MIMES DOGGY-PADDLE.

GUY: (POINTING AT MAC) He can't swim.

▸▸ CORRIDOR

CAROLINE LEAVES HER CHOCOLATE BEHIND.

CAROLINE: I'll just leave this here for a passing diabetic. (LOOKS AT ANGELA'S ORANGE) Aren't you going to eat that?

ANGELA: Er yes, yes, I'm just going to use it for a bit of juggling practice first. They love it in the children's ward.

ANGELA JUGGLES WITH HER ORANGE.

▸▸ THEATRE

GUY LOOKS BORED.

GUY: Swimmin'...!

▸▸ X-RAY WAITING AREA

STATHAM SPOTS JOANNA .

STATHAM: Missing you already.

JOANNA: Morning Doctor Statham.

STATHAM: Morning.

MARK: Morning.

JOANNA: Morning Mark.

STATHAM: Um — I wondered if I could just pick your brains for a minute?

JOANNA: Can't it wait?

STATHAM: Well, it's just, you know, I've got some students later on and I just wanted to run something past you, as it were. Almost literally.

JOANNA: Yeah?

STATHAM: Does my coat sweep when I go round a corner?

JOANNA: Pardon?

STATHAM: Does my coat, when I walk, does it sweep?

JOANNA: Sweep?

STATHAM: Mm, you know. Does it sort of float out the back when I go round... with a sense of contained urgency, yet stylish élan?

JOANNA: I'll tell you what Alan, why don't you go back to where you came from and try walking with a sense of — what was it?

STATHAM: Yes. Contained urgency yet stylish élan.

JOANNA: Yeah, and I'll watch you and tell you what I think.

STATHAM: Good, good. You wouldn't mind?

JOANNA: No, no, not at all. (MAKES A BEEP NOISE) Oh, I think you're wanted Doctor.

STATHAM: Ah, I'll straight, er — this way.

STATHAM WALKS OFF TO GET READY FOR HIS COAT SWIRL.

JOANNA: Arse!

STATHAM: No, no.

JOANNA WALKS IN THE OPPOSITE DIRECTION, NOT LOOKING. STATHAM SWIRLS HIS COAT AS HE WALKS UP AND DOWN.

STATHAM: Oh my goodness!

▸▸ **RECOVERY WARD**

CAROLINE IS LEANING OVER A SEDATED PATIENT MAKING SLIT CHEST GESTURES. MAC COMES OVER.

MAC: Disappointed.

CAROLINE: What? What?!

MAC: How are you today?

CAROLINE: Fine.

MAC: Good. Any aches, groin strains?

MAC WALKS AWAY.

CAROLINE: Stop right there. Come back here.

MAC: Stop right there, come back here, which? I'm confused.

CAROLINE: Can I just say one thing?

MAC: Yes, you can.

CAROLINE: I don't know what you're talking about, and always check your facts. Good day.

MAC: That's two things. Three if you count the valedictory flourish. Think I hit a bit of a nerve. Can I go and cut people up now?

CAROLINE: Yes.

MAC: Excellent.

HE SPEAKS TO THE SEDATED PATIENT AS HE LEAVES.

MAC: Try and get some sleep.

▸▸ **STAFF LIAISON OFFICE**

SUE IS LYING ON HER BACK OVER HER DESK KEEPING A PING PONG BALL UP IN THE AIR BY BLOWING THROUGH A STRAW.

CAROLINE: Sorry, is this not a convenient time?

SUE BLOWS THROUGH THE STRAW AND THE BALL DISAPPEARS TOWARDS THE CEILING.

SUE: Always, always and at all times I'm here to soothe, to bathe, to listen to the workers' woes. Now do I sense a woe? Sense I do.

Subject: Re: I know it was you!
From: Astatham@ehtrust.gov.uk
To: BoycieBoyceBoyce@hotmail.com

Dear Mr Boyce,

You know full well I am not talking about that. Everybody "Goes to the Gents'", you fool. And DO NOT call me Alan.

CAROLINE: Well yeah, I am a bit worried, to be honest.

SUE: Yeah, yeah, well I would be, if I were you.

CAROLINE: Why? What do you mean?

SUE: Nothing, just carry on.

CAROLINE: Right. Well, it's just I'm not quite sure — sorry, what did you mean by that?

SUE: Just ignore me.

CAROLINE: Right. It's just, um — I'm not quite sure what I should do.

SUE: About last night?

CAROLINE: You know about last night?

SUE: Oh Caroline, Caroline, Caroline...

CAROLINE: What?

SUE: Oh Caroline, Caroline, Caroline...

CAROLINE: Can you stop saying my name please. Do you know about last night?

SUE: I'm sure everybody knows.

CAROLINE: Oh God, then it's a disaster.

SUE: Then I'm sure nobody knows.

CAROLINE: Well you know.

SUE: Yes, well of course I know; I know everything, that's my job.

CAROLINE: But how?

SUE: You know...

SUE MIMES BLOWING AND FLAPS HER HANDS.

CAROLINE: Sorry, no — what's that? Is that... what? You heard by carrier pigeon?

SUE: No. Smoke signals.

CAROLINE: Oh.

▶▶ **OUTSIDE MAIN ENTRANCE**

BOYCE AND RACHEL ARE OUTSIDE HAVING A CIGARETTE. THEY LOOK AT THE WARNINGS ON THE PACKETS.

RACHEL: What does yours say?

BOYCE: "Smoking lowers the sperm count."

RACHEL: "May cause miscarriage."

THEY THINK ABOUT THIS AND STUB OUT THEIR CIGARETTES. THEN THEY SWAP PACKETS AND LIGHT UP AGAIN.

CAROLINE: Oh you get all the gossip and then you pass it on. I could — I could report you for meddling.

SUE: Meddling? M... m... meddling? How dare you! Take that back.

CAROLINE: No.

SUE: Take it back.

CAROLINE: No.

SUE: If I've got to stand up, things are really going to kick off here.

CAROLINE: I can stand up quicker than you.

THEY BOTH STAND, EYEING EACH OTHER UP.

SUE: I could put a spell on you.

CAROLINE: What?

SUE: Nothing.

CAROLINE: No, you just said you were going to put a spell on me.

SUE: No I didn't, are you mad? Now out.

SUE QUICKLY WAVES HER FINGERS AT CAROLINE AS SHE GOES TO LEAVE.

CAROLINE: Did you just put a spell on me?

SUE: No.

CAROLINE: Well don't, because I'm a doctor, remember. A doctor.

THEY POINT THEIR FINGERS AT EACH OTHER ACROSS THE DESK.

CAROLINE LEAVES.

THE PING PONG BALL REAPPEARS AND BOUNCES ON THE DESK.

GUY SEES ANGELA IN THE CORRIDOR AND LIFTS UP HIS SCRUBS TO REVEAL HIS CHEST.

GUY: Well, I don't know! I've had some steamy sessions in my time, but...

ANGELA: Ooh, can I just stop you there? If you're about to claim sexual relations with Doctor Todd, then I know you didn't, so don't bother.

GUY: Oh you know do you? How do you know?

ANGELA: Yeah, well I happen to have had a little heart to heart with Caroline, that's how I know.

GUY: Already? She's only been here a day and a half.

ANGELA: Women are like that Guy, we bond easily.

GUY: Ooh that's working for me, that image, keep that going.

ANGELA: You don't stand a chance with Doctor Todd. I happen to know she's looking for caring, sharing and understanding. She's looking for the one.

GUY: The one what? The one freelance anaesthetist with his own pieds-a-terre in Zermatt and Nice?

ANGELA: Way out of your league.

GUY: Yeah, well no one is immune to my charm, Ange. Yes, and now I know what she wants, thanks to you, I can just give it to her, can't I.

ANGELA: No, well that's just it. You're not capable are you?

GUY: We shall see.

ANGELA: Out of interest, what does long-term mean to you?

GUY: It's an airport car park.

ANGELA: Monogamy?

GUY: Nice, dark sort of wood, sideboards.

ANGELA: What is the 'C' word?

GUY: Unt.

ANGELA LAUGHS AND WALKS AWAY.

GUY: Well? Did I pass?

ANGELA: Spectacularly.

GUY: Yes!

HE LIFTS HIS SCRUBS AGAIN.

KIM: Hufflepuff.

HARRIET: Oh bad luck. I'm Gryffindor, I'm very chuffed about that.

RACHEL: That makes two of us in Gryffindor.

KAREN APPROACHES.

KAREN: I'm Wimbletink.

RACHEL: What?

KAREN: Spumptybum. Niffyniffniff.

KIM: They're not houses at Hogwarts.

KAREN: What?

HARRIET: No, it's the Sorting Hat.

RACHEL: Yeah, Harry Potter website?

KAREN: Oh yeah, my neighbour's daughter made me do that.

HARRIET: Oh, what did you come out as?

KAREN: Um… Slytherin it was called.

THEY ALL LOOK AT HER.

KAREN: Is that bad? I haven't read the book.

KIM: It's really bad.

RACHEL: It's where the most evil wizards and witches have come from. It's the worst house there is.

KAREN: Can I change it?

KIM: No, you can not. The decision of the Sorting Hat is final. You cannot go again.

KAREN: I don't want to be in Slytherin.

KIM: Well it's too late for that.

KAREN BURSTS INTO TEARS AND RUNS OFF. HARRIET IS ABOUT TO GO AFTER HER.

KIM: Careful! It could be a Slytherin trick.

RACHEL: She's right, you never can tell.

HARRIET SITS BACK DOWN.

HARRIET: Oh, I hadn't thought of that.

RACHEL: Hmm.

STATHAM IS SWIRLING HIS COAT BEHIND HIM, WALKING UP AND DOWN THE CORRIDOR.

CAROLINE ENTERS AND FINDS GUY.

Subject: Re: I know it was you!
From: BoycieBoyceBoyce@hotmail.com
To: Astatham@ehtrust.gov.uk

Dear Betty,

Everybody? Research has shown that more men than women "Go to the Gents'". Interesting bit of trivia.

Cheers, Boyce x

CAROLINE: There you are.

GUY: Oh yes, here I am, an anaesthetist in the anaesthetist's room. Da-dah! Have you been missing me?

CAROLINE: Everybody in this hospital knows where I was last night.

GUY: Caroline! You weren't supposed to tell anybody!

CAROLINE: It wasn't me!

GUY: Are you sure?! You know how one little boast leads to another.

CAROLINE: You are very very irritating. Yes you are.

GUY: And do you know what you should do with an irritation? You should rub it with cream.

CAROLINE: I think I'd prefer to scratch it very hard.

GUY: It won't get any better.

CAROLINE PRODUCES A NOTE.

CAROLINE: I want you to sign this.

GUY: (READS) "I hereby declare that Doctor Caroline Todd was given the sole use of my bedroom last night, whilst I myself spent the entire night on the sofa." I can't sign this, it would leave my reputation in tatters.

CAROLINE: Yeah, and what about my reputation?

GUY: Enhanced. You ensnared the legendary Guy Secretan on day one. How cool is that?

GUY STUFFS CAROLINE'S NOTE DOWN HER BLOUSE. SHE GETS IT BACK AND FOLLOWS HIM.

GUY: I'm not signing it.

CAROLINE: Well that's a shame, because I think I know something I shouldn't about you.

GUY: Really?

CAROLINE: Yeah, and it wasn't my fault; I just sort of stumbled on the information.

GUY: What do you know?

CAROLINE: And I can understand why you're embarrassed about it and why you wouldn't want to tell anybody.

GUY: Oh God, you've been talking to Sue White, haven't you?

CAROLINE: Er — well I have, yes...

GUY: Oh brilliant. She can't keep her fat mouth shut!

CAROLINE: No no no, that's a bit harsh, I'd say she's got quite a thin mouth, sort of like that... (SUCKS HER CHEEKS IN AND ATTEMPTS A SUE WHITE VOICE) "Hello, hello, how are we today? Would you like a sooky sweet?"

GUY: Yeah, well listen, we... we had the very briefest of encounters and any stories she may be spreading, well — hell hath no fury like a woman scorned.

CAROLINE: Did you scorn her?

GUY: Yeah, well I — yes, I called it a day, yeah. One day, one night. Urgh. And any, any of that bollocks, you know, you know, about what she did to me and how I really enjoyed it, all that anal penetration shit, you can take all that with a huge pinch of salt.

CAROLINE: You didn't!

GUY: Huh. Didn't I.

PAUSE.

CAROLINE: That's not what I thought I knew.

GUY: What? Not the Sue White thing?

CAROLINE: No. I only had some frankly rather weak stuff regarding your middle name. No, definitely didn't know the Sue White thing.

GUY: Ah.

CAROLINE: I do now though.

GUY: Yeah.

CAROLINE: What a lot of things I know.

GUY: Yes indeed.

CAROLINE: I'm a walking encyclopedia.

SHE WAVES THE NOTE IN FRONT OF HIM.

GUY: Yeah. Right, pen, I need a pen! This is really childish.

CAROLINE: I am much younger than I look.

GUY HOLDS THE NOTE AGAINST CAROLINE'S CHEST.

GUY: Yeah, do you want me to sign it here or here? (PRESSING ON EACH BREAST IN TURN)

CAROLINE GLARES AT HIM AND QUICKLY TURNS ROUND. HE SIGNS IT ON HER BACK.

GUY: I'm signing, I'm signing, look, watch, see how I sign. Oh, signy, signy, sign, sign. I've signed it. Take it, take it.

HE KEEPS OFFERING HER THE PEN, BUT SNATCHING IT AWAY AT THE LAST SECOND.

CAROLINE: Give me the pen!

GUY: You can have the pen. Wait, wait, one sec, watch.

HE CLICKS THE PEN CLOSED AND GIVES IT TO HER. THEY PAUSE,

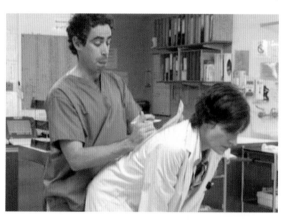

"Aaah the **lion's mane**. Truly the **king** of **beasts**.

LOOKING AT EACH OTHER AND THEN CAROLINE RUNS OFF. HE MIMICS HER RUN.

▸▸ STAFF LIAISON OFFICE

MAC ENTERS.

MAC: You, er — you wanted to see me?

SUE: Oh yes, of course, silly me. I got lost in your eyes there for a minute.

MAC: Right.

SUE: Now then, now then, Doctor Mac, that's...

MAC: Yes, yes, yes.

SUE: Oh now, here we are. I see I've got something of a delicate nature to discuss with you.

MAC: Right.

SUE: And now before I start, I want to make it quite clear that I do not agree with or support what I am about to say, but the powers that be have issued a memo and it falls to me to pass on that information.

MAC: I see.

SUE: It's about your hair.

MAC: Yeah. What about my hair?

SUE: Well, they think it's too long. I, on the other hand, don't think it's long enough. I imagine a woman can only just hang onto it. May I?

MAC: May you what?

SHE SPRAWLS ACROSS THE DESK AND GRABS HIS HAIR ON BOTH SIDES.

MAC: Aaargh! Actually that um, that quite hurts.

SUE: Oh, I am sorry. Sorry about that.

MAC: So what do they suggest I do?

SUE: Cut it, you know, for... for hygiene. Well, you know, I was thinking that perhaps I could give it a trim.

SHE NIPS ROUND THE SIDE OF THE DESK WITH A PAIR OF SCISSORS AND CUTS OFF A SMALL LOCK OF MAC'S HAIR.

MAC: Argh! No, no no no no. Okay. Shall we leave that to the professionals?

SUE: Yeah, well. As you wish.

MAC: Is that all?

SUE: For now.

MAC: Okay. Okay. I'll um — I'll see you later, yeah?

MAC GOES.

SUE: Aaah the lion's mane. Truly the king of beasts.

SHE PUTS HIS LOCK OF HAIR DOWN THE FRONT OF HER TROUSERS.

▸▸ CORRIDOR

AT THE NOTICE BOARD, MARTIN IS PINNING UP A POSTER WHICH READS: "HAVE YOU SEEN THIS YOGHURT?".

BOYCE: That is fantastic.

MARTIN: Thanks very much.

BOYCE: No no, not that, that's just weird. This.

MARTIN: What?

BOYCE: That. It.

MARTIN: Wow.

BOYCE: What would make someone do something like that?

MARTIN: I don't know.

BOYCE: It's unbelievable.

MARTIN: Yeah, that is amazing, eighty quid for a cello, I'm tempted to ring myself. I don't even play the cello.

BOYCE: No, no, not that. This. Look. (LIFTING MARTIN UP) "To whom it does not concern..." Signed by Guy down the bottom there, see?

MARTIN: Oh wow, that's brilliant news! That is great news.

Subject: Re: I know it was you!
From: Astatham@ehtrust.gov.uk
To: BoycieBoyceBoyce@hotmail.com

Dear Mr Boyce,

Stop being needlessly difficult. You know my complaint is not about you per se, but more about what happened in my office, which I might add caused me great embarrassment.

And please use my proper medical title in future correspondence.

BOYCE: It's — it's — she must have forced him.

MARTIN: Yes, that — oh good for Caroline. See, she's, she's powerful in her own way, do you know what I mean? She's, she is strong, yet she's sort of, I don't know, somehow kind of feminine.

BOYCE: Steady on.

▶▶ **CORRIDOR**

STATHAM IS SWIRLING HIS COAT ALONG THE CORRIDOR.

▶▶ **THEATRE**

MAC IS PERFORMING AN OPERATION. GUY IS USING A HAND PUMP FOR A PATIENT'S BREATHING, HE GETS FASTER AS HE TALKS TO MAC.

GUY: ...Yeah, and the bastards are still saying that I mistreated the fabric of the course, that club equipment was damaged — not true — and that I broke the basic etiquette of golf. And the point is, a) they have no bloody proof that it was me, b) they have no idea if I was driving the buggy willingly, I could have been forced at gun point, and c) since when is an ornamental squirrel part of the fabric of the course, for fuck's sake?!

MAC: Hey, calm down, calm down.

GUY: Yeah, well I know it doesn't do any good, but...

MAC: Yeah, plus she's blowing up like a bloody balloon! (INDICATING THE PATIENT) Look at her, look at her.

GUY: Oh yeah. I thought she was having a nightmare.

MAC: She is having a bloody nightmare, with you as her anaesthetist.

▶▶ **HOSPITAL GROUNDS**

MARTIN AND CAROLINE ARE SITTING ON A BENCH.

MARTIN: So do I call you Caroline, or — ?

CAROLINE: Most people do. Apart from patients and my parents, they call me Doctor Todd.

MARTIN: Oh. My name's Martin.

CAROLINE: I know.

MARTIN: (PLEASED) Oh you know?

CAROLINE: It says so on your little badge. Martin Dear.

MARTIN: (DISAPPOINTED) Oh right. Yeah.

CAROLINE: So, any nicknames I should know about?

MARTIN: No, well...

CAROLINE: What?

MARTIN: Well no, it's just school, that's all. Not any more.

CAROLINE: Oh school nicknames are great. Go on, tell me.

MARTIN: It's just — well, my name's Martin — as you know — and um... well at school they used to call me Chuzzlewit, because they said I looked Dickensian and we were doing Dickens, and um — Chuzzlewit became Chuzzletit... and Chuzzletit got shortened to just Tit. And then that got lengthened again to Titbrain. Um, yes. I mean, it wasn't derogatory or anything, it's just a literary reference. To Dickens.

CAROLINE: You were called Titbrain?

MARTIN: Mmm, but I mean, yeah, in an affectionate kind of way, do you know what I mean? They — they loved me, you know, it was just; "Hey, Titbrain", you know, it's just, it's not...

CAROLINE CAN'T QUITE BELIEVE WHAT SHE'S HEARING.

▶▶ **THEATRE**

GUY IS STILL HAND-PUMPING A PATIENT.

MAC: Haven't you got alarms and stuff that let you know when all this is going to kick off?

GUY: Yeah, of course, but I never use them. I mean if you do, all you

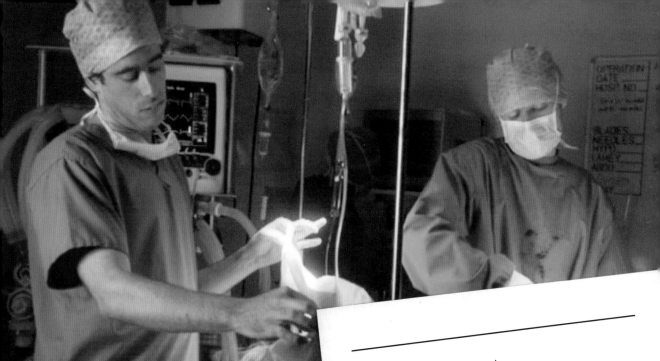

get all day is "bleep, bleep, bleep". It's a complete pain in the arse.

MAC: Yeah, well maybe today you should turn them on, just for a laugh.

GUY: Oh all right.

HE TURNS THE MONITOR VOLUME ON AND IT STARTS BLEEP-ING LOUDLY.

GUY: See? A complete pain in the arse.

HE TURNS THE VOLUME OFF AGAIN.

MAC: (TO THE UNCONSCIOUS PATIENT) You are very fortunate to be in the skilled hands of Doctor Secretan today, he's an extremely professional man and not in fact a reckless tit-end, or anything like that.

GUY: She's fine. Actually, she's a bit of a babe, this one.

MAC: Yeah, not my type. I prefer the ones without the great big gash across the abdomen.

GUY: Yeah, and that is why, my friend, you are no good at relationships.

MAC: Er — excuse me?

GUY: You heard.

MAC: Hello? Have you ever had a relationship? At least I managed

---

Subject: Re: I know it was you!
From: BoycieBoyceBoyce@hotmail.com
To: Astatham@ehtrust.gov.uk

Dear *Dr* Betty,

Sorry to hear that you embarrassed yourself in your office. Maybe you should do that at home before coming to work? I could lend you a Littlewoods catalogue if you like. Thirty pages of underwear. Phwoarr, eh?

    Bx

Subject: Re: I know it was you!
From: Astatham@ehtrust.gov.uk
To: BoycieBoyceBoyce@hotmail.com

Must you always be this flippant, Boyce?

Subject: Re: I know it was you!
From: BoycieBoyceBoyce@hotmail.com
To: Astatham@ehtrust.gov.uk

Why, how flippant would you like me to be?

Hugs and kisses, Bx

six years. What is your personal best? I think it was six hours.

GUY: A little bit unfair. Sometimes they get tea in the morning.

▸▸ **RADIOLOGY**

STATHAM IS LECTURING A GROUP OF STUDENTS.

STATHAM: All right ladies and gentlemen, boys and girls, and Boyce. We're going to look at the diagnostic benefits afforded us by the use of barium. I have here some before and after pictures. Here is an image of the lower intestine of a forty-eight-year-old woman. Let's call her patient X...

BOYCE: (COUGHS) ...boring.

STATHAM: You find the use of barium boring do you Mr Boyce?

BOYCE: Not at all, not at all, just your choice of name. Patient X. I think it would be really helpful if we gave her a proper name.

STATHAM: All right everybody, shall we make it easier for Mr Boyce? Let's give our lovely patient here a name. What's it to be? Miriam? Or Delilah? What is it?

BOYCE: Can we call her Joanna?

THERE IS SOME GIGGLING FROM THE STUDENTS. STATHAM SUDDENLY LOSES HIS SENSE OF HUMOUR.

STATHAM: No.

BOYCE: Well, why not?

STATHAM: Because er... we can't.

BOYCE: Well, why can't we?

STATHAM: Because I say so.

BOYCE: It's a nice name though, isn't it?

STATHAM: Yes, it's a beautiful name, and that is why it, it is inappropriate.

BOYCE: Why?

STATHAM: Because it doesn't look like Joanna — any — any Joanna...

BOYCE: Oh, I think it does. Yeah, yeah, definitely. Look, let's put it to the vote, okay? Who here thinks we should call her Joanna? Yeah? Hmm?

THE STUDENTS ALL RAISE THEIR ARMS.

BOYCE: Yes sir?

STATHAM: All right, we'll call her Joanna.

BOYCE: All right.

STATHAM: So, in the second image after the introduction of the barium...

BOYCE: So does Joanna take it up the bottom?

STATHAM: What?

BOYCE: The barium? Hmm?

MORE GIGGLING IN THE BACKGROUND. STATHAM IS GETTING MORE AND MORE UNCOMFORTABLE.

STATHAM: Well yes, it is a barium enema, in this case. In some cases it would be a meal, but more usually... an enema.

BOYCE: Right — so she takes it orally as well, does she?

Subject: Re: I know it was you!
From: Astatham@ehtrust.gov.uk
To: BoycieBoyceBoyce@hotmail.com

Did you, or did you not conceal a fax machine in my office ceiling then during an important meeting fax a large drawing of a penis to it, ending with said drawing dangling in the face of several senior NHS consultants? It's very simple. Just answer the question.

STATHAM: Yes, yes, yes, but as I say, this is an — an enema.

BOYCE: (WRITING NOTES) Joanna takes it up the bottom...

STATHAM: Stop that.

BOYCE: I'm just taking notes.

STATHAM: Stop it!

BOYCE: Well you always said we should take notes.

STATHAM: You've never taken any bloody notes before, have you?!

HE FURIOUSLY SNATCHES BOYCE'S NOTES AND SCREWS THEM UP.

STATHAM: So, why are you taking them now?!

BOYCE: Well, I just thought it was particularly important.

STATHAM LOSES IT AND ROUGHS UP BOYCE'S HAIR, AND SLAPS HIM ROUND THE HEAD. JOANNA APPROACHES.

JOANNA: What are you doing Doctor Statham?

STATHAM: He — er — there was a fly and now it's gone.

JOANNA: Could I — could I have a word?

STATHAM: Yes. Um... excuse me.

STATHAM AND JOANNA WALK AWAY FROM THE GIGGLING STUDENTS.

STATHAM: They were teasing you.

JOANNA: Teasing *me*, were they?

JOANNA AND STATHAM GO INTO HIS OFFICE.

▶▶ **DAY WARD**

GUY FINDS MARTIN.

GUY: The cardiac unit wants to see you.

MARTIN: The cardiac unit? Why? I've not been there this week.

GUY: Well, when they saw an e-mail with a big attachment, they thought they were getting extensive details of a donor heart.

MARTIN: Yeah, so?

GUY: So, what they actually received was a three-megabyte digital photo of a fruits of the forest yoghurt, and the words "hands off!".

MARTIN: Well, yeah, they sent me a really caustic e-mail actually, so what do they expect?

GUY: You do realise that a man has died because of your e-mail?

MARTIN: You're jok... — how? When...?

GUY: It stopped details of the real heart coming through on time.

MARTIN: Fucking hell! What, I've killed someone?! Really — have I killed someone? Tell me!

GUY: Ye—, nnn, ye—, nn, ye—, n...

MARTIN: Have I killed someone? Just say yes or no?

GUY: Y, n, ye—, nn, ye—, nn...

MARTIN: Guy, just tell me, did I kill someone?

GUY CONTINUES TO NOT QUITE SAY YES OR NO AS HE LEAVES THE WARD, FOLLOWED BY MARTIN.

MARTIN: Did I...? Did I kill someone or not? Guy! Have I! Guy, tell the truth, yes or no?

▶▶ **STATHAM'S OFFICE**

STATHAM IS STANDING BEHIND JOANNA, FONDLING HER NIPPLES.

STATHAM: Radio 3.

JOANNA: Ah, I'm not sure this is an appropriate moment.

STATHAM: Or else there might be a concerto in B minor or a little fugue, just waiting for us to tune in?

HE PINCHES HER NIPPLES.

JOANNA: No, it's too hard, it's too hard.

Subject: Re: I know it was you!
From: BoycieBoyceBoyce@hotmail.com
To: Astatham@ehtrust.gov.uk

Por favor pode você dizer-me a data em que esta aconteceu?

Subject: Re: I know it was you!
From: Astatham@ehtrust.gov.uk
To: BoycieBoyceBoyce@hotmail.com

And *not* in Portugese.

HE GENTLY BRUSHES THEM INSTEAD.

JOANNA: Well I can't feel anything now.

HE CONTINUES TO RUB HER BREASTS.

STATHAM: Yes, oh yes, I can, I can hear Bartok's music for strings, percussion and...

JOANNA: No no no, it's Puccini.

STATHAM: Puccini.

JOANNA STARTS TO SING HIGH NOTES. STATHAM JOINS IN.

JOANNA: Don't join in!

JOANNA SINGS A BIT MORE (FROM *MADAM BUTTERFLY*).

JOANNA: Oh, I'm losing reception now.

STATHAM RUBS HER MORE. JOANNA CARRIES ON SINGING.

JOANNA: Not the lips.

SHE GETS MORE AND MORE FRANTIC AND SINKS TO THE FLOOR. THERE IS A KNOCK AT THE DOOR.

STATHAM: Yes. Oh my goodness! It's up there. Yes. Lots to do, lots to do.

THEY TRY AND RECOVER THEMSELVES.

▸▸ GENERAL MEDICAL RECEPTION

BOYCE: I read an interesting item on the notice board this lunch time.

GUY: What, "cello for sale"?

MARTIN: No no no, not cello for sale, underneath that actually.

BOYCE: Yeah, something about you sleeping on a sofa.

GUY: Yes, well you don't want to believe everything you read on notice boards, mate.

BOYCE: Oh ho ho, I think you do. Mate!

GUY: Yeah, well in that case, I'm forced to believe that *Puss In Boots The Chemist* will be "a hilarious evening's entertainment" and "a bargain at five pounds a ticket".

MARTIN: But... but I'm going to see that actually.

GUY: Oh but, but, but, that doesn't surprise me.

MARTIN: Yeah, well. It doesn't surprise me either... Valery.

GUY: Grow up.

GUY LEAVES THEM.

MARTIN: He's really hurting inside, isn't he?

BOYCE: Hmm.

▸▸ MESS

ANGELA AND MAC ARE IN THE KITCHEN AREA; MAC IS USING THE TOASTER.

ANGELA: I spoke to Holly yesterday.

MAC: Oh yeah. Holly who?

ANGELA: The one you spent six years with? She sends her love.

MAC: Really? And what am I supposed to do with that?

ANGELA: Accept it as a friend?

MAC: She's *your* friend.

ANGELA: She can still be *your* friend.

MAC: Whatever.

ANGELA: Oh come on Mac, don't throw the baby out with the bath water... Oh — oh no.

MAC: No really, lovely, beautiful. Lovely turn of phrase. Excellent.

ANGELA: Oh gosh — a hideous, hideous turn of phrase. You know, you've just got to put this behind you, it was a hard decision for her.

MAC: Yeah, yeah.

ANGELA: She had some other news.

MAC: Yeah, what's that? Did she accidentally mow down fifty people with a machine gun because they were standing in the way of her career? It's not totally out of character, but I expect it was still quite a hard decision for her.

ANGELA: She's getting married.

MAC: Really?

HIS TOAST POPS UP — HE PICKS IT OUT, BUT IT IS VERY HOT.

MAC: Ow!

ANGELA: Ow! Is that painful?

MAC: No.

ANGELA: Are you all right?

MAC: Yes.

ANGELA: Are you sure about that?

MAC: Yes.

▶▶ OUTPATIENTS RECEPTION AREA

GUY TALKS TO SUE WHITE BY A RECEPTION DESK.

GUY: Just to let you know, that new Doctor Todd is quite something.

SUE: Oh do you know what? You come in here every week with your sordid little tales, but I know whatever you're doing, whoever you're doing, it's my face you see before you.

GUY LAUGHS. SUE SITS ON THE DESK AND PULLS HIM TOWARDS HER WITH HER LEGS.

SUE: Yeah, yeah, yeah. Because you see, I was the one that broke you first. Wasn't I? And you just can't get me out of your head.

GUY: That is...

SUE: (STARTS TO SING KYLIE MINOGUE SONG) La la la, la la la la la...

SHE USES HER TONGUE PROVOCATIVELY.

GUY: Yeah. That is...

SUE: (CONTINUES SINGING) La la la, la la la la la...

GUY TRIES TO SAY SOMETHING, BUT CAN'T. HE HEADS OFF DOWN THE CORRIDOR, FOLLOWED BY SUE WHO IS STILL TORMENTING HIM.

▶▶ X-RAY RECEPTION/WAITING AREA

CAROLINE: Can I have a quick word?

MAC: Zoom and whoosh. There you are, quick words. Words that are quick.

CAROLINE: Oh I get it.

MAC: Got it?

CAROLINE: Yeah, no, very good.

MAC: Yes, go on. I promise not to confuse you this time.

CAROLINE: Okay. I just want to say that despite signed confessions and so on... some people still have slightly the wrong idea, so just to clarify, I did stay at Guy's, but nothing happened. I was going to book into a hotel...

MAC: Can I stop you there?

MAC WALKS OFF, CAROLINE FOLLOWS.

CAROLINE: So, if anybody mentions it, I'd be grateful if you'd... put them straight?

MAC: Nothing to do with me.

CAROLINE: No, if anybody does mention it...

MAC: Why do you think I'm interested?

CAROLINE: No, I never said you'd be interested, I...

MAC: So why bore me with all the details?

CAROLINE: Don't be so bloody rude!

MAC: I have a job to do, I am not interested in your personal life. If that offends you, if it bothers you, then I apologise. Staff at your previous hospital might have found you totally fascinating, I don't.

CAROLINE: If anything, that's an increase in rudeness.

MAC: Oh, oh, I hope nobody starts gossiping about me, because I'd hate to be the centre of attention.

CAROLINE: That is not fair.

MAC: I don't care. I'm not bothered, I don't — I'm sick of hearing about you and Guy and your night of passion or non-passion.

CAROLINE: So people *have* been talking.

MAC: Yeah, talking and not concentrating on their jobs. Do your job Doctor Todd, keep your personal life personal, allow my staff to concentrate on their work. I think there's enough soap operas set in hospitals, don't you think? (CHECKING A FILE) What? I don't need this.

HE WALKS AWAY, LIFTING HIS WHITE COAT TO SHOW A HOLE HAS BEEN CUT IN HIS SCRUBS, REVEALING A BARE BOTTOM. CAROLINE DOESN'T SEE.

CAROLINE: You're the drama queen if anyone is.

SHE ANGRILY RUFFLES UP THE FILES HE WAS USING.

▸▸ OFFICE

HARRIET: Shit! Shit, shit, shit! Oh God!

RACHEL: Calm down.

HARRIET GETS OUT A LARGE WHITE BOARD WITH INFORMATION ABOUT HER CHILDREN'S WHEREABOUTS. THE OTHERS GATHER ROUND TO HELP HER.

HARRIET: Oh, I can't look. I know I should be picking someone up or dropping someone off. Okay. Oh, deep breath, no need to panic. Right, Oscar is with the nanny until four o'clock, and then he's...

RACHEL: (READING FROM CHART) He's getting collected by Ian.

HARRIET: Okay. Oh great. Um, right now, Jamie, Jamie Jamie... Um. Oh.

KIM: Tiny Tots.

HARRIET: Tiny Tots! Right, okay! Robbie is um... well, Robbie is lost! Shit, I can't believe I've lost Robbie. Oh my God!

KAREN: Calm down, he'll be on here somewhere. We'll find him.

HARRIET: Oh it's just sometimes I lose track of them. I can't believe I've lost Robbie!

RACHEL: Yeah, we'll find him.

▸▸ OUTSIDE MAIN ENTRANCE

CAROLINE IS PICKING BOYCE'S BRAINS.

CAROLINE: You're friends with Mac and Guy, who's the biggest scum-bag?

BOYCE: Guy. Guy. Guy. Guy...

CAROLINE: Guy, Guy — why Guy?

BOYCE: He once ethically objected to resuscitating a woman with an A cup.

CAROLINE: An egg cup?

BOYCE: No no, an A cup, you know, little puppies? No point in saving less than a handful, apparently.

CAROLINE: Dear God!

GUY COMES OVER WITH A PRESENT.

GUY: Hey — oh I'm so glad I caught you.

CAROLINE: Speak of the devil.

GUY: Me?

CAROLINE: Yeah. Apparently it's not just me you've treated despicably, you've got previous form.

GUY: Um...

CAROLINE: It now seems like you're some sort of deranged madman.

GUY: House-warming gift. I know you've had a dreadful day and I also know that I'm partly responsible. I am deeply sorry. And I'll try and set the record straight, yeah? I'll see you whenever. (TO BOYCE) Oh, and Boyce, well done today. You carry on like that and you're going to make a top-notch doctor. (TO CAROLINE) Oh — and as for my previous form, well I mean, I think you know better than most that rumours aren't always to be believed...

CAROLINE GOES TO SPEAK.

GUY: Sssh. And, you know, I think we've all made mistakes in the past, started a relationship with someone and then realised they're not to be trusted. And at times I have been cruel, you know, I've lashed out, but it's because I was hurt and of that I am guilty. See you whenever.

HE WALKS AWAY, LEAVING THE OTHER TWO STARING AFTER HIM.

BOYCE: He is, of course, good, very good.

CAROLINE RIPS OPEN THE WRAPPING PAPER ON THE GIFT.

CAROLINE: Oh my God!

BOYCE: What, one for the boot fair?

CAROLINE: No, I've wanted one of these for ages. I have hard toe nails, I think I mentioned it once in an anecdote about my mum. He remembered.

BOYCE: He's better than good!

» OFFICE

HARRIET IS STILL TRYING TO REMEMBER WHERE ROBBIE SHOULD BE.

HARRIET: Oh, I know I took three morning-after pills to try and flush him out, but it doesn't mean I don't love him, does it? He's just 'blinky'... (SHE BLINKS)

KIM: (SUDDENLY POINTS AT THE CHART) Bingo! I've got the fucker, he's with the school therapist till five.

HARRIET: Oh! Oh!

KAREN: There, you see? It's all fine. Everyone's where they should be.

KIM: Right, let's get the fuck out of here.

HARRIET PACKS UP HER THINGS. ON HER BACK IS A POST-IT NOTE WHICH READS: "DON'T FORGET. COLLECT STUART FROM SCHOOL TRIP AT 5.30"

» STREET

IT'S GETTING DARK. STUART IS SITTING ON A BENCH, WAITING.

» CAROLINE'S HOUSE

MARTIN HELPS CAROLINE TAKE A FEW THINGS INTO THE HOUSE THAT CAROLINE IS RENTING FROM HER BROTHER.

CAROLINE: This really is very kind of you.

MARTIN: Well, it's on my way home, so... How did you get this place?

CAROLINE: Oh it's, it's not mine, it's my brother's.

MARTIN: Yeah, what does he do?

CAROLINE: Oh, whatever he can get his hands on.

SHE UNPACKS THE FOOT SPA.

CAROLINE: So, tell me what you know.

MARTIN LOOKS AT THE FOOT SPA.

MARTIN: Well... you just, I guess you plug it in and put your feet in here...

CAROLINE: No no, about Guy.

MARTIN: Oh, Guy.

CAROLINE: Hmm.

MARTIN: Um... well, he's an anaesthetist.

CAROLINE: Yep.

MARTIN: Er... his name's Swiss.

CAROLINE: Yeah, yeah. You see, what I really wanted to know is — is he the sort of doctor I should avoid?

MARTIN: Yes.

CAROLINE: Well, that was very definite Martin, not much mulling it over going on there.

MARTIN: No, well I just meant on reflection, thinking about it, yeah, you should avoid him. Well, he — I shouldn't say this, because he is a good mate of mine — but... it's just that... thinking about it, there are other doctors who work in, in the hospital... who, that — who are nice, for you, for you.

CAROLINE: Is English your first language?

MARTIN: Yeah it is, yeah, why?

CAROLINE: Yeah. No, you do have quite an exotic turn of phrase.

MARTIN: Oh, thanks. Well I have travelled quite a lot.

CAROLINE: Yeah, well that'll be it then.

MARTIN: Yeah, no, I've been all over. France... Boulogne, Paris.

CAROLINE: Yeah, it might be time to travel now. (MARTIN LOOKS BLANK) Homewards?

MARTIN: Oh, okay.

CAROLINE: Thanks for the help.

MARTIN WALKS OUT STILL HOLDING SOME OF CAROLINE'S THINGS. HE RETURNS THEM AND GOES.

▶▶ SPANISH RESTAURANT

STATHAM AND JOANNA ARE HAVING DINNER. THERE IS A 'SIZZLING' DISH IN THE MIDDLE OF THE TABLE.

JOANNA: Are you all right?

STATHAM: Hmm? Yeah. Yeah.

JOANNA: You seem a bit edgy.

STATHAM: Well, no. Yes. Well... actually um...

HE TAPS THE GLASS WITH HIS KNIFE.

STATHAM: Um... I would just like to say — take this opportunity to say a few special words... um — Joanna Yardley Clore, we've been intimately, you know, entangled now for some months, and let's be honest, it's become more than, more than just a, you know... especially for me. Um... you know, you may not be the, the youngest or even the prettiest lady in the hospital, but nevertheless, in this age of casual chlamydia and, and so forth, it seems a rather old-fashioned notion, and that's why, um... I'd like to say those um... those three special words...

JOANNA POURS SOME WINE ON THE SIZZLING PAN, DROWNING OUT STATHAM'S CRUCIAL WORDS.

STATHAM: I love you. Um... and I want people to say: look, oh look, there goes that lovely lovely couple. They must be so terribly...

JOANNA POURS MORE WINE ON THE SIZZLING PAN. STATHAM COUGHS.

STATHAM: ...In love. There, I've, I've said it. What do you think?

JOANNA: (TO WAITER) Can we turn the music up?

JOANNA GETS UP AND STARTS TO DANCE THE SALSA.

▸▸ **BAR**

MARTIN, GUY AND MAC ARE HAVING A DRINK.

GUY: Try drastically lowering your sights.

MARTIN: How do you mean?

GUY: You know, try God-botherers, phone-mast campaigners.

MAC: Women who smell of biscuits.

GUY: Yeah, lollipop ladies.

MARTIN: Yeah, but I don't really want a woman like that, do I?

MAC: If only we could somehow give you a bit of Guy's natural prowess with women, maybe a pheromone transplant, something like that.

GUY: You know how the Vikings used to get their fearsome fighting powers from eating hallucinogenic mushrooms?

MARTIN: So?

GUY: So, well the senior Vikings would eat the mushrooms, then the next level down would drink their urine, which contained the active substances, and so on down the line.

MAC: Are you saying what I think you're saying?

MARTIN: What?

MAC: You can't, you can't do that, no.

MARTIN: No go on, well tell me.

MAC: Well, Guy has a natural ability with women. There's something in him which makes him attractive to women, so...

MARTIN: So?

GUY: So the Vikings, remember?

MARTIN: What, I drink your urine and become a Viking? (REALISES) Oh — I get a girlfriend.

GUY: Drink my pee, pull like me.

MARTIN: Yeah, all right.

GUY: Yeah?

MARTIN: Yeah.

GUY: Right.

GUY GOES OFF WITH A GLASS.

MARTIN: Cool.

MAC IS TRYING NOT TO LET MARTIN SEE THEY'RE WINDING HIM UP.

▸▸ **CAROLINE'S HOUSE**

CAROLINE HAS SETTLED INTO AN ARMCHAIR WITH A TAKE-AWAY CURRY, HER FEET IN THE NEW FOOT SPA, WATCHING THE TELEVISION.

CAROLINE: (TALKING TO TV) You evil bitch! You've got to watch out for him, he's after your man.

A CAT COMES OUT OF NOWHERE AND JUMPS ON HER LAP. SHE DROPS HER CURRY INTO THE FOOT SPA.

CAROLINE: Argh! Oh, where did, where did, where did you come...? Oh shit!

▶▶ BAR

GUY RETURNS WITH A GLASS FULL OF YELLOW LIQUID. MARTIN DRINKS IT. THE OTHER TWO WATCH HIM. HE GROANS.

MARTIN: Right, I'm off to bag me a woman.

THE OTHER TWO WATCH HIM GO. GUY STARTS EATING A YOGHURT.

MAC: That wasn't really your urine?

GUY: No, of course not.

MAC: No. Phew, thank goodness.

GUY: I got it from the path lab. Corpse juice.

▶▶ RESTAURANT

STATHAM AND JOANNA ARE DANCING IN THE RESTAURANT. NO ONE ELSE IS.

▶▶ MESS, NIGHT-TIME

ON THE TABLE A YOGHURT IS IN THE GLARE OF AN ANGLE-POISE LAMP. MARTIN'S ARMS APPEAR, HE CHECKS HIS WATCH.

▶▶ THERAPY POOL

MAC AND GUY ARE AT THE THERAPY POOL, WEARING SCRUBS.

MAC: You know the rules?

GUY: Oh I know the rules. End and back. No hands.

▶▶ MESS, NIGHT-TIME

MARTIN CRASHES IN THROUGH THE BLINDS. NO ONE ELSE IS THERE. HE PLAYS WITH THE LAMP, INTERROGATION-STYLE.

MARTIN: Hey Mr Royce, are you familiar with the name Jimmy the Yoghurt?

▶▶ RESTAURANT

STATHAM AND JOANNA ARE STILL DANCING FRANTICALLY. THE WAITER LOOKS ON, BORED.

▶▶ THERAPY POOL

GUY: On your marks, get set —

GUY JUMPS IN, FOLLOWED BY MAC. THEY WALK THROUGH THE WATER.

▶▶ RESTAURANT

JOANNA AND STATHAM ARE STILL DANCING.

JOANNA: It's Darcy Bussell!

▶▶ CAROLINE'S HOUSE

CAROLINE: (TO THE CAT) You little — chicken dhansak!

▶▶ THERAPY POOL

GUY PUSHES MAC UNDER THE WATER.

▶▶ RESTAURANT

STATHAM LIFTS UP JOANNA'S SKIRT. THE WAITERS ARE PUTTING CHAIRS ON TABLES.

▶▶ THERAPY POOL

MAC PULLS GUY UNDER THE WATER.

▶▶ MESS, NIGHT-TIME

MARTIN CAREFULLY PLACES THE YOGHURT AND SPOON UNDER THE LAMP, THEN DISAPPEARS UNDER THE TABLE.

▶▶ STREET, NIGHT-TIME

STUART IS LYING DOWN ON THE BENCH, STILL WAITING FOR HARRIET TO PICK HIM UP.

EPISODE 3

▶▶ STREET

JOANNA WALKS PAST SOME WORKMEN WHO COMPLETELY IGNORE HER.

▶▶ CAROLINE'S HOUSE

CAROLINE IS INTERVIEWING A MAN.

POTENTIAL LODGER: I thought I'd find myself a new place after my wife died.

CAROLINE: Oh I'm so sorry. Was it sudden?

POTENTIAL LODGER: Well, I didn't notice it straight away, you know. Sex was the same, but the dishes kept piling up.

▶▶ STREET

JOANNA IS ANNOYED THAT THE WORKMEN HAVEN'T NOTICED HER AND WALKS PAST THEM AGAIN, HITCHING UP HER SKIRT A LITTLE AND TAKING HER JACKET OFF.

▶▶ CAROLINE'S HOUSE

POTENTIAL LODGER: I like a laugh me.

CAROLINE: Right.

▶▶ STREET

JOANNA TRIES WALKING PAST THE WORKMEN HITTING HER ARSE. THEY STILL IGNORE HER.

▶▶ CAROLINE'S HOUSE

CAROLINE: Yeah, well thinking about it, the room is on the tiny side, and has ridiculously low ceilings for a tall chap like you. And quite smelly.

▶▶ STREET

JOANNA IS REALLY ANNOYED NOW.

JOANNA: Oi! Wankers!

SHE OPENS HER BLOUSE AT THEM. THEY STARE AT HER.

SHE WALKS OFF, DOING UP HER BLOUSE.

JOANNA: Yeah, still got the magic.

▶▶ ROAD OUTSIDE HOSPITAL

MAC ARRIVES ON HIS BIG DUCATI MOTORBIKE AT THE SAME TIME AS MARTIN ON HIS SCOOTER. MAC DRIVES IN FRONT OF MARTIN AND THE TURBULENCE CAUSES MARTIN TO VEER OFF INTO A BUSH.

▶▶ CORRIDOR

LYNDON ARRIVES — HE CLEARLY INSPIRES GREAT RESPECT AND AFFECTION IN ALL THE STAFF HE WALKS PAST. HE IS VERY COOL.

LYNDON: Hey.

STAFF: Hi Lyndon!

LYNDON: (HELPING SOMEONE OUT) Hey, just let me do that... All right?

STAFF: Hi Lyndon!

LYNDON: Hey. Hey doc...

▶▶ ROAD OUTSIDE HOSPITAL

MARTIN REVERSES HIS SCOOTER OUT OF THE BUSH.

▶▶ CORRIDOR

BOYCE WALKS ALONG AND BOWLS AN IMAGINARY CRICKET BALL. HE MEETS CAROLINE AT THE NOTICE BOARD.

BOYCE: Oh — if you see a really pretty blonde girl, about five-seven, green eyes, slightly foreign accent, can you tell her I've gone to Radiology?

CAROLINE: Yeah, I suppose so. What's her name?

BOYCE: I've no idea, she might not even exist, but you know, just in case.

CAROLINE: I see.

BOYCE: (READS CAROLINE'S ADVERT) Oh... are you looking for a lodger?

CAROLINE: Yeah. All I've had so far are loonies. I thought I'd see if the staff here are a bit more normal, you know, ten fingers, no fur. Why, are you interested?

BOYCE: No. I know someone who will be, though. There you go — (HE POINTS OUT ANOTHER NOTICE ON THE BOARD) "Desperately seeking accommodation."

CAROLINE: (SHE LOOKS AT IT) Angela...

BOYCE: Yeah, she was sharing a house, but she wants to go a bit more exclusive.

CAROLINE: Oh.

BOYCE: Do you want me to track her down for you?

CAROLINE: Oh no no. No, it's all right, I'll see her later. And she'll... she'll probably see this anyway.

BOYCE: Don't forget, five-seven, green eyes.

CAROLINE: I'll keep a look out.

BOYCE GOES. CAROLINE TAKES DOWN HER LODGER ADVERT.

▸▸ **LOCKER AREA**

MARTIN AND MAC TAKE OFF THEIR CRASH HELMETS. MARTIN MAKES NOISES WITH MAC'S RATHER FLASHY HELMET.

MAC: Wow. It's never done that for me.

MARTIN: What?

MAC: I said it's never done that for me.

MARTIN: Alloy isn't it?

MAC: Yeah, yeah. It's a Kevlar-carbon composite, you need the protection if you're going to sit astride what is basically a big kid's stupid and very dangerous toy, so...

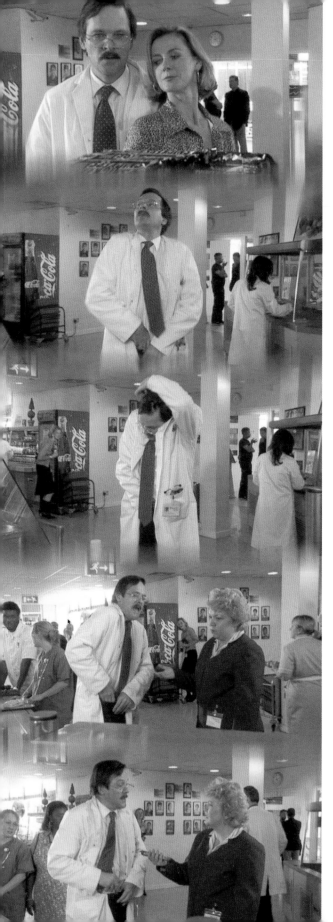

MARTIN: Hmm. Yeah, I'm thinking about getting an Adamantium helmet.

MAC: Yeah?

MARTIN: Mmm.

MAC: That's the stuff that Wolverine's skeleton's made out of, isn't it?

MARTIN: Yep. Hardest metal in the world.

MAC: Indeed, indeed, yeah. Sadly, of course, a fictional metal. So, that would probably reduce its effectiveness in a crash-style scenario.

MARTIN: Good point. Good point. Still. Hardest metal in the world.

MARTIN WALKS OFF.

MAC: Fictional.

▸▸ CANTEEN

JOANNA IS LOOKING ALONG A LINE OF CHOCOLATE BARS. STATHAM JOINS HER.

JOANNA: Too close.

STATHAM: You smell lovely, of beautiful garden centres. It makes me want you right now.

JOANNA: Oh do shut it Alan, unless you've got something useful to say, don't bother.

STATHAM THINKS FOR A MOMENT.

STATHAM: If you boil a kettle with vinegar, it gets rid of the unpleasant residue.

JOANNA: Nick it.

SHE POINTS TO A SNICKERS CHOCOLATE BAR.

STATHAM: What?

JOANNA: Nick the chocolate bar.

STATHAM: I'll buy it for you.

JOANNA: No, if you really wanted me, you'd nick it. Come on Alan, where's your sense of danger? It might make me horny.

STATHAM: Oh God!

JOANNA: Go on, just nick it.

STATHAM MAKES A GREAT FUSS OF STUFFING THE CHOCO-LATE BAR DOWN HIS TROUSERS. THE CATERING MANAGER SUDDENLY APPEARS.

Ha ha, Losers,

I'm on holiday — you're not.
Renewed membership of Mile
High Club. Twice. Three
times if you count frottage
with a trolley.
Kiss my Swiss.

Guy the Impaler
XXX
(WITH HARDCORE TONGUES + SPITTLE).

Zürich, Schiffstation Bürkliplatz

RUDI SUTER, OBERRIEDEN-ZCH

Odd, Stem Ginger,
Fartin etc.

Surgical 9 Deviants
East Hampton NHS
Trust
Blighty
EB2 4NL

CATERING MANAGER: Excuse me.

STATHAM: Are you — you talking to me?

JOANNA WATCHES IN THE BACKGROUND.

CATERING MANAGER: Yes, could I have a word? Could you put the tray down and step to one side?

STATHAM: No!

CATERING MANAGER: Pardon?

STATHAM: No, I won't!

CATERING MANAGER: Well, I don't think you'll want this discussed in front of everyone.

STATHAM: Yes, yes I do.

CATERING MANAGER: Okay, what have you got down the front of your trousers?

STATHAM: Trousers?

CATERING MANAGER: A Snickers fifty percent bigger size, I saw you through the two-way mirror.

STATHAM: Yes. Yes, yes you did.

CATERING MANAGER: Hand it over.

STATHAM: Um — yes I will, I will, yes, because there we, there we have it. So, other colleagues, putting, er — for reasons best known, and that's why we have this situation.

CATERING MANAGER: Urgh, it's all melted.

STATHAM: Yes, those, those were my exact words to — to them. And therefore I — I accept your apology, goodbye!

HE WALKS OFF, VERY EMBARRASSED.

▸▸ CORRIDOR

GUY WALKS ALONG AND SNATCHES A MAGAZINE FROM BOYCE.

GUY: Ooh, oh *Men's Health*? (HE PERUSES THE ARTICLES AT GREAT SPEED) 'Ten steps to a flatter stomach' — no need. 'Sex: what she wishes you knew' — yes, yes, duhh, obviously — how? Oh they like that, sucking's better and they like it hard and rough. 'Combat hair loss' — hah! 'Get a harder body in ten minutes a day' — already got one. 'How to click with women' — already can: clickety click click click.

GUY THROWS THE MAGAZINE IN THE AIR AND BOYCE CATCHES IT.

▸▸ HOSPITAL SHOP

CAROLINE ENTERS.

CAROLINE: Do you have some cigarettes? I need cigarettes, do you sell them?

ASSISTANT: You do know this is a hospital?

CAROLINE: Well yes, yes I know, I work here. Look, my badge says Dr Caroline Todd.

ASSISTANT: Well you should know better then, shouldn't you?

CAROLINE: Perhaps you can tell me where I can get some?

ASSISTANT: Don't they say seventy percent of all ill people are ill because they smoke?

CAROLINE: Did I say lecture? Sorry, I meant directions, to the nearest shop. Real shop that is.

ANGELA COMES UP BEHIND HER.

ANGELA: Caroline...

CAROLINE: Careful Angela, I might bite.

ANGELA: Really?

CAROLINE: Somebody might be about to die if I don't find some cigarettes.

ANGELA: Oh, I see. How's your house, is it okay?

CAROLINE: My house?

ANGELA: Yeah.

CAROLINE: Yeah, it's great.

ANGELA: Are you going to be all right living there all by yourself?

CAROLINE: Yeah, yeah, I'm a big girl. Figuratively.

ANGELA: So you're not looking for lodgers any more?

CAROLINE: Sorry?

ANGELA: Boyce told me about your advert.

CAROLINE: Yes, yes, yes, I'm looking for lodgers, yes, sorry, yes, sorry, I misunderstood you. Nicotine deficiency.

ANGELA: Da-dah! Am I too late?

CAROLINE: No... all I've had so far is psychopaths.

ANGELA: Oh great. Well I'm not a psychopath. (SHE LAUGHS HYSTERICALLY) I'm not. So can I come and see the room?

CAROLINE: Well no, you see — I mean the thing is... do you smoke?

ANGELA: No I don't.

CAROLINE: I do. I did, I gave up, but it's just my lungs are sentimental, and when I'm under pressure they, they start to woo me.

ANGELA PRODUCES A CARD.

ANGELA: Quitline! So, can I come and see the room?

CAROLINE: Yes, please do. Yes, please do come. Absolutely. I won't take no for an answer.

ANGELA: Thanks Caroline.

ANGELA BLOWS A KISS AT CAROLINE AND GOES. CAROLINE THROWS THE QUITLINE CARD ON THE FLOOR.

▶▶ **LIFT**

BOYCE IS TALKING TO A FELLOW STUDENT IN THE LIFT. JOANNA IS STANDING WITH HER BACK TO THEM, LISTENING.

BOYCE: You know the main health risks obviously, but I wasn't aware that the actual act of smoking a cigarette causes lines to form around the mouth.

STUDENT: Oh what, because of the...? (SUCKS IN)

BOYCE: Well yeah, I mean you do that twenty times a day, it's going to have an effect isn't it?

STUDENT: Yeah.

THE LIFT DOORS OPEN AND JOANNA RUSHES OUT IN A PANIC.

►► OFFICE

RACHEL: Bloody hell!

KIM: Are you all right?

RACHEL: No, I'm not. I hate it when men say "I can't remember saying that" or "I was only joking".

KIM: Yeah. Or "I didn't mean it like that".

RACHEL: Yeah, and what about "You only hear what you want to hear".

KAREN: Yeah. Or "I'm actually a woman".

RACHEL: Exactly.

KIM AND RACHEL PAUSE AND REALISE WHAT KAREN HAS SAID.

KIM: A man's actually said that to you?

KAREN: Yep.

JOANNA RUSHES IN.

JOANNA: Oh Harriet, did you manage to get the contract document sorted last night for the smoke unit? — Stroke unit? Yeah? Great.

HARRIET LOOKS IN THE FILE AND SEES HER CHILDREN'S ART-WORK IN THERE INSTEAD OF THE CONTRACT. SHE SITS ON THE FILE TO HIDE IT. JOANNA GOES INTO HER OFFICE AND CLOSES THE BLINDS. SHE GETS OUT A CIGARETTE AND LOOKS IN A MIRROR. SHE PUTS MOISTURISING CREAM ALL AROUND HER MOUTH AND TRIES TO SMOKE.

JOANNA: Stop smiling, dear.

SHE PUTS THE CIGARETTE UP HER NOSE AND SMOKES THAT WAY, LEANING BACK IN HER CHAIR.

►► CORRIDOR

LYNDON, HOLDING A COMPUTER CIRCUIT BOARD, WALKS PAST A NURSE.

LYNDON: Hey.

NURSE: Hi!

HE PASSES GUY WHO IS TALKING TO NURSE DEBS.

LYNDON: Hey Debs.

NURSE DEBS: (BIG SMILE) Hi!

GUY FOLLOWS LYNDON.

GUY: Er — my domain.

LYNDON: Sorry?

GUY: You are entering my territory, yeah? I am the master of all I survey. In here, in here I perform the most delicate and intricate operations and procedures on the human body. If, God forbid, something should go wrong, somebody dies. That's it. The end.

LYNDON: You've killed them.

GUY: No... but it's over. You can't just buy another one. Yeah? You can't just, you can't just...

HE TOUCHES LYNDON'S CIRCUIT BOARD. LYNDON REMOVES HIS FINGER.

GUY: Sorry. You can't just swap up to a G4 megahertz kilodrive whopper thing, whatever, okay? I'm at the cutting edge. Stand aside please, information technology boy, somebody needs my help.

A PATIENT IS BEING WHEELED INTO THE OPERATING THEATRE.

GUY: Nurse, what have we got?

THEATRE NURSE: Knee arthroscopy.

GUY: Right, tricky, yeah. You see, it's not all about a pretty-boy face around here. All right little lady, let's get this show on the road.

GUY POKES THE NURSE, WHO IS SMILING AT LYNDON.

THEATRE NURSE: Oi! Back off, butcher!

LYNDON WALKS AWAY. GUY PUSHES A TROLLEY OF INSTRUMENTS AFTER HIM, BUT IT HITS SOMEONE ELSE EMERGING FROM A DOORWAY.

▶▶ STATHAM'S OFFICE

STATHAM IS IN HIS OFFICE PLAYING THE RECORDER. BOYCE ENTERS.

BOYCE: I just came to get the Jarvis MRI file for Doctor MacCartney?

STATHAM: Yes.

BOYCE: I didn't know you were a recorder player.

STATHAM: Yes, I have many strings to my bow — recorder.

BOYCE: Great. So, can I have the file?

STATHAM: Er, yes.

BOYCE: Okay. Um, I think Mac needs it quite urgently.

STATHAM WON'T GET UP BECAUSE HE HAS AN ERECTION.

STATHAM: Nearly there.

BOYCE: Right.

STATHAM: Ready in a minute.

BOYCE: Okay. Shall I get it?

STATHAM: No, no, it's complicated, it's one of many. I'll um...

HE GETS UP, BENT OVER. BOYCE GOES TO TOUCH THE RECORDER.

STATHAM: Don't touch my sopranino!

HE GETS THE FILE, BUT COVERS HIS ERECTION WITH IT.

STATHAM: I have it.

BOYCE TAKES THE FILE.

STATHAM: Um — no — no!

BOYCE: Oh my God! What the fuck is that?!

STATHAM: Um... You're probably thinking that in some bizarre way that my playing the recorder has caused um — an expansion down... down below.

BOYCE: Well I wasn't thinking that, but I am now.

STATHAM: Really? If you were, you'd be sorely mistaken.

BOYCE: Of course, because most people just think of freely bouncing breasts.

STATHAM: As, as I do.

BOYCE: Good, good. Good. So, does it work if anyone plays it?

HE PICKS UP THE RECORDER.

STATHAM: No! Don't put my instrument in your lips!

BOYCE PLAYS A NOTE.

STATHAM: Oh dirty! Filthy!

BOYCE: Cheerio.

BOYCE LEAVES THE RECORDER AND GOES.

STATHAM: Man spittle...

STATHAM PULLS THE RECORDER APART AND PUTS IT IN A MUG.

▶▶ CORRIDOR/STAFF LIAISON OFFICE

SUE COMES UP TO JOANNA.

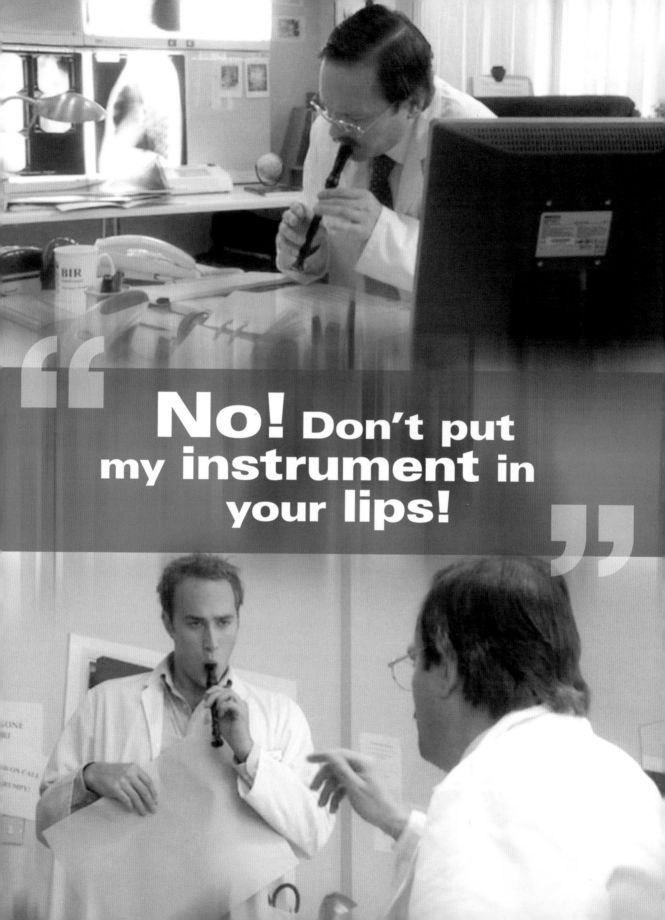

SUE: You know that thing about bringing in animals for patients to stroke?

JOANNA: Oh God, yeah, cancelled. Lack of funds, more important things to worry about.

JOANNA WALKS OFF.

SUE: What?! What?! What? Fuck!!

SHE GOES BACK TO HER OFFICE.

SUE: O-oh. Okay, come on now, shoo. Shoo shoo. Come on, shoo fly. Come on, kum ba yah.

THERE'S A CAMEL IN HER OFFICE.

SUE: You want to think a wee bit about personal hygiene you know, darling. Now come, let's get out of here.

▸▸ FIRE ESCAPE

CAROLINE SNEAKS OUT ONTO THE STEPS AND TRIES TO LIGHT A CIGARETTE, BUT THE LIGHTER WON'T WORK. SHE SCREWS UP THE CIGARETTE AND THROWS IT AWAY IN A TEMPER.

CAROLINE: Aarrgh! I want nicotine!! And then I would like to meet a very nice man and have a sexually charged, no speaking affair.

SHE TRIES THE LIGHTER ONCE MORE, WHICH NOW LIGHTS — SHE THROWS IT AWAY IN A TEMPER. SHE TRIES TO GET BACK IN THROUGH THE EMERGENCY EXIT DOOR, BUT IT WON'T OPEN FROM THIS SIDE — SHE IS LOCKED OUT.

▸▸ CORRIDOR

SUE LEADS THE CAMEL DOWN THE CORRIDOR.

▸▸ NOTICE BOARD

JOANNA IS PINNING NOTICES ON THE BOARD. STATHAM COMES UP TO HER AND PATS HER ON THE BOTTOM.

STATHAM: Guess who?

JOANNA: No idea. Jack Nicholson?

STATHAM: No.

JOANNA: God, you're so predictable!

STATHAM: What do you mean?

JOANNA: Every day you do this 'hand on my arse' thing.

STATHAM: Well I thought you — I thought you liked it.

JOANNA: It wouldn't be so bad if you changed things a bit, if you — I don't know — used something other than your hand. But oh no, hand on arse, hand on arse, every bloody day!

STATHAM: Um, I was just... Oh, I've dropped my pen there.

STATHAM TOUCHES HER ARSE WITH HIS FOREHEAD.

JOANNA: No, no, no, that's no good. It was my suggestion, it's got to come from you.

STATHAM: Yes, hmm.

A COLLEAGUE WALKS PAST. JOANNA AND STATHAM TRY TO ACT PROFESSIONALLY.

JOANNA: Derek...

STATHAM: Wednesday.

THE COLLEAGUE HAS GONE — THEY BECOME CONSPIRATORIAL AGAIN.

JOANNA: You've got to be more exciting, a bit more, you know, spontaneous.

STATHAM: Yes, all right, well I'm sure that can be arranged.

JOANNA: No, no no. It can't be arranged, that's the whole point. You've got to just do it.

STATHAM: All right, but when?

JOANNA: Don't ask me, it's up to you, it's supposed to be spontaneous.

STATHAM: Right, I'll have a think.

JOANNA: No, don't think.

STATHAM: What do you mean, don't think? Where would we be if nobody thought? You know — no art, no literature, no music, no medicine, you know, we'd just be in the jungle like rutting, sweaty, dirty beasts.

JOANNA: Well that's a start.

SHE WALKS OFF.

▸▸ MESS

ANGELA IS WITH MARTIN AND GUY.

ANGELA: Can I just warn you both, Mac's had some difficult news.

MARTIN: Oh really, news?

ANGELA: Yes, about Holly.

MARTIN: Ah, Holly the tear-your-life-apart, break-your-heart, baby-killer? Oh.

ANGELA: Yeah, she is a friend of mine Martin. And that's a little bit unfair. She just wasn't ready to start a family.

MARTIN: That's what Mac calls her.

ANGELA: Yes, well it broke his heart splitting up with Holly, he was probably under a great deal of stress.

GUY: What about her?

ANGELA: Well look, I'm only telling you this so you can be supportive to Mac should he need it. Um — she's getting married, and also, although I haven't found the time to tell him this, she's pregnant.

MAC ENTERS.

MAC: Who's pregnant?

MARTIN: Holly the baby-killer.

ANGELA: I'm sorry Mac, I was going to tell you and I haven't found the moment.

MAC: I think we're out of milk, so I'll probably steal some from the nurses.

MAC GOES.

GUY: Oh well done Fartin! Nice and subtle, I like your style! Who's she marrying?

ANGELA: John James Wyard. He's a hot consultant at St Thomas'.

GUY: Yeah, I know him, he's a really good bloke. Absolutely loaded.

MAC RETURNS.

MAC: Who's loaded?

ANGELA & GUY: (WARNING HIM) Martin...

MAC: Martin is?

GUY: No. Holly's fiancé. Loaded. John James Wyard? Really really decent chap. Tall, muscular, plays rugby.

MAC: Yeah, he sounds like a really great bloke.

GUY: Oh yeah, he is, yeah, yeah. Yeah. Spent, you know, a year in Kenya curing sick children and he leads his field.

MAC: Cool. They'll probably be very good together.

GUY: Yeah. Hmm. And he's obviously got really good genes. That is going to be one good-looking baby.

MAC: Fuck you.

MAC LEAVES.

GUY: Huh! Well! Sense of humour failure there from the quipmeister.

GUY NOTICES MARTIN AND ANGELA STARING AT HIM.

GUY: What?

MARTIN AND ANGELA REFUSE TO SPEAK.

GUY: I'm going to... I'm going to get a thing from the — from the whatsit.

GUY GOES.

▶▶ **OFFICE**

JOANNA PUTS SOME PAPERS ON KIM'S DESK AND GOES INTO HER OFFICE. WHILE HER BACK IS TURNED, ALL THE STAFF IN THE OUTER OFFICE CHANGE DESKS. JOANNA COMES BACK OUT AND THEY'RE ALL IN DIFFERENT PLACES. THIS HAPPENS SEVERAL TIMES, BUT SHE DOESN'T CATCH THEM OUT.

▶▶ **THEATRE**

MAC: Okay, swab on a stick.

GUY: So, Doctor MacCartney.... this man that Holly is um — is marrying, she's only been with him since Christmas, hasn't she? And yet you were with her for, ooh... six years?

MAC: Leave it. I'm serious, leave it. Scissors.

GUY: He must be quite something. A real man. The kind of man a woman can imagine spending the rest of her life with. (HE GETS A NASTY LOOK, AND AGREES TO 'LEAVE IT') Okay. (PAUSE. GUY THEN STARTS TO SING TO HIMSELF) "All that she wants... is another baby. All that she wants is another baby, yeah."

MAC: Scalpel.

Kim,

Report car stolen. (Caught speeding on way here and don't want to pay fine.) Then move car to the usual place, but make sure no one sees you. Bring me back a Frappe Latte, Fruit Pastilles and Pepto-Bismol.

Joanna

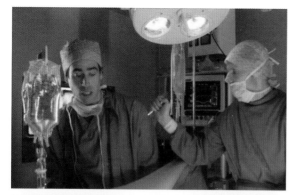

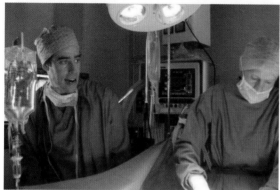

GUY: Yeah, have you ever seen that film *The Terminator*? It's about this cyber woman that gets pregnant and...

MAC SUDDENLY STABS GUY IN THE ARM WITH THE SCALPEL.

GUY: Ow!

MAC: (TO THE OTHERS) Good, thank you very much. I think we're ready to close here. Let's close her up, thank you very much. (TO GUY) I'll deal with you in a minute.

GUY GASPS. CAROLINE COMES OVER TO FINISH THE OPERATION.

GUY: Hi Caroline...

GUY CREEPS OUT, HIDING HIS ARM.

▶▶ STATHAM'S OFFICE/JOANNA'S OFFICE

STATHAM IS REVOLVING ON HIS SWIVEL CHAIR, SPEAKING INTO THE PHONE.

STATHAM: Joanna? It's me. That should get you wondering. Er — if you come down to my office in five or six minutes, then something entirely spontaneous may be occurring.

HE HAS NOW WRAPPED HIMSELF UP IN A TANGLED MESS OF TELEPHONE CABLE.

JOANNA: (PUTTING PHONE DOWN) Wanker.

▶▶ THEATRE

GUY'S ARM IS NOW IN A SLING.

MAC: Okay guys. Can you finish him off for me?

GUY: Yeah, can you finish me off?

MAC: Not you.

CAROLINE: I'll be fine.

MAC: Thank you.

CAROLINE STITCHES THE PATIENT AND WHEN MAC GOES SHE TALKS TO GUY.

CAROLINE: I wasn't sure at first, but I reckon he's all right.

GUY: Who, Mac?

CAROLINE: Yeah.

GUY: It depends what you mean by all right I suppose.

CAROLINE: Well, you know, he seems to have his heart in the right place.

GUY: Yeah... Outwardly, I suppose.

CAROLINE: What, something I should know?

GUY: I shouldn't really say.

CAROLINE: What?

GUY: Hmm. He went out with this girl called Holly, told her he loved her, she got pregnant, he dumped her, I'll say no more.

CAROLINE: Is that true?

GUY: Yeah, on my life. I shouldn't really go into details, and don't say I told you.

CAROLINE: God. You never can tell. Is there something wrong with your arm?

GUY: Ah no, it's — Mac stabbed me.

CAROLINE: Did he?

GUY: Yeah, I'm all right.

CAROLINE: Bastard... You never can tell.

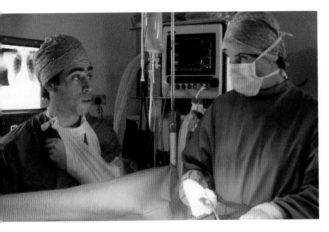

GUY: No you can't. You're doing a great job there.

CAROLINE: Thanks.

▶▶ STAFF LIAISON OFFICE

MARTIN IS SITTING ACROSS THE DESK FROM SUE WHITE.

MARTIN: Well, what I'm trying to say is, I'm getting stressed out about my exams.

SUE: All right, okay, I've got you.

MARTIN: Yes. And that stress is just getting bigger and bigger, like kind of snowballing into more stress.

SUE: Snowball?

MARTIN: Well yeah, something that gets bigger as it rolls along.

SUE: No, just leave the snowball out.

MARTIN: Okay, well I'm just saying that...

SUE: Snowball, snowball.

MARTIN: Well, it's just, I'm, it's a vicious circle of stress and I want to be able to, to break that circle, and — and I don't know how to.

SUE: Right. Well, it seems to me you're under stress.

MARTIN: Yes.

SUE: If you stopped being stressed, things really would be a lot easier for you.

MARTIN: Yes.

SHE JUST LOOKS AT HIM ACROSS THE DESK.

▶▶ THEATRE CORRIDOR

EMMY GOES UP TO GUY.

EMMY: Doctor Secretan, some post for you, it went to the department office by mistake. They're from abroad.

GUY: Yeah, from Switzerland, from my father.

EMMY: Gosh, is he Swiss?

GUY: Yeah, I'm half Swiss.

EMMY: What's the other half?

GUY: English, as far as I know.

EMMY: You don't know your mother?

GUY: No, she died when I was born.

EMMY: Oh my God, how awful.

GUY: Mmm.

EMMY: You never knew her. How sad.

EMMY GETS INCREASINGLY DISTRESSED FOR GUY.

EMMY: As you came into the world, she departed, so in fact she gave her life for you. God, that's beautiful, yet so...

GUY: Yeah, whenever I close my eyes, all I can see is her.

EMMY: Stop!

GUY: Yeah, yeah, and you know, but I sense her presence, I feel her soft eyes and her loving face.

GUY MOVES CLOSER TO EMMY.

GUY: You know, apparently she used to sing to me when she was pregnant, when I was in the womb.

EMMY: (CRYING) What did she sing?

GUY: You know that song, "Where's your mother gone? Where's your mother gone? Far far away." SINGS: "Last night I heard my mother singing a song, ooee, chirpy chirpy cheep cheep."

EMMY: Yeah, I think it might have been before then...

GUY: Yeah, well anyway, she loved me and she died. And I will never know a mother's love, never.

EMMY: Stop it, it's too sad!

GUY: It's so sad, you know. Snow fell, carpet of white as they took out her young body, leaving behind her newborn son.

EMMY IS GASPING IN GRIEF.

GUY: I know. I know. I know. I know. Would you like to go out with me some time? You know, I could really do with a friend, and you kind of remind me of her, you're young, you have all your life to lead.

EMMY: Yes. Yes.

GUY: Thank you.

EMMY GOES OFF CRYING.

GUY: Nice. Must try that again on someone with smaller teeth.

➤ **STAFF LIAISON OFFICE**

MARTIN: Yeah, thanks. You've been really helpful.

SUE: No I haven't.

MARTIN: Well, you've tried.

SUE: No, I didn't try either. No, we just filled a space in time really, didn't we?

MARTIN: Yeah, but that's all we can do I suppose.

SUE: Yeah, that's the spirit.

THEY LAUGH, INCREASINGLY HYSTERICALLY.

SUE: Now fuck off!

MARTIN: Mmm.

SUE CONTINUES TO LAUGH.

MARTIN: Look, can I just ask, do you — do you get stressed-out?

SUE LOOKS AT HIM AND THEN STARTS TO PULL SILK SCARVES OUT OF HER MOUTH. HE WATCHES HER, TRANS-FIXED.

MARTIN: No thanks.

SUE STUFFS THE SCARVES BACK INTO HER MOUTH.

SUE: Next!

STATHAM'S OFFICE

THE OFFICE IS SEEMINGLY EMPTY. HARRIET ENTERS AND STATHAM, WEARING ONLY HIS UNDERPANTS, COMES OUT OF THE CUPBOARD AND DANCES AROUND PLAYING THE RECORDER. HE SUDDENLY JUMPS AS HE REALISES IT'S HARRIET RATHER THAN JOANNA. HE'S VERY EMBARRASSED.

STATHAM: Come in — Oh...

HARRIET: Joanna said you had something for her.

STATHAM GIVES HARRIET A MUG. HE IS TOO EMBARRASSED TO SPEAK PROPERLY.

STATHAM: (BARELY INTELLIGIBLE) It's this... On you go, because she'll be waiting...

HARRIET GOES OUT AND SHUTS THE DOOR. STATHAM FALLS TO THE FLOOR.

CANTEEN

LYNDON IS EATING HIS MEAL. JOANNA IS SITTING VERY CLOSE TO HIM.

JOANNA: So Lyndon, computers. Oh, they're funny old things aren't they?

LYNDON: Oh, not if you speak kindly to them.

JOANNA: I think you have to be immensely clever to really get to grips with the fundamentals of the IT world.

STATHAM COMES PAST AND SEES THEM TOGETHER. HE DELIBERATELY DROPS HIS TRAY OF FOOD ALL OVER LYNDON.

STATHAM: Oh dear!

LYNDON: Oh Jesus!

STATHAM: Yes, so — oh, I must have...

LYNDON: Man!

JOANNA GETS A CLOTH.

STATHAM: I must have tripped over your enormous... Neanderthal feet.

JOANNA: Go away, go away.

STATHAM: It could have been your great big head with your shiny...

JOANNA: Sorry Lyndon, I'm so sorry.

LYNDON: No, it's fine, no...

STATHAM: Oh dear.

JOANNA RUBS DOWN LYNDON WITH THE CLOTH.

LYNDON: No, it's fine. No, don't worry. Stop now.

JOANNA: Such a terrible thing. I'm so sorry.

STATHAM GOES.

LYNDON: It's all right.

▸▸ STAFF LIAISON OFFICE

CAROLINE ENTERS. SUE WHITE IS WEARING BLACK LEATHER GLOVES AND TALKING RATHER STIFFLY.

SUE: You wanted to see me?

CAROLINE: Yes. Now I know it's sort of against hospital policy, but I've been thinking...

SUE: Ah yes, thinking. This is good. You may proceed.

CAROLINE: You see, I had an idea...

SUE: (LAUGHS LIKE A NAZI) I think you'll find me a reasonable woman. So please, tell me this idea of yours.

CAROLINE: Right, well I was thinking about an indoor smoking area for staff, if they smoke. I know it might seem a bit retrogressive, as policies go...

SUE: Yes, I would say it was unacceptable. A sign of weakness.

CAROLINE: Well I know we shouldn't really do it. But I think these smoking areas would definitely make people's lives easier.

SUE: Well, as I see it, there's only one thing for it. We must contact Berlin without delay... (INTO PHONE) Vorsprung?

CAROLINE: Berlin? Oh, what — some sort of centralised EU decision type thing? ...Hang on — are you talking to me like a Nazi from a film?

SUE: Um — well... nothing could be further from the truth.

CAROLINE: If you're talking to me like a Nazi from a film, I am going to complain to someone.

SUE: (IN GERMAN ACCENT) I think zat zese things you are imagining!

CAROLINE: Right, you...

CAROLINE LOSES HER TEMPER AND TRIES TO RIP UP A 'YEAR PLANNER' CHART, BUT CAN'T BECAUSE IT'S LAMINATED, SO SHE THROWS IT AT SUE AND STORMS OUT. SUE THROWS THE PLANNER ON THE FLOOR AND LIGHTS UP A CIGARETTE, RELISHING IN IT.

SUE: Good luck, Tommy!

▸▸ CORRIDOR

BOYCE AND ANGELA ARE WALKING ALONG THE CORRIDOR.

ANGELA: Bet you can't.

BOYCE: Bet I can.

ANGELA: Go on then.

BOYCE: After you.

ANGELA: Promise you will too?

BOYCE: Sure.

ANGELA AND BOYCE CARTWHEEL THE LENGTH OF A CORRIDOR AND STAND UP TRIUMPHANT AT THE END.

ANGELA: That was — not bad.

BOYCE: Cheers.

▸▸ **STAFF LIAISON OFFICE**

SUE TAKES OFF HER GLOVES AND GOOSE-STEPS ROUND HER OFFICE.

▸▸ **CANTEEN**

GUY AND MAC ARE AT THE SAME TABLE.

GUY: No, the point about public school is that it's character forming.

MAC: Yes indeed, well it certainly did form you into a rude, arrogant, selfish bastard with no interest in anybody but yourself.

GUY: Thanks!

MAC: That's okay.

GUY: Yeah, but it also means that I know that "selfish" and "no interest in anyone but yourself" mean *the same thing*.

MAC: Yes, yes. But, so does "fuck off" and — (HE FLICKS A V-SIGN AT GUY).

GUY: Piss off.

MAC: No, no, *you* piss off.

GUY: No, you piss off!

MAC: Interesting, that's very interesting.

CAROLINE JOINS THEM.

CAROLINE: What is?

MAC: We are just discussing the role of the public school in the creation of the *Guy-Wanker*.

CAROLINE: Oh, I always think it's terribly sad those tiny kids being left to fend for themselves at school like that.

GUY: That's the point. I mean that sort of education teaches you to be self-reliant.

CAROLINE: Yeah, but I always imagine these tiny kids turning up at this big Victorian building with their little shorts and all this luggage, and they're just left there by their parents and they're not going to see them again for months.

GUY: No, well now you see, no, because, well — I mean it wasn't like that, for a start my school was Edwardian.

CAROLINE: They don't know anyone, they're not sure where to go, and they're scared of being bullied or being homesick or crying and letting the side down. It's just very sad.

MAC: Sad, yeah, very very sad.

GUY: Yeah, well I don't know what you mean, because they were — it was the happiest days, the happiest...

CAROLINE: I mean what sort of a mother could do that to her own child?

MAC: Guy's probably.

GUY: I have to go.

GUY WALKS OFF, TAKING A NAPKIN TO BLOW HIS NOSE.

CAROLINE: Okay, see you later.

MAC: Yeah, see you. I'll see you after double Latin. I think Pongo's going to bring some tuck up to the dorm actually.

▸▸ STATHAM'S OFFICE

STATHAM IS ATTACKING AND STAMPING ON HIS COMPUTER KEYBOARD. THERE IS A KNOCK AT THE DOOR. HE ADOPTS A STRANGELY ULTRA-COOL MANNER AND PUTS HIS FOOT UP ON THE DESK.

STATHAM: Yeah. Ah, come, come in.

LYNDON: Hi. You paged me? Having problems?

STATHAM: (IN A BIZARRELY FAUX-HIP VOICE) Yeah, with the computer, er yeah... Er, but with my personal life, no. This little computer's, you know, fucked itself up, and I'll be, you know, right up the shitter if I don't get these notes to surgical. Oh make way, stand aside for information technology man, is he the coolest guy in the hospital?

LYNDON: (EXAMINING THE SCREEN) God, someone's done a real job on this, it looks like a two year-old's just gone mad. Sorry, it's going to take me some time, I'm sorry.

STATHAM: Okay, no probs big boy. Yes. I understand you're quite a hit with the hospital staff? Attractive man, big... big bits. Joanna Clore, I think her name is, Personnel Manager, I think probably has need of you, of your... your skills, does she? (UNDER HIS BREATH) She's mine.

LYNDON: Yeah, she has been having quite a few problems lately. Had to work late a couple of nights, she keeps losing her files.

STATHAM: (HISSING) She's mine.

LYNDON: Sorry?

STATHAM: She's mine — it's fine, just lime. You know.

LYNDON: Yeah?

STATHAM: Yeah, well I'd better — I'd better go and split. I save lives.

LYNDON: Yeah, right. Listen, I'll page you when I've sorted this mess out.

STATHAM: She's... she's mine.

STATHAM GOES.

STATHAM (OOV): She's mine!

LYNDON LOOKS AFTER HIM.

▸▸ STAFF LIAISON OFFICE

SUE'S MOBILE PHONE RINGS. INSTEAD OF ANSWERING IT, SHE DANCES TO THE TUNE AND THEN CUTS THE CALLER OFF.

SUE: Fuck off!

THE PHONE RINGS AGAIN. SHE DOES SOME MORE DANCING AND AGAIN CUTS OFF THE CALLER.

▸▸ CORRIDOR

GUY IS WALKING DOWN THE CORRIDOR, SINGING AND SOBBING.

GUY: "Through fortitude and character, We'll thwart the knavish hordes! And show through our resilience, of our destiny we are lords! Something something something, each and every day, For Whiteleaf School, we'll fight as one; Hooray! Hooray! Hooray!

SOMEONE STARES AT HIM AS THEY PASS.

GUY: What? Pleb!

▸▸ DAY WARD

CAROLINE IS READING A MAGAZINE, SUCKING ON A PEN. MARTIN IS PRETENDING TO BE BUSY NEAR HER.

CAROLINE: Apparently, if you eat lots of pineapple, it makes your sperm taste nice.

MARTIN: Right, well I'll keep that in mind, for the future.

CAROLINE: And pubic topiary is the new pashmina.

MARTIN: Ah yeah... yeah, you could... you could have a heart done or, or your initial, or a lovely swan.

CAROLINE: I could have a C for Caroline. Oh no no, they might get the wrong idea, they might think it's C for something else.

MARTIN: Oh, crazy or...

THE C WORD DAWNS ON MARTIN.

MARTIN: Oh, yes, the — the nasty C word. Oh.

CAROLINE: Yeah, I wouldn't want that.

MARTIN: No. Well, I mean you don't want to signpost it anyway, do you? It would be obvious to... to any... you know — visitors... there.

CAROLINE: Well, I'd hope so.

THEY'RE NOT QUITE SURE WHAT TO SAY TO EACH OTHER.

NURSE: Mr Howell's ready in cubicle three.

CAROLINE: Thank fuck for that.

CAROLINE SNATCHES THE FILE FROM THE NURSE AND GOES. MARTIN PICKS UP THE PEN SHE HAS BEEN SUCKING AND WALKS OFF, ENJOYING THE FACT THAT HE CAN NOW SUCK IT.

▸▸ STORE ROOM

SUE WHITE IS WALKING PAST THE STORE ROOM. SHE HEARS WEEPING COMING FROM THE RACKS OF COATS. SHE FINDS GUY 'HANGING' ON A COAT HANGER AMONG THE COATS.

SUE: Doctor Secretan? Are you okay?

GUY: Don't touch me.

SUE: And you're hiding in the coats because — ?

GUY: I feel safe here, it reminds me of...

SUE: Being locked up when you were a boarding school boy for being caught tampering with your down-belows?

GUY: Yeah. No! I just wanted some space, could you just go away!

SUE: No. Now what's the problem? I'm here to help, to listen, to soothe.

GUY: My mother's womb is no more.

SUE: Oh dear. Hysterectomy?

GUY: No, she died when I was very young, I'm motherless, and my life is just a shambles without her and it's getting worse. I mean, look at my eyes.

SUE: Well, there's nothing wrong with your eyes, you have very nice eyes, if a little on the pokey side.

GUY: Don't be nice to me.

SUE: Oh all right. Pull yourself together, you cretinous fuck-wit! What sort of a man hides in other people's coats, rocking and whinging to themselves? I'll tell you what sort of a man, a self-centred, egotistical wank-pot! Now unhook yourself and stop being so weak. Men don't cry, they're strong, hunter-gatherers. So go hunt, go gather, go be a total cunt, because that's what you do best!

GUY: Fuck you, you ugly bitch!! Oh that feels so much better. Do you fancy a quick fiddle now we're in here?

SUE: I am tempted, because I'm all fired up, but no thanks, I'd rather lick my own armpit.

SHE SLAPS HER BOTTOM AND GOES. GUY IS REALLY TURNED ON AND DROPS HIS TROUSERS, DISAPPEARING INTO THE COATS.

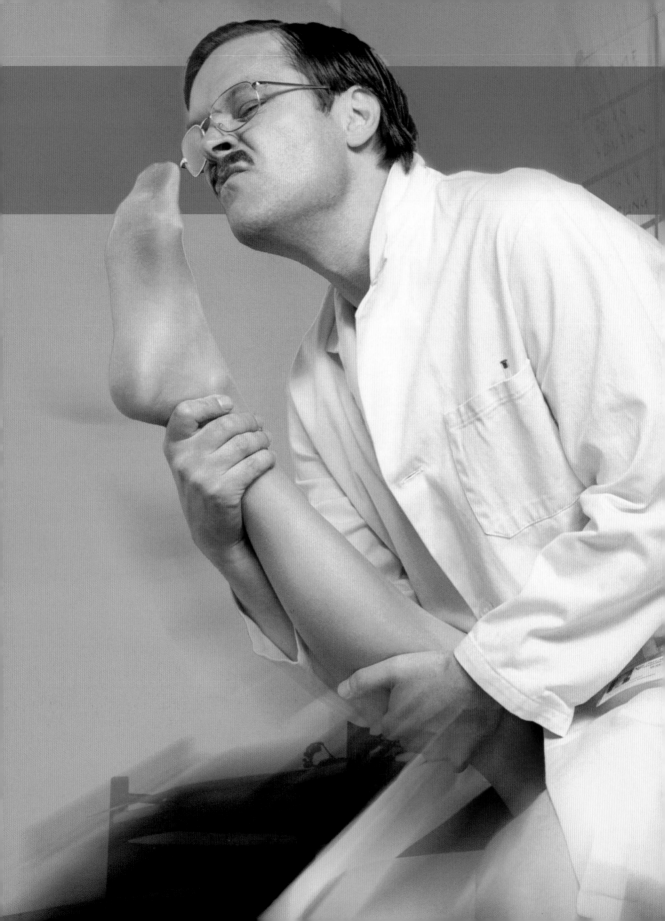

"Using the er... the old **pre-radiology diagnostic technique** of checking for broken bones... **orally.**"

RACHEL IS STOOPED, PULLING TWO SUITCASES DOWN THE CORRIDOR.

KIM: Are you going on holiday?

RACHEL: I wish! No, I'm just staying at a mate's tonight.

KIM: Rach.

RACHEL: Yeah?

KIM PULLS THE SUITCASE HANDLES OUT, ALLOWING RACHEL TO STAND UP AND PULL THEM ALONG.

RACHEL: That's so much better!

▸▸ **X-RAY PREP**

CAROLINE IS LOOKING AT A CHEST X-RAY.

CAROLINE: Oh Doctor MacCartney, Mac, Mac, er Doctor Mac, can I — can I ask your professional opinion?

MAC: Yes, it's definitely a chest.

CAROLINE: Yeah, yeah, I know that.

MAC: Good, be a bit of a worry if you didn't know that, so shall we have another look? I would say it's the chest of maybe a ten-, eleven-year-old boy.

CAROLINE: Fuck off! It's my chest.

MAC: Really? Can you see why I thought it might have been a boy's?

CAROLINE: No I can't. I was just wondering if um — if you could see anything wrong?

MAC: No, it looks pretty clear. Of course you shouldn't really be using hospital equipment for your own diagnosis, unless you are ill, and even then you should really be consulting another doctor.

CAROLINE: Well I'm consulting you aren't I? I also have a very... very sore throat. Do you think it could be cancer of the oesophagus?

MAC: I er... no, I don't think it is.

CAROLINE: Well you haven't even examined me, I mean — don't you want to check my throat to be sure?

MAC: Yeah, okay fine, go on, open up. Yeah.

HE LOOKS DOWN HER THROAT.

MAC: Hmm, say ah.

CAROLINE: Ah.

MAC: Say aah.

Rachel,
LEAVE YOUR HAIR
ALONE — you're not
Jennifer fucking Aniston.
Please tell me you don't
use L'Oreal, I can't
think of anyone less
worth it. (Except
Karen, obviously.)

Joanna

CAROLINE: Aaah.

MAC KEEPS GETTTING HER TO COPY AAAH NOISES, SOUND-ING MORE ORGASMIC EACH TIME. MAC ENDS UP PANTING.

CAROLINE: You're a bastard!

MAC: You are completely fine. You are completely fine. Do you know what you want to do? Maybe think about investing in some mouthwash.

HE BREATHES IN AND WALKS AWAY. CAROLINE TRIES TO SMELL HER OWN BREATH.

CAROLINE: Ha ha, minty fresh.

▶▶ JOANNA'S OFFICE

STATHAM IS SUCKING FRANTICALLY ON JOANNA'S TOES. HARRIET ENTERS.

HARRIET: Oh God! God, sorry! I'm sorry.

STATHAM QUICKLY TRIES TO LOOK PROFESSIONAL.

STATHAM: Good, good, no that's good, that's um — that's excellent. I can assure you Miss Clore that your um — your toe bone is certainly not broken, it's probably just strained, so there we are.

JOANNA: Oh thank you, thank you Doctor Statham.

STATHAM: Using the er... the old pre-radiology diagnostic tech-nique of checking for broken bones... orally. Now I'd better get on

my way, plenty more bones to suck — check!

HE GOES.

▶▶ BAR

MARTIN AND CAROLINE ARE AT THE BAR.

MARTIN: So what's your favourite colour?

CAROLINE: Right now? Black.

MARTIN: Black, ah I love black.

GUY JOINS THEM.

GUY: Hi. Long day?

GUY PUTS HIS HAND ON CAROLINE'S SHOULDER.

CAROLINE: If you're going to try and give me a shoulder massage, you can piss off.

GUY: (TO BARMAN) I'll have whatever's making her hostile and suspicious please.

CAROLINE: Sorry, sorry. Yes, long day and it's just about to get worse.

GUY: Oh, am I that terrible? I'll go.

CAROLINE: No, not you. I've got to go back and interview potential lodgers.

GUY: Yeah, so I heard.

CAROLINE: One of them I'm going to find really hard to reject.

GUY: Why?

CAROLINE: A friend. Sort of.

GUY: Put them off.

CAROLINE: I can't.

GUY: No, it's easy. Get yourself down to Research Faculty, get a nice big rat.

CAROLINE: Oh please!

GUY: No no, really, dead rat, by the toaster, bye bye friend. I'll sort you something out.

CAROLINE: A very kind and thoughtful offer, but, at the same time, also quite disgusting.

MARTIN: It does work, because Guy uses it in his flat to get rid of bunny boilers.

GUY: Are you still here?

MARTIN: Yeah, actually.

GUY: Yeah, good joke Mart!

GUY SLAPS MARTIN HARD ON THE BACK, CAUSING HIM TO NEARLY CHOKE ON HIS BRITVIC.

GUY: I got you something.

GUY HANDS CAROLINE A PACKAGE.

CAROLINE: What is it?

GUY: What is the most valuable thing in the whole world?

CAROLINE: Plutonium?

MARTIN: Christ, where did you get that from?

GUY: Your privacy.

CAROLINE HAS OPENED THE GIFT.

CAROLINE: A lock?

GUY: Well it's bound to happen, Roger the lodger accidentally stumbles into your room — oh what a surprise, he catches you just at the moment you're down to your underwear and it's all, "Oh I'm so sorry, I seem to have got the wrong room, I haven't quite got my bearings yet."

CAROLINE: Oh I don't know, it might be quite nice having a man around. I could pretend I don't know how to unblock a U-bend. He could shake the spiders from my shoes.

GUY: Yeah, you see, a spider here, a friendly word there, a nightcap, you know, one thing leads to another, before you know it, you're up against the kitchen units with your tongues down each other's throats and rice all over the floor.

MARTIN: Who's Roger?

GUY: The thing is — and you've got to trust me here — not all men are gentlemen, like me and Mart. You know, I really don't want to scare you, but I would feel terribly guilty if I didn't try and warn you, as a friend.

CAROLINE: Well thank you. I do appreciate your concern. Thanks for the lock, there isn't one on the bathroom and it'll be really useful.

GUY: Now you take care.

CAROLINE: I will.

MARTIN: See you.

CAROLINE GOES.

MARTIN: That was really thoughtful Guy.

GUY: Yeah, well, I'm not having some teenage runt porking her before I've had my turn.

MARTIN: I'm going to tell her you said that.

GUY: Ooooh, well it'll make a change from "What's your favourite colour?"

▶▶ CORRIDOR/LIFT

ANGELA MEETS MAC OUTSIDE THE LIFT, WHICH HAS AN 'OUT OF ORDER' SIGN ON IT.

ANGELA: Coming for a drink?

MAC: Er, probably not.

Do you want a ride?

MAC STARTS THE BIKE UP.

▸▸ **CAROLINE'S HOUSE**

CAROLINE IS INTERVIEWING ANOTHER POTENTIAL LODGER.

CAROLINE: I don't have much storage space here. Do you have a lot of clothes?

THE INTERVIEWEE DOESN'T ANSWER OR CHANGE EXPRESSION TO ANY OF CAROLINE'S QUESTIONS.

CAROLINE: Do you have any pets? Children?

CAROLINE GRINS AT HER AND THE WOMAN BEGINS TO LAUGH AND GRIN BACK.

▸▸ **LIAM'S CAR**

LIAM IS WAITING FOR ANGELA IN HIS CAR OUTSIDE THE HOSPITAL.

ANGELA: Hello.

LIAM: Hi.

ANGELA TALKS TO LIAM, BUT HE DOESN'T LISTEN BECAUSE HE'S LISTENING TO FOOTBALL COMMENTARY ON THE RADIO.

ANGELA: I'm going to see a room tonight. Yeah, it's in a really good area, and it's very handy, so it would be stupid to ignore it. The landlady's a bit weird. I don't think I'm going to mention you just yet though. I don't want to put her off, you know what these single saddos can be like about couples. So I think what I want to say is that, you know, I just see you from time to time. What do you think? (NO RESPONSE) What do you think?

LIAM: (TO THE CAR RADIO) Oh come on!

ANGELA: Oi!

SHE SWITCHES OFF THE RADIO.

LIAM: What are you doing?

ANGELA: You weren't listening to me.

LIAM: No, I was listening to that.

ANGELA: Yes, I could see the way you were trying to stick your ears into the radio, despite the fact that the speakers are actually in the doors.

THEY DRIVE OFF.

▸▸ **CORRIDORS**

MAC IS DRIVING ROUND THE HOSPITAL CORRIDORS ON HIS MOTORBIKE.

ANGELA: Really?

MAC: No, I'm going to go for a spin.

HE HITS THE LIFT DOOR BUTTON. THE LIFT OPENS AND HIS MOTORBIKE IS INSIDE.

MAC: Ah, lovely.

MAC GETS INTO THE LIFT AND SITS ON HIS BIKE.

MAC: Do you want a ride?

ANGELA: Isn't that a health hazard? And you wonder why they won't make you a consultant!

▸ **CAROLINE'S HOUSE**

A MAN HAS COME TO SEE THE ROOM IN CAROLINE'S HOUSE.

MAN: Have you got an internet connection? Because what it is, right, I like talking to the internet ladies, you know, on the internet, with names like... "Hot 4-u", you know? Like Hot 4 and then a little U. I love all that.

CAROLINE JUST LOOKS AT HIM. HE PLAYS WITH HIS CROTCH.

▸ **STATHAM'S HOUSE**

JOANNA IS STRETCHING HER LEGS ON THE COUCH. STATHAM HAS GOT OUT SOME PHOTO ALBUMS.

STATHAM: All right then, here's the choice. Um... a bit of er — Peter up the panty passage, or um... holiday snaps of Crete 1976?

JOANNA: Oh, Crete.

STATHAM: Sure?

JOANNA: Yeah.

▸ **CAROLINE'S HOUSE**

THE MAN IS STILL TALKING TO CAROLINE ABOUT THE INTER-NET. HE TURNS HIS BACKSIDE TO HER.

MAN: And that sort of thing, which is nice, because you can see what they look like.

A WOMAN HAS COME TO SEE THE ROOM.

WOMAN: I'm an only child.

SHE BANGS THE CUSHIONS AND CHAIR.

WOMAN: Mummy and Daddy and me! (RECOVERED) Oh, I'm a bit better now.

CAROLINE STARES AT HER.

▸ **STATHAM'S HOUSE**

STATHAM: That's the taverna and there I am... eating some calamari and tzatziki, actually... well it may actually be tara-masalata, I'm not sure...

JOANNA: Oh, is it taramasalata? Hmm.

STATHAM: Um... er — there's Cathy again, in the Minoan palace of Knossos.

JOANNA: Knossos.

STATHAM: Knossos, yes.

JOANNA: Knossos.

STATHAM: Yes, yes, Knossos. And you can see she's got a bit of sun, sunburn on the upper arms there.

JOANNA: Ooh, poor Cathy's upper arms. Oh boo hoo.

STATHAM: Yes, poor — could you just stop it! Just stop that, stop it.

JOANNA: Stop it.

STATHAM: No no, don't say stop it when I'm saying stop it!

JOANNA: Stop it. Stop it.

STATHAM: No, stop it. No, I said stop it. Stop it! You're just

spoiling it. You're just like Simon shitting Mason! You know, "Oh, I'm so clever, I can, I can make everybody in the class laugh at stupid Alan." Well well Simon, hmm, the picture was interesting and some people, Colin Cann, for instance, found it very interesting, so you can just shut it!

STATHAM LOSES IT. JOANNA IS TURNED ON.

STATHAM: Just bloody shut it! You just bloody shut it, and if you don't, I'll, I'll, I'll…

JOANNA: You'll what?

STATHAM: I'll tell a man about you, a — a — not my dad, a big foreign uncle with big hands, which are bigger than your fffff-face! And then, and so — Simon shitting Mason — you just, you just shut it, or you'll crap your pants and then everyone will smell your fear and then… You just shut up! Shut up!

JOANNA PULLS STATHAM ONTO THE FLOOR. HE IS STILL RANTING "SHUT UP". HER LEGS STICK UP IN THE AIR.

STATHAM: I love you Simon!

▸▸ **CAROLINE'S HOUSE**

CAROLINE IS SHOWING ANGELA AROUND HER HOUSE.

▸▸ **GUY'S FLAT**

GUY IS READING THE MEN'S HEALTH MAGAZINE. HE PICKS UP THE PHONE AND MAKES A CALL.

GUY: Oh, oh hello, sorry to call you so late. Is Tony Phillips still there please? Thank you. Tony, hello. I was just reading your article about, about you know… Yeah, yeah, that one. Sorry? No, no, I'm a doctor. Yeah. No no, I really am. No, I really am a doctor. Listen Tony, I was just, no I was just wondering, do you, you know, when you measure it, do you measure it from where it joins the stomach, or do you measure it from the actual base itself, you know the bit that goes down towards the general arse area? (PAUSE) From the actual base itself, yeah, I thought so. Thank you…

THE CALLER HAS HUNG UP.

GUY: Yes!

▸▸ **CAROLINE'S HALLWAY**

CAROLINE IS STILL GIVING ANGELA A TOUR OF THE HOUSE.

CAROLINE: These floorboards are still a bit loose. I don't think the police ever did put them down properly.

ANGELA: The police?

CAROLINE: Yeah. Four bodies I think it was. You'd never think there was space under there, would you? Still, the smell's gone now, pretty much. The checkout girl murders…

ANGELA: How exciting!

CAROLINE: Sometimes you can hear cash registers in the night.

ANGELA: We could have a séance.

CAROLINE GIVES UP TRYING TO PUT ANGELA OFF.

CAROLINE: Okay, when do you want to move in?

East Hampton Hospital Trust

Urophagia – The Quaffing Of Urine

Preliminary Research by:
Dr. A.R. Statham (Consultant Radiologist)
BMedSci. MMed. DDR. FFR. SHO.

Points For:	Points Against:
• Contains melatonin – sleep well.	• Pissy breath
• Anti-bacterial	
• Anti-fungal	
• Gandhi drank it	
• Tastes nice	
• It's a bit rude	

ANGELA: Tomorrow?

CAROLINE: Hooray!

ANGELA: Were you — were you trying to put me off?

CAROLINE: Just er — testing your commitment. I only want someone who really wants to be here.

ANGELA: Very wise.

▶▶ **STATHAM'S HOUSE**

JOANNA IS SNORING, FAST ASLEEP.

STATHAM: It looks like I myself shall have to charm the mighty python.

HE ADJUSTS HIS CROTCH AND PLAYS THE RECORDER.

STATHAM: Oh Princess Joanna darling, the snake has risen from the basket and awaits your tender caress.

JOANNA CONTINUES TO SNORE.

▶▶ **GUY'S FLAT**

GUY TRIES ANOTHER PHONE CALL.

GUY: Suzy? Babe? (HE GOES INTO A WELSH-ISH ACCENT) Oh hello, oh hello Frank. No no, it's Geoff. Yeah. No, I'm an old school friend of Suzy's. I know she did, but I moved down when I was twelve. From... (HIS ACCENT CHANGES AGAIN) ... Derbyshire. Oh do they? Which part? Which part? Which bit? Oh I know I don't, but because I've got a bit of a cold at the moment and I'm a bit... sad. About... well about my hedgerows. Yeah. I've got to go now, I've got to go to the Vale. The Vale of Pewter. Near Derby. Okay. Okay, bye.

HE PUTS THE PHONE DOWN.

GUY: I think I got away with that.

▶▶ **CORRIDORS**

MAC IS DRIVING AROUND THE HOSPITAL CORRIDORS ON HIS MOTORBIKE — NAKED.

EPISODE 4

▶▶ OFFICE/JOANNA'S FLAT

STATHAM PHONES JOANNA ON HIS MOBILE. INTERCUT SCENE BETWEEN JOANNA AT HOME, GETTING READY FOR WORK, AND STATHAM IN HER OFFICE. THE PHONE RINGS IN HER FLAT:

JOANNA: Go away! No one's going to know you've got a forty-eight-year-old fuffie!

SHE LETS THE PHONE RING AND SHOVES SOME CREAM DOWN HER PANTS.

JOANNA: Happy birthday Fuffie. "Happy birthday Joanna."

THE ANSWERPHONE STARTS, STATHAM'S VOICE IS ON THE LINE.

STATHAM: Um, hello, it's me, Enobarbus, your humble servant, calling, with birthday greetings. (SINGS) "Why do birds suddenly appear, every time you are near?"

STATHAM GOES INTO JOANNA'S OFFICE, KISSES A SMALL GIFT AND PUTS IT ON HER DESK.

STATHAM: (SINGING) "Just like me, hmm, they want to be... close to you."

HE SNIFFS JOANNA'S CHAIR.

JOANNA GETS ANNOYED WITH LISTENING TO STATHAM ON THE ANSWERPHONE.

STATHAM: "Aa-a-a-a-ah, close to you."

JOANNA SPRAYS THE PHONE.

STATHAM: "Just like me, they long to be..."

JOANNA WHACKS THE PHONE OFF THE SOFA AS SHE LEAVES.

▶▶ OFFICE

STATHAM: "...close to you."

STATHAM IS STILL SINGING ON THE PHONE WHEN RACHEL AND KIM WALK IN.

STATHAM: Ah, aah, ah yes, ah ha. Ah ha, yes, yes, yes. Bye, goodbye to you, yes.

HE PUTS THE PHONE DOWN.

STATHAM: That's a — it's a very very interesting, er — why, why do birds, er the gulls, you know, Jenny wrens, Tommy tits... No, not, not actually, no, I wouldn't say that as such, but um, good morning to you.

OLIVER: Good morning.

STATHAM: Er, nice to see that you're um, I was explaining... Right.

▶▶ SUPERMARKET

▶▶ JOANNA'S FLAT

JOANNA IS GETTING READY FOR WORK. SHE LOOKS IN THE BATHROOM MIRROR.

JOANNA: I'm forty-two. I'm forty-two, I'm forty-two, I'm forty-two, I'm forty-two. Oh Christ! Forty-two.

▶▶ OFFICE

EARLY MORNING. STATHAM SNEAKS IN WHILE NO ONE'S THERE.

▶▶ JOANNA'S FLAT

JOANNA IS RUBBING LOTS OF ANTI-WRINKLE CREAM ON HER-SELF WHILE SHE'S GETTING DRESSED.

JOANNA: Oh face it Joanna, you're forty-eight!

THEY WALK TO THE CHECKOUT. KAREN HAS SECOND THOUGHTS AND SWAPS THE TIT CAKE FOR THE BORING ONE.

▸▸ **CAROLINE'S HOUSE**

CAROLINE IS EATING BREAKFAST. SHE CALLS UPSTAIRS TO ANGELA.

CAROLINE: Angela, do you want coffee?

ANGELA (OOV): Yes!

CAROLINE: (TO HERSELF) What did your last slave die of?

CAROLINE CAN HEAR ANGELA CALLING OUT. SHE TAKES THE MUG OF COFFEE INTO ANGELA'S BEDROOM.

HARRIET AND KAREN ARE LOOKING AT THE SHELVES.

KAREN: Okay, birthday cake. What about this one?

HARRIET: No, a bit stuffy. How about this?

KAREN: A bit childish.

HARRIET SPOTS A CAKE IN THE SHAPE OF A PAIR OF TITS.

HARRIET: Oh, this one.

KAREN: That's more Rachel, it's not really Joanna.

HARRIET: We can put a candle on each nipple. I've always wanted to do that. Either that or run away and join the circus.

KAREN: Maybe we should get the iced cake.

HARRIET: Oh no, go on, let's be daring.

KAREN: Okay.

CAROLINE: Angela, what are you doing? Are you all right?

ANGELA: Yeah.

LIAM POKES HIS HEAD UP FROM UNDER THE DUVET.

CAROLINE: Argh! Oh my God! Oh! Have I just seen you come?

ANGELA: Almost. I think I just missed.

CAROLINE: Oh, I'm so sorry. Sorry. Look, I'll just, I'll just leave your coffee there. Morning Liam.

LIAM: Morning.

▶▶ **LOCKER ROOM**

GUY COMES IN.

GUY: Buggering wank!

MAC: No no, don't tell me that the Swiss water polo team has lost again?

GUY: No. The bloody woman from Obstetrics is wearing knee-length patent leather boots!

MAC: In a month with an R in it. You know what we should do, we should march on Obstetrics with flaming torches and we should kill her.

GUY: Yeah, I knew you wouldn't understand.

MAC: Who is this woman anyway?

GUY: I don't know, she just is.

MAC: Join me again next week on this episode of Let's Make No Fucking Sense, when I will be waxing an owl.

GUY: Just when I'd nearly finished putting all the data in as well, it's just... grrr.

MAC: What are you talking about?

GUY HAS A PALM PILOT MINI-COMPUTER.

GUY: The league table.

MAC: You haven't got a league table just for Obstetrics?

GUY: Don't be stupid! It's for all hospital females. And knee-length patent leather boots bump her up to a six in kinkiness. You just never bloody know with women, do you?

MAC: I know, it's crazy isn't it, soon they'll be telling us that we can't thrash our own wives.

GUY: Yeah. Look what it's done to the graph, look, it's knocked it out of whack. Obstetrics is now kinkier than Personnel. And the cute Chinese nurse from Fincham Ward is down to nineteenth. Jesus!

MAC: Have you ever thought — this is just a shot in the dark really — you may be taking this a little bit too seriously?

GUY: What do you mean?

MAC: Have you thought that maybe your life might be a bit easier if you just didn't bother with it?

GUY: Mac, if I didn't do this, how in God's name am I supposed to put women in the proper order?

MAC: Oh my God, look, look, there is a coach-load of Swedish physios.

GUY: (TAKEN IN FOR A SECOND) What? Shut up!

MAC: That, of course, would raise some very interesting, but conflicting issues for you; very exciting sexually, on the other hand, a lot of admin.

GUY: Yeah, I actually did have a coach-load of Swedish physios once. They smelt of herring, surprisingly, and flat-pack furniture. And Rolf Harris.

MAC: Rolf Harris isn't Swedish.

GUY: That's what was so surprising.

▶▶ **OFFICE**

THE GIRLS IN THE OFFICE FINISH LIGHTING THE CANDLES ON JOANNA'S CAKE AS SHE ENTERS.

KIM: Oh, she's coming. Quick.

HARRIET: Quick!

OFFICE STAFF: (SING 'HAPPY BIRTHDAY' TO JOANNA)

JOANNA: Right, right, thanks yeah, surprise surprise! Hmm, same banner as last year. Hope it's a fresh cake!

KIM: We didn't know how old you were so...

KIM POINTS TO THE BALLOONS WITH '30', '40' AND '50' ON THEM. JOANNA BURSTS THE '50' BALLOON ON THE CANDLES.

JOANNA: Ha, bloody ha ha ha!

JOANNA HEADS INTO HER INNER OFFICE.

KAREN: What's that on your coat?

RACHEL: What?

KAREN: Silver lines, on there.

RACHEL: Oh, snails. Yeah, I went to a party last night and woke up in the garden.

HARRIET TAKES LARGE BITES OUT OF THE CAKE, WITHOUT SLICING IT.

▶▶ **PAYPHONE, CORRIDOR**

FUMBLING WITH HIS STETHOSCOPE, MARTIN IS TRYING TO USE THE PHONE.

MARTIN: Hello Mum, it's me. Martin. Martin Dear, M-A-R- You know who it is. No, I'm in the corridor, no one can hear me. I just want... Hello?

SHE HAS HUNG UP ON HIM.

▶▶ **THEATRE CORRIDOR**

GUY: A luxury penthouse apartment in the Docklands, panoramic views, yours for a year.

MAC: Would it have electronic swipe card entrances?

GUY: Yes, and a concierge on the door twenty-four hours a day, and there will probably be a swimming pool in the basement with a gym and sauna for residents.

MAC: Probably or definitely?

GUY: Can't say at this stage, but there would be underground parking.

MAC: Will it have a glass lift?

GUY: No. It'll have a normal lift.

MAC: Okay, what's the price?

GUY: Two weeks as Esther Rantzen's love-bitch.

MAC: Is that a five-day week or are weekends included?

GUY: No no, weekends are included, fourteen days, fourteen nights.

MAC: Okay, um... no, because every time I look through the panoramic windows, I would have flash-backs of how I got there.

GUY: All right, okay, so five days and she gets to film it with the possibility it might end up on the internet.

MAC: Will it probably or definitely be on the internet?

> *karen,*
>
> *No i can NOT remove the words 'depressing wanker' from your Annual Review.*
> *Sue me.*
>
> *Joanna*

GUY: I can't say at this stage, that's the gamble you take with the five-day option.

MAC: Okay. Yes, as long as at some stage in the future a glass lift was installed.

GUY SUDDENLY HIDES BEHIND MAC AS SOMEONE GOES PAST THEM.

MAC: Who was that?

GUY: Oh, shagged his mum. Highest sag factor in the league. I left my watch inside her.

▸▸ DAY WARD

MARTIN GOES TO TALK TO CAROLINE, WHO IS READING A MAGAZINE. HE IS WEARING NEW SHADES AND CAN'T SEE VERY WELL. HE BUMPS INTO THE DESK.

CAROLINE: At least you *look* cool.

MARTIN: Yeah, well I'm taking them back. They said they were photochromic, right.

CAROLINE: Right.

MARTIN: Yeah, well they go dark when I come inside and light when I go...

CAROLINE: When you go outside.

MARTIN: Yeah.

CAROLINE: Oh, right.

MARTIN: I got them from the market. Still, they do look cool though.

CAROLINE: (LOOKING AT HER MAGAZINE) This psychologist, Carol Rothwell, claims to have devised a formula for happiness.

MARTIN: Can you do that?

CAROLINE: Well she seems to think so. Apparently happiness = $(p + 5\ e^2 - \sqrt{3}) - dq$, where p equals personal hygiene, e equals entertainment value and d equals density.

MARTIN: What does that mean?

CAROLINE: I've no idea, it's put me in a really bad mood, I know that much.

MARTIN: Yeah, well, bloody happiness eh? Huh...! You know, it's more trouble than it's worth, that happiness.

CAROLINE: You are so right Martin. I never wear sunglasses, I can always see the giant reflections of my own eyes staring back at me. It's too spooky.

MARTIN: Yeah well, you know... you've got really nice eyes.

CAROLINE LAUGHS.

CAROLINE: Martin! You think I've got really nice eyes?

MARTIN: Yeah, well I mean — you know, the whole head is, is good, but — but it's your eyes... They're top eyes.

CAROLINE TAKES MARTIN'S HAND.

CAROLINE: Aww! Aww, you are really sweet.

SHE LETS GO OF HIS HAND.

CAROLINE: ...Sweaty.

SHE GOES.

▸▸ OFFICE

JOANNA OPENS THE GIFT WHICH STATHAM LEFT FOR HER FIRST THING IN THE MORNING. IT'S A LOCKET, BUT SHE CAN'T FIND OUT WHO IT'S FROM.

JOANNA: Has anyone been in my office this morning?

KIM: Just Lyndon.

JOANNA: Lyndon?

KIM: Yeah, he did that anti-virus thing.

JOANNA: Lyndon?

KIM: Uh-huh.

JOANNA GOES INTO HER OFFICE AND STRUTS AROUND, LOOK-ING THRILLED.

KAREN: I didn't see Lyndon this morning...

▸▸ MESS

CAROLINE COMES IN AND FINDS ANGELA, WHO IS EXAMINING GUY'S PALM PILOT.

CAROLINE: Ah. Morning again. Nice to see you with some clothes on.

ANGELA: What? Oh gosh, I'm sorry about the live bed-show with Liam. I don't know what it is, it just keeps getting better and better. I guess we just click.

CAROLINE: Yeah. It sounded like you put your hip out.

ANGELA: Yeah, I tell you, I could have done the way he's been...

CAROLINE: Enough! Enough of your clickety clicking. I don't care if he snapped your pelvis. From now on, all clicking is to be done behind closed doors.

ANGELA: Sorry Mrs Landlady.

CAROLINE: And don't call me that. It makes me sound like a spinster with a hair net, smelling of wee, who hasn't had a good click in ages.

ANGELA: Don't be silly. Anyway, you're not a spinster, you're a babe.

CAROLINE: You think I'm a babe?

ANGELA SHOWS HER THE PALM PILOT.

ANGELA: No, I don't, Guy does. It's one of the categories in this report thing, it's like a chart with all women staff and there are scores. And look, here's you. Arse.

CAROLINE: Arse? Has he called me an arse?

ANGELA: No no, it's the arse category. And you've scored four.

CAROLINE: Out of five?

ANGELA: Er no, ten.

CAROLINE: What did you get?

ANGELA: I don't know, and to be honest, I couldn't care less, it's just utter nonsense.

CAROLINE LOOKS FOR HERSELF.

CAROLINE: Eight, you got an eight for arse.

ANGELA: I got an eight? Did I really? Well, that can't be right, can it? I mean, you only getting a four, and me getting an eight, that's nearly — nearly full marks.

CAROLINE: Oh good for you! If it meant anything, which it doesn't, because you're right, it's utter nonsense.

ANGELA: Utter nonsense.

▸▸ STAFF LIAISON OFFICE

SUE WHITE IS SMELLING HER ARMPITS. MARTIN ENTERS.

MARTIN: You... you arrange um — courses to help staff with personal development and all that don't you?

SUE: I do.

MARTIN: Well, because I was wondering...

SUE: Yes?

MARTIN: Um — is there some sort of... male/female inter-relationship creation course? I mean I'd go halves, so...

SUE: What, a course for getting a girlfriend?

MARTIN: Well yes, I suppose, in a sense...

SUE: Well, why didn't you say, eh? You don't need to go on a course Martin, I can help you now.

MARTIN: Really?

SUE: It's easy.

MARTIN: Really?

SUE: Yeah. Let's have a look in here. (SHE LOOKS IN HER DESK)

Oh right, here we go, just the ticket. Now, you just take these magic beans, but mind out for the ogre.

SHE PUTS SOME IMAGINARY BEANS IN HIS HAND.

MARTIN: Look, I'm not going to plant any of your bloody beans! They don't work!

SUE: No?

MARTIN: I...

SUE POINTS HER MOBILE PHONE AT MARTIN AND IT PLAYS A TUNE, WHICH SHUTS HIM UP.

MARTIN: It's not your job to...

AS HE SPEAKS, SHE PLAYS ANOTHER TUNE AT HIM.

EAST HAMPTON FEMALE LEAGUE 9:33a

Total Hazard Current [uA]

Transformer load [%]

CATEGORY: ARSE

ANGELA HUNTER:	8/10
CAROLINE TODD:	4/10
CUTE CHINESE:	7/10
TITTY BLONDE BIG TEETH:	10/10

New File Session ?

MARTIN: All I'm asking from you, okay...

SUE PLAYS ANOTHER TUNE. MARTIN LEAVES.

▶▶ **MESS**

ANGELA IS READING GUY'S LEAGUE TABLE.

ANGELA: Yes, here's you, nine. Nine! Congrats.

CAROLINE: Really? Nine for what?

ANGELA: Easiness.

CAROLINE: Yeah, what the hell is that?

ANGELA: It's easy-going, easy to get on with, it's very good.

CAROLINE: No, it's appalling. It's degrading, it's sexist, it's untrue. And we should probably report it.

ANGELA: Yeah. I know. Gosh, I can't believe your arse only got a four and mine got an eight. What about breasts? Is there a mark for pertness?

CAROLINE LAUGHS. THEY BOTH GRAB FOR THE COMPUTER, CAROLINE GETS IT.

▶▶ **OFFICE**

KIM: Karen, where's the Ward 2B file?

KAREN: In the filing cabinet.

KIM: Yes, but where?

KAREN: Under Ward 2B.

RACHEL: Karen, are you going to the snack machine?

KAREN: Probably.

RACHEL: Can you get me a Toffee Crisp and a packet of Quavers? Oh, and a carton of Ribena.

KAREN: Yeah.

KIM: Can you get me a yoghurt from the canteen and a frothy coffee, no sugar?

KAREN: Can't you get it yourself?

KIM: No Karen, it's a bit pointless us all going down. You can get a tray.

HARRIET: Oh actually, I'd like a frothy coffee, two sugars, and a banana.

KAREN LOSES IT.

KAREN: No I won't! I am not your slave!

RACHEL: Hark at her! Who rattled your cage?

KAREN: You lot, I am sick of it! Taking advantage, just because I haven't got any breasts!

▶▶ **WARD RECEPTION AREA**

GUY BUMPS INTO CAROLINE

GUY: Have you seen...? Hi.

CAROLINE: (FROSTY) Hello.

GUY: Hi.

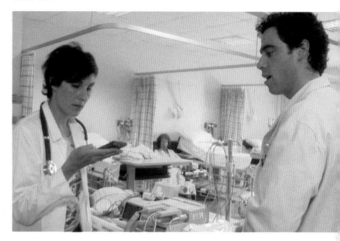

CAROLINE: Lost something?

GUY: Um... maybe.

CAROLINE: This, by any chance? It was lying around.

SHE IS HOLDING HIS PALM PILOT.

GUY: Ah.

CAROLINE: It makes very interesting reading. It seems I score quite highly in all-round easiness, though I lose a few marks on cleanliness and mental attitude.

GUY: Yes, the thing is...

CAROLINE: Additional comments: "Probably looks up at you in a pleading way during intercourse."

GUY: Yeah, I er — suppose you're wondering what I've got to say about that.

CAROLINE: Yeah, it crossed my mind.

GUY: Well... The thing is that...

CAROLINE: What?

GUY: Well, the — what you — what you have to bear in mind is...

CAROLINE: Yes, is...? What? Is what?

Prizegiving Guest

We are greatly indebted to former pupil Guillaume Secretan (Whiteleaf 77-90) for his attendance and speech at the recent Prizegiving ceremony. It should be made quite clear, however, that some of the views expressed by Dr Secretan are not necessarily shared by the board of governors of the school, nor by members of the Old Whiteleafian Association committee. In particular, references to 'girlie subjects' do not reflect school policy on curriculum, and as Head of Art, Mr Beresford has written to Dr Secretan to express his dismay.

With regard to the introduction of Drama courses, we are quite sure that the use of the expression 'poofs-ville Arizona' was not meant to cause offence to either Mr Latimer or Mr Ramone personally, but was rather an attempt at 'post-modern' humour. Equally, Dr Secretan has assured us that his description of Mademoiselle Renard as 'quite fit' was a reference to her time in this year's London Marathon (3hrs 39mins). The pelvic thrusting movements which accompanied the ... was deemed

Latin Club News

Salvete Amici!

Next Thursday's forum has been postponed; id est; it will take place at a later date. There is no actual date per se, as all future fora will be held on an ad hoc basis. Ergo, look out for further news. And it would really help if either of you bloody bastards would turn up.

ARS

Grammar Club News

It has been decided that it would be better if EHT Grammar Club were (NB SUBJUNCTIVE MOOD) henceforth to merge (NB AVOIDING SPLIT INFINITIVE) with the EHT Latin Club. At Monday night's meeting a motion to this effect was put to the floor. The motion was carried by 1-0, with the Chairman exercising his casting vote.

AR Statham (Chairman)

Comedy Club

With Dr Statham

Want to learn a few tricks of the trade? (Nothing too zany, just proper comedy)

All those interest in joining A spanking new Comedy Club, please sign below:

Boycie
can we forget the new Comedy and just have a spanking club?

Karen Ball.

Martin Dear

U.R. Atwat

Professor P. Niss

Ray Diologysucks

Bob Monkhouse (deceased)

The 2 Minute Challenge

This is a two-player game. You will need a stopwatch or a very accurate (atomic) sundial.

In less than two minutes you must name:

- Five famous homosexuals
- Five fascist dictators/politicians
- Five phallic vegetables
- Five fetishes
- Five countries where anal sex is a crime

Check your answers via the internet, or by asking an old person. Two points for each correct answer. One point for a wrong answer, but only if it is libellous. You score an extra point for every ten seconds you completed the challenge under the two minutes.

The loser must atone for his/her stupidity with a forfeit. The winner will devise the forfeit, but it must involve either syrup, lipstick, or syrupy lipstick.

GUY: Is... It's Mac's.

CAROLINE: That this... that this is Doctor MacCartney's?

GUY: Yes it is.

CAROLINE: Well, you — you shouldn't look like a man who has one of these.

SHE WALKS AWAY.

GUY: Do you look up pleadingly during inter—? Yeah. She probably does.

▸▸ GENERAL MEDICAL RECEPTION

LYNDON IS SITTING ON A NURSE'S DESK. THEY ARE LOOKING AT HER COMPUTER SCREEN.

LYNDON: Control, alt, delete, lock your system and prevent the data getting wiped, you see?

NURSE: I only went to the loo.

LYNDON: Sure. But just remember, control, alt, delete and then it doesn't matter if someone sits on your keyboard, all your files are safe.

NURSE: Show me again.

LYNDON: You try.

NURSE: Well, okay then. This one, this one and... Gosh, they all look the same don't they? Um — it's a bit of a stretch; I've only got tiny hands.

LYNDON: Use the other one.

NURSE: Oh, okay.

JOANNA JOINS THEM.

JOANNA: Psst.

LYNDON: Okay, if you just...

JOANNA WHISPERS AT LYNDON.

JOANNA: Psst. Thank you. Cheeky boy! Yeah, I just wanted to say thanks.

SHE FINGERS THE LOCKET ROUND HER NECK.

JOANNA: I love it, love, love, love it.

LYNDON: For?

JOANNA: I love it.

SHE KICKS THE NURSE'S CHAIR OUT OF THE WAY, TO GET NEARER TO LYNDON.

JOANNA: The er... e-mail was spot on — yeah, very thoughtful. You're a bad boy. Bad, bad, bad, bad, bad boy. Laters?

LYNDON: Sorry?

JOANNA: Catch you laters. Later, birthday drinks in the bar, about sixish. (TO THE NURSE) Yeah, not you. Just him.

LYNDON: I don't think I...

JOANNA PUTS HER HAND OVER HIS MOUTH SO HE CAN'T REFUSE AND WALKS OFF.

LYNDON: (TO NURSE) Okay, do you just want to try again?

LYNDON TURNS TO LOOK TOWARDS WHERE JOANNA WENT. HE DOESN'T UNDERSTAND. THE NURSE SMELLS HIS ARMPIT WHILE HE'S NOT LOOKING. STATHAM COMES ROUND THE CORNER TO CHECK WHAT'S GOING ON.

MAC: Okay, you have the chauffeur-driven car, twenty-four hours a day, 365 days a year, seven days a week.

GUY: So, if I wanted to go to any pub at any hour of the day in any part of the country, it would take me?

MAC: Yes.

GUY: Would the driver be parked outside my house twenty-four hours a day?

MAC: Hmmm, no.

GUY: Well that's ridiculous, how would I contact him?

MAC: Okay, whatever, whatever, okay, he's outside twenty-four hours.

GUY: Well one man couldn't stay awake twenty-four hours a day for a year.

MAC: All right, there are several drivers; they're working in shifts.

GUY: Would he have a uniform?

MAC: Yes.

GUY: Designed by me?

MAC: Yes.

GUY: What make of car?

MAC: You would have... a Bentley, but more than a Bentley, you would have a Bentley with diplomatic immunity.

GUY: The price?

MAC: Three nights of passion with Doctor Alan Statham.

GUY: I'll do it.

MAC: Really?

GUY: Yeah, course. Diplomatic immunity? Bargain.

MAC: Okay, what about the same thing without immunity?

GUY: Only if I can have a little Swiss flag on the front of the Bentley like ambassadors do.

MAC: Every day you're going to go to work, you're going to see him; you're going to be reminded of the horrors of those three nights.

GUY: Yeah, but I'd have a flagged-up, chauffeur-driven Bentley!

MAC: Fair point.

GUY SINGS TRIUMPHANTLY.

MAC: Yes, fair point.

GUY SWINGS THE OPERATING TABLE LIGHTS ABOUT.

MAC: (REFERRING TO PATIENT) He's waking up.

GUY: Oh yes.

MARTIN: Hello Mum, it's — it's me again... Don't hang up, I know you're there, I just want...

SHE HANGS UP. HE DIALS AGAIN.

MARTIN: Hi Mum, it's me again...

SHE HANGS UP AGAIN.

STATHAM IS OPPOSITE SUE WHITE. SHE IS EATING CHOCOLATE CAKE.

SUE: Celebrating Joanna's birthday. Piece of cake?

STATHAM: No, I'm here to discuss Lyndon.

SUE: Oh right, the Prince of Darkness.

STATHAM: Yes, and that's partly — no, absolutely nothing to do with it, it's just that I — I think we're going to have to let him go.

SUE: Lovely, lovely. Lovely Lyndon.

STATHAM: The female contingent in the hospital feel unable to talk about it, so I have designated myself their voice. Um... he looms.

SUE: Looms?

STATHAM: Yes.

"**Men are such dopes, don't they realise women who are too nice are secretly evil?**"

SUE: Cake?

STATHAM: No. He creeps out of dark corners, in frankly a predatory fashion, you know, with his ulterior ways, and he slips into their still warm seats. He... he unsettles them.

SUE PUTS CHOCOLATE ICING ON HER CHEEKS.

SUE: Does he now? And who exactly does he unsettle?

STATHAM: Well, I'm speaking for — for many anonymous women.

SUE: I need names.

STATHAM: Er... well — um, Joanna Clore, for one — she is unsettled by his loomingness. Er — she becomes breathy and skittish around him and moisture forms on her brows. Um...

SUE SINKS HER WHOLE FACE INTO THE TOP OF THE CHOCOLATE CAKE. SHE LIFTS HER HEAD AND LOOKS AT HIM.

SUE: Would you say that I'm looming now?

STATHAM: No. You remain completely unscary, in spite of your — and don't think I don't know what you're getting at, with — with your face-paint!

▸▸ CORRIDOR/PHYSIOTHERAPY

ANGELA AND CAROLINE MAKE THEIR WAY ALONG THE CORRIDOR TOWARDS THE PHYSIOTHERAPY DEPARTMENT.

ANGELA: She's in there, apparently.

CAROLINE: Well, I can't wait to meet this perfect woman, who scores top in everything, including personality. Men are such dopes, don't they realise women who are too nice are secretly evil?

THEY WATCH EMMY THROUGH THE WARD WINDOW. SHE IS HELPING A CHILD TO WALK. THE CHILD'S GRATEFUL PARENTS WATCH IN WONDER.

EMMY: Come on Thomas. Yes. Very slowly. Slowly. Yes, come on. Very good. Oh yes. Come on. Yes.

EMMY HANDS THE BOY TO THE PARENTS AND CRIES WITH JOY.

CAROLINE: You see? Pure evil.

ANGELA: Yeah. Look at her, playing on the emotions of those people, and turning on the tears so people like her more.

CAROLINE: Hmm. She's not that attractive, she's got a big mouth.

ANGELA: Yeah, but men like that. You know, it's voluptuous...

CAROLINE: Yeah, but not like a letterbox. Actually, you've got quite a big mouth.

ANGELA: No I haven't.

CAROLINE: Yes you have.

ANGELA: (SUCKING HER CHEEKS IN) No, I haven't.

CAROLINE: You have.

ANGELA: I have not!

THEY MAKE THEIR WAY BACK DOWN THE CORRIDOR.

CAROLINE: Well that's not your real mouth.

ANGELA: This is a pert mouth.

CAROLINE: No, that's not your real mouth.

▸▸ STAFF LIAISON OFFICE

STATHAM: Um... I'm not.

SUE: Not what?

STATHAM: One of those people who thinks ill of someone because of their — their... I think we've all of us learned from the — the pop group Showaddywaddy, that the story goes that out of the entire pop group, they had only nine 'O' levels between them. Obviously the result of a comprehensive education, but it transpired that the Caucasians hadn't passed any exams at all, and it was in fact the darker, the darkest chap who in fact passed all of the — all of the exams himself. And so of course everyone was amazed, you know; who would have thought it of the — the er.... but not me. I wasn't surprised in the least. So.

SUE: You weren't?

STATHAM: No, well because the rest of the group were clearly um — um... Well, not... And so, that's — that's why.

STATHAM LEAVES. SUE PUTS HER FACE BACK INTO THE CHOCOLATE CAKE.

▸▸ RADIOLOGY

MARTIN AND BOYCE HAVE SEVERAL BOXFULS OF CRISPS AND ARE PASSING EACH PACKET THROUGH A SCANNER.

BOYCE: No. No. Nein.

MARTIN: That's it for the prawn cocktails. Ready salted...

BOYCE: Okay. No. No. Yes, yes, direct hit! Open it up, open her up.

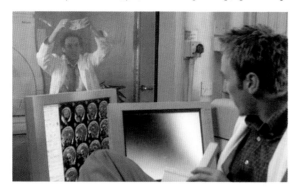

MARTIN: Yes! twenty quid!

BOYCE: Twenty quid!

MARTIN: Twenty quid.

BOYCE: Twenty British quid.

MARTIN: That's eighty quid now.

BOYCE: Right, stick it with the others, there's plenty more to come. (LOOKS BACK AT MONITOR) No...

STATHAM ENTERS. BOYCE JUMPS UP.

STATHAM: This is out of bounds Mr Boyce, what do you think you're doing?

BOYCE: Me? I er — just wanted to be at the helm. I just wanted to feel what it was like to be like you.

STATHAM: Dream on Mr Boyce, dream on, you will never know what it's like to be like me.

BOYCE: Well I know that now. It takes someone special to control a ship like that.

STATHAM: Yes, it does.

BOYCE: You're special. You're special; you're like Obi-Wan Kenobi to my Luke Skywalker.

MARTIN CARRIES OFF THE BOXES OF CRISPS, DROPPING THEM. STATHAM AND BOYCE HEAD TOWARDS THE LIFT AND GET IN.

BOYCE: So er, what makes me special then?

STATHAM: What?

BOYCE: What makes me special? I mean, you know, you have the whole effortless charm thing going for you.

STATHAM: Do I?

BOYCE: Yeah, of course you do. Everyone can see it a mile off. But you know, what have I got?

STATHAM: Don't know.

BOYCE: You must do, I mean I know what makes you attractive, so surely you must sense what my special gift is.

PAUSE WHILE STATHAM CONSIDERS.

STATHAM: Charts, you do nice charts.

BOYCE: Do I?

STATHAM: Yes, very neat handwriting.

BOYCE: Really?

SOMEONE GETS OUT AND THEY ARE LEFT ALONE IN THE LIFT.

BOYCE: Anything else?

STATHAM: Um... Er — well, eyes like — like... blue...

BOYCE: Are they?

STATHAM: Like chipped blue ice.

BOYCE LOOKS PLEASED.

▸▸ CANTEEN

SOME OF THE OFFICE GIRLS ARE HAVING LUNCH AT A TABLE.

KIM: What have you got there?

KAREN: Soup.

KIM: What kind?

KAREN: Minestrone flavour.

KIM: Minestrone *flavour*? Minestrone's not a flavour.

KAREN: It is.

KIM: No. A flavour's like strawberry or salt and vinegar or sour cream and chive.

HARRIET: Vanilla.

KIM: Yeah, vanilla. Or lemon.

HARRIET: Pistachio.

KIM: We could say, what flavour is the minestrone? Is it tomatoey or garlicky?

HARRIET: Or oniony.

KAREN: It's minestrone-ey.

KIM: No it fucking isn't!

HARRIET: Please don't swear.

KAREN: You haven't tried it.

KIM: I don't care. There's no such thing.

KAREN: It's my soup!

KIM: It's not a bloody flavour, all right?!

KAREN: (RELISHING HER SOUP) Hmmm… minestrone-ey.

KIM PICKS UP THE KETCHUP AND SQUIRTS IT INTO KAREN'S SOUP.

KIM: Tomatoey.

▸▸ MESS

GUY AND MAC ARE GOING TO ARM-WRESTLE.

GUY: Bring it on. Left hands, unless you want to sort your hair out.

MAC: Prepare to burn.

GUY: All right, light the flames. (BOYCE HOLDS A LIGHTER ON ONE SIDE AND MARTIN STRIKES A MATCH ON THE OTHER) Er, right, yes, that's good. Are you ready? Okay, don't go until I say. Okay.

MAC: I'm ready.

GUY: Okay, three, two…

HE STARTS TO WRESTLE.

MAC: You fucker!

GUY: Burn, you titty!

MAC: Find the extra gear. Ah yes.

MAC IS WINNING.

GUY: No.

MAC: Feel the heat. Feel the heat.

GUY IS CLEARLY LOSING, BUT MARTIN'S MATCH BURNS HIS FINGERS.

MARTIN: Ow!

MAC: Yes!

GUY: Void. Void.

GUY BREAKS AWAY FROM THE WRESTLING.

MAC: No it's not.

GUY: It is, it's void.

MAC: No it's not.

GUY: Because the Fartin dropped the match.

MAC: No, I won!

GUY: I'm sorry, that's my final word on the matter.

MARTIN: Sorry Mac, but it was burning my finger. See? It throbs.

MAC: Do you want a re-match?

GUY: No.

MAC: Why not? Why not?

GUY: Because I don't want to.

MAC: Yeah, because you're afraid to lose.

GUY: No.

ANGELA AND CAROLINE MARCH IN.

CAROLINE: Right, we want a word with you!

GUY: No, I won't go out with you both.

CAROLINE: Not you, him. About this. (SHE WAVES A SHEET OF PAPER AT MAC) This ridiculous league table of women in this hospital.

GUY: Where did you get that?

ANGELA: It's a printout from Mac's poisonous gadget. It's childish and offensive.

GUY: Well actually, most women would be flattered at the attention.

ANGELA: He gave Caroline's bum a four out of ten!

CAROLINE: Shut up!

ANGELA: What? He knows what he gave you.

MAC: Do I?

GUY: Well actually — in that skirt — you are a four out of ten.

MARTIN: I would give you a nine.

CAROLINE: Thank you Martin!

GUY: I mean if you were wearing little cuppy pants or something, you might have the arse of a seven. But in those, it's a four, that's a fact. So we were — he was — just stating a fact, end of story.

CAROLINE: Er no, no no, it's not the end of the story, because I don't go around saying — Guy, you look like the donkey from *Shrek*, or ginger freak to Mac, or, Martin, you look like a vole, do I? Or you, Boyce, you look like a porcelain lady-boy sometimes. Do I? Do I?

MAC: No, you don't, because that would be offensive and that would be personal abuse as stated in the discrimination policy of this hospital.

CAROLINE: What?

MAC: You heard. You've just made discriminatory remarks about each one of us.

CAROLINE: No I didn't.

MAC: Yes you did. You just said that he looked like the donkey from *Shrek*, that is making fun of physical deformity. You said Boyce looked like a lady-boy, that is homophobic. You said I was a ginger freak, that is — well that's colour-blind for a start, it's also racist.

MARTIN: You said I looked like a vole.

THEY ALL LOOK AT MARTIN.

MAC: Yeah... You said all these things in front of witnesses. I think you're lucky that we don't report you.

GUY: I might report you.

CAROLINE: You can't, I've done nothing wrong.

ANGELA SKILFULLY SIDLES ROUND TO STAND WITH THE OTHERS.

ANGELA: You kind of have.

MAC: I suggest that you leave and we won't take this any further.

CAROLINE: Well, what about the table?

MAC: If you ignore the table, we will let the homophobic, the racist, the disability jibes slide.

ANGELA AND CAROLINE LEAVE.

BOYCE: Nice one Mac.

MAC: (HANDING HIM THE SHEET) Yours, I believe?

GUY: Yeah.

Let me drink from your Wondrous cup
Something something Hairy?
Nectar sup.

Tooth and Claw
I fight to be with you,
That tempting slice twist moon
White thighs
Dripping hot sweet lady gravy
onto my face.
You are so sexy bad, ohhh
ohhh God. yes yes

Nipple frisky
Dusky musk
Sexy tickle
Back door thrust

Happy Birthday

A

Wondrous gash
Shimmering lips
Earth scent sniffly
Finger licky.
If only you could talk
And say
Here comes Alan
yum, yum, yum

Romeo and Juliet are fuck
all compared to us
Napoleon and Josephine are
fuck all compared to us
Bonnie and Clyde are fuck
all compared to us
Sooty and Sw

MAC: (THROWING THE PALM PILOT AT HIM) As is this?

GUY: Yeah.

MARTIN: Do you really think I look like a vole?

OTHERS: Yeah.

GUY: (TO MAC) Um... listen mate, I really appreciate that. Thanks. I won't forget it.

MAC: Yeah. Neither will I.

GUY: And there's nothing wrong with ginger pubes.

MAC: (DONKEY NOISE) Eee-ore.

▶▶ **CANTEEN**

JOANNA IS FINGERING HER LOCKET, WHICH IS STARTING TO LEAK SOME LIQUID.

JOANNA: Urgh...

STATHAM COMES IN.

STATHAM: Ah ha! Ah ha ha ha! There she is, there's the birthday girl.

JOANNA: Yes? What?

STATHAM: But, ah — you got my little token I see.

JOANNA: Your what?

STATHAM: My symbol of affection.

JOANNA: This isn't from you?

STATHAM: Yes it is. Yes, thank you very much, yes. I secretly put it on your desk this morning.

JOANNA: Bugger!

STATHAM: It's um — it's from Enobarbus to his Cleopatra. Sorry, you said bugger — why did you say that?

JOANNA: Well I suppose it had to be from you, the bloody thing's broken!

STATHAM: It can't be.

JOANNA: Well it is. Where did you get it from, the market?

STATHAM: Right...

JOANNA: It's shoddy.

STATHAM: Right.

JOANNA: I've got this gluey stuff all over me.

STATHAM: Yes, oh dear... no, but we'll have that fixed. Um...

JOANNA: What is it anyway?

STATHAM: Well, have a — have a guess. Go on, have a guess.

JOANNA: I don't know.

STATHAM: It's man's milk. It's my love-juice.

JOANNA: That had better be a joke.

STATHAM: But don't worry, I can easily refill it. Well, not — not here, obviously. I mean...

JOANNA: Are you telling me you've given me a spunk-filled locket for my birthday?

SUE WHITE SEES THEM.

SUE: (SINGS 'HAPPY BIRTHDAY') ...Now that you're fifty-two..." Joke! (SPOTTING THE LOCKET) Nice trinket — may I?

JOANNA PULLS THE TRINKET AWAY AS SUE TOUCHES IT.

JOANNA: No!

SUE: Oh. Well there seems to be a slight discharge there now. Now er... what is that? Perfume?

JOANNA: No. No, it's a special nectar.

SUE HAS SOME OF THE 'SPECIAL NECTAR' ON HER FINGER.

GUY: Well, broadly speaking, that's my point, Doctor Tit!

MAC: Maybe you have a hideous wasting disease.

GUY: Yeah, or maybe, Flopsy, somebody's spiked my lunch with something to make my wee blue.

MAC: We wouldn't do that.

GUY: Oh wouldn't you? Well let's put that to the test shall we? Eat some of that.

MAC: I don't want it.

GUY: Oh well! Guilt speaks.

MAC: No, I just don't like sweetcorn. Can I pick it out?

GUY: And remove the evidence?

MAC: Hang on, hang on. Are you seriously suggesting that by bribery or theft I got a syringe, injected individual pieces of sweetcorn with stuff that makes wee blue?

GUY'S BLEEPER GOES OFF.

MAC: Of course we didn't.

GUY: Yeah, well I...

MAC: Yeah. Of course not.

GUY: Yeah, well...

GUY LEAVES, LOOKING A BIT SHEEPISH.

SUE: Hmm.

JOANNA: It's an Indian, tribal, youth-giving... it's hippy-shit, you know.

SUE: Hmm.

SHE PUTS HER STICKY FINGER IN HER MOUTH.

SUE: Well, yum yum. We could all do with a bit of "youth". Are you in the market for a bun?

STATHAM: No, I'm not.

SUE WALKS OFF, PULLING A DISTASTEFUL EXPRESSION.

JOANNA: (TO STATHAM) Thank you so much!

STATHAM: Yes, well don't worry, I've got you something else, you know, you get your main present later.

HE INDICATES HIS FLIES.

▸▸ **MESS**

GUY JOINS MAC AND MARTIN. HE IS HOLDING A BOTTLE OF BLUE LIQUID.

GUY: Okay, why has my wee gone blue?

MARTIN: Blue? Oh, it shouldn't be that colour.

MAC: It was in your Fanta.

MARTIN: Doctor Tit.

▸▸ **RADIOLOGY**

STATHAM IS POINTING AT AN X-RAY.

STATHAM: Good, now then here we are Mr Boyce, I think this

demonstrates perfectly the hip screw I was discussing yesterday morning...

BOYCE: It's cold in here.

STATHAM: Yes, there's a problem with the heating, I've contacted Maintenance.

BOYCE: I can see your nipples through your shirt.

STATHAM: Um... can you?

BOYCE: They're like little bullets pointing at me.

STATHAM: Just stand behind me so you can't see them!

BOYCE: Yeah, sorry, yeah.

STATHAM: So, something may be caught, for instance, the iliopsoas muscle may be entrapped between the overhanging cup component on the hand, and the...

BOYCE: The thing is, I still know that they're erect.

STATHAM: Look, Mr Boyce, it's a perfectly unremarkable, involuntary physical response. Kindly pay attention and stop thinking about my nipples.

BOYCE: Right, I'm sorry. Of course, I'll concentrate now.

STATHAM: So we're looking for an abnormality of some sort, possibly, in this case, specifically, er... There's... I think yours are erect now, by the way. Yes.

BOYCE: Are they?

STATHAM: Yes, yes. They're like beady eyes.

BOYCE: It must be the cold.

STATHAM: Er — there's a nip in the air, as it were.

BOYCE: Um... okay, so why don't we go back to the x-rays, but this time we could maybe rub our nipples to bring them down?

STATHAM: Yes, that's good, that's good, very good. And er...

THEY BOTH RUB THEIR NIPPLES. BOYCE TRIES NOT TO LAUGH.

BOYCE: They're retracting.

BOYCE HAS A PIECE OF PAPER STUCK ON HIS TONGUE WHICH SAYS: "HOMO". HE KEEPS PUTTING HIS TONGUE IN WHEN STATHAM LOOKS AT HIM.

STATHAM: When, and er — if an infiltration of, um... into the painful muscle, of local anaesthetic, would... Some relief, um — obviously. (EVENTUALLY STATHAM READS WHAT IS WRITTEN) And er... good, goodbye. Um... correct, Doctor, well done. That's er, that's cleared, cleared that. Ship shape and um... I'll check, I'll, yes...

▶▶ **PAYPHONE, HOSPITAL CORRIDOR**

MARTIN IS ON THE PHONE.

MARTIN: (SINGS THE OPENING LINES OF 'HAPPY BIRTHDAY')

THE OTHER PERSON HANGS UP.

▶▶ **STAFF LIAISON OFFICE**

SUE WHITE IS IN HER OFFICE. SHE STUFFS BALLS OF SCREWED-UP NEWSPAPER UP HER T-SHIRT. THERE IS A KNOCK AT THE DOOR.

SUE: Enter.

CAROLINE ENTERS.

SUE: Ah, Doctor Todd, come in, take a seat.

CAROLINE: Thank you. (NOTICES SUE'S CHEST) Oh God I — you've, well you've — they've, well they're...

SUE: Bigger?

CAROLINE: Yes.

SUE: How odd you noticed.

CAROLINE: Not really, they're hard to miss.

SUE: Ooh. Like you, I'm drawn to large breasts. Full ones.

CAROLINE: Right. Only I'm not drawn to them.

SUE: Ah, you noticed mine.

CAROLINE: Well, yes, but...

SUE: Comforting aren't they? I think I want to touch a big woman's breasts. I'm not a lesbian, it's just they look so inviting, don't they? Actually, maybe I am a lesbian.

CAROLINE IS UNCOMFORTABLE.

CAROLINE: (TO HERSELF) Breathe, breathe...

SUE: Now, how can I help?

CAROLINE: Er, it doesn't — well, I just have some concerns about attitudes to female staff. Some of the male doctors are... You know what, I don't think it matters now.

CAROLINE GOES TO THE DOOR. SUE TAKES ONE OF THE BALLS OF NEWSPAPER OUT OF HER TOP AND THROWS IT AFTER CAROLINE.

CAROLINE: Did you just throw your breast at me?

SUE: No. Do you want me to?

CAROLINE: No.

OUT OF VISION, CAROLINE THROWS BACK THE 'BREAST', WHICH HITS SUE IN THE FACE, AND SHE LEAVES. SUE PUTS THE OTHER BALL OF NEWSPAPER IN THE BIN.

▸▸ CORRIDOR

MARTIN AND BOYCE ARE PASSING EACH OTHER.

BOYCE: Martee.

MARTIN: Boycee.

BOYCE: Martee.

MARTIN: Boycee.

BOYCE: Marteeah.

MARTIN: Boyceee.

BOYCE: Marteeee.

MARTIN: Boyceee.

BOYCE: Martee.

MARTIN: Boyceee.

BOYCE: Marteeee.

THEY CONTINUE TO SAY "MARTEEE" AND "BOYCEEE" FOR SOME TIME, DOING WHAT LOOKS ALMOST LIKE A DANCE ROUTINE AS THEY PASS EACH OTHER.

BOYCE: Marteeah!

MARTIN: Boyceee!

BOYCE: Martee.

MARTIN: Boyceee.

BOYCE: Stop it.

THEY WALK ON. MARTIN STOPS AT THE END OF THE CORRIDOR AND TURNS BACK.

MARTIN: (SHOUTS) Boyceeeee!

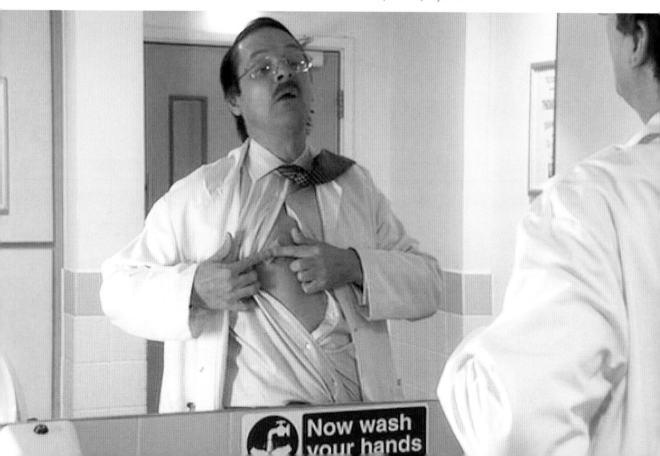

▸▸ MEN'S TOILETS

STATHAM IS PUTTING ELASTOPLASTS ON HIS NIPPLES. SOMEONE COMES IN TO USE THE URINAL.

STATHAM: Um, you're — you're probably thinking that um... In some way, um... That er...

STATHAM LEAVES.

▸▸ OFFICE

RACHEL: Ooh, Karen! Martin Dear "Isn't He Queer" is on his way up.

KAREN: Oh my God! How do I look?

RACHEL: Rough.

KAREN: Oh!

RACHEL: I know — crouch down. It makes you look less ugly.

KAREN: Okay.

KAREN BENDS.

RACHEL: No, crouch.

KAREN CROUCHES.

RACHEL: Hmm, still ugly? Yes.

KAREN CROUCHES RIGHT DOWN. MARTIN COMES IN. JOANNA HIDES.

MARTIN: Is Joanna — Joanna Clore in the...? Hello ladies.

RACHEL: Martin.

MARTIN: Doctor Dear.

RACHEL: Whatever.

MARTIN: Is um — is frizz-head around? The one with the curly hair? I need some T & D forms.

KAREN: I'm here.

MARTIN: What are you doing down there?

KAREN: Searching.

MARTIN: For what?

KAREN: Something.

MARTIN: Can I get some forms please?

KAREN DOESN'T WANT TO STAND UP.

KAREN: They're — they're over there.

MARTIN: Where?

KAREN: I'll get them.

KAREN WALKS WITH BENT KNEES TO THE FILING CABINET AND GIVES MARTIN THE FORMS.

KAREN: There you go.

MARTIN: Thanks. So... you've got lots of hair, haven't you?

KAREN: Yeah.

MARTIN: Curley wurley sort of... Is it — is it like that... all over? Do you, do you... (MARTIN IS STUCK) Can you tell Joanna Clore that

I have passed by please? Thanks.

MARTIN GOES. KAREN STANDS UP.

RACHEL: See? I told you you look better crouched down.

▶▶ RADIOLOGY

STATHAM IS TEACHING A GROUP OF STUDENTS. HE POINTS TO AN X-RAY.

STATHAM: And what is this? Mr Boyce?

BOYCE: It's a bone.

STATHAM: Of course it's a bone, you fool, the question is, which bone is it?

BOYCE: That's not the question you asked.

STATHAM: Oh yes it is.

BOYCE: No, you said, "What's this?"

STATHAM: Yes, well I meant, what bone is this?

BOYCE: Hmm, don't know.

STATHAM: Well then I suggest you don't waste people's time by raising your nipple — hands — to er… ask a question, answer that you have no idea about!

BOYCE: Yes, well I knew the answer to the question you actually asked, so I was right to raise my hand.

STATHAM: Yeah, but that wasn't the question I meant, so you got it wrong.

BOYCE: Oh, is that not a bone then?

STATHAM: Yes, but you didn't get the question right, so you were wrong to raise your hand.

BOYCE: But I didn't raise my hand to answer that question.

STATHAM: Well just — just, that's, that is beside the point! And just cease now!

BOYCE: Do I still have chipped ice blue eyes?

STATHAM: Moving on.

BOYCE: And neat handwriting?

STATHAM: Moving on! Does anybody know what this is?

BOYCE: It's a bone.

STATHAM: Mr Boyce, you…

STATHAM GETS HIS POINTER STUCK BEHIND HIS GLASSES AND KNOCKS THEM TO THE FLOOR.

STATHAM: Nobody move!

HE CAN'T SEE WITHOUT HIS GLASSES.

▶▶ OFFICE

JOANNA COMES IN, ONLY HARRIET IS THERE, PACKING UP HER THINGS.

JOANNA: Where is everyone?

HARRIET: Gone.

JOANNA: What, to the bar?

HARRIET: No, home I think.

JOANNA: Good, oh what a relief. God. I was dreading having to make conversation with you lot — you know, pretend we all like each other!

HARRIET: Yes, well have a nice night.

JOANNA: This isn't a joke, is it? You know, a surprise party? Make me think you've all gone home and then find you're all in the bar?

HARRIET: No.

JOANNA: Because I'd hate that.

HARRIET: Yes. Well you should be all right, because that's not the plan.

JOANNA: Good, good. What a relief!

JOANNA IS DISAPPOINTED.

▶▶ LOCKER AREA

CAROLINE COMES IN TO FIND MARTIN, GUY AND MAC TALKING AMONGST THEMSELVES.

GUY: There's not one bloody colour photo in the whole thing!

MARTIN: That's an old one, that one.

CAROLINE: (INDIGNANT) I mean...!

MAC: "I mean"... yes?

CAROLINE: No no, nothing.

MAC: No, go on.

CAROLINE: I mean, how would you boys feel if I'd been compiling a league table about you?! Reducing you to mere physical attributes listed in cold numerical order, ignoring everything else about you and just concentrating on sex, sex, sex?!

THE BOYS REPLY ENTHUSIASTICALLY AND SIMULTANEOUSLY.

GUY: I'd like that.

MARTIN: (EXCITED) Have you really?

MAC: That would be fascinating.

CAROLINE: Unbelievable! All right, all right, we'll make one up shall we? Hmm? Arses, out of ten: Guy — six, Mac — four, Martin — seven. Hair: Martin — three, Mac — three, Guy — six. Fuckosity: (TO GUY AND MARTIN IN TURN) Nil. Nil. (TURNING TO MAC) Guess what?

MAC: What?

CAROLINE: Nil. Okay? Happy boys?

MAC: Yeah, very.

CAROLINE STORMS OUT.

MARTIN: Did you hear that? I got seven for my arse.

MAC: Oh shut up!

GUY: She was making it up Martin, she said so.

MARTIN: Yeah, well she still said it; those words came out of her mouth.

GUY: Yeah, well the word "vole" came out of her mouth earlier.

MAC: Remember the words "face" and "donkey".

MARTIN: Yeah, well I still got a seven.

MAC: No, you didn't get a seven. You didn't get a seven because that was made-up. Yeah? She was just saying the first thing that came into her head, it's not real.

GUY: Yeah, mind you, it is hard to suppress your inner

Guy's Occasionally Medical Rhyming Slang

Pubic hair - Gas and air. As in "Give her a blast of pubes".

Betty and Mabel - Dead on the table. As in "Leave him, I think he's Betty."

Hangman's rope - Stethoscope. As in "Lend us your hangman's."

Sweaty Bra - Hospital bar. As in "I'll see you down the sweaty."

Martin Dear - Queer. As in "You fucking Martin" or, "How Martin, I was sure I left my glasses on the bookcase."

Age - Pee. As in "Drink my age" or, "Bring your brolly, it's going to age it down."

Billy Goat - Scrote. As in "Shit, I've found a lump in my billy."

Blue Peter Badge - Vag. As in "What a capacious Blue Peter" (ECHO) Peter, Peter, Peter

Postman Pat - Twat. As in "May I stroke your postman?"

thoughts completely and she did do it very quickly, so there might be something in it. I mean, after all, you do have the shittest hair.

MAC: No, because if you actually listened, you would actually remember that I tied with Martin on hair.

GUY: Yeah, but I won it! And what's more, with a clear three — *three-point* — margin.

GUY CHANGES HIS TWO FINGERS TO THREE TOWARDS MAC.

GUY: And I had the highest aggregate combined total. That is it. I think there might be something in it after all.

THEY HEAD OFF DOWN THE CORRIDOR.

MARTIN: Yeah, we still got nil for fuckosity though, didn't we?

GUY: Yeah, we did.

MARTIN: Still, I've got the nicest arse.

▸▸ STATHAM'S OFFICE

STATHAM IS AT HIS DESK. HE CAN HEAR A STRANGE WHIRRING NOISE. HE CHECKS THE PHONE. A REMOTE-CONTROL, SILVER AIRSHIP FLIES INTO THE OFFICE WITH THE WORD "HOMO" WRITTEN ON IT IN PINK. HE IS COMPLETELY FREAKED OUT. HE THINKS ABOUT ATTACKING IT, BUT THEN RUNS OUT OF THE OFFICE.

▸▸ BAR, TABLE — LATER

STATHAM SITS BETWEEN JOANNA AND LYNDON.

STATHAM: I — I said, you do not know the difference between Diphenhydramine Hydrochloride and Nucleic Acid. Ha ha ha!

LYNDON: (ANYTHING TO GET AWAY FROM THIS) Who's for another drink?

JOANNA: (ANYTHING TO BE ALONE WITH LYNDON) Oh Alan, you go.

STATHAM: No, no.

LYNDON: No, it's all right, I don't mind.

JOANNA: No no no, it's Doctor Statham's turn.

STATHAM: No, no it isn't.

JOANNA: Yes it is, you know it is.

STATHAM: No. Well actually, it's just that I'd rather not go to the bar. It might be rather awkward, because um — the staff and I had a bit of a disagreement.

JOANNA: About what?

STATHAM: Um... bringing a dog into the bar.

JOANNA: You haven't got a dog.

STATHAM: No, that's right... and that's why they wouldn't serve me, because they said they were only serving dog owners. Yeah, that was — that was it.

LYNDON: That's bizarre.

JOANNA: Oh dear.

STATHAM: Yes, yes, quite mad they are... (TO LYNDON) and there's some money, if you wouldn't mind...

JOANNA: Yes, he does mind.

STATHAM: No, he doesn't mind.

JOANNA: Yes he does.

STATHAM: No, he doesn't.

JOANNA: Yes he does.

LYNDON: I don't.

STATHAM: He doesn't.

LYNDON GOES TO THE BAR.

JOANNA: What's the matter with you?! Can't you just do your own thing for one minute?

STATHAM: What, and leave you alone with him? You must be mad. He's got methods.

JOANNA: Oh what are you talking about?

STATHAM: You know, he's got — he's got devious ways, you know, one minute you're having a perfectly nice drink in the bar, the next minute — whoof, you're spread-eagled on a rug in the woods, without knowing how you got there, while he — he — he's rutting on top of you and ploughing his mucky little furrow.

JOANNA IS QUITE TURNED ON BY THIS.

JOANNA: Hmm.

STATHAM: What?

JOANNA: Oh, nothing.

▶▶ **BAR**

MARTIN IS WATCHING MAC MAKING NOTES — GUY COMES UP TO JOIN THEM.

GUY: What are you doing?

MAC: Writing a speech.

GUY: Oh yeah? Are you resigning?

MARTIN: No, it's his best man's speech.

GUY: Are you going to be a best man?

MAC: Yeah, this weekend.

GUY: Fuck!

MARTIN: Yeah, he's been asked to do it seven times. That is popularity for you.

GUY: Seventh time, eh? You want to watch it mate. My dad used to say to me — careful, always the bridesmaid, never the bride.

MAC: You were a bridesmaid were you?

GUY: What? No, I...

MAC: You just said your father said, "Always the bridesmaid, never the bride."

MARTIN: "Never the bride."

MAC: That would imply that you were a bridesmaid.

GUY: It was a turn of phrase.

MAC: A turn of gender?

GUY: Well actually, in Switzerland it's quite common for men to be bridesmaids.

MAC: No it isn't.

GUY: Are you Swiss?

MAC: No.

GUY: Then you don't know.

MAC: No, I do know that bridesmaids are women. What did you wear?

GUY: Fuck off.

MAC: A dress?

GUY: No, it was a long sort of tunic.

MAC: A dress.

GUY: No, I was five.

MAC: I don't care how old you were, that is a thing that girls do.

GUY: You tell anyone, I'll cut your heart out with a spoon.

MAC: Whatever.

MARTIN: Always a bridesmaid, that's brilliant!

GUY: I said shut up.

MAC: Oh dear.

GUY: I'm going to go and strain the greens.

MAC: Yep.

GUY GOES TO LEAVE. MARTIN AND MAC SING 'HERE COMES THE BRIDE'. MAC THROWS PEANUTS AT GUY. GUY GRABS

SOMEONE'S BAG OF CRISPS AND THROWS THEM AT MAC.

MAC: Huh! Yeah, I bet you look lovely in a tunic.

▶▶ BAR, TABLE

JOANNA: If you want to go to the loo, just go.

STATHAM: I don't want to go to the loo.

JOANNA: Yes you do, I know you do, you're sitting there jiggling with your legs crossed, like you always do.

LYNDON: Maybe I should go.

JOANNA: Oh no no no, please Lyndon, it's my birthday.

LYNDON: Well maybe just a few minutes.

JOANNA STARTS TO POUR DRINK FROM HER GLASS TO STATHAM'S AND BACK AGAIN. STATHAM STARTS TO LOOK EVEN MORE UNCOMFORTABLE.

JOANNA: So, the world of IT, what a mystery it is to the rest of us. How long have you been doing it for now Lyndon?

LYNDON: Four years.

JOANNA: Four years, hmm.

STATHAM: All right, you win. Just — you know, remember what I said, be careful, he's got methods.

STATHAM GOES TO THE TOILET. JOANNA CLOSES THE GAP BETWEEN HER AND LYNDON. HE LOOKS WORRIED.

LYNDON: Okay...

JOANNA: Oh Lyndon, Lyndon, I don't think I got my birthday kiss.

BOYCE SUDDENLY CLIMBS OVER THE SEAT AND SLIPS BETWEEN THEM.

BOYCE: Hello.

JOANNA: What the hell do you want?!

BOYCE: Doctor Statham said he'd give me twenty quid if I sat here for five minutes. Peanut?

LYNDON: I'd better go.

JOANNA: Oh no, Lyndon...

LYNDON LEAVES.

JOANNA: Oh fuck!

▶▶ CAROLINE'S HOUSE

LIAM IS HELPING ANGELA TO MOVE IN A FEW REMAINING

THINGS. CAROLINE WATCHES WITH GROWING CONCERN.

ANGELA: Just bring it straight through. Careful Liam.

CAROLINE: I thought you'd moved all your stuff in already.

ANGELA: Yeah, just, you know, all the little bits and bobs that I couldn't manage.

CAROLINE: Right.

ANGELA SEES CAROLINE'S FLUTE.

ANGELA: Is this yours?

CAROLINE: Yes actually, oh — oh, I'd rather you didn't play with that. Sorry, it's just that it was quite expensive.

ANGELA: How long have you been playing?

"The thing
is, it's
such a —
it's such a
part of me
that I
sometimes
forget that
it's
**quite
big.**"

CAROLINE: Oh, let me see, God, um, it was when I was, yeah... about six months.

ANGELA: Have you taken any grades?

CAROLINE: Oh no no no, it's, it's purely for relaxation. I'm completely self-taught. You know, the thing about the flute is that it's a far more complicated business than you'd imagine. You see, it actually takes about, oh, three months to get any sound out of it at all.

ANGELA: Really?

CAROLINE: Yeah, yeah... but yeah, I'm getting quite good now, so maybe I will take an exam.

ANGELA: Brilliant. You know I used to play the flute when I was little.

CAROLINE: When you were little? Are you sure you're not thinking about the recorder? This one goes out to the side; the recorder goes up and down.

ANGELA: Oh well let me think, I'm pretty sure it was one of those long silvery tube things. Good job you didn't go for the nickel-plated one.

CAROLINE: Why?

ANGELA: You get terrible problems with acidic perspiration; it makes all the plating come off very quickly.

CAROLINE: Well, that would be no good to a sweaty old pig like me. The whole thing would just dissolve!

ANGELA: No no no no no no, I didn't mean that you were a sweaty...

CAROLINE: So, maybe we could play together, do you still have your flute?

ANGELA: No.

CAROLINE: Aah. Yeah, it gets a bit difficult after the first year, doesn't it?

ANGELA: I just sort of moved on.

CAROLINE: Yeah? Bit daunting was it?

LIAM ENTERS.

LIAM: Where do you want to put the harp?

ANGELA: Hang on; let me give you a hand.

LIAM: Okay.

▶▶ **MEN'S TOILETS**

STATHAM IS USING THE URINAL. GUY COMES IN AND WAITS.

STATHAM: So. Not waiting to take drugs I hope?

GUY: What?

STATHAM: That's what people do; they take drugs in the cubicles. I read it in a report.

GUY: Are you —? Are you accusing me of taking cocaine on duty?

STATHAM: No, no no, just probably fully understand you're just waiting to do — to do a private poo.

GUY: No, I'm not waiting to do a private poo. I er... just, normally I like using a cubicle, but just to prove to you that I'm not doing drugs, or wanting to do a poo, I will use the urinal, okay?

STATHAM: Yes, yes.

GUY USES THE URINAL. STATHAM HAS A LOOK.

STATHAM: Um... you do realise that your — your wee is fluorescent?

GUY: Yes, thank you. Yes. (TO HIMSELF) Fuck, shit! (TO STATHAM) It's not a discharge.

▸▸ **BAR**

ON HIS WAY BACK FROM THE TOILETS STATHAM BUMPS INTO LYNDON.

STATHAM: Stealer.

LYNDON: What?

STATHAM: You've got a rug in the woods, haven't you? Warmed and waiting.

LYNDON: I beg your pardon?

STATHAM: You heard. It didn't work this time though, did it, Mister!

STATHAM GOES.

LYNDON: Mental.

▸▸ **CAROLINE'S HOUSE**

CAROLINE: I just think it's something you might have mentioned before you moved in, that's all. That's all.

ANGELA: Yeah, I know, I know. And gosh I'm so sorry.

CAROLINE: A harp?

ANGELA: I really am. The thing is, it's such a — it's such a part of me that I sometimes forget that it's quite big.

LIAM: Well I think it's terribly exciting.

LIAM IS CARESSING ANGELA WHILE SHE HOLDS THE HARP.

CAROLINE: And you can play it can you? Or do you just jam?

ANGELA: Well I wouldn't say that I could play to a professional standard.

CAROLINE: No.

ANGELA: I got distinction at grade seven.

LIAM: Oh, what a clever baby.

ANGELA: But when I made the decision to do medicine, well I — I just play for pleasure now.

LIAM: That I want to see.

ANGELA: But listen, if it's going to cause a row, then I can just pop it straight into storage.

LIAM: Oh woah, woah, woah. No.

CAROLINE: No no no. No no, it's fine, it's fine, I wouldn't dream of it. I'm really looking forward to hearing you play. Although, isn't it a shame you didn't get grade eight!

ANGELA: I know!

▸▸ **CAR PARK**

MARTIN JUMPS OUT AND SURPRISES JOANNA OUTSIDE THE HOSPITAL.

MARTIN: Hi there!

JOANNA: Oh God. Don't *do* that.

MARTIN: Sorry, did I scare you?

JOANNA: No no, I just meant don't come near me.

MARTIN: Yeah, well I've got something for you.

JOANNA: Well go on then, make it quick.

MARTIN: Well, happy birthday — Mum.

HE GIVES HER A "HAPPY BIRTHDAY MUM" BALLOON. JOANNA BURSTS THE BALLOON WITH A CIGARETTE.

JOANNA: Bugger off!

MARTIN: What about a birthday hug?

JOANNA: Yeah, sounds great, go and find me a fireman.

MARTIN: No, I meant from your son?

JOANNA: No.

MARTIN: Please!

JOANNA LOOKS AROUND TO SEE THAT NOBODY IS LOOKING. MARTIN PUTS HIS HEAD ON JOANNA'S CHEST.

MARTIN: Oh, happy birthday Mum.

JOANNA: Yep.

MARTIN: Oh, you're lovely.

JOANNA: No I'm not.

▸▸ CAROLINE'S HOUSE

CAROLINE IS DESPERATELY TRYING TO GET A NOTE OUT OF THE FLUTE. SHE HEARS LOVELY HARP MUSIC COMING FROM ANGELA'S ROOM ABOVE.

▸▸ CAR PARK

MARTIN IS HOLDING JOANNA TIGHT.

MARTIN: You're like a big pink furry hot water bottle.

JOANNA: Yeah, thanks very much!

JOANNA SEES STATHAM AND PUSHES MARTIN AWAY.

JOANNA: (SO THAT STATHAM CAN HEAR) Right, so the er — Heimlich manoeuvre from the front is... basically a non-starter?

MARTIN: Yes, yeah, that's right, the Heimlich manoeuvre from the front is... is not going to work. It's dangerous, so...

JOANNA: Yeah, so nice talking to you Doctor Dear.

MARTIN: Yeah, good.

JOANNA: (HISSING AT MARTIN) Just go away!

JOANNA GOES OVER TO STATHAM.

JOANNA: You're lurking.

STATHAM: Yes.

JOANNA: Right. Meet me at my car, front car park, five minutes.

STATHAM: As it's your birthday, are you going to let me touch it?

JOANNA: Maybe.

SHE WALKS AWAY. STATHAM STROKES THE CAR.

▸▸ CAROLINE'S HOUSE

THERE IS STILL LOVELY HARP MUSIC COMING FROM ANGELA'S ROOM. CAROLINE PUTS ON A FLUTE CD AND MIMES ALONG TO IT.

▸▸ CAR PARK

JOANNA IS IN HER CAR. STATHAM COMES OVER TO HER.

ALAN: Shall I go round?

STATHAM GOES ROUND TO GET IN THE CAR, BUT JOANNA DRIVES OFF AT SPEED WITHOUT HIM. HE STARES AFTER HER.

ALAN: God I love that woman!

▸▸ CAROLINE'S HOUSE

CAROLINE IS SINGING REALLY BADLY AND LOUDLY.

CAROLINE: La la la la la!

▸▸ CAR PARK

STATHAM IS STANDING, LOOKING LONGINGLY IN THE DIRECTION IN WHICH JOANNA HAS DRIVEN OFF. HE EVENTUALLY WALKS AWAY.

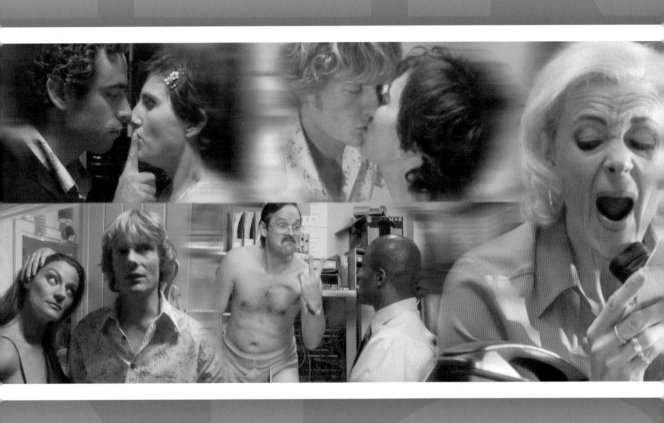

EPISODE 5

MAC ON HIS DUCATI AND MARTIN ON HIS SCOOTER ARRIVE AT THE SAME TIME.

▸▸ CAROLINE'S HOUSE

CAROLINE IS LOOKING IN THE HALL MIRROR, TRYING TO GET HER HAIR RIGHT. SHE CAN'T DO ANYTHING WITH IT. SHE PICKS UP A STRAY RUBBER BAND, BUT THAT DOESN'T HELP MUCH. SHE TRIES A HAT AND THEN A BULLDOG CLIP. ANGELA JOINS HER AT THE MIRROR AND OPENS A HUGE CASE WHICH HAS SEVERAL COMPARTMENTS LINED WITH FOAM, WITH HAIR CLIPS ALL NEATLY ARRANGED (LIKE A FISHERMAN'S FLY BOX). CAROLINE LOOKS AT IT WITH DISTASTE.

▸▸ CAR PARK

MARTIN DROPS HIS CRASH HELMET AS HE PUSHES HIS SCOOTER INTO THE PARKING SPACE. HE CAN'T GET IT ONTO ITS STAND.

▸▸ CAROLINE'S HOUSE

LIAM COMES UP TO ANGELA AND CAROLINE IN A STATE OF DISTRESS.

LIAM: I've got bowel cancer.

ANGELA: What is it, sweet?

LIAM: I've told you, I've got bowel cancer. I've got blood clots in my...

ANGELA: Okay, well we'd better go and have a look.

ANGELA FOLLOWS LIAM UPSTAIRS. CAROLINE MESSES UP HER BOX OF HAIR EQUIPMENT. SHE TAKES A HAIR GRIP AND HIDES IT IN HER MOUTH.

▸▸ CAR PARK

MARTIN PARKS HIS SCOOTER IN THE HOSPITAL CAR PARK AND RETRIEVES HIS HELMET.

▸▸ CAROLINE'S HOUSE

ANGELA REJOINS CAROLINE AT THE MIRROR.

ANGELA: Sun dried tomatoes.

▸▸ CAR PARK

MARTIN IS SITTING ON MAC'S DUCATI, TRYING TO IMPRESS A COUPLE OF NURSES.

MARTIN: Yeah, so thank God I had this filthy bitch between my thighs! She is a beast, but you've got to become one with that beast, yeah? You've got to control the beast, okay?

▸▸ CAROLINE'S HOUSE

ANGELA FLICKS HER HAIR ALL OVER THE PLACE.

ANGELA: I don't think I need it.

ANGELA WALKS OFF, SMACKING CAROLINE ON THE BUM.

▸▸ CAR PARK

MAC COMES OVER TO WHERE MARTIN IS SITTING ON HIS BIKE, STILL TALKING TO THE NURSES.

MARTIN: It was a nightmare, everyone was panicking, I just said, "You've got to calm down guys", you know? Because they were, we had to intubate nasally, and there was house red everywhere, okay? And you would have probably fainted. That kind of thing does not bother me at all.

MARTIN SEES MAC.

MARTIN: Sorry.

MAC: No, go on, sit on it. Go on, sit on it.

MARTIN: (TO THE NURSES) I have *got* a bike. It's a scooter. It's not — it's similar, but...

THE NURSES LEAVE.

MAC: It's a great scooter.

MARTIN: Yeah, cheers.

MARTIN PRETENDS TO REV MAC'S BIKE UP AND MAKES ENGINE NOISES.

MAC: That's probably enough.

MARTIN: Yeah.

▸▸ **MAIN ENTRANCE**

JOANNA WALKS INTO THE HOSPITAL. SHE HAS DYED HER HAIR STARTLINGLY BLONDE — IT IS ALMOST WHITE. TWO MEN LOOK AT HER. SHE APPROACHES CAROLINE.

JOANNA: Ah, Caroline Todd. Still sleeping rough I see.

CAROLINE: Well no actually...

CAROLINE STARES AT JOANNA'S HAIR.

JOANNA: Bit of advice, hairdressers are alive and well, you know.

CAROLINE: (UNDER HER BREATH) Clearly all blind...

▸▸ **CAR PARK**

MARTIN DROPS HIS HELMET AGAIN.

▸▸ **OFFICE**

KAREN IS WATCHING MARTIN FROM THE OFFICE WINDOW.

KIM: Where do you want these admissions lists Karen?

KAREN: Put them in my in-tray.

KIM: (PICKING UP A PIECE OF PAPER) What's this?

KAREN: Give it back to me.

KIM: What is it?

KAREN: It's mine!

KIM: Can't I look at it?

KAREN TRIES TO RETRIEVE HER PIECE OF PAPER.

KAREN: No!

RACHEL: Oh, it looks like a poem to me.

KIM: Oh, have you written a poem Karen?

KAREN: Can I have it back now, please?

RACHEL: Let's hear it.

KIM: "Ode to Martin", Martin who?

RACHEL: Martin Dear, he's the queer.

KAREN: He is not!

KIM: (READS) "There was a time I had not seen you, I don't know how I coped. Now every day I want to watch you, and help you with your moped." Help you with your moped? What does that mean?

KAREN: Mo-ped. It's mo-ped.

KIM: That doesn't rhyme.

KAREN: Yes it does.

KIM: No it doesn't!

KAREN: Well it's assonance.

KIM: What?

KAREN: It's a half rhyme. Michael Caine taught Julie Walters about it in *Educating Rita*.

KIM: Bollocks.

KAREN GRABS THE POEM, SCREWS IT UP AND PUTS IT IN HER MOUTH. SHE SOON TAKES IT OUT AGAIN.

HARRIET: I tell you what you could do Karen, in the second line, coped — co-ped. I know not how I co-ped. No. A bit florid perhaps.

THE PEROXIDE BLONDE JOANNA ENTERS.

JOANNA: Morning mumsie. Morning Rachel. Morning Kim.

KIM: Jesus!

JOANNA: What?

KIM: Oh, sorry, nothing, you took me by surprise.

JOANNA: Right. Oh Kim, I need you to sort out everyone's holiday rota at some point, okay?

KIM: It looks very striking by the way.

JOANNA: What does?

KIM: Your hair.

JOANNA: Yeah, what about it?

KIM: Well...

JOANNA: Oh that, yeah, it always gets a little lighter in the summer with the sun. What do you think?

KIM: Well it's amazing!

JOANNA: Oh, I wouldn't go that far. I'm surprised you've noticed actually, I don't think anyone else has.

▸▸ CORRIDOR

SUE WHITE IS TAKING SOME SIXTH FORMERS ON A TOUR OF THE HOSPITAL.

SUE: Right. Full attention please, tiny tots. As you've seen from your actual in-depth bowel tour of an actual working hospital, it's basically full of sick people who desperately want to get better, but a lot of them don't and they die in pain. Any questions?

SIXTH FORM BOY: Can we see the morgue?

SUE: No. Anything else?

NOBODY SAYS ANYTHING.

SUE: Good. Now, we are going to meet a very competent doctor and a close personal friend of mine. Doctor

MacCartney. This way, youths.

▶▶ **OFFICE**

JOANNA COMES OUT OF HER OFFICE TO FIND THAT ALL THE OFFICE STAFF HAVE COVERED THEIR HAIR IN YELLOW POST-IT NOTES.

JOANNA: Right, Kimmy, I'm just off to this IT seminar, if anybody... (SHE SEES THE POST-IT NOTES) Oh you all think you're so titting funny, don't you? Of course you realise I'll have to dock your wages for stationery wastage.

▶▶ **THEATRE**

MAC MEETS THE STUDENTS.

MAC: Hiya. You're Highfield sixth form, yeah? I hear you want to ask me some questions. About medicine. No? Right, I'll piss off then.

SIXTH FORM BOY: Do you cut people up?

MAC: Yep, but only if they're asleep and if they ask me nicely.

SIXTH FORM BOY: Do you get to sleep with the nurses?

MAC: Yeah, it's in their contract.

SIXTH FORM GIRL: Are you married?

MAC: No. Are you?

SIXTH FORM GIRL: No.

SIXTH FORM BOY: Oh she's just saving herself for 'the one'.

SIXTH FORM GIRL: Oh shut up!

MAC: Oh yeah.

CAROLINE JOINS THEM.

CAROLINE: Sorry Mac, they're bringing Mrs Foyle round, you wanted to be there?

MAC: Yeah, I'll be right there, I'm just going to put a few people off a life in medicine.

CAROLINE: Oh. Hello.

SIXTH FORM BOY: Are you a doctor?

CAROLINE: Er, yes.

SIXTH FORM BOY: And are you married?

CAROLINE: Goodness, no.

MAC: She's still looking for 'the one'.

▶▶ **SEMINAR ROOM — LOBBY**

STATHAM JOINS JOANNA AS SHE COMES OUT OF AN IT SEMINAR.

STATHAM: Can I just say you're looking absolutely fantastic.

JOANNA: Thank you.

STATHAM: My God, look at you! You look like a cross between Debbie Harry and Linda Evans from *Dynasty*.

JOANNA: Oh you flatterer.

STATHAM: I used to think dyed hair was a bit trashy. On you it's...

JOANNA: Yeah, yeah, it's not dyed actually; it just gets a little lighter in the summer.

STATHAM: Yes, yes, absolutely. We had a dog that did exactly that.

JOANNA: Well there we are.

LYNDON WALKS PAST.

JOANNA: Ah, morning Lyndon.

LYNDON: Hi.

STATHAM: "Morning Lyndon."

JOANNA: Wassup?

LYNDON: Hmm?

JOANNA: What's up, what's going down, what's the buzz?

LYNDON: Oh I don't know. Oh — there's a house-warming, one of the doctors.

JOANNA: Oh, which doctor?

STATHAM: Oogaga, oogaga! It's *witch* doctor... Oogaga... (THERE IS AN AWKWARD SILENCE) Carry on.

LYNDON: It's Caroline Todd.

JOANNA: Ah, the ragamuffin one. Yeah. Are you going?

LYNDON: I can't I'm afraid.

JOANNA: Aww. What about you Mr Voodoo man, are you invited?

STATHAM: Oh I don't think so; she's not going to invite someone of my seniority. I think she'll be sticking to the lower forms of pond life.

LYNDON: And what form of pond life am I?

STATHAM: I'd say you were a water boatman.

LYNDON: Cool.

STATHAM: Er no, not "cool", actually, because a fish would probably eat you.

▸▸ THEATRE

MAC AND CAROLINE ARE STILL TALKING TO THE SIXTH FORM STUDENTS.

MAC: Any final thoughts Doctor Todd?

CAROLINE: Don't get ill, we make you all sleepy and do terrible things.

MAC: Wise words indeed.

SIXTH FORM GIRL: She could be your 'one'.

MAC: Well okay, that's all we've got time for. Very good. Enjoy yourselves, have good lives. It's been real.

SUE: Right young people, chippy choppy. Your coach awaits, choppy choppy.

SIXTH FORM GIRL: I love him.

SUE: (DEEPLY THREATENING) Hands off!

THE STUDENTS GO.

CAROLINE: Well, that's them fucked-up for life.

MAC: Yeah, well done.

CAROLINE: Thanks.

▸▸ MESS

MARTIN IS REVISING FOR HIS EXAMS. GUY IS 'HELPING'.

GUY: What would you do?

MARTIN: They don't ask questions like that.

GUY: They can, it's called ethics, it doesn't have to be about medicine, they can throw anything at you.

MARTIN: Right, so what was it, there was a five-year-old girl in a house?

GUY: Yeah, the house is on fire, you can run in and save the girl, but if you do, the dangerous psychopath will shoot the mother in the head, what are you going to do?

MARTIN STUTTERS.

GUY: What are you going to do?!

MARTIN: Right, okay, um — right, I'm going in, I'll try and save both of them.

GUY: You can't save both, that's the point!

MARTIN: Oh right, okay. Well I'd save the girl.

GUY: Why?

MARTIN: Because she's younger, she's got more years of human life ahead of her. I am saving more years of human life.

GUY: Okay, the girl's got an incurable disease; she's got five years to live tops.

MARTIN: Nightmare, um...

GUY: Come on Martin, that fire's really catching hold!

MARTIN: Yes, no, okay, right I'm in, I'm — I'm still going for the kid, that's what the mother would want.

GUY: No, the mother is very selfish.

MARTIN: Oh well then she deserves to die.

GUY: Oh — oh, they won't like that!

MARTIN: No no, she doesn't deserve to die.

GUY: Come on Martin! You're losing points!

MARTIN: Yes, right, I'm going in, and I'm still getting the kid, I'm getting the kid.

GUY: What about the mother?

MARTIN: Well I just hope the psychopath changes his mind.

GUY: Why would he change his mind?

MARTIN: Because I would talk to him.

GUY: What would you say?

MARTIN: I would say, um — hey, calm down, don't do anything stupid Steven, give me the gun.

GUY: Steven?

MARTIN: Yeah, well I'd find out his name first.

GUY: What's his star sign?

MARTIN: Um...

GUY: I'm joking!

MARTIN: Right, yeah, no, calm down Steven, I'm a doctor, I'm going to...

GUY: Aaarrrgh!!

MARTIN: What's that?!

GUY: That's the girl dying horribly in the fire, you took too long, she burnt to a crisp.

MARTIN: Oh my God! She was quite poorly though, wasn't she?

GUY: Bang!

MARTIN: What's that?

GUY: Mummy's dead.

MARTIN: Oh...

GUY: Bang!

MARTIN: Steven?

GUY: No, his name was Jason, you lose. Work!

MARTIN: They don't ask questions like that.

▶▶ **DAY WARD**

CAROLINE: What if nobody comes?

ANGELA: Why wouldn't they?

CAROLINE: Well, I haven't been here that long, and I'm not exactly Miss Popular.

ANGELA: Oh, don't be silly. Anyway, I am.

STAFF LIAISON OFFICE

SUE WHITE IS WAITING FOR MAC TO WALK INTO HER OFFICE. SHE IS POISED ON A CHAIR, PUTTING A FILE BACK ON THE SHELF, WITH HER ARSE STICKING OUT.

OUTPATIENTS CORRIDOR

MAC AND GUY ARE WALKING TOGETHER.

GUY: I am just saying that my genes come from intellectuals and yours come from potato-digging shillelagh strummers.

MAC: Right, a shillelagh is a stick. Why would you want to strum a stick?

GUY: Yeah, well exactly, I mean that's my point, how stupid can you get? (HE SEES MARTIN) Martin, what do you think of when I say the word Switzerland to you?

MARTIN: I don't know, you've never said Switzerland to me before.

GUY: Yeah, well I'm saying it to you now and don't say that Phil Collins lives there.

MARTIN: Does he?

GUY: Shut your eyes, think of Switzerland, what do you see?

MARTIN: Nothing.

GUY: Nothing? You must see something!

MARTIN: No, I don't have a visual memory, sorry.

MAC: I see something, I see something...

GUY: What?

MAC: I see a chocolate Phil Collins coming out of a clock every hour to tidy up his Nazi gold.

GUY: Yeah, well that is a big lie. Oh look, here comes Jimmy Savile.

JOANNA AND STATHAM COME PAST.

MARTIN: I like Phil Collins...

GUY: (JIMMY SAVILE) "Now then, now then."

JOANNA: Yeah, what the hell are you lot laughing at? (TO MAC) Yeah, you of all people! Well at least I don't look like a girl.

MAC: Yeah, touché, touché, very good.

GUY: Absolutely.

JOANNA: Yeah, well, what I mean is, I don't look like a man-girl, I mean of course I look like a girl. In fact only this morning someone said I looked like a Hollywood star.

STATHAM: It was Linda Evans actually.

GUY: Oh well she should know.

MAC: Really? What, Linda Evans said that?

STATHAM: No, she should, she should...

JOANNA: Yeah, Linda Evans from *Dynasty*, no less, so stick that in your orange pipe and choke on it, Doctor...

MAC: Doh! Hey, hey.

JOANNA: Lena Zavaroni.

JOANNA AND STATHAM WALK AWAY.

STATHAM: You were absolutely brilliant!

JOANNA: I know. Will you just fuck off!

GUY DOES IRISH FOLK DANCING IN FRONT OF MAC AS HE WALKS OFF.

DAY WARD

CAROLINE: What are you wearing?

ANGELA: It's called a white coat. It's identical to the one you are wearing; only a tiny bit whiter.

CAROLINE: Tonight, tonight, what are you wearing tonight?

ANGELA: Oh God, I hadn't really thought. I've probably got something new in the cupboard.

CAROLINE: New? New? How can you just have something new in the cupboard?

ANGELA: Oh — forward planning. I often pick up the odd outfit on my day off. I hate panic buying. What about you?

CAROLINE: Yeah, I've got plenty of odd outfits.

▶▶ **STAFF LIAISON OFFICE**

SUE IS STILL POISED, WAITING FOR MAC TO ENTER HER OFFICE. MAC KNOCKS ON THE DOOR AND ENTERS.

MAC: Hi. How are you?

SUE: Hi.

MAC: You did say twelve didn't you?

SUE: Hmm, you're right Mac, I did say twelve and you're bang on time. Now could you hold this chair steady? It keeps swivelling around here?

MAC: Yeah, sure.

SUE: I just need to put something up here.

MAC: Okay, I've got you, I've got you.

MAC HOLDS THE CHAIR. HIS FACE IS VERY NEAR SUE'S BOTTOM. SHE PROLONGS THE UNNECESSARY ACTION OF PUTTING THE FILE ON THE SHELF.

SUE: All right, okay, okay, okay. And it's in.

MAC: Lovely. I er...

SUE: Lovely, right, well thanks, thanks for that. Thanks Mac. Now, how can I help you?

SUE LEANS ALL OVER MAC.

MAC: I was wondering if you could sign this application form for me?

SUE: Yeah, of course I can, let's have a look at those details shall we?

MAC: Great.

SUE: Oh.

MAC: It's just, yes, at the bottom there.

SUE: Still — still single I see?

MAC: Yeah.

SUE: I find that — I find that hard to believe.

MAC: Yeah.

▶▶ **DAY WARD**

CAROLINE IS COVERING HER NOSE WITH HER HANDS. SHE TRIES TO GET ANGELA TO LOOK AT HER.

ANGELA: What?

CAROLINE: Angela.

ANGELA: Hmm?

CAROLINE: Angela.

ANGELA: Hmm?

CAROLINE: Angela.

ANGELA: Hmm?

CAROLINE: I might have got a pen top stuck in my nose.

ANGELA: Let's have a look. Ouch! Ah, how on earth did you do that?

CAROLINE: No, I wasn't picking! No, my hand was on my head and I slipped and the top of my pen just went up my...

ANGELA: Okay, let's have a look, let's have a look. Oh. Try blowing it out.

CAROLINE BLOWS OUT THROUGH HER MOUTH.

ANGELA: No, like blowing it out through your nose.

CAROLINE BLOWS OUT THROUGH HER NOSE TOWARDS ANGELA.

ANGELA: No, no, you see, no. Okay, come along.

ANGELA LEADS CAROLINE AWAY.

▸▸ STAFF LIAISON OFFICE

SUE IS LOUNGING ON THE DESK.

MAC: So, perhaps if you could just sign here, just at the bottom.

SUE: Okay, all righty, here we go.

SHE SIGNS THE FORM, BUT WON'T GIVE IT BACK.

MAC: That's great.

SUE: Right.

MAC: Thank you very much.

SUE: No, thank you. Thank you.

MAC: Very good. Er...?

SUE: There you go, there you go.

SHE GIVES HIM THE FORM.

MAC: Yeah.

SUE: All right.

MAC: Thank you.

SUE: Thank you Doctor MacCartney.

MAC: Thank you.

SUE: Thanks very much. You know something?

MAC: Yeah?

SUE: You are going to make a wonderful consultant.

MAC: That's very kind of you. See you later, bye bye.

SUE: Bye bye. Bye bye now.

SHE LEANS ACROSS HER DESK AND SNIFFS THE CHAIR WHERE MAC WAS SITTING.

▸▸ OFFICE

ANGELA LEADS CAROLINE INTO THE OFFICE.

ANGELA: Hello girls.

KIM: All right?

RACHEL: Oh, what's up with her?

CAROLINE: I thought we were going to A & E.

ANGELA: Well we are, sort of. Is Harriet around?

KIM: I think she's feeding the guinea pigs.

HARRIET: Are my ears burning?

HARRIET COMES UP FROM UNDER HER DESK, WITH HAY STUCK TO HER CLOTHES.

ANGELA: Oh hello Hatty. We've got a pen top, left nostril, slightly protruding.

HARRIET: (HOLDING CAROLINE'S FACE) Hello snooks.

CAROLINE: Hello, I'm Doctor Todd. I'm very pleased to meet you all.

HARRIET SPINS HER ROUND AND MAKES HER LEAN BACK.

HARRIET: Look at the fairies!

CAROLINE LOOKS AT HARRIET'S FINGERS, HARRIET VERY SKILFULLY EXTRACTS THE PEN TOP.

HARRIET: There, done.

CAROLINE: What? That was incredible.

HARRIET: Beads up noses, scraped knees or splinters, come to me.

CAROLINE: Thank you. Thanks very much. Um, look, I'm having a party tonight and you're all invited.

ANGELA: Back to work, back to work. Right.

THE GIRLS ALL GIVE EACH OTHER THE THUMBS UP SIGN AS CAROLINE AND ANGELA LEAVE.

▶▶ **RADIOLOGY**

STATHAM IS GIVING A LECTURE TO SOME STUDENTS.

STATHAM: So the second stage of the scan is the powerful pulse of radio waves which knock the protons out of alignment.

A MOBILE PHONE TEXT MESSAGE SOUND IS HEARD.

STATHAM: Oh! Is that a mobile phone?

NOBODY ANSWERS.

STATHAM: Come on!

BOYCE: Was — was what a mobile phone?

STATHAM: That noise.

BOYCE: I didn't hear a noise.

STATHAM: Well I did.

BOYCE: Can you describe it?

STATHAM: Yes, it was a kind of chirrup.

BOYCE: Chirrup?

STATHAM: Yes. Like, um, "chi- chi- chirrup."

BOYCE: Could it have been a chaffinch? Stuck in a ventilation shaft?

STATHAM: No, it wasn't a chaffinch Mr Boyce; a chaffinch goes "t-t-t-twee twe tu tu."

BOYCE: Chiff chaff?

STATHAM: A chiff chaff. I wonder what noise the onomatopoeic-ally named chiff chaff might make.

BOYCE: A sort of chirrup noise?

STATHAM: "Chiff chaff." "Chiff chaff."

STATHAM REPEATS HIS CHIFF CHAFF IMPRESSION.

BOYCE: Now you're beginning to sound a bit like a tit.

STATHAM: Come here. Come on, come here. Arms up.

BOYCE: I'm unarmed, I swear to God.

STATHAM: Assume the position. Right.

STATHAM BODY SEARCHES BOYCE. BOYCE GROANS AS IF AROUSED.

STATHAM: No, stop that!

BOYCE: I can't help it; you've got really masterful hands.

STATHAM: No I haven't. Ah ha, here we are.

HE FINDS A MOBILE PHONE.

STATHAM: Now, I can only assume this is of the utmost importance and can therefore be shared with the entire class.

BOYCE: Oh, I'm not sure that um...

STATHAM READS OUT THE TEXT MESSAGE ON BOYCE'S PHONE.

STATHAM: "Hello bc..."

BOYCE: Hello Boyce.

STATHAM: Oh "hello Boyce", yes, "hello Boyce, I wnt..."

BOYCE: Want.

STATHAM: Oh it's "want u" with a u, very clever, yes, "I want u to cm...?"

BOYCE: Come.

STATHAM: "I want u to come on my t, ts, t..."

STATHAM REACTS WITH DISGUST WHEN HE REALISES THE LAST WORD IS SUPPOSED TO BE "TITS".

BOYCE: It's quite forward isn't it? She's a primary school teacher as well.

STATHAM: Come here, come here.

STATHAM TAKES BOYCE ASIDE.

STATHAM: Are you telling me a primary school teacher sent you this poorly spelt barrage of filth?!

BOYCE: Yeah. I haven't phoned her for a while.

STATHAM: What are they like in your depraved world?!

BOYCE: You know what women are like, eh, Rambo? The way they get keener when you get meaner — and less available, more mysterious. They love all that, you know. They'll do anything to a man they think is mysterious.

STATHAM THINKS ABOUT THIS. HE SEEMS TO DRIFT OFF FOR A MOMENT.

BOYCE: Enigmatic.

STATHAM: Stop, finish! Enough! (TURNING BACK TO THE OTHER STUDENTS) Because of Mr Boyce's diversion, we've run out of time for today, so um — er, shoo! Yes, shoo, shoo shoo. Go on. And you, shoo.

▶▶ **STAFF LIAISON OFFICE**

MARTIN IS WITH SUE WHITE.

SUE: Something's troubling you Martin.

MARTIN: No, nothing, honestly.

SUE: Don't lie to me Martin, do not lie to me.

MARTIN: I am not lying!

SUE: Is it the party?

MARTIN: Oh, you know about the party?

SUE: Is the little party bothering you Martin?

MARTIN: Yes, yes it is.

SUE: Ha ha, I knew it. You see, it wasn't that difficult, was it?

MARTIN: Are you going to go?

SUE: Well I haven't, yeah, yeah — haven't been invited.

" What are they like in you

depraved world?!"

MARTIN: Hmm.

SUE: I thought maybe perhaps you could possibly perhaps maybe er... have a word with them perhaps.

MARTIN: I could do, yeah, that's a good idea.

SUE: Is that um... what's his name? Doctor... Doctor... Doctor MacCartney — is he going?

MARTIN: I think so, yes.

SUE: Yep. I see, I see, I see.

MARTIN: You see, the thing is, I think I need to get some clothes.

SUE: You've got no clothes? No, well don't worry Martin, just go in your white coat, you look splendid.

MARTIN: No no no, I have got clothes, but I mean, you know, I just haven't got anything cool. You know, I don't know what kind of clothes women like.

SUE: You're going to go in women's clothes?

▸▸ STATHAM'S OFFICE/JOANNA'S OFFICE

STATHAM IS WEARING MAGNIFYING GLASSES LOOKING AT AN X-RAY.

STATHAM: Hmm, mysterious. Hmm.

AN INTERCUT PHONE CONVERSATION BETWEEN STATHAM AND JOANNA IN THEIR OFFICES. JOANNA ANSWERS HER PHONE.

JOANNA: Yeah?

STATHAM: Hello, it's me.

JOANNA: Yeah, what do you want?

STATHAM: I'm not in your office.

JOANNA: Yeah, so what about it?

STATHAM: Normally I would have come to see you, but today, well...

JOANNA GETS OUT AN ELECTRIC SHAVER AND SHAVES HER FACE.

STATHAM: (LAUGHS MYSTERIOUSLY) I have better things to do.

JOANNA: So?

JOANNA SHAVES BELOW THE LEVEL OF THE DESK.

STATHAM: So...

JOANNA: So piss off and do them!

SHE PUTS THE PHONE DOWN.

STATHAM: Hmm... I rather think the lady hath a fishhook in her lip.

JOANNA CHECKS THE EFFECTS OF THE SHAVING IN A HAND MIRROR. STATHAM TRIMS A TINY PIECE OFF HIS BONSAI TREE.

STATHAM: That's it.

▸▸ STAFF LIAISON OFFICE

MARTIN IS STILL WITH SUE.

SUE: Get your kit off. Kit off! Right, now if it's clothes you're after, how about these for starters?

MARTIN GETS HIS SHIRT OFF AND TRIES ON ONE OUT OF SUE'S BOX.

SUE: Okay, how's that?

MARTIN: Well, it's a bit crispy here.

SUE: Crispy?

MARTIN: Yeah, and here.

SUE: Crispy?

MARTIN: Hmm.

SUE: Creeping Jesus! These are supposed to have been washed!

MARTIN: Washed? Washed, what — it's not new?

SUE: No, it's not new! Why would I have a box of new clothes in my office? No, no Martin, it's not new. This is the dead box.

MARTIN: What — these are the clothes of dead people?

SUE: Name hasn't fooled you then.

MARTIN: That is disgusting!

HE THROWS THE SHIRT BACK IN THE BOX.

SUE: Oh don't be so soft, there's nothing wrong with it.

SUE POINTS TO WHAT SHE'S WEARING.

SUE: Look, fatal RTA, fatal RTA, stroke victim. I waited three days for these, saves me a fortune. But if it's not good enough for you Martin, I'll just have to take you shopping.

MARTIN: Oh brilliant!

SUE: Yes, well not now, you fucking twat! Out! Go and dance with your midget elf friends!

MARTIN GOES.

▸▸ LYNDON'S OFFICE

JOANNA COMES IN 'SEDUCTIVELY'.

JOANNA: Hello.

To Whom It May Concern

Stop making llama noises
outside my office.

Dr. A. R. Statham

(Consultant Radiologist)
BMedSci. MMed. DDR. FFR. SHO.

LYNDON: Hey.

▸▸ **THEATRE**

GUY AND MAC ARE PERFORMING AN OPERATION.

GUY: So if you had to kill someone out of work, do you reckon you could?

MAC: What? Kill an unemployed person?

GUY: No no, outside of work, not at the hospital?

MAC: Hmm, I don't know.

GUY: I reckon I could if they came at me.

MAC: Yeah? What, hand-to-hand?

GUY: Yeah, well you know, if they had a sword or something. I reckon reflexes would take over.

MAC: Hmm, but you see, if somebody came at me with a sword, my reflex would be to run away.

GUY: Yeah, but sometimes you're just not in a running away mood, you know, or maybe I've got a sword as well.

MAC: How come you both have swords?

GUY: Maybe we're in a sword shop.

MAC: Oh right, what, that local sword shop down the road in the high street?

GUY: Yeah, you know, so we're in a sword shop and he comes at me. I reckon I'd be ready. I reckon I could take him...

GUY THRUSTS AND KNOCKS A PIPE OUT OF A RESPIRATION MACHINE.

GUY: Oh shit! I've got the blower thing. Where do I — ? Just poke it in somewhere...

▸▸ **LYNDON'S OFFICE**

JOANNA IS ALL OVER LYNDON.

JOANNA: What if you had an important ally, you know, someone high up in the hospital management, someone sophisticated and slightly older maybe, who could help you, if you get my meaning?

LYNDON: Well, that would be unfair, and like I say, my wages really are fine, thanks.

JOANNA: Oh Lyndon, Lyndon, Lyndon... you're forgetting, I am head of Human Resources, I know exactly how much you earn. (SHE LAUGHS)

LYNDON: And you forget I'm head of the database, I know exactly how slightly older you are.

JOANNA FALLS UNDER THE DESK AT LYNDON'S FEET.

JOANNA (OOV): Hmm, what gorgeous shoes...

HER HEELS APPEAR ABOVE THE DESK TOP AS SHE PICKS HERSELF UP OFF THE FLOOR.

LYNDON: Excuse me. Watch your head.

JOANNA: Sorry. That's a very interesting article.

LYNDON: Yeah.

JOANNA GOES.

▸▸ **THEATRE**

GUY: I could happily kill everyone with a baseball cap.

MAC: Yeah, what — with one baseball cap?

GUY: No, if you get everyone, loads of people together who are all wearing baseball caps, I'd happily kill them.

MAC: With a sword?

GUY: Yeah.

MAC: Of course you could.

GUY: What if you had to kill your own dad?

MAC: Okay, she's out of here, thank you very much. You know what, we're very very lucky I think to have people like you working in the caring profession.

GUY: That's right.

THE LIFE SUPPORT MACHINE MAKES A TONE.

GUY: Oh shit! That's...

GUY TAPS THE MONITOR AND IT SOUNDS NORMAL AGAIN.

GUY: Oh yeah but, yeah — you don't fool me sleepy.

GUY DOES A PRETEND HEAD-BUTT ON THE UNCONSCIOUS PATIENT.

▶▶ **CLOTHES SHOP**

SUE AND MARTIN ARE SHOPPING.

SUE: Do you like this? Like this? Look. Hmm? Have you got a hoody? Well?

MARTIN LOOKS A BIT UNCERTAIN.

MARTIN: I'm circumcised actually.

SUE: A hoody.

SHE POINTS TO A TOP WITH A HOOD.

MARTIN: Oh, a hoody. Hood, yes. Well, this makes you look like you're in a gang, so. I know what you're thinking. I'm not Jewish.

▶▶ **LYNDON'S OFFICE**

STATHAM ENTERS.

LYNDON: Take a seat.

STATHAM STANDS AND SAYS NOTHING.

LYNDON: Look, has this got something to do with Joanna Clore? Do you want to talk about it?

STATHAM JUST MAKES GESTURES AT LYNDON.

LYNDON: Look, if there's a problem, I'm sure we can... No, really, I think we can...

STATHAM PUTS HIS FINGER TO HIS MOUTH AND STRIPS DOWN TO HIS UNDERPANTS.

LYNDON: I'm not sure that I'm with you here.

STATHAM INDICATES FOUR GESTURES TO LYNDON. FIRST HE SHOWS HIS MUSCLES, THEN HE DOES KARATE ACTIONS. HE THEN FLICKS VS AND LASTLY, HE SLIPS THE BACK OF HIS PANTS DOWN AND SLIDES HIS BUM ROUND LYNDON'S DESK. LYNDON CAN'T BELIEVE WHAT HE'S SEEING. STATHAM LEAVES.

LYNDON: Fucking hell!!

▶▶ **HOSPITAL ENTRANCE**

CAROLINE RUNS OUT OF THE BUILDING AND HEADS FOR THE SHOPS.

▶▶ **MAIN ENTRANCE/CORRIDOR**

MARTIN IS PRACTISING HIS DANCING FOR THE PARTY.

GUY: Are you all right Fartin?

MAC: Don't listen to him. (TO GUY) I think he's quite excited about the party.

MARTIN: Yeah, just — just practising my dancing. I think my moves are getting a little bit funky.

MAC: Funkeh.

MARTIN: Funky.

MAC: No, funkeh.

MARTIN: Funky.

MAC: No, funkeh.

MARTIN: Funky.

MAC: Funkeh.

MARTIN: Funky.

MAC: Say it with me, say it with me: funkeh.

MARTIN: Funky.

GUY: Oh for Christ's sake!

GUY WALKS OFF.

MAC: Funkeh.

MARTIN: Funky.

MAC: No, funkeh.

MARTIN: Funky.

MAC: No. Ready? Funkeh.

MARTIN: Funky.

MAC: Funkeh.

MARTIN: Funky.

MAC: Funkeh. Funkeh.

MARTIN: Funky.

MAC: Funkeh.

GUY RETURNS.

GUY: Funkehy!!

MAC: Yeah, right.

MARTIN: Funky!

MAC: Funkeh!

⏩ **STATHAM'S OFFICE**

JOANNA GOES TO SEE STATHAM.

JOANNA: Alan, what the fuck have you been up to?!

STATHAM: Oh you know, things, my own secret things.

JOANNA: Yeah, why?

STATHAM: Ah. Ha ha.

JOANNA KICKS A CHAIR.

JOANNA: Are you ever going to stop being such an utter wanker!?

STATHAM: Joanna, I — I don't care what you're thinking or feeling, but please don't damage hospital property.

JOANNA: Yeah, why?

STATHAM: Well, all I'm saying is that this is a hospital, not some kind of a stunt show.

JOANNA PINCHES ALAN'S NIPPLES.

JOANNA: What do you think you're doing?!

STATHAM: Ow! Ow! Don't. Ow, ow, ow, ow, ow!

JOANNA: Alan!

STATHAM: All right, all right, I've been being mysterious, all right?

JOANNA: Why?

STATHAM: You don't want to know why.

JOANNA: Yes I do.

BOYCE HAS WALKED IN UNNOTICED. JOANNA PULLS STATHAM'S HAIR AND TIE.

STATHAM: Ow! All right, all right, so you'll give me Mr Wanky with your finger in my back door, all right!

THEY SEE BOYCE.

BOYCE: Er — well, we've finished the modules, so I'll just put them there, shall I?

STATHAM: Yes. Nearly finished rehearsing the play.

JOANNA: Just learning through our lines.

BOYCE GOES. STATHAM AND JOANNA LOOK AT EACH OTHER. JOANNA SLAPS STATHAM ACROSS THE FACE AND LEAVES.

⏩ **MAIN ENTRANCE/CORRIDOR**

CAROLINE RUNS INTO THE HOSPITAL. SHE HAS BOUGHT SOME NEW SHOES. SHE STUFFS THE OLD ONES INTO A BIN AND PUTS ON THE NEW ONES. SHE CAN'T WALK IN THEM VERY WELL AND ENDS UP CRAWLING DOWN THE HOSPITAL CORRIDOR. MAC AND GUY SEE HER.

MAC: Aah, I thought I hadn't seen much of you this afternoon. Do you need a doctor?

GUY: Or will Mac do?

CAROLINE: No no, I'm just wearing my shoes in for tonight. You are both coming aren't you?

MAC: Oh yeah, yeah, yeah. Will there be many vertical people there?

CAROLINE: Yeah, I hope so.

MAC: Then so shall we. Cool.

MAC AND GUY WALK OFF, LEAVING CAROLINE STILL CRAWLING ALONG THE FLOOR.

▸▸ CAROLINE'S HOUSE, EVENING

THERE AREN'T MANY GUESTS AT CAROLINE'S PARTY.

CAROLINE: Two lab technicians and a porter? I told you no one would come. Everyone's probably having a great time in the pub right now.

ANGELA: No no no, they wouldn't do that.

LIAM COMES OVER TO THEM WITH A BOTTLE OF BEER.

ANGELA: Oh, beer number two. We could get some dancing going.

LIAM: Yeah, in a while, it's a bit early for that.

ANGELA: Have a little nibble.

LIAM: Not right now.

ANGELA: Just to line your stomach.

LIAM: No, not right now.

CAROLINE GRABS A HANDFUL OF SNACKS AND STUFFS THEM IN HER MOUTH.

▸▸ BAR

RACHEL AND KIM ARE SITTING EITHER SIDE OF BOYCE AT THE BAR.

KIM: I can match you drink for drink, sad boy.

BOYCE: Oh she's got spunk, but can she back it up? Another?

KIM: Let's do two, straight down.

RACHEL: Oh God!

BOYCE: Oh ho ho, fighting talk from the brunette. Barman, six of your finest morphine mind warpers please. This will blow your tits off.

RACHEL: I'm going to be sick!

THEY DOWN A SHOT. RACHEL RUSHES OFF.

BOYCE: So, it's just you and me. I tell you what, if you're still standing after this, I'll let you put my hand in your pants.

THEY DOWN ANOTHER DRINK. KIM STANDS UP.

KIM: Still standing.

▸▸ OFFICE, NIGHT

JOANNA IS IN HER OFFICE. STATHAM CREEPS TO THE DESK OUTSIDE HER OFFICE AND PHONES HER.

JOANNA: Yeah?

STATHAM: I can see you.

JOANNA: What?

STATHAM: I ask the questions!

JOANNA: Go on then.

STATHAM: I can see everything you're doing.

JOANNA: I have to do my own abduction?! Do I have to do everything?

STATHAM: Well no, it'll be all right, because it'll be very unpleasant for you.

JOANNA: Yeah.

▶▶ CAROLINE'S HOUSE — HALLWAY, KITCHEN

THE PARTY IS GETTING BUSIER. GUY AND MAC ARRIVE. GUY HAS A CASE OF WINE.

THEY SEE MARTIN AND BOYCE. MARTIN IS WEARING BRIGHT PINK TROUSERS AND A T-SHIRT WITH LARGE GREEN STUDS ON THE SLEEVES.

GUY: Hello, Boycee's pulled. (HE LOOKS AT MARTIN'S OUTFIT) Er, cool.

MARTIN: Yeah?

GUY: No, shit! (GOING INTO THE KITCHEN) Brace yourself girls, the class has arrived.

GUY KISSES KIM ON BOTH CHEEKS. HE IS ABOUT TO KISS KAREN BUT RECOILS.

GUY: Ooo!

HE TRIES TO KISS KIM AGAIN BUT SHE RECOILS.

GUY: Oh, all right.

HE KISSES RACHEL ON BOTH CHEEKS.

JOANNA: Who are you supposed to be exactly?

STATHAM: My name is irrelevant, and you asked there, you asked a question — I asked you not to ask it. Don't, otherwise there...

JOANNA COMES OUT OF HER OFFICE AND SEES STATHAM CROUCHING OUTSIDE.

STATHAM: Oh, hello.

JOANNA: Ah, you must be Mr Irrelevant. What are you going to do to me now then, mystery man?

STATHAM: I'm going to push you into a car and drive you to a secret location and do unspeakable things to you.

JOANNA: Ooh, unspeakable things.

STATHAM: Yes.

JOANNA LIFTS HER SKIRT UP TO HER WAIST.

JOANNA: Really?

STATHAM: And actually, could you drive? Because I've just got the bike and I'm not insured.

To Whom It May Concern

Please remove your llama from my office.

Dr. A. R. Statham

(Consultant Radiologist)
BMedSci. MMed. DDR. FFR. SHO.

GUY: Hmm. Rachel.

RACHEL: Well remembered.

GUY: Yeah, have you got a dog Rachel?

RACHEL: Yeah, a Westie actually, well it's my mum's, but I sometimes look after it.

GUY: Yeah, do you ever let it lick your face?

RACHEL: Yeah, sometimes.

GUY: Yeah, thought so, yeuch. (TO MAC) Oh look, there goes a BFB.

MAC: What's that?

GUY: (WATCHING A GIRL GO PAST) BFB, better from behind.

MAC: Oh, you're so sensitive!

GUY: (TO RACHEL AS SHE PASSES) Fashion tip, if you're getting skin wings, bra's too tight.

HE TWANGS HER BRA STRAP AND SHE GIVES HIM THE FINGER. THREE GOTH GIRLS WALK PAST.

MAC: Goths are superb.

GUY: Yeah, the point of them is...?

MAC: Goths, superb. What I love is the way they pretend they're being ugly on purpose. It's genius.

GUY SEES MARTIN.

GUY: Yeah. Oh hey, look — it's the love child of Wayne Sleep and Godzilla. What are you, the eighth dwarf? Twatty? You know, even if you were from the future, you'd still be wrong. Actually, do you know what I like about this outfit?

MAC: What's that?

GUY: Fuck all.

GUY SUCKS ON ONE OF MARTIN'S SHIRT SLEEVE STUDS.

▶▶ OFFICE

STATHAM IS STILL KIDNAPPING JOANNA.

JOANNA: Yeah...

STATHAM: And I thought because I would wear the balaclava and...

JOANNA: Yeah, yeah, that might help actually. Can you put it on?

STATHAM: Um, well I'd rather save it until later, because I've got...

JOANNA: Show me.

STATHAM: ...An intolerance to wool. Well I'll do it for a bit. I go blotchy. I don't know if... I can do it, I can do it.

STATHAM FUMBLES WITH THE BALACLAVA AND PUTS HIS GLASSES BACK ON OVER THE TOP.

JOANNA: Yeah, yeah, no that might help. I'll just get my coat.

JOANNA GOES INTO HER OFFICE.

STATHAM: (DEEP SCARY VOICE) It's going to be very bad for you in the woods.

SOMEONE COMES INTO THE OFFICE.

COLLEAGUE: Evening Doctor Statham.

STATHAM: Er, um — yes, good evening.

THE COLLEAGUE GOES.

JOANNA: Can you do any other voices?

STATHAM: Um... Mexican bandit...

JOANNA AND STATHAM MAKE THEIR WAY OUT OF THE OFFICE.

JOANNA: No, I don't think so.

STATHAM: An American. This is very — this is very itchy. Well, um...

JOANNA: Anyone else?

STATHAM: (STRANGELY ASIAN ACCENT) Marlon Brando...

▸▸ CAROLINE'S HOUSE, LIVING ROOM

KAREN JOINS MARTIN.

KAREN: Hi.

MARTIN: Have you seen Caroline?

KAREN: No. I'm Karen.

MARTIN: I'm Martin.

KAREN: I know.

MARTIN: How do you do?

THEY DON'T SAY ANYTHING FOR A WHILE.

▸▸ CAROLINE'S HOUSE, LIVING ROOM

CAROLINE IS TALKING TO LIAM. ANGELA IS DANCING IN THE BACKGROUND BEHIND THEM.

CAROLINE: So, you and Angela...

LIAM: Me and Angela.

CAROLINE: Angela and you. You seem to be seeing quite a lot of each other.

LIAM: Oh yes. Funny, I wasn't really looking for a relationship, but she is irresistible, isn't she?

CAROLINE: Well, I have managed to resist so far.

LIAM: Do you know, I don't think I've ever been out with anyone so absolutely perfect. (PAUSE) Although, she does dance a bit like a wolf.

ANGELA IS DANCING IN A VERY STRANGE WAY, WITH ODDLY CANINE PAWING MOVEMENTS.

CAROLINE: Yeah, odd that.

THEY WATCH ANGELA DANCE.

▸▸ CAROLINE'S HOUSE, LIVING ROOM

KAREN: You're a doctor aren't you?

MARTIN: Yeah.

KAREN: You look just like one. Is your wife a doctor?

MARTIN: Wife? No, not — I mean I don't — I don't have a wife.

KAREN: Is your girlfriend a doctor?

MARTIN: (MUMBLES) I don't have a girlfriend.

KAREN: What?

MARTIN: (SHOUTS) I don't have a girlfriend!

JUST AS MARTIN SHOUTS THIS, THE TRACK THAT HAS BEEN PLAYING ENDS AND THE ROOM GOES QUIET. EVERYONE HAS HEARD MARTIN.

RACHEL: Shame.

▸▸ OFFICE

IT IS DARK. HARRIET GOES TO HER DESK AND PUTS THE DESK LAMP ON. THE CLEANER IS THERE.

HARRIET: Morning Lesley.

LESLEY: Evening, you mean!

IT DAWNS ON HARRIET THAT IT'S STILL THE EVENING.

HARRIET: I fell asleep. Wrong sort of nine o'clock.

CAROLINE: You're funny.

MAC: Yeah? Trick of the light.

A PARTY GUEST IS OFFERING LINES OF COCAINE ON A CD CASE. THE WOMAN TAKES A LINE OF COKE. HE OFFERS THE CD CASE TO MARTIN, WHO TAKES IT AND TIPS IT OVER TO LOOK AT THE TRACK LIST, SPILLING ALL THE COKE ON THE FLOOR.

MARTIN: That is fucking brilliant.

▸▸ CAROLINE'S HOUSE, KITCHEN

SUE WHITE FINDS MAC. SHE IS ALL OVER HIM.

SUE: Wah!

MAC: "Wah!"

SUE: Have I... ever told you about the little pink rabbit?

MAC: Er no, no, I don't think you have.

SUE: The... you know, little pink rabbit that lives down a little magic rabbit hole?

MAC: I think I'd have remembered that. Yeah.

SUE: Some people think the little pink rabbit doesn't exist, because they haven't been able to find it.

MAC: Really?

SUE: Yeah. Do you think you'd be able to find it?

MAC: I could have a guess.

SUE: I don't mind you having a stab in the dark.

MAC: Does the rabbit live in an enchanted forest?

SUE: Yeah.

MAC: Yeah?

SUE: Yes, yes, yes it does.

MAC: Does the rabbit only pop his little head out every once in a while?

SUE: Yes!

MAC: Yeah. Does the rabbit like a nice big carrot?

SUE: Absolutely!

MAC: Can I say one thing at this point, yeah?

SUE: Yep.
MAC: Haven't got a clue what I'm talking about.

SUE: Yeah, you have.

MAC: I haven't.

SUE: You have.

MAC: Have not, have not.

SUE: You have!

MAC: No, have not.

MAC LEAVES.

SUE: Well, don't you worry Mr Bunny; we're not finished yet.

▸▸ CAROLINE'S HOUSE, KITCHEN

GUY, MARTIN AND SOME GUESTS ARE IN THE KITCHEN TASTING SOME WINE.

ROYSTON
Snack Foods Ltd.

Subje____ ____MacCartney

____3567/5298NNB

Area: Medical
Dept: Surgical

Dear Ms White,

Thank you for your letter of the 19th.

Please be assured that we strive to maintain and improve the quality of all our products, and as part of this ongoing process we listen to customer feedback most carefully. Nonetheless, we find it hard to accept your claim that a multipack of our Salt and Vinegar crisps contained the Ghost of a Headless Horseman.

Furthermore, tests have confirmed that your letter, far from being written in your own blood "that spurted from my neck, high, high up the wall as his sword snicker-snacked through the air, in the ill light of a pale moon," is actually scrawled in red ink from a standard 'Bic' biro.

Therefore we feel we cannot accept any responsibility for the "traumatic banshee damage" you claim was caused to yourself, your home, your car, your elderly grandparents, your pond, your lock up, or indeed your dog 'Simon' by an otherworldly spirit contained in our snack product.

Yours truly,

Graham Deeds, Royston Snack Foods Ltd

Complaints filed:	Complainant	Date:
Length of hair	Dr AR Statham	03.10.04
Earring	Dr AR Statham	14.10.04
Earring	Dr AR Statham	15.10.04
Length of hair	Dr AR Statham	17.10.04
Attitude	Dr AR Statham	17.10.04
Length of hair (too short)	S White	17.10.04
Jelly theft	Dr GV Secretan	24.10.04
Attitude	Dr AR Statham	28.10.04
Being a poof	Dr GV Secretan	02.11.04
Silly slippers (like Aladdin)	Dr AR Statham	07.11.04
Too gorgeous by half	S White	08.11.04
Suspiciously pale (vampire?)	Dr GV Secretan	17.11.04
Attitude/lack of pants	Dr AR Statham	22.11.04
Annoyingly enigmatic	Dr C Todd	23.11.04
Sarcasm	Dr AR Statham	28.11.04
Motorcycle attack	Dr AR Statham	01.12.04
Offensively ginger	Dr GV Secretan	03.12.04

Staff Liaison Officer's Comments:

Words fucking fail me. What a super duper young man – a credit to the hospital! But I can't help thinking he's wasted in Surgery – perhaps a spell in Staff Liaison might be beneficial?

S. White

MARTIN: Well... oh yeah, I bought that.

GUY LOOKS AT MARTIN'S BOTTLE OF WINE.

GUY: Yeah, oh wise choice Martin, yeah. Chateau de la Shite, yeah.

GUY MAKES A HUGE FUSS OF TASTING THE WINE AND SPITTING IT INTO HIS GLASS.

MARTIN: Nice?

GUY: Yeah, pure tramp juice.

MARTIN: Well yeah, I've got my own criteria actually, so...

GUY: Oh really? Let me guess, yeah, anything that's £4.99, because £2.99 is a bit low, a tenner's too much, so you stand there and you think, I really should buy a Chablis, but fuck it, it's only a party, I can't be bothered. So what you end up with is this. I mean, Vin de Pays for what you get. And what you get is shite. Now, am I right?

MARTIN: No.

GUY: Yeah, well I am actually mate, because I have exactly the same...

GUY FEELS MARTIN'S STUDS.

GUY: They're weeping. I have exactly the same criteria myself.

MARTIN: Yeah, well — no I admit it, I did. Yeah.

GUY: Yeah. I fucking knew it, you pleb!

▶▶ CAROLINE'S HOUSE, BATHROOM

BOYCE IS SITTING IN THE BATH WITH KIM.

BOYCE: All right, it's my turn. It is my turn. And if you get this one wrong, you have to, have to... (LIKE A GAME SHOW HOST) "Take a shower". Okay, are you ready? Are you ready?

KIM: All right.

BOYCE: Okay, Kim, on an x-ray of which organ would you find endocarditis of the tricuspid valve?

KIM: Is it Brazil?

BOYCE: I'm sorry, that's the incorrect answer.

KIM: Damn.

BOYCE: I'm afraid I'm going to have to make you wet.

THEY GET IN THE SHOWER.

▶▶ CAROLINE'S HOUSE, LIVING ROOM

GUY IS DIRTY-DANCING WITH A GIRL. MARTIN IS TRYING TO TALK TO CAROLINE, WHO IS TALKING TO SOMEONE ELSE.

CAROLINE: There are some neurologists over there, I think they can help you.

MARTIN: What's the difference between jumping on a trampoline and jumping on a baby?

CAROLINE: Um...

MARTIN: You have to take your shoes off to jump on a trampoline.

CAROLINE: Not if it's your trampoline.

MARTIN: True. Funny though isn't it?

CAROLINE WALKS AWAY AND SEES KAREN STARING AT MARTIN.

▶▶ JOANNA'S CAR

STATHAM IN HIS BALACLAVA IS IN THE CAR WITH JOANNA.

STATHAM: (SUPPOSEDLY MENACING) Drive!

JOANNA: I am.

STATHAM: Well... keep doing so.

JOANNA: Where?

STATHAM: Go right here. Now! Right.

JOANNA: Right. I'll go right.

STATHAM: Did you indicate?

JOANNA: Yes!

STATHAM: Into second gear.

JOANNA: You're sounding like a driving instructor now.

STATHAM: Shut up! I make the rules here.

JOANNA: You'll be tapping the dashboard with your clipboard in a minute.

STATHAM: You — you shut up! I'm in charge! I'm getting quite itchy.

JOANNA: Keep it on.

STATHAM: Just… I'm your worst nightmare.

JOANNA: Yeah, you're telling me. The degree of menace is killing me.

STATHAM: I'm steaming up. Can we have the heater off?

▸▸ CAROLINE'S HOUSE, LIVING ROOM

THE PARTY IS WARMING UP NOW, THERE ARE MORE PEOPLE. GUY'S DANCING IS GETTING MORE EXTRAVAGANT.

▸▸ CAROLINE'S HOUSE, HALLWAY

KAREN SITS NEXT TO MARTIN ON THE STAIRS. MARTIN IS PLAY-ING WITH A SLINKY.

KAREN: Are you okay?

MARTIN: Yeah, I'm all right. (MARTIN LOOKS WORRIED) Listen, you're a woman — well a female… if someone fancied you, well more than fancied you, they loved you and they wanted to tell you, but they weren't sure of the response, but they did it anyway, would you slap them?

KAREN: Maybe I'd be pleased.

MARTIN: I don't think she's going to be pleased.

KAREN: You don't know that.

MARTIN: I do know that. Because no woman's ever fancied me before, ever.

KAREN: What about me?

MARTIN: What, has no woman ever fancied you either?

KAREN: I really like you.

MARTIN: Yeah, well no offence, but I'm a bit sick and tired of girls saying they "like" me. It's not the same as "fancy" is it?

KAREN: Well, I'd sleep with you if you wanted.

MARTIN: Yeah, as a friend.

KAREN: You're very very attractive.

MARTIN: Yeah, I know, but she doesn't think so. She just thinks I'm nice.

KAREN GRABS MARTIN'S CROTCH. HE DOESN'T KNOW WHAT TO DO.

MARTIN: Do you want to play with my Slinky?

MARTIN GIVES THE SLINKY TO KAREN.

MARTIN: Drink.

MARTIN GETS UP AND GOES, LEAVING KAREN ON HER OWN. HIS WAY IS BLOCKED BY THREE GOTH GIRLS, HE GOES THROUGH THE LEGS OF ONE OF THEM.

▸▸ JOANNA'S CAR

STATHAM: Stop the car now!

JOANNA: All right Mr Forceful, time to have your mysterious way with me.

STATHAM: Are you telling me that Mr Frankfurter can look inside the bun?

STATHAM GOES TO KISS JOANNA.

JOANNA: Ah ah ah ah ah. Out there, in the park.

STATHAM: No, the gates are locked.

JOANNA: Yeah, well we can climb the fence.

STATHAM: But we're not allowed to do that, my sexy darling!

JOANNA: Allowed? Allowed?! What sort of a mystery kidnapper are you?

STATHAM: Well, one that's loath to contravene the local byelaws.

JOANNA: Oh, you're a bloody local councillor now.

STATHAM: Can we not have it, have — in here?

JOANNA GETS OUT OF THE CAR.

STATHAM: All right, yes, get out of the car you! Get out! Right, over there!

▶▶ CAROLINE'S HOUSE, LIVING ROOM

GUY AND MAC ARE WATCHING CAROLINE DANCE — SHE'S HAD A LOT TO DRINK.

MAC: So have you given up on her?

GUY: Far from it, it's all part of the grand scheme. Anyway, she's TDTF.

MAC: She's certainly TDTD.

GUY: Er... too drunk to dig? Doodle? Defecate...?

MAC: Dance.

GUY: Yeah? Watch and learn.

GUY GOES OVER AND JOINS IN WITH CAROLINE'S DANCING. HE LEADS HER INTO WHAT LOOKS LIKE A KISS, BUT THEN SIDE STEPS AND WALKS OFF. MARTIN COMES OVER TO CAROLINE, BUT SHE FOLLOWS GUY.

MARTIN: Caroline, Caroline...

CAROLINE: Not now Martin.

MAC WATCHES CAROLINE AND GUY.

▶▶ PUBLIC PARK

STATHAM AND JOANNA ARE TRYING TO CLIMB OVER A WALL INTO THE PARK.

STATHAM: Up you go.

JOANNA: Oh!

STATHAM: Up. Why don't I be Robert Kilroy Silk?

JOANNA: No. Fuck!

STATHAM: What about Charlton Heston?

JOANNA: No.

STATHAM: Or, or — no wait, he'd be too small. Um...

JOANNA MANAGES TO GET OVER THE WALL.

JOANNA: Get off!

STATHAM MANAGES TO CLIMB OVER AFTER HER, BUT HE FALLS OVER.

▶▶ CAROLINE'S HOUSE, HALLWAY

GUY IS AT THE FRONT DOOR.

CAROLINE: Shit, are you going?

GUY: Yeah, I thought I'd better.

CAROLINE: You don't want to stay here?

GUY: In the hall?

CAROLINE: You could sleep in my bed; you let me sleep in yours once.

GUY: And where would you sleep?

CAROLINE: Maybe I wouldn't be doing much sleeping.

CAROLINE LEANS SEDUCTIVELY AGAINST THE DOOR, BUT IT MOVES BACK AND SHE LOSES HER FOOTING.

GUY: Are you all right?

CAROLINE: Yeah. So, do you want to spend the night?

GUY: Yes. But only when it's right.

CAROLINE: When would it be right?

GUY: Soon.

CAROLINE: It's not right now?

GUY: No.

CAROLINE: Are you sure it will be all right?

GUY: I'm sure, yeah, we just need to spend some special time together and we just need to work up to it, until we feel we're about to explode.

HE KISSES CAROLINE.

CAROLINE: I think I might explode now.

GUY: You have to wait.

CAROLINE: We have to wait.

GUY: Yes.

GUY GOES. CAROLINE REJOINS THE PARTY. GUY REAPPEARS AND THEN GOES AGAIN.

▶▶ CAROLINE'S HOUSE, LANDING/BEDROOM

MARTIN TRIES TO GET PAST SUE WHITE ON THE STAIRS.

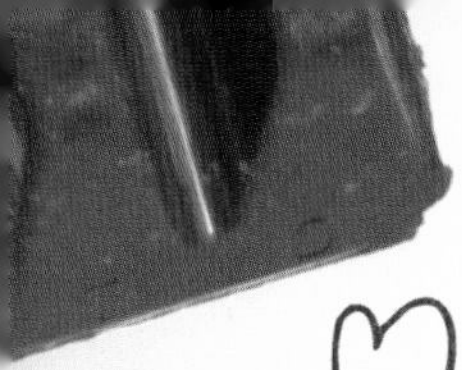

MOUNTAIN RANGE CAKE

INGREDIENTS:

2 TBL. SP. COCOA POWDER DISSOLVED IN WATER

8OZ SOFT MARGARINE (SWISS)

4 EGGS (FROM HIGH ALTITUDE HENS)

1 TSP. BAKING POWDER

8OZ GOLDEN CASTER SUGAR

ICING/DECORATION

4OZ SWISS COOKING CHOCOLATE

2OZ SOFT BUTTER

3 TBL. SP. MILK (COW/ATTRACTIVE WOMAN)

6OZ ICING SUGAR (SIFTED)

1 LRGE. TOBLERONE

1 SML. BAR OF WHITE SWISS CHOCOLATE

CAKE:

PREHEAT THE OVEN TO 180 C/GAS MARK — NO IDEA. PREPARE TIN (LARGE CAKE VARIETY) BY GREASING AND LINING. HURL ALL THE INGREDIENTS INTO A LARGE BOWL AND BEAT WELL FOR FOUR MINUTES. IF YOU'VE HURLED THE ICING AND DECORATIONS INTO THE BOWL, YOU'VE SCREWED UP. NO CAKE FOR THICKOS. HALF FILL THE TIN WITH MIXTURE AND SMOOTH IT OUT. BAKE FOR APPROX. FORTY MINS. IT SHOULD NOW BE BOTH FIRM AND RISEN LIKE A NEWLY BORN BOSOM. COOL IN TIN FOR FIVE MINS. TURN GENTLY ONTO WIRE RACK. OR, IF YOU DON'T HAVE A WIRE RACK, A BACTERIA-INFESTED WORK SURFACE.

CHOCOLATE ICING:

PLACE HEATPROOF BOWL INTO A PAN OF SIMMERING WATER. LOB IN THE COOKING CHOCOLATE (IF YOU CAN DO IT FROM THE OTHER SIDE OF THE ROOM, ALL THE BETTER). ADD THE BUTTER AND THE MILK AND STIR GENTLY (THE LADIES KNOW WHAT I'M TALKING ABOUT). COOL SLIGHTLY, THEN GRADUALLY ADD YOUR ICING SUGAR AND BEAT UNTIL THE MIXTURE IS SMOOTH. SPREAD OVER THE COOLED CAKE.

DECORATIONS:

CARVE THE TOBLERONE INTO INDIVIDUAL TRIANGLES. WAIT UNTIL THE ICING HAS COOLED SLIGHTLY THEN ADD YOUR TRIANGLES/ MOUNTAINS. CREATE ANY MOUNTAIN RANGE YOU LIKE. ALLOW TO SETTLE. MELT THE WHITE CHOCCY AND DRIZZLE FROM A GREAT HEIGHT ONTO YOUR MOUNTAINS. (GET IT RIGHT AND IT LOOKS LIKE SNOW; GET IT WRONG AND IT LOOKS LIKE A MONEY SHOT.)

MARTIN: I'm just going to get something from my coat.

SUE: Crack cocaine?

MARTIN: No thank you.

MARTIN GETS PAST SUE AND GOES INTO A BEDROOM. HE SITS ON THE BED, WHICH IS COVERED IN COATS.

MARTIN: (TRYING TO CONVINCE HIMSELF) All right. You are a strong manly man. You are a strong manly man.

BOYCE APPEARS FROM UNDER THE COATS.

BOYCE: Well thanks very much.

MARTIN: Boycee! What, are you going to crash here? Great, we could have a slumber party! Talk about girls, just kind of...

KIM APPEARS.

KIM: Piss off will you, Martin!

MARTIN: Kim, what are you doing here?

KIM: Having sex.

MARTIN: Good, well okay, I'll go somewhere else.

BOYCE: We'll have that slumber party thing another time though, yeah mate? See you later.

MARTIN GOES OUT OF THE BEDROOM.

SUE: Yeah man.

SHE FOLLOWS A MAN DOWNSTAIRS.

▸▸ CAROLINE'S HOUSE, BATHROOM

MARTIN IS PSYCHING HIMSELF UP, TALKING TO THE MIRROR.

MARTIN: Right, show no fear, no fear. Grrrr!

THERE IS A KNOCK AT THE DOOR.

MARTIN: Yeah? Yeah, fine, um... I love you. No, I love you.

MARTIN GOES OUT OF THE BATHROOM.

▸▸ CAROLINE'S HOUSE, HALLWAY

CAROLINE IS AT THE DOOR SAYING GOODBYE TO HER GUESTS.

CAROLINE: Bye. Bye. Oh. Who are you?

GUEST: Thanks for the party.

CAROLINE: Thanks for coming.

SUE WHITE COMES TO THE DOOR TO LEAVE.

CAROLINE: Oh — you were here? Well, thank you for coming.

SUE: Thank you Doctor Trodd, for inviting me to your party.

CAROLINE: I didn't know I did, but you're here and now you are going, so that's all that matters.

SUE GRABS CAROLINE AND KISSES HER ON THE MOUTH. SUE PULLS AT HER OWN BREASTS WHILE SHE'S TALKING TO CAROLINE. MARTIN WATCHES.

CAROLINE: I've been sick.

SUE: Well, so have I. And I am completely shaved.

CAROLINE: Oh my God.

SUE: Bye bye then, I'll see you at work.

CAROLINE: Bye.

SUE GOES. MARTIN COMES UP TO CAROLINE.

MARTIN: I'm partially shaved.

CAROLINE: Are you leaving?

MARTIN: Well no, not necessarily.

CAROLINE: Oh God, so I don't have to kiss you then.

MARTIN: Although I have got exams, so perhaps I should.

CAROLINE: Aww, have you?

MARTIN: Yeah.

CAROLINE: Oh. Oh well night night then Martin, and thank you, thank you for coming.

CAROLINE KISSES MARTIN ON THE MOUTH.

CAROLINE: Oh sorry, I'm so sorry, I'm a little bit stupid, I — it wasn't you I wanted, it was — it was the kitten.

CAROLINE STAGGERS OFF.

MARTIN: Thank you. Thank you!

MARTIN CALLS AFTER CAROLINE.

MARTIN: Maybe I could stay a bit longer and leave again later, it's actually not that late.

▶▶ **PUBLIC PARK**

STATHAM AND JOANNA ARE HAVING SEX ON THE GROUND.

STATHAM: Oh yes, at last, here we… Oh, the infidel is at the gates.

JOANNA: Well you're going to have to knock a bit harder.

STATHAM: Right, hmmmm!

JOANNA: Oh, yeah, yeah…

▶▶ **CAROLINE'S HOUSE, KITCHEN**

CAROLINE IS DRINKING SHOTS WITH MARTIN.

CAROLINE: Okay, what shall we drink to now Martin?

MARTIN: Um…

CAROLINE: I know, goats, with hooves.

MARTIN: Okay.

CAROLINE: Goats with hooves. May they always be sure-footed and never fall from the mountain and break their spindly legs.

CAROLINE DOWNS ANOTHER DRINK. MARTIN CAN'T DRINK HIS. CAROLINE FALLS BACKWARDS, BUT MAC APPEARS FROM NOWHERE AND CATCHES HER.

MAC: Ooh, could she be drunk?

MARTIN: Yeah. She's had twenty shots of Tequila.

CAROLINE: Twenty-two.

MARTIN: Four shots of undiluted orange squash. I bloody love her.

MAC: Yeah. I think we'd better get her up to the bathroom. Come on.

▶▶ **PUBLIC PARK**

STATHAM AND JOANNA ARE MID-COITUS.

STATHAM: Oh yes, oh yes…

JOANNA: No, you're going to have to pretend you're someone else.

STATHAM: Right, right.

JOANNA: Perhaps you've come to mend something.

STATHAM: Right, hello? I've come to mend an appliance for you.

JOANNA: Be more specific and use a deeper voice.

STATHAM: Right, hello, I've come to fix some problem in your fax modem. Oh let's have a feel where it...

JOANNA: Oh, that's more like it.

STATHAM: Ooh, there it is.

JOANNA: Yeah, go on sort me, sort me.

STATHAM: Yes. Oh yes, oh yes!

JOANNA: Oh, oh!

▸▸ CAROLINE'S HOUSE, BATHROOM

MAC IS HOLDING CAROLINE, WHO IS KNEELING OVER THE TOILET BOWL.

CAROLINE: Oh no, it's okay.

MAC: Yeah?

CAROLINE: It's okay, it's gone again. Oh, I'm so sorry. I'm so so sorry. I'm okay now.

MAC: Yeah?

CAROLINE: I've only eaten Hula Hoops today.

HE STROKES HER HAIR.

MAC: Very good.

CAROLINE: You're a very attractive man aren't you?

MAC: Yeah, yeah, okay.

THEY KISS.

CAROLINE: That was nice.

MAC: Mmm.

CAROLINE: But I feel I should remind you that you have just kissed a sicky mouth.

▸▸ CAROLINE'S HOUSE, GARDEN

KAREN IS PLAYING WITH MARTIN'S TANGLED SLINKY OUTSIDE. SHE'S CRYING.

KIM: He's not worth it, Karen.

KAREN: Yes, he is.

KIM: No he isn't.

KAREN: Yes he is, Kim.

KIM: No he isn't.

KAREN: Yes he is!

KIM: He's got pink trousers on, Karen!

KAREN: I like them.

KIM: Oh, get over it. He's not even a proper doctor.

KAREN HAS THE SLINKY STUCK IN HER HAIR. SHE'S DISTRAUGHT.

▶▶ CAROLINE'S HOUSE, BATHROOM

MARTIN COMES INTO THE BATHROOM WHERE MAC AND CAROLINE ARE ABOUT TO KISS.

MARTIN: Um, I've got the — the glass of water.

MAC AND CAROLINE SPLIT APART.

MAC: Excellent, excellent. Come on then, let's get you up. I'm going to leave you in the very capable hands of Doctor Martin Dear, okay?

CAROLINE: Okay.

MAC: Hope you feel better soon.

CAROLINE: Thank you, I feel much better already.

THEY SHAKE HANDS.

MAC: Thank you for coming to see me.

CAROLINE: Thank you Doctor.

MAC: See you.

CAROLINE: Right.

MAC: Doctor?

MARTIN: Yes, um...

MARTIN HELPS SUPPORT CAROLINE, BUT CAN'T QUITE MANAGE.

MARTIN: Oh sorry — oh... Listen, shall I just carry you to your room?

CAROLINE: No. I think I'd probably crush you if you did.

MARTIN PICKS CAROLINE UP AND BANGS HER HEAD AGAINST THE SHOWER.

MARTIN: Oh sorry, sorry.

HE BANGS HER AGAINST THE DOOR ON THE WAY OUT.

MARTIN: Oh sorry. Sorry. Sorry...

▶▶ PUBLIC PARK

STATHAM AND JOANNA ARE STILL HAVING SEX. STEAM IS NOW RISING THROUGH THE COLD NIGHT AIR MIXED WITH THE SMOKE FROM JOANNA'S CIGARETTE.

STATHAM: And, oh — and have you taken an extended warranty out madam?

JOANNA: A what?

STATHAM: An extended warranty, it's well worth the extra money, as it covers even accidental damage.

JOANNA: What? Oh God!

JOANNA CALLS OUT.

STATHAM: The five — the five — the five — the five year warranty! Arrgh!

THEY REACH ORGASM.

STATHAM: Golly, oh my golly. Oh my golly. Oh, a little bit left there, hmm, there it is...

EPISODE 6

▸▸ **LARGE GYMNASIUM**

MARTIN ENTERS. THERE IS A PANEL OF THREE JUDGES SITTING AT A TABLE.

MARTIN: Just me?

JUDGE: We can only do one at a time.

MARTIN: Er, can I have a chair?

JUDGE: Well, we can have one brought in, but most people don't need one.

MARTIN: Won't bother then, won't bother.

ONE OF THE PANEL GETS OUT A CD/TAPE PLAYER AND PUTS ON SOME MUSIC. MARTIN TAKES OFF HIS WHITE COAT AND DOES A DANCE ROUTINE WHICH GETS INCREASINGLY AMBITIOUS. MARTIN PUTS IN AN IMPRESSIVE FINISH AND THE MUSIC STOPS.

JUDGE: When did you realise you were in the wrong exam room?

MARTIN: Well quite early on... but then I thought I was in a dream I once had and that if I kept dancing, one of you would turn into Michaela Strachan and kiss me. Has this ever happened before?

JUDGE: Oh, actually it happens surprisingly often.

▸▸ **MARTIN'S ROOM**

MARTIN'S ALARM IS GOING OFF. HE WAKES UP IN A SWEAT WITH REVISION NOTES STUCK TO HIS FACE. HIS ROOM IS A COMPLETE MESS, WITH PAPERS ALL OVER THE FLOOR. HE FUMBLES AROUND AND GETS DRESSED IN A HURRY.

MARTIN: Yes...

▸▸ **OUTPATIENTS RECEPTION**

KIM SEES RACHEL AT THE VENDING MACHINE. SHE IS WEARING A LONG PAIR OF FLARED JEANS WHICH DRAG ON THE FLOOR. THEY ARE SOAKING UP TO THE KNEE.

KIM: I like your trousers, are they new?

RACHEL: Yeah. I shouldn't have worn them in the rain though; they're really heavy now.

AS THEY WALK AWAY, RACHEL LIFTS UP THE LEGS OF HER JEANS TO HELP HER WALK.

KIM: Make your thighs look really tiny.

RACHEL: Do they?

KIM: Yeah.

STATHAM SEES JOANNA IN THE CORRIDOR. HE HIDES AT THE VENDING MACHINE UNTIL SHE COMES PAST.

STATHAM: Ah, morning, morning my sweet, you are looking glorious as ever.

JOANNA: Oh do shut it Alan, I'm feeling queasy as it is.

SHE HITS HIM WITH HER BAG.

▸ **ACCOMODATION BLOCK/ CAR PARK**

MARTIN COMES OUT OF HIS FRONT DOOR AND LOADS ALL HIS FILES ONTO HIS SCOOTER. HE DOESN'T NOTICE THAT ONE FALLS OFF. HE DRIVES OFF ALONG THE ROAD, TURNS INTO THE CAR PARK AND DRIVES ALL THE WAY ROUND IT LOOKING FOR A SPACE. ONCE HE HAS PARKED, HE SPOTS A COUPLE OF WOMEN PASSING BY. HE LEANS AGAINST THE SCOOTER IN A SUPPOSEDLY COOL WAY.

MARTIN: Morning ladies.

HE THEN UNPACKS HIS FILES AND NOTICES ONE'S MISSING. HE WALKS ACROSS THE ROAD TO RETRIEVE IT, AND WE REALISE THAT HIS PARKING SPACE IS ABOUT TEN YARDS AWAY FROM WHERE HE FIRST STARTED.

▸ **CANTEEN**

JOANNA COMES IN AND STOPS SUDDENLY. SHE LOOKS LONGINGLY AT A PLATE OF DOUGHNUTS FOR SOME TIME AND THEN STUFFS ONE IN HER MOUTH. SHE THEN SCOOPS THE REST OF THE PLATE INTO HER HANDBAG AND PUTS THE GRAPEFRUIT SHE'D CHOSEN ONTO THE EMPTY DISH. SHE GOES UP TO THE CASHIER.

JOANNA: Do you know how long it is since I've eaten carbohydrate?!

▸ **LOCKER AREA, MESS**

MARTIN IS TRYING TO STUFF THINGS IN HIS LOCKER. HE STARTS JUMPING UP TO SEE WHATS ON TOP OF THE LOCKER.

GUY: Yeah, all right Lord of the Dance, what's the er — which midget are you playing?

MARTIN: Look, I'm nervous, okay!

GUY: Oh, what are you scared about Marty?

MARTIN: Oh well, failing my exams again and everyone I know realising what a loser I am and always will be and losing any self-esteem that I ever had and hating myself and beating myself for the rest of my life!

GUY: Oh, fair enough.

MARTIN: Still, I suppose everyone feels like that about exams, don't they?

GUY: Er no, not me.

MARTIN: Why not?

GUY: Ooh, let me think. Is it because exams are easy peasy, lemon squeezy? Or is it because I am brilliant? It's both! You see the Secretans have never been at home to self-doubt; I have no idea what you're feeling.

MARTIN: Well it's bloody horrible.

MARTIN PUTS ON HIS WHITE COAT. THERE'S A TIGER'S TAIL ON THE BACK OF IT, WHICH HE DOESN'T SEE.

GUY: Um, Martin...

MARTIN: What?

GUY: Nothing.

GUY SINGS AS THEY GO INTO THE MESS. EVERYONE LOOKS AT HIM.

GUY: (SINGS) "Examinations, examinash-ha-ha-hions, examinations — that's what you need. If you want to fail the test, if you wanna be depressed, wo-ho... examinations are what you need. If you wanna be a record failure? Yeaaah!"

A WOMAN SMILES AS SHE LEAVES THE ROOM.

GUY: Stop flirting with me!

▶▶ MAIN ENTRANCE/CORRIDOR

CAROLINE HAS DRAGGED HERSELF INTO WORK. SHE IS WALKING WITH A PRONOUNCED STOOP, AND LOOKING DEEPLY THE WORSE FOR WEAR. MAC APPEARS.

MAC: Ah ha, if I'm not mistaken, it's the brave explorer returning from the uncharted regions of drunkenness.

CAROLINE: No no, stop saying words.

MAC: Okay. We could try Morse, but I don't know any. It's a very interesting new walk you've got there.

CAROLINE: Invisible hangover hat.

MAC: Do what now?

CAROLINE: Hovering above my head is an invisible hangover hat. You can't see it.

MAC: Because it's invisible?

CAROLINE: So if I straighten up, I am wearing the invisible hangover hat and then I will be very sick.

MAC: Okay, I'm assuming you've taken painkillers.

CAROLINE: I want something stronger. I want the stuff you use to kill people.

MAC: I'm saving all that for Guy.

CAROLINE: Why are you all right? How can you be all right?

MAC: Because I am the chosen one.

CAROLINE: Look, no, why? Why really?

MAC: Because I didn't drink any of Guy's ethanol punch. Okay, let's have a look at this hat of yours.

CAROLINE: Wait, no, what are you doing? Too much movement.

MAC: Woah.

CAROLINE: Oh...

MAC: Okay, I'm swapping your hangover hat for my "I knew when I'd had enough" hat. There we go. Now...

CAROLINE SLOWLY STANDS UP.

CAROLINE: Thank you. Again. Mac, look — um... about last night, I just wanted to say, look — I need to clear up...

MARTIN WALKS PAST.

MAC: Ah, exam boy. What time's kick-off?

MARTIN: Oh, two o'clock. I'm just trying to find a place to do some last minute cramming.

MAC: Right, right. Good plan, good plan.

CAROLINE: See you later loud people. Martin, I like your tail.

MARTIN CAN'T SEE THE TIGER'S TAIL ON HIS WHITE COAT.

MARTIN: Well! Caroline likes my arse.

MAC: Yeah. Yeah, that'll help. Yeah.

MARTIN: Wow.

MAC: How are you feeling?

MARTIN: Oh, Jesus, I just forgot for a minute.

MAC: Only exams, you've got to lighten up.

▸▸ **OFFICE**

KIM AND RACHEL ARE THROWING SCRUNCHED UP BALLS OF PAPER AT KAREN WHO HAS A WASTEPAPER BASKET OVER HER HEAD. KAREN PICKS UP ALL THE MISSILES.

HARRIET: (SUDDENLY WAILS) Oh no!! Oh, I'm pregnant!

KIM: What?

HARRIET: I am pregnant.

KIM: What again? Have you done a test?

HARRIET: No, I just know.

KIM: How can you just know?

HARRIET: Oh I can, I can sense it, it's in there and it's another boy!

KIM: I really don't think it's possible for someone to just know they're pregnant. Rach?

RACHEL: No way.

JOANNA COMES INTO THE OFFICE UNNOTICED, EATING A DOUGHNUT, AND LISTENS TO HARRIET.

HARRIET: Oh it is. There's a sort of low-level nausea in your belly, accompanied strangely by this overwhelming desire to eat fatty foods.

JOANNA THROWS THE REST OF A DOUGHNUT AWAY.

HARRIET: And total lethargy, like you've had fifteen Mogadon, or been involved in a road traffic accident. (IN THE BACK-GROUND, JOANNA COLLAPSES BRIEFLY AGAINST THE WALL) And then, on the plus side, your boobs swell, but on the down

WANTED
Revision buddy

Must be very tolerant, non-cynical and likely to pass.
Lady preferred though not essential. Nothing pervy,
I just think ladies smell nice and that helps me concentrate.

Contact Martin Dear.

Spleen → v. v. important.
Absorbs fat
Clears blood   Maybe not that important
Remember
ask Mac

side, they're too tender for anyone to touch and then you're snappy, a bit like a Jack Russell, but bigger!

JOANNA: I trust you're all focused on the day's workload everyone. (SNAPPILY) Or are you just tossing your one brain cell around the room as usual?! Hmm? Thickos. (SHE BARKS LIKE A BIG JACK RUSSELL) Woof!

SHE GOES INTO HER OFFICE.

▸▸ **STAFF LIAISON OFFICE**

SUE IS SUCKING A LOLLIPOP. GUY LEANS OVER HER DESK.

GUY: Do you know what I like about you?

SUE DOESN'T ANSWER.

GUY: Fuck all.

GUY LEAVES. SUE CARRIES ON SUCKING.

▸▸ **OFFICE**

KIM: So, weren't you using anything?

HARRIET: Oh yes, we just seem to be incredibly unlucky with condoms. They always come off and then we can never find them. Unless the cat's in the bed, then he finds them. There was a night last week when Ian was on the home brew and it completely disappeared, and I keep hoping it's going to pop out any day, but it hasn't.

KAREN: Yeah, but if a man's had too much to drink, the spermatozoa isn't that strong.

KIM: What do you know about sperm? You've never been near any.

KAREN: Yes I have. I had some on my skirt once, on the tube. It was a pencil skirt too.

KIM: Have you done a test?

KAREN: I don't think you can get pregnant from it getting on your skirt.

KIM: Not you.

HARRIET: No I haven't. I just know. It would be a waste of money.

RACHEL GIVES HARRIET A TISSUE AND A PLASTIC CUP.

RACHEL: Here. I'll take it to the guy in the path lab, I'm a bit of a regular, so you won't have to pay. Just fill that.

HARRIET: I've just been.

RACHEL GIVES HARRIET A BOTTLE OF WATER. HARRIET GOES TO DRINK SOME.

▸▸ JOANNA'S OFFICE

JOANNA STUDIES HER CALENDAR.

JOANNA: Oh fuck shit! Fucking shit!! Oh shit, fuck, bollocks!

SHE FEELS HER BREASTS.

▸▸ OUTPATIENTS CORRIDOR

ANGELA GOES UP TO CAROLINE.

ANGELA: Caroline, excuse me — can I have a quick word?

CAROLINE: Yeah, of course.

ANGELA: Um... in private if that's okay?

CAROLINE: Er, yep.

THEY GO INTO THE CORRIDOR.

ANGELA: Sorry, maybe I should have waited until we got home, it's just that it's sort of been bugging me and it's sort of getting me a bit annoyed and — and I don't want to get all stressed out and angry, because it makes me look ugly.

CAROLINE: What is it? Have I done something to upset you?

ANGELA: Are you wearing my pants?

CAROLINE: What?

ANGELA: My very white Tanga briefs, they're plain cotton, not sexies, but they're my cute sportsies.

CAROLINE: No, I haven't got them.

ANGELA: Ah, because I think you have. Um — I put them in the tumble drier last night, but they weren't there this morning when I came to iron them.

CAROLINE: You iron your pants?

ANGELA: Of course. So if you could just return them to me, then I'll say no more about it.

CAROLINE: But I haven't taken them.

GUY, MAC AND BOYCE COME ROUND THE END OF THE CORRIDOR. THEY STOP TO WATCH THE GIRLS.

ANGELA: Oh, you're wearing them now aren't you? Oh Caroline, you let your dirty washing stack up, you were desperate for a fresh pair, I understand — but it's the principle you see. It's theft. Obviously I will not wear them after your vagina has been in them. I'll burn them, but I want what is legally mine.

CAROLINE: Shut up!!

ANGELA: What?!

CAROLINE: I haven't taken your pants, I wouldn't want to. Stop being so anal!

ANGELA: Give me back my pants. Don't make me get cross.

You see, you've obviously got something to hide. Give me back my pants.

ANGELA ATTACKS CAROLINE. CAROLINE TRIES TO FEND HER OFF.

GUY: Yes, I have died and gone to heaven. Females fighting over their pants. They're going to rip each other's clothes off.

BOYCE: I'm getting a semi.

GUY: A semi? What's wrong with you boy? I'm like a flagpole.

MAC: Come on ladies, come on, come on. Woah, woah, woah, come on...

MAC STEPS IN AND SEPARATES ANGELA AND CAROLINE.

ANGELA: She's wearing my pants, even though they're too small for her. She wants to be me!

MAC: No, she's — come on. Hey hey hey hey!

CAROLINE: I'm not wearing your pants; you wear children's clothes!

GUY: Mac, set them free, let them fight!

MAC: Gently, gently, gently...

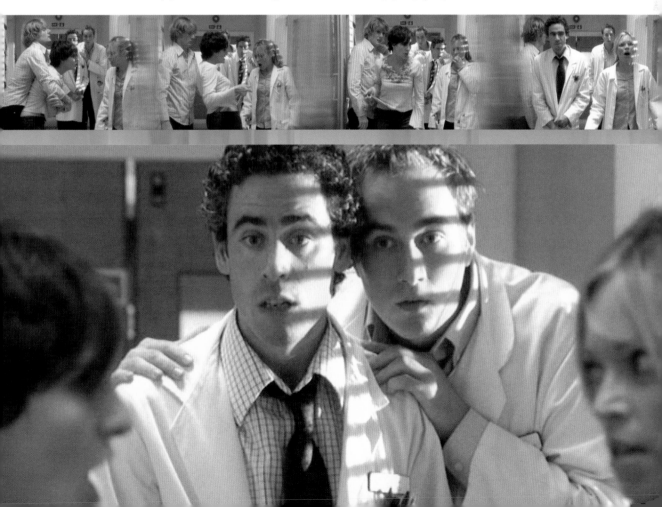

CAROLINE: You are mad. Look!

CAROLINE PULLS UP THE SIDE OF HER PANTS, WHICH ARE PURPLE.

ANGELA: Ooh!

CAROLINE: Why don't you try asking your boyfriend? He looks the type to wear women's pants.

CAROLINE WALKS OFF, VERY ANGRY.

ANGELA: Oh, I'm sorry Caro. I'll make it up to you. I'll — I'll buy you lunch!

▸▸ CORRIDOR

JOANNA FINDS STATHAM.

JOANNA: I'm late! Fucking late!

STATHAM: Well, that's your prerogative, you're the boss.

JOANNA: No, idiot, feel my breasts!

STATHAM FEELS JOANNA'S BREASTS.

STATHAM: Oh my beautiful, demanding Aphrodite. You are so exciting when you want me.

JOANNA: Well?

STATHAM: Well what?

JOANNA: Do they feel different?!

STATHAM: Well, Mimi's slightly weightier than Charlotte, but I...

JOANNA: Dear God... I'm late! And I may need you to get me something.

STATHAM: What, a taxi?

JOANNA: Look, I presume you must be a reasonably intelligent man, otherwise they wouldn't let you work in a hospital...

STATHAM: Well thank you, thank you, and nice to know that somebody's on my side.

JOANNA: ...But there are times when you can appear remarkably thick.

STATHAM: I don't understand.

JOANNA: Well there you are, you see? How can you not understand that?

STATHAM: No, I understand you think I'm thick, but I don't understand why. I — I have an IQ of 139, I'm a member of MENSA, I can sing 'Baa Baa Black Sheep' in Latin...

JOANNA: But even so, I'm just not sure that you should have any children.

STATHAM: I haven't got any children.

JOANNA: Well that's what you think.

STATHAM: No, I can assure you, I have no children.

JOANNA: Well there's a grave danger of you having one soon! All right?!

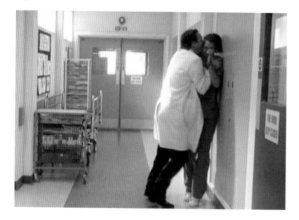

SHE GOES. STATHAM HEADS OFF LOOKING PUZZLED, BUT THEN THE PENNY DROPS. HE DOES A LITTLE DANCE OF CHILDISH DELIGHT, CLAPPING HIS HANDS TOGETHER WITH EXCITEMENT. HE SUDDENLY GRABS A PASSING NURSE AND KISSES HER.

▶▶ THEATRE

MID-OPERATION — AND MID-GENERAL KNOWLEDGE QUIZ.

MAC: Okay, thank you Claudette. To what are the French referring when they speak of a woman's *cassolette?*

GUY: Um, her make-up bags.

MAC: Wrong.

GUY: Sacks. Er... very large baskets.

MAC: Utterly utterly wrong. The sortilege of odours emanating from a woman is known as her *cassolette.*

GUY: What?

MAC: And the smell of her perfume mingling with her skin, her bodily fluids, her shampoo, which all come together to make...

GUY: A dirty, minging woman. Trust the bloody French to make it sound romantic!

MAC: Eight points to one! Thank you very much.

CAROLINE: Sssh, sssh.

MAC: Bow down to the master.

CAROLINE: Shush.

MAC: Okay, I'll give you an easy one. Who wrote *Paradise Lost?*

GUY: We said no book questions. What am I, a girl?

MAC: Yes you are, but I'll tell you anyway. The answer is...

GUY: I don't care; it's irrelevant to the quiz and mankind.

CAROLINE: John Milton.

MAC: Thank you very much. Bring on the next contestant please.

GUY: Well what an absolute tragedy there. By posing an illegal question, he loses ten points. So it's another handsome victory for the young anaesthetist, by one point to minus two.

MAC TURNS AWAY.

GUY: Get in! I love your *cassolette.*

GUY SNIFFS.

▶▶ LAB WINDOW

JOANNA TAKES A URINE SAMPLE AND HANDS IT TO A BESPEC-TACLED LAB TECHNICIAN AT A HATCH.

LAB TECHNICIAN: What is it?

JOANNA: Oh — straw-coloured liquid in a sample pot? We work in a hospital?

LAB TECHNICIAN: Eurgh, is it wee?

JOANNA: Oh come on, come on.

LAB TECHNICIAN: I need a name.

JOANNA: Big geeky nerdy twat face.

LAB TECHNICIAN: I need a name for the sample.

JOANNA: Well, it's for a friend of mine, who wishes to remain anonymous. Is that going to cause problems in your weird little techno-brain?

LAB TECHNICIAN: No, it's just that we'll have to go up on the roof and shout "Pregnancy test results for the stupid lanky old bitch who's not learned to take basic precautions in her forty-odd years on this planet!" You know, assuming that your friend is quite lanky.

JOANNA SEES HARRIET STEALING NAPPIES FROM THE STORE CUPBOARD NEARBY.

JOANNA: Um, Harriet Schulenburg, that's my friend's name.

LAB TECHNICIAN: Right. Are you sure about that?

JOANNA: Yes, quite sure, thank you.

LAB TECHNICIAN: Right, how are you spelling Schulenburg?

JOANNA: Any way you like.

LAB TECHNICIAN: You've got to sign.

JOANNA SCRIBBLES ON THE PAD AND WALKS OFF.

LAB TECHNICIAN: Don't leave, I think I love you!

▶▶ OUTSIDE THEATRE

CAROLINE TAKES MAC TO ONE SIDE.

MAC: Yes?

CAROLINE: I er... I just wanted to say, I'm sorry about what happened at — at my party, you know, the thing.

MAC: Thing? What thing exactly?

CAROLINE: Yeah, the — the thing, you know, the um... the incident between... between you and me.

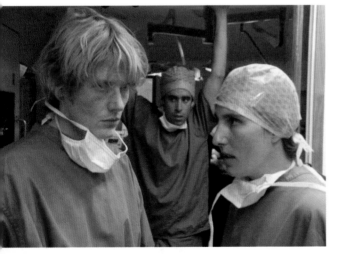

MAC: We had an incident?

CAROLINE: Yeah, yeah, a sort of... lip on lip incident. Yeah, er — accident possibly.

MAC: Oh that. That, yeah, yeah... no.

CAROLINE: Yeah, well I'm sorry. I'm sorry.

MAC: That's perfectly all right.

CAROLINE: No it isn't you see, the thing is, I don't really like you.

MAC: Well yeah, I was wondering why you'd done it.

CAROLINE: Yeah, well we were very close together and then I just lost my balance and fell forwards and er... and we ended up quite close together with our mouths open. It was an error.

MAC: No.

CAROLINE: It was.

MAC: No, I mean that's not... how we ended up together, no it's not, it wasn't me.

CAROLINE: It was, it was.

MAC: No. No, that was how you ended up kissing Guy.

CAROLINE: I — I kissed Guy?

MAC: Yes, in the hall. We kissed in the loo.

CAROLINE: No, no, that was Sue White.

MAC: I kissed Sue White?

CAROLINE: No no, I kissed Sue White.

MAC: You kissed Sue White?

CAROLINE: Possibly.

MAC: Blimey! What, and you — you kissed Sue White and you don't remember us in the toilets?

CAROLINE: No. Well, no — but hang on, you, first you say you don't remember any kissing at all, and now you're saying that there was kissing in the toilet, which one is it?

GUY COMES OVER.

GUY: Kissing in the toilet?

CAROLINE: Yes, er... who sang 'Kissing In The Toilet' in 1978?

GUY: Um... was it a young George Michael?

CAROLINE: Yes.

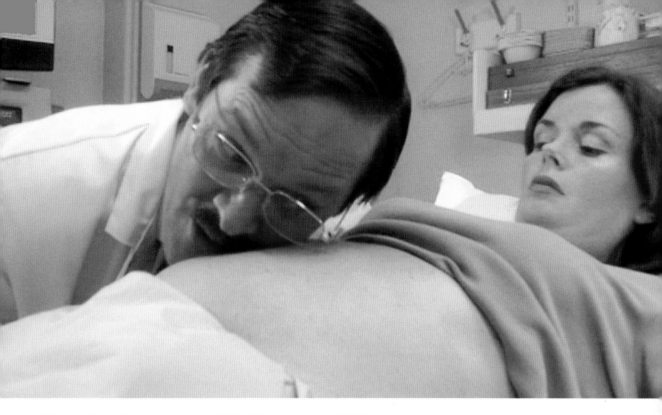

GUY: Fucking hell! That was a guess! (SINGS) "Kissing in the toilet, don't flush, it's lush."

▶▶ **OFFICE**

JOANNA TALKS TO KIM OUTSIDE HER OFFICE.

JOANNA: Any internal mail for Harriet, give it to me first, okay?

KIM: Yeah, okay. Why?

JOANNA: Because um... hate mail.

KIM: What?

JOANNA: Yeah, she's been getting hate mail, death threats, you know, so I need to, you know — intercept her mail first.

KIM: Why does she get death threats?

JOANNA: Well isn't it obvious?

HARRIET IS STRUGGLING TO GET A PIECE OF PAPER OFF HER SLEEVE.

KIM: No...

JOANNA: Well I can't think of a single reason why anyone wouldn't want to kill her.

▶▶ **ULTRASOUND DEPARTMENT**

A WOMAN IS HAVING HER STOMACH SCANNED. STATHAM

ENTERS.

STATHAM: There you are. There you are.

ULTRASOUND TECHNICIAN: Something wrong Doctor Statham?

STATHAM: No no, just overseeing here. Hello, how are you?

PATIENT: Well I'm not so...

STATHAM: Good. Good. Alan Statham, Consultant Radiology and Imaging. Just keeping an eye on my flock. Let's have a look. Hmm. Could be a little bit sharper. Um, back off a bit.

HE PUSHES THE TECHNICIAN OUT OF THE WAY.

STATHAM: Yes, yes, a baby is there.

STATHAM PUTS HIS HEAD ON THE WOMAN'S STOMACH.

STATHAM: A tiny little tiny baby. Hmm, you are there aren't you? Yes you are, yes you are. What are you going to be when you grow up?

HE IS RUBBING HIS FACE INTO HER BELLY. SHE LOOKS CONFUSED.

STATHAM: Are you going to be a radiologist like your Uncle Alan? Are you? Is it a big tickly moustache? Is it a bit tickly? (SINGS) "You shall have the fishy on a little dishy, you shall have a fishy when the boat comes in." Here comes the foghorn.

HE BLOWS A RASPBERRY ON HER STOMACH.

STATHAM: You are a lovely little boy. You are a lovely little boy. Yes you are. Oh yes you are. Oh you are, you are, you are, you are, you are... (HE TRIES TO GET BACK INTO PROFESSIONAL MODE) It's a very — that's good, well done. And you, well done. Where's he gone? (TO THE TECHNICIAN) Come on, in you go, on with your work. Right...

HE LEAVES, LOOKING PLEASED.

▸▸ JOANNA'S OFFICE

MARTIN: I want to know what would happen if I didn't pass my exams this time.

JOANNA: If??

MARTIN: What would happen to my position in the hospital?

JOANNA: Look, this isn't a good time Martin.

MARTIN: That's so unfair.

JOANNA: Yeah, life's unfair. Go and run along and pretend to do some doctory stuff, eh?

MARTIN: Oh come on Mum...

JOANNA: Don't you *ever* say that word!

MARTIN: Sorry.

JOANNA: Nothing will ensure that you are turfed out of this hospital quicker than saying that out loud! Is that what you want? Hmm? Hmm? It's up to you, you just have to say the word. We had a deal, remember?

MARTIN: Sorry, but it's just, it's really hard, 'cause... I love you.

JOANNA SNATCHES THE SELLOTAPE MARTIN HAS BEEN PLAYING WITH.

MARTIN: And I know deep down you love me too.

JOANNA: Oh be quiet.

MARTIN: I know you pretend to be ashamed of me.

JOANNA: No, it's quite genuine.

MARTIN: Well, underneath I know you've got some mother's pride. And I don't mean the bread.

JOANNA FLINGS THE DOOR OPEN.

JOANNA: Get out!

MARTIN: I love you, I always will, and you can't change that.

HARRIET HAS BEEN STANDING AT THE DOOR.

HARRIET: Shall I come back later?

JOANNA: Er yeah, Doctor Dear was just telling me what a patient had said to him earlier today. A psychiatric patient, obviously.

MARTIN GOES, GETTING HIS FOOT CAUGHT IN THE WIRING AND PULLING THE PHONE OFF THE DESK.

JOANNA: Pick it up! Go on! Come on, come on, come on! (TO HARRIET) Get out mummy, go on.

HARRIET LEAVES.

▸▸ STAFF LIAISON OFFICE

SUE IS CHECKING HER PONYTAIL. THERE'S A KNOCK AT HER DOOR.

SUE: Hang on a minute. Come.

CAROLINE ENTERS.

SUE: Just tugging the squirrel.

CAROLINE: What?

SUE: Now what can I do for you Doctor Trodd? Although I suspect I know you well enough now to call you Caroline.

CAROLINE: Yes, well that's what I've come about, the... the incident at my... at my party. The... the um — the...

SUE: The?

CAROLINE: The...

SUE: The?

CAROLINE: The...

SUE: The what, dear?

CAROLINE: Well the... You know when you left, when you left and we were in — in the doorway and you... and you, and we, and we...

SUE REACHES ACROSS THE DESK AND KISSES CAROLINE ON THE LIPS.

SUE: Is that what you mean?

CAROLINE: Yes. Yes, well, the thing is I — oh God! The thing is, I — I didn't want there to be any... any awkwardness or, or — or misunderstandings.

SUE: No no, there's none, none. I don't have a problem with that at all, do you?

CAROLINE: No.

SUE: Good. Good.

CAROLINE: Glad we cleared that up then. Fine, well I'll be off then.

SUE: Yeah, bye then.

▸▸ CORRIDOR

KIM SEES BOYCE.

KIM: All right, fucker?!

BOYCE: Not bad, bitch!

BOYCE IS LIMPING SLIGHTLY.

KIM: What's with the leg shit? On the lookout for a sympathy shag?

BOYCE: Might be, might have been shot. Good party at the weekend.

KIM: Oh, were you there?

BOYCE: Oh yes.

KIM: Get hold of anyone?

BOYCE: Just some treacle with top tits.

KIM AND BOYCE GRAB EACH OTHER AND EMBRACE PASSIONATELY. HE WALKS OFF DOWN THE CORRIDOR, LIMPING.

▸▸ CANTEEN

MARTIN HAS HIS BOOKS ALL OVER A TABLE. MAC AND GUY JOIN HIM. GUY PUSHES SOME OF MARTIN'S FILES ONTO THE FLOOR TO MAKE ROOM FOR HIS TRAY.

MAC: You know what you need? You need a system. Like I used mnemonics when I was revising.

GUY: Yeah, me too. Take the bones of the head, all right? You've got the frontal, parietal, occipital, zygomatic, sphenoid, temporal, maxilla, mandible, vomer and nasal.

MARTIN: Jesus! How did you remember that?!

GUY: I just took a simple, everyday phrase, where the words begin with the same letters as the bones.

MARTIN: Okay.

MAC: Go on then, what is it?

GUY: Foreign... politicians... often... zing stereotypical tunes... mayday, mayday, Venezuela neck.

▸▸ HOSPITAL GROUNDS

ANGELA IS EATING HER LUNCH. CAROLINE IS LYING ON THE GROUND MOANING.

CAROLINE: Ohhhhhhh........

ANGELA: You've said that.

CAROLINE: Oh have I? Sorry. Did I tell you I'm never ever going to drink again?

ANGELA: What did you do before alcohol became the centre of your universe?

CAROLINE: Homework.

ANGELA: You know what you really need to do...

CAROLINE: Hmm?

ANGELA: ...is go for a walk.

CAROLINE: Where to?

ANGELA: I don't really care, just stop whining!

▸▸ **CANTEEN**

MAC: Relax, relax, yeah. Breathe. Try it again.

MARTIN: Um... French politicians...

GUY: *Foreign* politicians!

MARTIN: Foreign! Foreign politicians often zing... No, it's gone. Um — I know it begins with an S and a T.

MAC: Yeah.

MARTIN: Um...

MAC: Hang on, hang on. How do you know it began with an S and then a T?

MARTIN: Because it begins with the same letters as the bones, so

I know, you know — sphenoid, maxilla, mandible, vomer, nasal. Er — er — stereotypical, stereotypical!

GUY: Yes, yes, yes!

MARTIN: Yes! Right.

GUY: You see, all you have to do, just think of the bones and the phrase will come back.

MARTIN: Brilliant!

GUY: Okay.

MARTIN: Um — yes, the bones and...

HE PICKS UP HIS STUFF, DROPPING THINGS ON THE FLOOR.

MARTIN: Sorry, sorry Mac.

MAC: All right?

MARTIN: Yeah, I've got it in, it's fine.

GUY: You're all right, it'll be fine. We'll do the leg later.

MARTIN: Okay.

MARTIN GOES.

GUY: That's how I remembered your name when I first met you.

MAC: What?

GUY: Massively Annoying Chap.

MAC: Massively Annoying Chap?

GUY: Yeah, Mac.

MAC: Hmm.

GUY: I was going to say Massively Annoying —

▸▸ **RECOVERY WARD**

CAROLINE GOES UP TO MAC.

CAROLINE: That was it though, wasn't it?

MAC: Hello. Hang on, I didn't realise I'd just turned into Uri Geller, I'll just adjust my mind reading psychic antennae...

CAROLINE: The full list of those I had lip contact with — you, possibly, Guy and Sue White, possibly?

MAC: Yeah, that's it, yeah. If you don't count Martin.

CAROLINE: I kissed Martin? Oh no. Oh yes I did. Oh God! Am I a slut?

MAC: Yes.

CAROLINE: Oh God!

MAC: No, it's fine, it's absolutely fine.

CAROLINE: How can it be fine?

MAC: Because you were a pissed slut.

CAROLINE: Ah. Thanks.

MAC PULLS THE BED CURTAIN ACROSS CAROLINE'S FACE. SHE KISSES THE CURTAIN WHERE HE WAS.

▸▸ STAFF LIAISON OFFICE

SUE IS CHASING A WASP AROUND HER OFFICE. EVENTUALLY SHE TRAPS IT IN A GLASS.

▸▸ RADIOLOGY

STATHAM IS GIVING A LECTURE IN A DAZE.

STATHAM: ...Whereas in radionuclide scanning, the radioactive substance injected into the body emits what kind of rays? Anyone?

STUDENT: Gamma.

STATHAM: Precisely. Gamma rays which produce images of I'm having a baby, or can be expressed in numerical form. Tiny pink little baby, moving on to diagnostic preferences in let's say soft tissue trauma, who's the daddy? I think you'll find that I am the daddy.

▸▸ CORRIDORS/CANTEEN

SUE TRANSPORTS THE WASP IN THE GLASS ALONG THE CORRIDORS AND INTO THE CANTEEN. SHE SETS IT FREE — RIGHT UNDER AN INSECT 'ZAPPER'.

SUE: Adios!

THE WASP FRIES.

▶▶ OFFICE

JOANNA IS POKING HER STOMACH. KIM ENTERS.

KIM: You wanted internal mail for Harriet?

JOANNA: Yeah, yeah, yeah, thanks Kimmy. Yeah yeah, that's all, thanks.

JOANNA HAS AN ENVELOPE WITH PREGNANCY TEST RESULTS IN IT. MEANWHILE, IN THE OUTER OFFICE, RACHEL IS AT KAREN'S DESK.

RACHEL: Hmm, you haven't got many e-mails have you? Oh...

SHE SEES SOME 'CRUMBS' ON KAREN'S DESK. SHE LICKS HER FINGER, PICKS SOME UP AND EATS THEM.

RACHEL: Coconut macaroons?

KAREN: Eczema.

RACHEL: Ah...

RACHEL RUNS OUT, ABOUT TO BE SICK.

KIM: Another internal mail for Harriet.

JOANNA: Yeah, yeah, she can have it.

KIM: I thought it might be a death threat...?

JOANNA: What? No, shouldn't think so. Oh, well — no no, there was a death threat, but then they rang up and they said they were sorry and they weren't going to do it any more. So that's good, isn't it? Yeah, yeah, yeah.

KIM GOES, A LITTLE CONFUSED.

▶▶ **DAY WARD**

MAC AND GUY ARE SPINNING ROUND AND ROUND ON SWIVEL CHAIRS.

ANGELA: Hey, can one of you give me a hand? I've got a squealer in cubicle four.

MAC: Yep.

THEY STAND UP AND IMMEDIATELY FALL OVER — COMPLETELY DIZZY.

ANGELA: Seriously!

MAC MANAGES TO MAKE IT OUT OF THE ROOM. GUY FALLS OVER THE DESK.

▶▶ **OFFICE**

HARRIET OPENS HER ENVELOPE.

HARRIET: Yes! It's negative! I'm not! Hurray!

EVERYONE IS HAPPY.

HARRIET: Booze.

SHE OPENS A BOTTLE OF BEER. THEY ALL CELEBRATE. HARRIET HAS SIX CIGARETTES IN HER MOUTH. THEY HEAR A TERRIBLE SCREAM AND DAMAGE BEING CAUSED BY JOANNA IN HER OFFICE — SHE HAS JUST OPENED THE TEST RESULTS SHE WAS GIVEN BY KIM.

▶▶ **MESS**

MARTIN IS TRYING TO CHOOSE A MASCOT FOR HIS EXAMS. HE HAS THREE SOFT TOYS.

GUY: Not gone to the gallows yet then?

MARTIN: No! I'm trying to think of a mascot to take. Um... Right, I've decided for Mr Ratty.

GUY: Oh my God, you're a child.

GUY RIPS THE HEAD OFF THE RAT.

GUY: Plague carrier.

MARTIN: Shit! I didn't think of that.

GUY: Yeah, well lucky Uncle Guy is here. Next?

MARTIN HOLDS UP A TOY BEAVER.

MARTIN: Um, Lord Chisel-tooth.

GUY: Jesus!

MARTIN: A hard-working, industrious social animal.

GUY: No! Builds dams, yeah? Blocks off the flow of inspiration. You'll be sitting in the exam room trying to think of the proper word for leg, and you'll dry up, all because of your poor mascot choices.

GUY THROWS THE BEAVER INTO THE BIN.

MARTIN: What, you can't — you just... What is the proper word for leg?

GUY: Can't tell you that.

MARTIN: Thank Christ I've got B.

MARTIN HOLDS ONTO A TOY BUMBLE BEE.

GUY: Oh what's he called, Emperor Bumble Wank? Buzzy Buzzy Penis?

MARTIN: No, he's called B, right? And this is the clever bit — just the letter B.

GUY: Hive worker, doesn't stand out from the crowd, short life-span and sterile.

GUY THROWS B INTO THE BIN.

MARTIN: Oh Christ, I need a mascot!

GUY PRODUCES A NAPKIN.

GUY: Da-dah! Clean, orderly, a blank sheet.

MARTIN: It doesn't even have a name.

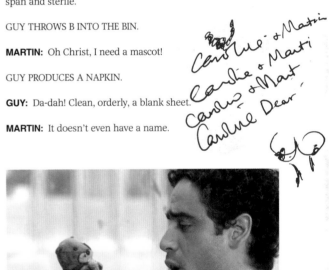

Dear The Jim Henson Company

My name is ▓▓▓▓▓▓ MacCartney, but my parents call me Mac. I am 8 years old, and my favourite programme is

Fraggle Rock. My favourite Fraggle out of all the different Fraggles is called Red. I like her because she has red hair, and I have almost red hair ↙
(although actually is a different colour called 'frezz blondé).

I always get teased because my hair is red (although it isn't).

I am writing to you because I wanted to know if Red Fraggle currently has a boyfriend, because if she hasn't, I would like to be her boyfriend, because she is kind and funny, and has a funny walk and wouldn't tease me because I have red hair (even though I don't). Also, I am being teased by a Swiss

boy through pen pal letters which is stupid because I haven't even met him yet.

Your sincerely, 'Mac'

My Hair
↓

Red and me holding hands

GUY: Yes it does. Captain Wipey.

MARTIN GOES TO FOLD IT UP AND PUT IT IN HIS BAG.

GUY: Don't fold your mascot! That's really bad luck.

GUY GOES. MARTIN GOES TO RETRIEVE HIS STUFFED TOYS FROM THE BIN.

GUY: Leave them!

MARTIN WAITS UNTIL GUY HAS GONE AND THEN GETS THE MASCOTS OUT OF THE BIN.

▶▶ **OUTSIDE BOARDROOM**

MAC IS SITTING NEAR THE BOARDROOM DOOR. CAROLINE FINDS HIM.

CAROLINE: Ah ha. Where have you been? Aren't you supposed to be back in theatre? I've been looking for you.

MAC: Here, no, and well done, you've found me. It's your turn to hide.

CAROLINE: Um... I don't think we've quite finished our chat.

MAC: If you're looking for more names for your roll call of conquests, I am out, and actually I am quite busy.

CAROLINE: Oh, are you in trouble or something?

MAC: Not yet, no, but if you must know, I'm here for an interview.

CAROLINE: Oh?

MAC: Hmm.

CAROLINE: Interview for what?

MAC: Consultancy vacancy. Preliminary only, internal post, so nothing major.

CAROLINE: Wow! I had no idea, nobody said.

MAC: Nobody knows.

CAROLINE: Sorry. Right, er well — I guess now is not quite the moment.

MAC: No.

SHE LOOKS HIM UP AND DOWN FOR A MOMENT.

CAROLINE: Casual is all right is it?

MAC: Casual is good, yeah, yeah, because it's really about how good you are at the job, not about how you dress. And I think wearing suits displays a certain lack of imagination.

CAROLINE: Right.

MAC: Yeah.

CAROLINE: Well, good luck.

MAC: Thank you.

CAROLINE: Are you sure you want to go in there with your hair like that?

MAC: Like what?

CAROLINE: Nothing. Good luck.

MAC: Yeah.

CAROLINE GOES. SUE WHITE COMES OVER.

SUE: Doctor MacCartney!

MAC: Sue — Sue White, can I ask you a quick question?

SUE: Yes, of course.

MAC: Um — my hair, does it look okay?

SUE: Yeah. A lion's mane has never looked so free.

MAC: Thank you very much, thank you.

SUE: Oh, you're welcome.

MAC: Do you think I could borrow that hair thingy?

SUE: My whaty?

MAC: Clippy thing you put in your hair, it's an emergency.

SUE UNDOES HER HAIR AND MAKES A BIG THING OF SWIRLING HER LOOSE HAIR AROUND.

SUE: Well okay then, but I want you to know, I don't let the squirrel out for just anybody.

MAC: Thank you.

SUE: Knock yourself out.

MAC TIES HIS HAIR UP AT THE BACK.

MAC: What do you think?

SUE: Yeah, lovely. Just give it a bit of a tidy. There we are, just stick that in.

SHE PUTS COMB GRIPS IN MAC'S HAIR ON EITHER SIDE.

MAC: Thank you.

SUE: Right. Thank God for the dead box.

MAC: Yes, yes.

SUE: There.

MAC: Yeah, how do I look?

SUE: Excellent.

MAC: Brilliant.

SUE: Yes, d'Artagnan! The big musketeer.

MAC: Great. You are a life-saver. Thank you very much.

SUE: Okay.

ASSISTANT: Doctor MacCartney?

MAC: That's me, thank you. Great, wish me luck.

SUE: Good luck, good luck. Just try not to turn side on.

MAC: Okay.

MAC GOES INTO HIS INTERVIEW, EDGING SIDEWAYS.

MAC: Hello there, hi.

▸▸ STATHAM'S OFFICE

STATHAM IS PUTTING TOGETHER PICTURES OF BABIES' BODIES UP ON HIS LIGHT BOX AND ADDING HEADS WHICH ARE PHOTOS OF HIMSELF AND JOANNA. BOYCE COMES IN SUDDENLY.

BOYCE: Question — would it be okay to x-ray my penis? I think I might have dislocated it.

STATHAM: Get out!

BOYCE: No really, I think I have.

STATHAM: Get out!

▸▸ OFFICE

THE OFFICE STAFF ARE ALL CELEBRATING NOISILY.

JOANNA: I'm sorry everyone, it seems that Harriet's mistaken this office for a children's party. Shall I call the medics in, or would someone just stab her for me?

KIM: No it's okay, she's just had a bit of good news. She thought she was pregnant and she just got the lab results back and it's negative.

JOANNA: She — ? She had a pregnancy test done today??

KIM: Yeah.

JOANNA: A real one?

KIM: What do you mean?

JOANNA: I mean — here, today?

KIM: Yes.

SHE GIVES JOANNA THE
RESULT SHEET.

JOANNA: Hmm... That's not how you spell Schulenburg. Fan-bloody-tastic!

SHE GETS THE POSITIVE RESULT.

JOANNA: Oh Harriet, um — the lab just sent this up for you. It's marked urgent. I'm afraid I opened it by mistake and er... congratulations!

SHE PATS HARRIET'S STOMACH. HARRIET IS DISTRAUGHT. JOANNA CELEBRATES BY DANCING IN HER OFFICE.

▶▶ **STATHAM'S OFFICE**

STATHAM IS STILL COMPILING BABY PICTURES ON HIS LIGHT BOX.

▶▶ **EXAM ROOM**

MARTIN ARRIVES — EVERYONE ELSE HAS ALREADY SAT DOWN. HE FINDS A DESK AND PUTS OUT HIS NAPKIN AND BROKEN RAT MASCOTS.

INVIGILATOR: Right, ladies and gentlemen, you may turn over your papers and begin.

▶▶ **STAFF LIAISON OFFICE**

SUE WHITE IS AT HER DESK. GUY ENTERS.

SUE: Yes?!

GUY: I haven't asked the question yet.

SUE: Yes.

GUY: Is the answer?

SUE: What?

GUY: Is yes the answer?

SUE: Is the question?

GUY: But is yes the answer? Take a gamble.

SUE: I don't know, is it?

GUY: Take a gamble.

SUE: No.

GUY: No is the answer?

SUE: No is the answer. Yes is never the answer.

GUY: So no is the answer?

SUE: No is the answer.

GUY: So if I were to say are you going to ever have sex with any other man apart from me, then your answer is no?

SUE: Do you want to have sex with me? I mean do you want to just have — do you want to just fuck me now? Do you want to do that? Do you want to just get your cock out and fuck me now? How about that, yeah? Shall we? Here, on the table? Yeah, how about whopping it up my arse, what about that Mr Secretan? Doctor. Mr. Yeah? One above Doctor, how about that, yeah?

GUY DOESN'T SAY ANYTHING.

SUE: Mr Secretan whopping it up Staff Liaison's arse. So wipe yourself down and come back and tell me what you think about that. Okay?

GUY: I'm not sure I can stand up.

SUE: No. Well, I'll leave for a few moments, shall I?

GUY: Okay. Shut the door.

SUE: Yeah.

▶▶ **EXAM ROOM**

MARTIN SWEATS PROFUSELY IN HIS EXAM. HIS PAPER STICKS TO HIS FINGERS AND RIPS DOWN THE MIDDLE. THE INVIGILATOR GIVES HIM A TOWEL AND ANOTHER PAPER.

▶▶ **OUTSIDE BOARDROOM/CORRIDOR**

CAROLINE IS WAITING FOR MAC TO FIND OUT HOW THE INTERVIEW WENT. HE COMES OUT OF THE BOARDROOM.

MAC: No thank you, thank you very much.

CAROLINE: Fuck!

MAC: What?

CAROLINE: Your hair — you look like a Girl's World doll.

MAC: No, I don't know what you're talking about, this is regulation.

CAROLINE: Where at, St Augustine's Girls School?

MAC: No no no, here, here, just been introduced, did you not get it, no?

CAROLINE: No. How was the interview?

MAC: Not sure, I think I might have used the words "job", "stick", "up" and "arse" all in one sentence. Is that a bad thing?

CAROLINE: Well, I think tone of voice is very important.

MAC: Is it, is it? Damn. Shit. If you'll excuse me, I have some patients to see...

CAROLINE: Yeah.

▶▶ **BAR**

LUNCHTIME — JOANNA IS CELEBRATING THE FACT THAT SHE'S NOT PREGNANT. STATHAM ENTERS, EQUALLY ECSTATIC — BUT FOR VERY DIFFERENT REASONS.

JOANNA: Hi.

STATHAM IS CARRYING A 'CONGRATULATIONS' BALLOON, A SOFT TOY AND SOME FLOWERS.

STATHAM: Ah ha, what's this? In the bar in the middle of the day?

JOANNA: Yeah, celebrating.

STATHAM: Yeah, lots to celebrate! Yeah.

JOANNA: Hmm, yeah... (TO BARMAN) Vodka, double.

STATHAM: Er — no, no, mummy, I think not, I think we'll stick to the mineral water if you don't mind.

JOANNA: Why?

STATHAM: Well, you know, we want to do what's best don't we?

JOANNA: Yeah, double vodka, pronto, I'm gagging.

STATHAM: No no, come on now, let's look after the unborn Statham minor. Give it to me.

THEY WRESTLE OVER THE GLASS OF VODKA.

STATHAM: No, give it, give it...

THE DRINK GOES ALL OVER STATHAM'S FACE.

STATHAM: Never mind, no, never mind.

JOANNA: Oh sweet Jesus! Didn't you get my text? It's not me who's pregnant, it's Harriet Schulenburg.

STATHAM: What? Harriet...? Harriet is having my baby?

JOANNA: Oh please! She's upset enough as it is, that might just be enough to tip her over the edge.

STATHAM: We're...? We're not?

JOANNA: No, no, false alarm. I was a bit windy this morning, got my knockers in a twist over nothing, that's all. (SHE LOOKS AT HIS FLOWERS) What's all this bollocks then? Has somebody died?

JOANNA LAUGHS AT STATHAM.

JOANNA: Oh God!

STATHAM: No, no never mind, no, never mind. No, we'll just have to... we'll just have to try again.

JOANNA: Is that one of your jokes?

STATHAM: No, it'll be good for our relationship to just...

JOANNA: Er, hang on a minute. Hang on a minute. (VERY SERIOUS) You and me are not an item. Never have been, never will be. What have you got to say about that then, eh?

STATHAM TAKES THIS IN.

STATHAM: I.

JOANNA: What?

STATHAM: You and *I* are not an item, not you and me.

JOANNA: Listen to *I*. I not in a relationship with you no more.

STATHAM: A-hah, a-hah! At least you admit it's a relationship.

JOANNA: Yeah, *was*.

STATHAM: Well, all right, I see, okay...

JOANNA: And remember, if you ever want to talk about this — you know, pick over the good times and the bad, you know, so you can learn from it — please please please don't come to me.

JOANNA STORMS OUT OF THE BAR.

STATHAM: So... oh dear.

JOANNA COMES BACK.

STATHAM: (JOVIALLY TO BARMAN) Oh — here she comes!

JOANNA: Forgot my fags.

STATHAM: Right.

STATHAM GRABS JOANNA'S BREASTS.

JOANNA: Get your dumped mitts off my tits!

STATHAM: I want — I don't want to...

JOANNA: Stop it, stop it.

STATHAM: I'm not going to...

JOANNA: Get off me, get off!

STATHAM: I'm not going to, no one can see...

JOANNA GOES TO THE DOOR WITH STATHAM HANGING ONTO HER. HE SLIDES TO THE FLOOR, FINALLY, HOLDING ONTO AN ANKLE.

JOANNA: Get off!

STATHAM: I'm not going to, please...

JOANNA: Alan...

STATHAM: Stay, stay...

JOANNA: Listen...

STATHAM: No one can see.

JOANNA: Get off.

STATHAM: Please.

JOANNA: Sorry.

▶▶ EXAM ROOM

MARTIN THINKS HE'S FINISHED HIS EXAM AND LEANS BACK, SMUGLY LOOKING AROUND. HE THEN SEES ANOTHER CANDIDATE TURN A PAGE OVER. HE TURNS HIS OWN SHEETS OVER, REALISES THERE'S A LOT MORE TO DO — AND PANICS.

▶▶ SUPPLIES CUPBOARD

CAROLINE: So now that I might remember the kiss that did or did not take place between us, but say that it did, as you did — what was it like? I don't want you to hold back, just... tell me what it was like.

MAC: It was average. Yeah.

CAROLINE: Oh.

MAC: I remember we were both standing on the scales and you were looking down a lot saying, "Oh my God, I think I've put on twelve stone!" That was a little bit off-putting.

CAROLINE: But that kiss — how did that happen for God's sake?

MAC: Kiss, the kiss, yeah, I remember that. Er — you had your head over the loo like this, and then you came up like this and then you turned round and I was there. I was on the floor next to you, stroking your hair — the time-honoured means of preventing sickness, obviously.

AS MAC RE-ENACTS THE KISS, HE AND CAROLINE GET CLOSER AND CLOSER TOGETHER.

MAC: I remember you had your hand on my cheek like this, and then...

CAROLINE: And then I looked into your eyes?

MAC: Yeah and then I looked into your eyes. There was a lot of looking going on.

CAROLINE: Yes. And then I kissed you. Clearly not on purpose.

MAC: Clearly.

CAROLINE: And then you kissed me back.

MAC: And then I kissed you back, um — equally accidentally.

CAROLINE: And then?

MAC: And then —

AT THE CRUCIAL SECOND, MAC BREAKS THE MOMENT AND PULLS AWAY.

MAC: — and then I left.

CAROLINE: Well I was totally wasted, I mean otherwise, why would I have kissed you, for God's sake?

MAC: Yeah, exactly.

CAROLINE: I must have been totally totally wasted.

MAC: Totally, totally, I guess, I guess.

CAROLINE WALKS DOWN THE CORRIDOR WATCHED BY MAC, SHE CAN HARDLY STAND UP.

▸▸ STATHAM'S OFFICE

STATHAM IS PUTTING AWAY THE BABY PICTURES. KAREN APPEARS.

KAREN: Hello.

STATHAM: Hello. Can I help you?

KAREN: Well, Joanna says you're to stop ringing her and she meant what she said.

STATHAM: Oh, about what?

KAREN: About how she doesn't want to go out with you any more.

STATHAM: Hmm?

KAREN: It's not a joke, Joanna told me to tell you.

STATHAM: Oh and what were her reasons?

KAREN: She said you'd ask. She said to say boredom. She said the only reason she went out with you was because she was bored and, well she's still bored. You're boring.

STATHAM: Right. You may leave.

KAREN: I'm very sorry.

STATHAM: (SHOUTS) No, don't be nice!

KAREN: Okay. Bye then.

KAREN GOES. STATHAM IS DISTRAUGHT. HE GETS SOME SCISSORS AND GOES TO CUT OFF HIS PENIS, BUT THEN CUTS OFF HIS TIE INSTEAD.

▸▸ OFFICE, END OF DAY

A MOROSE HARRIET HAS BUILT A TOWER OF NAPPIES ON HER DESK. KIM IS LEAVING.

KIM: Perhaps you should call it a day.

HARRIET: A day? Is that a boy or a girl?

KIM: No, I think you should go home, stop thinking about it.

HARRIET: Oh, sorry, my brain's a bit squidgy. I was up five times in the night.

KIM: (SYMPATHETIC) Kids?

HARRIET: No, I was just really hungry.

KIM: See you.

KIM GOES.

HARRIET: Bye.

▸▸ BAR

GUY, MAC AND MARTIN ARE BY THE SHOOTING ARCADE MACHINE. GUY HAS THE MACHINE'S GUN POINTED AT MARTIN.

GUY: So if you're using a handgun of any kind, you do not want to aim here, there's no guarantee of death, bullet lodged in the auditory cortex, you can forget your Dolby and Nicam stereo, pre-frontal cortex wrecked, it's porridge and rubber pants and an exploitative documentary on Channel 4.

MAC: Okay, so you would use a...?

GUY: Magnum.

MAC: Ice cream. Could be a bit messy, if that's your weapon of choice.

GUY: No, toss-pot, a Magnum gun. Probably the most powerful handgun in the world. Imagine, that baby's got a kick on it like a fat girl in heels. Down side, it's very easy to miss, so where would you aim?

MAC: I would aim obviously for the brain, which in your case would be here.

HE POINTS THE GUN AT GUY'S CROTCH.

MAC: I think womankind would applaud me.

GUY: No they wouldn't, they'd hunt you down and kill you with Hoovers.

MARTIN: What about up the nose?

MARTIN MAKES EXPLOSION/DEATH NOISES.

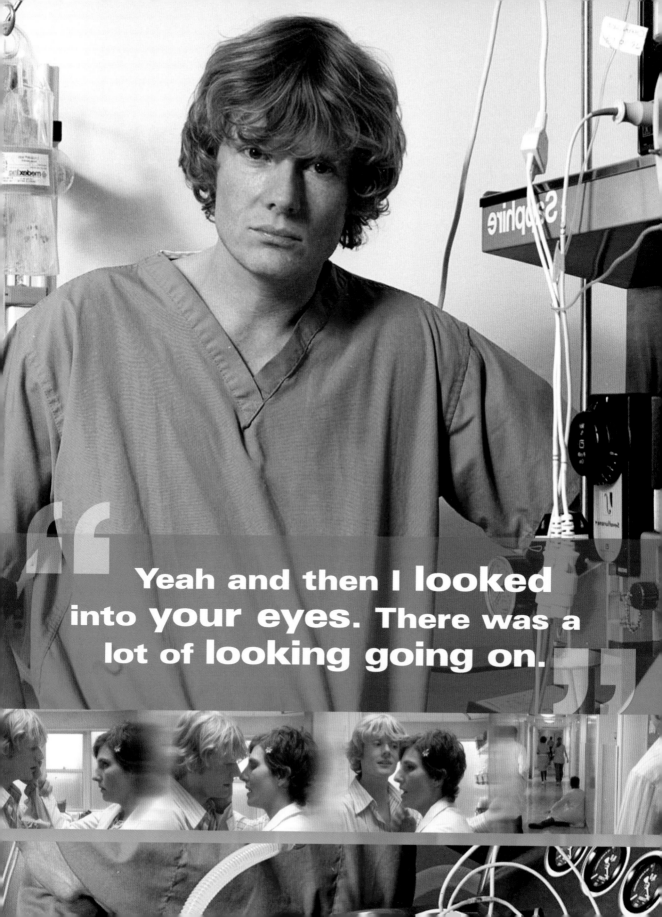

"Yeah and then I looked into your eyes. There was a lot of looking going on."

"What is this, some sort of ginger-dwarf alliance?"

GUY: Yeah, no the bullet has gone in further, but you know, it's survivable, you're a veg. No, what you really need to take out the cerebral cortex is...

MAC: A haircut.

GUY: No, a shotgun, held under the throat. And slash!

MAC: Bang. Or have you now swapped the shotgun for some sort of sword?

GUY: Yeah, bang, slash, blam, whatever. Listen, Martin, you can either do it my way or you can be wrong.

GUY HAS THE GUN IN MARTIN'S MOUTH.

MARTIN: (MUMBLES) Mmrgh...

GUY: What?

MARTIN: Crisp?

GUY: No.

▸▸ STREET, NIGHT

STATHAM IS DRIVING A MILK FLOAT. HE IS SHOUTING, SWEARING, THROWING MILK BOTTLES AND FLICKING V'S AT SOME PASSING WOMEN.

STATHAM: Sod off you, you Jezebel whores! Go on you slutty tarts! Go on with your slitty, slutty, slitty, slutty slots! Go on, sod off, you're all the bloody same!

▸▸ BAR

GUY IS HOLDING THE 'GUN' AT MARTIN AS IF HE WERE A HOSTAGE.

MAC: Put the gun down.

GUY: Put the gun down or the midget gets it.

MAC: I said, put the gun down.

MARTIN: I'm not a midget.

GUY: Or dwarfy here's going to — what is this, some sort of ginger-dwarf alliance?

MARTIN: I'm not a dwarf.

▸▸ STREET, NIGHT

STATHAM IS STILL SHOUTING OUT OF THE MILK FLOAT. HE SEES TWO WOMEN WALKING ALONG THE STREET.

STATHAM: There's a dirty Jezebel! Right, you two dirty whore bitches! Right, I can see you, you dirty sluts! Come here, I'll get you!

HE CHASES AFTER THEM, THROWING MILK BOTTLES, ETC.

STATHAM: What in God's... Off to a nunnery! You slutty tarts! Go on.

▸▸ BAR

GUY: I'm blowing his brains out when I find them...

▸▸ STREET, NIGHT

STATHAM IS STILL IN THE MILK FLOAT, RANTING AT WOMANKIND.

STATHAM: You're all the same, with your filthy bras and your pants and your peep-holes and...

▸▸ BAR

GUY IS POINTING TWO GUNS INTO HIS MOUTH.

▸▸ STREET, NIGHT

STATHAM DRIVES OFF IN THE MILK FLOAT, GOING OVER ROAD HUMPS.

STATHAM: Slutty panties... and you haven't even got a cock! You haven't even got a cock! You whores! You dirty... Ow! You dirty bumpy bastards! Bloody bumps!

EPISODE 7

▶▶ **CAROLINE'S HOUSE, BATHROOM**

CAROLINE IS IN A BUBBLE BATH DREAMING IMAGES OF HOW SHE KISSED MAC AND GUY AT HER PARTY. MARTIN'S VOICE WAKES HER UP.

MARTIN (OOV): Caroline, are you in there?

CAROLINE: I do! Er — I mean... I mean, I am. I'll be out in a minute.

SHE FROTHS UP THE BUBBLES TO LOOK LIKE A PAIR OF BREASTS.

CAROLINE: Meet the girls: Pinky and Perky.

SHE BLOWS THE BUBBLES.

▶▶ **GYM**

JOANNA IS DOING A PILATES CLASS. STATHAM COMES IN.

INSTRUCTOR: And we'll start the side stretch. Breathe in. And just take the ball...

JOANNA: Bloody shitting — ! Who let you in here?!

STATHAM: A word, you and I...

STATHAM FALLS OVER A BALL.

▶▶ **CAROLINE'S HOUSE, BATHROOM**

CAROLINE IS FLICKING WATER AT HER 'FOAM' BREASTS.

▶▶ **GYM**

STATHAM: You've got one last chance.

JOANNA: Get out!

STATHAM: One last chance to have me back.

▶▶ **CAROLINE'S HOUSE, BATHROOM**

CAROLINE IS LOOKING IN THE MIRROR, CLEANING HER TEETH.

CAROLINE: I'm Caroline Secretan, hi. (SHE TRIES OUT THE SOUND OF THAT AGAIN) "Caroline Secretan."

▶▶ **GYM**

JOANNA: Leave me alone Alan, or I'll get a restraining order.

▶▶ **CAROLINE'S HOUSE, BATHROOM**

CAROLINE IS STILL AT THE MIRROR.

CAROLINE: Hello, I'm Caroline MacCartney. "Caroline MacCartney."

THERE'S A KNOCK AT THE BATHROOM DOOR. CAROLINE OPENS IT.

MARTIN: Hi. Um... thanks for letting me stay.

CAROLINE: Yeah, you're welcome. Where did you sleep?

MARTIN: Oh on the sofa.

CAROLINE: Oh.

STATHAM: Look at the state — look at the state of me!! Every moment — well look, what, what do you think I've become?!

JOANNA: What have you become?

STATHAM: I'll — I'll tell you what! A shadow of my former self.

JOANNA: What, a shadow of a pompous arse?!

» CAROLINE'S HOUSE, BATHROOM

MARTIN IS EXAMINING THE BATH. HE FINDS A HAIR AND PUTS IT BETWEEN HIS TEETH.

» GYM

STATHAM: Yes, well if something bad happens, then — then on your head it be.

JOANNA: Oh, if what happens? If somebody steals all your pens again?!

» CAROLINE'S HOUSE, BATHROOM

MARTIN IS TALKING TO THE BATHROOM MIRROR. THE HAIR IS STILL STUCK BETWEEN HIS TEETH.

MARTIN: Hey, how are you doing there? Um... what's that? What, in my teeth? Oh — ah, that's probably one of Caroline's pubes. That is embarrassing.

CAROLINE CALLS THROUGH THE DOOR.

CAROLINE (OOV): Martin, did I leave my watch in there?

MARTIN: Um, yeah...

MARTIN FRANTICALLY TRIES TO GET THE PUBIC HAIR OUT OF HIS TEETH.

CAROLINE: Can I just grab it then?

MARTIN: Um, hang on...

HE OPENS THE DOOR, BUT DOESN'T WANT TO OPEN HIS MOUTH WITH THE HAIR IN HIS TEETH. HE SMILES.

CAROLINE: Oh great, thanks.

MARTIN: Hmm hmm.

CAROLINE: Are you okay?

MARTIN: Hmm?

CAROLINE: Are you okay?

MARTIN: Hmm.

CAROLINE: I'm just going to go to work now. How are you getting there?

MARTIN MUMBLES WITH HIS MOUTH CLOSED.

CAROLINE: Sorry?

MARTIN HIDES HIS FACE BEHIND THE DOOR.

MARTIN: I'll probably get on my scooter. I'll see you there.

CAROLINE: Yeah, okay, right.

» GYM

STATHAM: If something really really bad happens to me, it'll

be your fault!

JOANNA: Oh you're just trying to cheer me up, aren't you?

STATHAM: Yes, you'll be sorry!

JOANNA: Wrong!

THE CLASS ARE WATCHING STATHAM. HE ADDRESSES THEM.

STATHAM: All right, you know — just, you know, don't worry, I'm not — I'm not looking at your leotards. And even if I was, I'm a d—

A BALL HITS STATHAM AND HE FALLS OVER. THE WOMEN LAUGH.

▸▸ LOCKER AREA

GUY HAS A STRANGE PIECE OF HEADGEAR THAT LOOKS LIKE

A WICKER BASKET ATTACHED TO OLD-FASHIONED FLYING GOGGLES.

MAC: What the fuck is that?

GUY: My topmiler.

MAC: Your what?!

GUY: My new topmiler. It needs a bit of cranking up; I've got a semi-final on Sunday.

MAC: Oh yeah? This is your Whiteleaf thing is it?

GUY: Whitliff.

MAC: No, I've seen it written down, it says Whiteleaf.

GUY: Um, I was there for twelve years, I think I know how it's pronounced, thank you.

MAC: So, semi-final eh?

GUY: World Championship semi-final.

MAC: I'm sorry, World Championship semi-final. How many people play Guy-ball?

GUY: It's 'Gee-Ball'.

MAC: Gee-Ball, Gee-Ball? Of course Gee-Ball is Guy-Ball isn't it, actually? It's... it's Guy Secretan Ball.

GUY: Yeah, you can laugh if you like.

MAC: Thank Christ for that.

GUY: This country could soon have a new World Champion. And God knows, we've got precious few of those.

MAC: To get to the semi-final, yeah — was it... *two* fixtures that you played?

GUY: Well, I had a walkover in the first round. Markus Geissler had shin splints, the big Austrian.

MAC: So that was what, one? One match?

GUY: Yeah.

MAC: One weedy match.

GUY: I did win it in five straight clappers.

GUY PUTS THE TALL HAT ON HIS HEAD.

GUY: What?

MAC PUTS AN EMPTY PAPER CUP IN IT.

GUY: Oi! Is that a...? Did you? Is that? Oi!

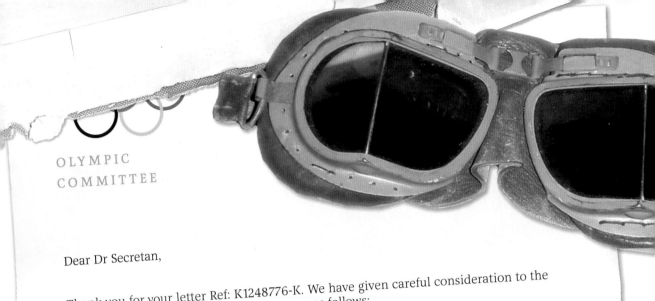

OLYMPIC
COMMITTEE

Dear Dr Secretan,

Thank you for your letter Ref: K1248776-K. We have given careful consideration to the matters you raised and our conclusions are as follows:

- We do not think that Guyball is 'the bollocks'.

- Guyball will not be included in the forthcoming Olympic Games.

- Contrary to whatever your friend 'Diggler' might have heard, we do not accept 'bungs'.

- We are not biased against Switzerland or any other nation.

- We do not care if you know where we live.

Your letter and emails have been forwarded to the appropriate authorities.

Sincerely.

Ram Pakrabathi
Administrator (Field Games) O.C.

HE EVENTUALLY GETS THE CUP OUT OF THE HAT. THEN HE WALKS UP AND DOWN IN IT, TRYING OUT SKILFUL MATCH MOVES.

▶▶ **MAIN CORRIDOR**

MARTIN IS HOLDING A LARGE ENVELOPE. BOYCE COMES UP TO HIM.

BOYCE: Martee. Ooh, results!

MARTIN: Yeah, I haven't managed to open it yet.

BOYCE: My fingers may be stronger than yours.

HE SNATCHES THE ENVELOPE. MARTIN SNATCHES IT BACK.

MARTIN: Oh no.

KIM JOINS THEM AS THEY WALK ALONG.

BOYCE: Martin's results.

KIM: Well open it.

MARTIN: I will.

BOYCE: When?

MARTIN: When I'm ready.

THEY HEAD UPSTAIRS.

BOYCE: I'll give you a fiver if you open it.

MARTIN: No.

KIM: I'll give you ten quid and a kiss. No tongues.

MARTIN: Oh no.

BOYCE: Twenty quid and a hand job?

MARTIN: No way.

BOYCE: So go on, name your price.

MARTIN: What, to open it now? Before I'm ready?

BOYCE: Yeah.

MARTIN: Before I am properly mentally attuned?

BOYCE: Yes.

MARTIN: 160 pounds.

KIM: I think I'll wait.

MARTIN: Yeah.

KIM WALKS AWAY.

BOYCE : Right, here you go.

BOYCE GETS OUT HIS MONEY.

BOYCE : 160? Twenty...

MARTIN : No no no no, no no, sorry, I meant half a million pounds.

BOYCE: Oh, too hot for me, I fold.

BOYCE WALKS AWAY.

▶▶ **DAY WARD**

CAROLINE COMES OVER TO MARTIN.

CAROLINE: Have you seen Mac?

MARTIN: No.

CAROLINE: Or Guy?

MARTIN: No.

CAROLINE: Typical! Even the available men aren't.

CAROLINE SEES A PICTURE OF JESUS'S FACE OUTSIDE THE WINDOW. SHE'S DISTRACTED.

MARTIN: I love you.

CAROLINE: What?

MARTIN: Nothing.

CAROLINE: I've just seen the face of Jesus at the window.

MARTIN: Okay.

▶▶ **RADIOLOGY CORRIDOR**

STATHAM IS WALKING DOWN THE CORRIDOR. A REMOTE

HER BAG. THERE IS MASHED POTATO ALL OVER EVERYTHING. KAREN LOOKS AT THE MESSY PILE.

HARRIET: Mashed potato.

KAREN: Right.

ON THE OTHER SIDE OF THE OFFICE, KIM IS WINDING A RULER ONTO THE BACK OF RACHEL'S THONG.

KIM: One...

RACHEL: Yeah.

KIM: Two...

RACHEL: Yeah.

KIM: Three...

RACHEL: Ow!

KIM: Ready?

RACHEL: Yeah.

KIM: Go.

KIM LETS GO OF THE THONG 'PROPELLER' AND RACHEL PRE-TENDS TO FLY ACROSS THE OFFICE, MAKING AEROPLANE NOISES.

KIM: Yeah!

CONTROL CAR IS DRIVING PAST, BEHIND HIM.

▸▸ OFFICE

HARRIET SITS DOWN AT HER DESK AND STARTS TO UNPACK

▸▸ STATHAM'S OFFICE

STATHAM PLAYS HIS ANSWERPHONE MESSAGE.

ANSWERPHONE: One new message. (BEEP)

JOANNA (OOV): It's over Alan. Never contact me. You will never feel my super vagina again.

STATHAM CONSIDERS THIS FOR A MOMENT.

STATHAM: (IRRITATED) I wish people would leave a name…

▸▸ **DAY WARD RECEPTION**

MAC: All work and no play…

CAROLINE: Do I get a medal?

MAC: Your reward will be in Devon.

CAROLINE: Devon?

MAC: Oh no, sorry. It's heaven isn't it, actually? Yeah, that's right. I used to get them confused when I was a kid, you know. When people die, they go to Devon.

CAROLINE: That's funny.

MAC: Well not really, no. It ruined my summer holidays; they'd be terrifying; I thought my whole family was dead.

CAROLINE: Mac, do you think you'll ever have kids?

MAC: Oh, whose are these do you think?

HE PICKS UP A PAIR OF GLASSES FROM THE DESK.

CAROLINE: I have no idea.

MAC: Here. Come here.

MAC PUTS THE GLASS ON CAROLINE.

MAC: Oh! Oh Nurse Todd, but you look beautiful with your glasses on.

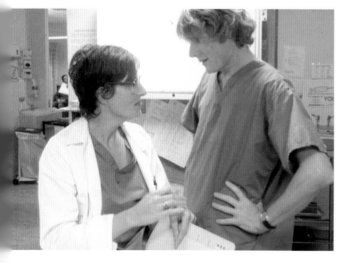

CAROLINE: Oh, oh no, they smell rough. Eurgh.

SHE TAKES THE GLASSES OFF.

MAC: See you later, smelly four-eyes.

HE GOES.

CAROLINE: Doctor Caroline MacCartney…

▸▸ **STAFF LIAISON OFFICE**

SUE WHITE IS AT HER DESK. GUY IS HOLDING A SMALL BOY UNDER HIS ARM.

SUE: What is that?

GUY: It's a kid. What do they eat?

SUE: Is it lost?

GUY: Er — no no no, I borrowed it off someone, because apparently women love it and I'm trying to pull. Do anything for me? Is it working?

SUE: Not really, no.

GUY: No, didn't think so.

HE PUTS THE BOY ON SUE'S DESK.

GUY: There, you have it.

HE LEAVES. SUE LOOKS AT THE BOY.

SUE: Huh. Hello.

BOY: Hi.

SUE: Hi there. Do you want to — do you want one of these?

SHE HOLDS OUT A LOLLIPOP.

BOY: Yes please.

SUE: Well you can't have it.

SHE PUTS IT BACK IN THE DRAWER.

▸▸ **OFFICE**

JOANNA ENTERS HER OFFICE TO FIND STATHAM HANGING BY A NOOSE AROUND HIS NECK. JOANNA IGNORES HIM, BUT JUST BEFORE SHE LEAVES SHE STICKS A POST-IT NOTE ON HIS TIE AND FEELS HIS CROTCH.

JOANNA: Don't forget you've got students waiting.

JOANNA GOES OUT OF HER OFFICE AND SHUTS THE DOOR, LEAVING STATHAM HANGING THERE.

KIM: We were going to stop him, but we thought you'd be cross.

JOANNA: Hmm.

JOANNA LEAVES THE OUTER OFFICE.

STATHAM: Well, I think I've made my point. Yes. Oh. Er, actually I might — I might need a bit of help. Hello?

THE GIRLS IN THE OUTER OFFICE IGNORE HIM CALLING OUT.

STATHAM: Hello? Anyone? Oh dear. Hello? I need a wee.

▶▶ NEO NATAL WARD

CAROLINE IS LOOKING AT THE BABIES IN THE NURSERY. GUY COMES ALONG AND LOOKS AT THEM THROUGH THE WINDOW. HE SECRETLY RUBS HIS EYES A LOT BEFORE CAROLINE COMES OUT.

CAROLINE: Hi.

GUY: Hi.

CAROLINE: Are you all right?

GUY: Yeah, I'm just looking at those children.

CAROLINE: I see.

GUY: I love children.

CAROLINE: Really?

GUY: Yeah. I'm not a paedophile or anything, obviously, I just think they're great. Oh. I hate to see them suffering. Do you like kids?

CAROLINE: Er, yeah.

GUY: Yeah. I'm just getting broody I guess. There's one hell of a dad in me bursting to get out.

CAROLINE: Crikey.

GUY: You know, I believe that children are our future.

CAROLINE: Teach them well and let them lead the way?

GUY: Sorry?

CAROLINE: It's Whitney Houston, "Children are our future, da da da…"

GUY: My God! My God! She knew what she was talking about.

GUY GOES. CAROLINE LEANS BACK AGAINST THE WINDOW.

CAROLINE: Doctor Caroline Secretan. Hi, I'm Doctor Caroline Secretan. I'm Doctor Caroline Secretan, hi.

SOMEONE WALKS PAST.

▸▸ **LYNDON'S OFFICE**

JOANNA ENTERS SEDUCTIVELY, WEARING A FUR COAT.

LYNDON: Hello.

JOANNA: I'm completely naked under here.

LYNDON: Okay.

JOANNA: Do you want to see?

LYNDON: Not really.

A SLIGHTLY GEEKY MEMBER OF LYNDON'S IT TEAM APPEARS FROM UNDER THE OTHER DESK.

YOUNG IT GUY: I wouldn't mind.

LYNDON SMILES. JOANNA GOES.

▸▸ **STAFF LIAISON OFFICE**

MARTIN IS WITH SUE WHITE, WHO IS SITTING ON THE DESK, PAINTING HER TOE NAILS.

MARTIN: I don't think I can go through with it.

SUE: Well don't.

MARTIN: No. If I fail, I'm dead meat, and I'm up to my ears in debt, so... What do you mean "don't"?

SUE: Well, just pretend it doesn't exist, you know, look.

SHE SITS ON THE ENVELOPE.

SUE: There. Out of sight, out of mind.

MARTIN: Right.

SUE: Right, blow.

SHE STICKS HER LEG TOWARDS MARTIN SO THAT HE CAN BLOW ON HER TOE NAILS.

SUE: Don't get any spit on them!

MARTIN: I've got a doctor's pubic hair in my tummy.

SUE: Okay. (SHE GIVES HIM HER OTHER FOOT) Blow. Right, fuck off. (PAUSE) Is it Mac's?

MARTIN: No. Oh, can I get my results envelope back please?

SUE: Your what?

MARTIN: Results envelope back? That you're sitting on? Please?

SUE: What envelope?

MARTIN: Right, I'm going to wait.

▸▸ **THEATRE**

MAC, CAROLINE AND GUY ARE PERFORMING AN OPERATION.

MAC: That part of the day that we've all been looking forward to. Nurse Richardson, perhaps you'd like to choose — movie genre or regional accent?

THEATRE NURSE: Regional accent please.

GUY LOOKS ANNOYED.

MAC: Excellent choice. Doctor Todd, perhaps you'd like to pick today's regional accent?

CAROLINE: Er...

GUY: Surrey. Buckinghamshire... er... Swiss...

CAROLINE: North East, Newcastle.

GUY: (VERY WORRIED NOW) Oh...

MAC: Tricky, but always very funny, good choice. (GEORDIE) All reet then, shall we get on and stort wur erperation?

GUY: (VERY STRANGE ATTEMPT AT GEORDIE) Yaahs, I think we showd. Yass, I think wee shood... (DROPPING THE 'ACCENT') Oh I'm not doing it, it's bloody silly.

CAROLINE AND MAC CONTINUE WITH THEIR REASONABLE MOCK-GEORDIE ACCENTS.

CAROLINE: Ah wus just gannin to fetch yus a bonny scalpel, pet.

MAC: Aye, thank you very much — would yus like a little fishy on a little dishy?

GUY: (NOT GEORDIE, BIG SULK) Why, aye.

MAC: Champion! Thou shalt have a mackerel! Alreet then, I divn't think we should wayest any more time, so it's eyes doon and let's errpen her up. Is she totally out?

GUY: Yows, I think she's tootally aaht, she's... yes, she's tortally... (HE GIVES UP AGAIN) Oh, I'm not playing.

CAROLINE: Oh come on man, come and play.

GUY: I'd have done it if it was movies.

GUY GOES TO LIGHT UP A CIGARETTE. THE OTHERS LOOK AT HIM.

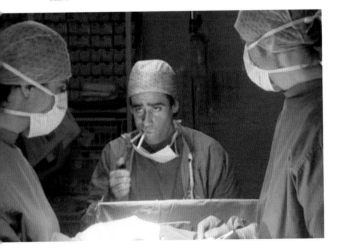

GUY: What? Does it say no smoking? ('GUY-GEORDIE') Dus it say no smorking? What way to the dole office? Do you know, I'm unemployed and I have a mullet?

▶▶ **STAFF LIAISON OFFICE**

MARTIN IS WAITING TO GET HIS ENVELOPE BACK.

SUE: Next!

PEOPLE COME AND GO, BUT HE STILL DOESN'T GET HIS ENVELOPE.

▶▶ **THEATRE, LATER**

GUY: Look, if you don't stop talking like bloody Jimmy Nail or Ant and Dec, I'm going to turn off the machine!

MAC: (GEORDIE) All reet pets, I want you all to resume normal accentage.

CAROLINE: (NORMAL VOICE) I'm just saying that if he's failed again, I think it might tip him over the edge, that's all.

GUY PLAYS WITH A RESPIRATION PIPE AND INFLATING BAG.

GUY: Yeah, survival of the fittest. Grrr! Martin needs to toughen up. Come on!

▶▶ **STAFF LIAISON OFFICE**

SUE SNOGS A MEMBER OF STAFF. MARTIN STILL DOESN'T GET HIS RESULTS ENVELOPE BACK.

▶▶ **THEATRE**

GUY: Maybe he's not cut out to be a doctor, maybe he should just, I don't know, stick to being like a nurse. I mean they can be as thick as pig-shit.

A METAL KIDNEY DISH HITS GUY IN THE FACE WITH SOME FORCE.

GUY: Ow! Fucking ow!

THEATRE NURSE: (UNCONCERNED) Sorry about that.

GUY: No! I could have got concussion!

CAROLINE: Toughen up Guy.

MAC: Survival of the fittest.

GUY: Grrrr!

▶▶ **STAFF LIAISON OFFICE**

SUE IS STILL SEEING PEOPLE WHILE MARTIN IS WAITING.

SUE: (HANDING SOMEONE A LEAFLET) Take that, 'Dealing With Difficult People' and fuck off!! Wanker!

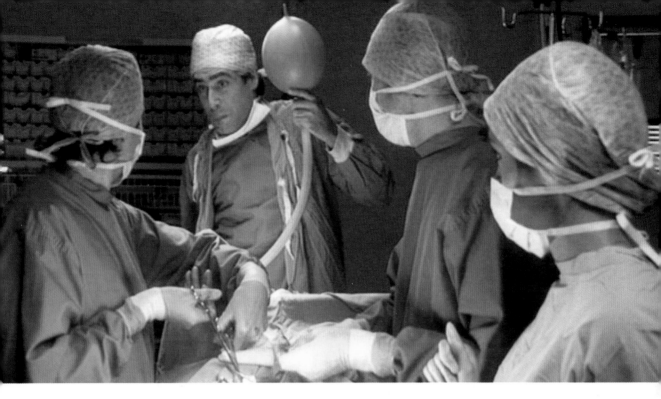

AT LAST SUE STANDS UP AND MARTIN GRABS HIS ENVELOPE AND LEAVES.

▸▸ THEATRE

GUY: Hold on, watch this.

GUY FARTS INTO THE TUBE AND INFLATES THE VENTILATING BAG.

GUY: Ooh. "Now that's magic! Magic!"

MAC: Magic?

GUY: "That's Magic."

HE GOES TO PUT THE TUBE IN HIS MOUTH TO INFLATE THE BAG AGAIN, BUT STOPS HIMSELF.

GUY: Oh, no! Oh that's been right on my anus.

▸▸ CAR PARK

GUY IS SELLOTAPING A WASTEPAPER BASKET TO MARTIN'S HEAD. MAC IS WITH THEM.

GUY: Up, up, up.

MARTIN: Look, I'm worried about my hair.

GUY: Don't be such a wimp.

MARTIN: Yeah, but why can't we use the proper thing with the leather strap?

GUY: We can't use an international standard topmiler, don't be ridiculous. Anyway, it's mine. Right, okay, this is a classic three-person variation of the game. Now tilt your head forward, forward, forward. Arret! Okay. And we just have to put the ball into the basket.

MARTIN: I can't go and see patients with a basket on my head, no way.

GUY: Don't leave the parish, all right? If you reach the maison, put your left arm in the air and shout "maison".

MAC: Maison!

GUY: Yeah. There are no burrow tactics and there are no hedgehogs, okay? Is that clear?

MARTIN: No, not really, I can't...

GUY: Right, okay. I won the toss, so Stickles are random, yes?

MAC: Oh yeah.

GUY: And it's a two-bounce Ubique. Right, go, move. Run! Run! Run, run! Move, damn it, or I'll towel whip you!

MARTIN RUNS OFF WITH THE BASKET ON HIS HEAD.

GUY: Right my friend, the game is on.

MAC: Yes. One thing...

GUY: What?

"There are no **burrow tactics** and there are no **hedgehogs**, **okay?**"

MAC: Martin likes me!

GUY: Go, ha ha!

MAC AND GUY CHASE AFTER MARTIN ROUND THE CAR PARK, CLAMBERING OVER CARS, TRYING TO GET BALLS INTO THE BASKET.

▶▶ CANTEEN

LYNDON IS HAVING A COFFEE. STATHAM COMES UP TO HIM.

STATHAM: You think you're clever, don't you?

LYNDON: Reasonably, yes.

STATHAM: Huh, you think — you think you're so clever. You think you're a real man because you've got Joanna trotting around after you like a little puppy!

LYNDON: If you say so.

STATHAM: Yes, well we are going to find out who the real man is, right here, right now!

LYNDON: I'll just drink my coffee, thank you.

STATHAM: Yes, oh well I bet you would mister, but that's not an option.

STATHAM GETS A ROPE OUT OF A BAG.

LYNDON: What's that?

STATHAM: This is how we're going to decide.

LYNDON: What?

STATHAM: Tug of war, get up.

LYNDON: Hey, you've got to be joking.

STATHAM: Get up, we're going to have a tug of war.

LYNDON: I don't want to.

STATHAM: Get up now! Get up for the tug of war, get up, get up, get up, get up, get up, get up...

LYNDON GETS UP, CAUSING STATHAM TO RECOIL WITH FRIGHT.

LYNDON: Right, give me that.

THEY CLEAR A SPACE AND TAKE AN END OF THE ROPE EACH.

STATHAM: Ready?

LYNDON: Ready.

STATHAM: And, go!

LYNDON EFFORTLESSLY PULLS STATHAM TOWARDS HIM, STATHAM'S FEET SLIDING HOPELESSLY ALONG THE FLOOR BENEATH HIM.

STATHAM: Wrong shoes. Wait there.

STATHAM GOES AND LYNDON SITS DOWN AGAIN.

▶▶ OFFICE

HARRIET PUTS SOME WIND CHIMES UP ON HER DESK LAMP AND BREATHES DEEPLY.

▶▶ THEATRE

MAC HAS JUST FINISHED AN OPERATION.

MAC: Having spread that little bit of joy, I'm out of here. Thank you, thank you, very very good. Goodbye.

GUY: Bye.

MAC: Bye.

MAC GOES, LEAVING GUY WITH CAROLINE.

GUY: Who was that again?

CAROLINE: Guy...

GUY: No, that can't be right, I'm Guy.

CAROLINE: No, listen, there's something I've been meaning to say to you.

GUY: We can't, not here, people are watching. And anyway, it wouldn't be hygienic.

THEY LEAVE THEATRE AND GO INTO THE ANAESTHETIST'S ROOM.

CAROLINE: No just stop it! For once will you?! You seem like a complete knob-head, obviously, and everyone knows you're a bastard...

GUY: Oh, thank you very much!

CAROLINE: ...But I think I know why you do it. Now in there, you're the only one who doesn't use a mask, right? But actually you do. There's layers and layers of mask. And I think that if you just peeled back the layers of mask, then — then the onion becomes a lot less of a red herring.

GUY: Does it?

CAROLINE: Yes. And you see, there are good bits to the onion, like... like at my party, and you know, your thoughtful presents, and um — and the man who thinks that children are the future. But it's all surrounded by this, these yucky layers that have all gone a bit yellow and this hard outer shiny skin of someone who's pretending to be unloveable, but well maybe he's just scared, I don't know. Maybe he needs to find someone who can peel back all the layers and look at the — look at the raw, sensitive vegetable in the mirror.

GUY: (GETTING EMOTIONAL) Oh my God... You're the first person who's ever really understood.

CAROLINE: What?

GUY: You're the first person to see under my onion layers and see the real me.

CAROLINE: Okay. Okay, right, so... maybe we can have a grown-up chat, you know, cut through all the bullshit?

GUY: Or — maybe we could go for a drive in the country, you know, fresh air, open spaces, meeee?

CAROLINE: I'm strangely aroused.

GUY: Inevitably.

CAROLINE: I assume we won't be heading too far north.

GUY: No. Well my car is instantly immobilised if I go past Luton.

THEY WALK OFF.

▸▸ OFFICE

SOMEONE WALKS PAST HARRIET'S DESK AND SETS OFF HER WIND CHIMES. SHE BREATHES DEEPLY. JOANNA IS IN HER OFFICE. SUDDENLY A LOUD HAILER STARTS UP OUTSIDE THE WINDOW. IT'S STATHAM STANDING ON A CAR.

STATHAM: (SINGS) "All by myself, don't want to be — all by myself... any more..." Still here. "All by..."

JOANNA GETS A POT PLANT AND HURLS IT AT STATHAM. IT MISSES AND SMASHES ONTO THE CAR.

▸▸ CANTEEN

BOYCE IS TRYING TO GET MARTIN TO OPEN HIS RESULTS ENVELOPE.

BOYCE: Open it. Open it, open it, open it, open it...

MARTIN: No.

GUY COMES IN.

GUY: Oi, I've written a song, it goes — (RAPS) "Who's the man, who's the man, is Guy the man? Yes, yes, I am."

BOYCE: Just going to get a salad.

BOYCE LEAVES THEM.

GUY: All right, wee man?

MARTIN: Yeah. You seem pleased with yourself. More than usual I mean.

GUY: Yeah, because I've cracked it. Me and Caroline. I thought you might like to be the first to know.

MARTIN: What — you and Caroline have…? You — no! What, you mean you, you and…? Where?

GUY: Not yet, but you're right, no point in wasting any time. Thanks Martin, tonight is the night.

MARTIN: No, I didn't mean it!

GUY: I wonder if you could pop out and get me some condoms. Yeah, I know what you're going to say, surely I've got condoms already? Well yes I have, but I need special ones. The pharmacy will know what I'm talking about, you don't need any money, I've got an account.

MARTIN: I'm not…

GUY: Go!

MARTIN: But…

GUY: Now!

MARTIN LEAVES, VERY DISTRESSED.

▶▶ OUTPATIENTS CORRIDOR

CAROLINE IS WITH MAC. A BOY IS PLAYING WITH A REMOTE CONTROL CAR IN THE CORRIDOR.

CAROLINE: Oh, I always wanted one of those.

MAC: What's that — a small boy?

CAROLINE: No, a remote control car.

MAC: Don't move.

MAC GETS THE REMOTE CONTROL CAR FOR CAROLINE.

▶▶ OFFICE

HARRIET IS GETTING INCREASINGLY ANNOYED WITH THE WIND CHIMES, WHICH ARE SUPPOSED TO CALM HER.

▶▶ OUTPATIENTS CORRIDOR

MAC GIVES THE CAR CONTROLLER TO CAROLINE.

MAC: Here we go, here we go.

CAROLINE: I can't believe you gave him a lighter!

MAC: No, it's all right, I got them in the market. They're only five for a pound.

CAROLINE: Mac?!

MAC: They only spark, he'll be fine. Ready? Live the dream.

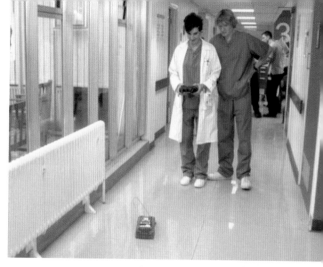

CAROLINE DRIVES THE CAR INTO MAC'S FOOT.

CAROLINE: Oh, sorry.

MAC: Nice one.

CAROLINE: No…

CAROLINE MESSES AROUND WITH THE CONTROLS, BUT THE CAR WON'T MOVE.

MAC: Living up to expectations?

CAROLINE: All right, just wait for a second. Oh, um…

THE CAR RACES OFF AND CRASHES INTO A WALL.

MAC: One early tip is to master the basic controls first and leave the big stunts until later on.

CAROLINE: Yeah, yeah, okay.

MAC: Let me show you, let me show you.

CAROLINE: No no no, I'll be fine.

MAC: No, go on, no, trust me, trust me.

MAC PUTS HIS ARMS ROUND CAROLINE TO SHOW HER THE CONTROLS.

MAC: It's forwards and backwards, yeah?

CAROLINE: Yeah.

MAC: That is left and right. Left and right, forwards and backwards.

CAROLINE: Ah ha. And is that the same as we grown-ups call reverse?

MAC: Was I being patronising?

CAROLINE: No no no, just childish.

MAC: Well thank God for that. Here we go. Forwards and backwards...

THEY BOTH TURN TO EACH OTHER AT THE SAME MOMENT AND FREEZE, LOCKED IN AN EMBARRASSING YET INTIMATE STARE. THEY ARE SUDDENLY AWARE THAT MAC'S ARM IS AROUND HER. MAC LIFTS HIS ARM BUT CAROLINE IS HOLDING ONTO THE CAR CONTROLLER, AND HIS ARM IS MOMENTARILY STUCK.

MAC: I'll remove my arm then.

CAROLINE: Yeah, if you wouldn't mind.

MAC: Yeah.

CAROLINE: Well yeah, thanks — thanks for the ride.

MAC: Thank you very much.

CAROLINE: Can you smell burning?

▸▸ OFFICE

SOMEONE HITS THE CHIMES ON HARRIET'S DESK. SHE CAN'T TAKE IT ANY MORE — SHE PULLS THEM OFF THE LIGHT AND SHUTS THEM IN HER DRAWER.

▸▸ STAFF LIAISON OFFICE

STATHAM SITS OPPOSITE SUE WHITE.

STATHAM: I don't know, I don't know, it's all the same, she hates me!

SUE: Okay, let's just calm down Doctor Statham, let's try to deal with this rationally. Right. Let's take a few moments to breathe deeply.

STATHAM: Right, well, all right, if you think that'll help.

STATHAM BREATHES DEEPLY.

SUE: That's it, that's it, close your eyes, close your eyes and just try... try to relax. That's it.

STATHAM: Yes.

STATHAM TAKES DEEP BREATHS AND CLOSES HIS EYES.

SUE: Just centre yourself.

SUE CRAWLS QUICKLY UNDER HER DESK.

STATHAM: Yes, yes... Oh, yes, yes... and in a sense, that does... that does...

HE OPENS HIS EYES TO FIND THAT SUE HAS APPARENTLY DISAPPEARED.

STATHAM: Oh you — you bloody bastard! You bloody bastard! You bloody, bloody, bloody, bloody bastard!

THE PHONE RINGS. STATHAM ANSWERS IT.

STATHAM: Yes, hello? ...No, no no no, I'm afraid she's just nipped out... to do a poo on a plate. No. ...Director of Finance, yes. Right, wait. Hmm? No, no it is not Alan Statham, it's somebody completely different.

HE PUTS THE PHONE DOWN.

STATHAM: Right.

HE ATTACKS SUE'S OFFICE, STAPLING HER CHEESE PLANT LEAVES TOGETHER AND MESSING UP HER TELEPHONE INDEX FILE. THE FACE OF JESUS APPEARS AT THE WINDOW. STATHAM ISN'T QUITE SURE WHAT HE'S SEEN.

▸▸ MESS

MARTIN IS CLUTCHING HIS UNOPENED RESULTS ENVELOPE.

CAROLINE: Think positively, breathe and just do it, it'll be fine.

MARTIN: Yeah, but what if it isn't?

ANGELA: (SOOTHING) We're here for you.

GUY: What the fuck is all this therapy shit?

MARTIN: It's here.

GUY: What is, Christmas? A new ice age? A cleaner, brighter wash, what?

ANGELA: Martin's got his results.

GUY: Oh, is it terminal?

ANGELA: His MRCP.

MARTIN: Oh, I feel sick.

GUY: Yeah, so do I. It's the aroma of 'women who care' mingled with Martin's fear.

MARTIN: If I've failed, that's going to be the end.

GUY: Oh thank God for that!

ANGELA: Look, this is actually quite a big deal, in case you hadn't noticed!

GUY: Okay, then. Well let's get it over with.

GUY SNATCHES THE ENVELOPE.

CAROLINE: No no, you can't do that!

GUY: No, come on, it's eating away at you like a cancerous growth, let's whip it out.

CAROLINE: Guy, you can't do that.

ANGELA: I'll do it.

CAROLINE: Angela!

GUY: Listen, you'll thank me for this later, let's get it over and done with.

MARTIN: No.

CAROLINE: Martin, maybe it's for the best.

MARTIN: Okay, right. Whatever I do, don't stop, just open it, okay?

GUY: All right.

GUY STARTS TO OPEN THE ENVELOPE.

MARTIN: No! No, I didn't mean it...!

GUY: Can you restrain him please, can you restrain him? Ready? Here I go.

HE OPENS THE ENVELOPE, RUSTLING IT IN MARTIN'S EAR.

GUY: Here it comes. You can hear that? That's the result, there it is. Oh yes, oh oh oh. (HE LOOKS AT THE LETTER) Ooh. I know the answer.

MARTIN: Oh God!

GUY: It's in my head, it exists. Do you want to hear it?

MARTIN: No. Yes. Go on tell me, quick.

GUY: Martin Dear...

MARTIN: Yeah?

GUY: You have...

ANGELA: Oh come on Guy, get on with it!

GUY: Okay, Martin Dear, you have...

BOYCE COMES INTO THE ROOM.

BOYCE: Who wants to suck my cock?

ANGELA: Sssh!

CAROLINE: No!

GUY: Well Martin might want to in a minute, because — congratulations Martin, you have passed with merit! You are now a proper doctor...!

GOING INTO SLOW MOTION, THEY ALL HUG EACH OTHER AND CELEBRATE. BOYCE DRINKS FROM A BOTTLE; GUY TAKES ADVANTAGE OF THE SITUATION TO TURN HIS HUGS WITH THE GIRLS INTO LECHEROUS ATTEMPTED SNOGS. THEY BREAK FROM SLOW MOTION.

GUY: Good boy! Martin's passed his exams!

ALL: Yes!!

MARTIN: Yes!

ALL: Wahay! Martin! Yes!

BOYCE: Martee! Martee!

A TRIUMPHANT MARTIN RUNS OFF WITH HIS RESULTS LETTER. THE OTHERS ARE STILL CELEBRATING.

GUY: Hey, hey hey hey, hey! Look, what's wrong with you? Are you mad? I was joking! Of course he didn't pass, he failed! What's wrong with you people?

GUY LAUGHS. NOBODY ELSE SAYS ANYTHING.

GUY: What? (SILENCE) What?! What?!! Oh — oh — so now I'm not allowed to make jokes about Martin and his exams, is that it? Is that — ? Oh Christ…!

▸▸ **MAIN CORRIDOR**

JOANNA SEES MARTIN. WHEN SHE'S SURE NO ONE'S LOOKING, SHE APPROACHES HIM.

JOANNA: Well?

MARTIN: I failed.

JOANNA: Oh boo hoo. God!

SHE PUSHES HIS STETHOSCOPE ONTO THE TOP OF HIS HEAD.

JOANNA: Tosser!

JOANNA WALKS OFF IN DISGUST. MARTIN IS UPSET AND LIES ON THE FLOOR WEEPING. NO ONE TAKES ANY NOTICE OF HIM.

▸▸ **MESS**

AN ANGRY-LOOKING MAC COMES IN TO FIND GUY, WHO IS EATING A BOWL OF CORNFLAKES AND TALKING TO SOMEONE.

GUY: …That's how I lost my virginity. She had nice tits for a forty-five-year-old. I haven't seen her since though.

MAC: Well?

GUY: Well what, you scrawny poof?

MAC SHOVES GUY'S FACE INTO HIS BOWL OF CORNFLAKES.

GUY: (QUITE SHOCKED) You're not a poof! You're not a poof! You're not a poof!

MAC: And…?

GUY: And — you are a poof!

MAC THROWS THE BOWL OF CORNFLAKES OVER GUY.

MAC: Come on!

> Harriet
>
> Health and Safety need you to erect a screen around your desk — your face is irritating other members of staff (me).
>
> Joanna

GUY: What?!

MAC: Come on!

GUY: What are you doing?! Get off.

THEY START TO FIGHT.

MAC: Not the hands, not the hands!

GUY: Yeah, well not the hair!

MAC PICKS UP A KNIFE.

GUY: That, Mac — that is really sharp.

GUY HAS A MUG OF HOT COFFEE.

MAC: That's hot.

GUY: Yeah, and I'll use it!

MAC SWAPS HIS KNIFE FOR A MUG OF HOT COFFEE AND STARTS SPILLING IT ONTO GUY.

GUY: Argh! Mac! Don't! Don't — put it down, put the coffee down.

MAC: Aargh!

GUY: Put it down! Put it down! We'll talk, I'm sorry. I'm putting it down.

THEY PUT THE COFFEE MUGS DOWN.

GUY: Look — okay? It's down, all right? Now just sit down, sit down and we'll talk, okay? No, the other chair, I'll sit on this chair. Sit down.

MAC GOES TO THE OTHER CHAIR.

GUY: All right?

GUY SUDDENLY PUSHES MAC INTO THE CHAIR AND MAKES A DASH FOR IT. MAC RUNS OUT AND CHASES HIM DOWN THE STAIRS.

GUY: Out of my way, baldy!

GUY KNOCKS FILES OUT OF A MAN'S ARMS.

▶▶ **CANTEEN**

THE FIGHT CONTINUES IN THE CANTEEN. GUY DELIBERATELY SITS WITH A MAN EATING HIS LUNCH, THINKING THIS MAKES HIM SAFE.

GUY: Hi.

MAC LAUNCHES HIMSELF AT GUY AND THEY FIGHT OVER THE TABLE.

GUY: Ow! You've got your knee on my balls! Ow! My — your knee, your knee! Ow!

MAC: Shit!

▶▶ **HOSPITAL CHAPEL**

STATHAM IS WAILING AND RANTING IN DESPAIR.

STATHAM: Oh, you big bitch! You bitches! So thank you, thank you God! Thank you so very much for ruining my life, if you exist, which — which I doubt that you do, otherwise you wouldn't have taken her from me. Right! One — one more chance! One more chance to bring her back. Look — I'll start counting. Right! One. Two. Three. Come on — four! Five!

A WOMAN COMES OVER, UNSEEN BY STATHAM.

CHAPLAIN: (GENTLY) Hello there.

STATHAM: Oh my fucksy! Oh. I — I thought you were her. But I suppose I have to face it, you know — God's a sod! She's — she's gone.

CHAPLAIN: Oh, I'm so sorry. Was it sudden?

STATHAM: Yes, yes and no. It's... in a sense I — I could see it coming and in another sense, I — I couldn't.

CHAPLAIN: It doesn't make it any easier does it?

STATHAM: No. No. And here I am, an empty... hole.

CHAPLAIN: Would you like to light a candle for her? Some people find that very comforting. Death is never easy.

STATHAM: My God, is she dead?!

CHAPLAIN: Who?

STATHAM: Joanna.

CHAPLAIN: Joanna?

STATHAM: Joanna.

CHAPLAIN: Joanna...?

STATHAM: She — no no. No no no no. No, she just dumped me, like a — like a piece of old furniture that...

CHAPLAIN: I assumed she'd died.

STATHAM: No, no no. No. Um... I'm a consultant here, by the way, Doctor Alan Statham, Radiology.

CHAPLAIN: Oh, Cordelia Denby, Chaplain.

STATHAM: Chaplain. Oh... the — the "God sod" business, that's... Could we light a candle for her anyway?

CHAPLAIN: Yes, of course.

STATHAM WON'T LET GO OF THE CHAPLAIN'S HAND.

▸▸ LOCKER AREA, MESS

MAC IS PUSHING GUY AGAINST A LOCKER. MARTIN IS WATCHING.

MAC: Properly.

GUY: Um... je suis désolé.

MAC: In English.

GUY: Um... oh God, Martin, I'm really, I'm really, I'm really sss-sorry that I told you you'd passed your exams when you hadn't.

MAC: Now hug.

GUY & MARTIN: What?

MAC: I said hug.

NOTHING HAPPENS.

MAC: Fucking hug!!

MARTIN AND GUY KIND OF HUG.

MAC: I said hug!

MARTIN AND GUY HUG. MAC GOES.

GUY: Yeah, all right, don't try and cop a feel. (HE RUBS THE BACK OF HIS HEAD) Ow!

MARTIN: Oh, are you all right?

GUY PICKS MARTIN UP AND THROWS HIM.

▸▸ CORRIDOR

A REMOTE CONTROL CAR IS IN THE CORRIDOR. IT MOVES EVERY TIME STATHAM TRIES TO GET PAST IT. STATHAM WALKS THE OTHER WAY AND THE CAR FOLLOWS HIM. STATHAM RUNS AWAY.

▸▸ STAFF LIAISON OFFICE

GUY: I want Mac struck off. He's gay and I've got proof, so if you

could please get out the appropriate form, I...

THE FACE OF JESUS APPEARS AT THE WINDOW.

GUY: Who's the bearded ponce? Is that Noel Edmonds?

THE FACE DISAPPEARS. GUY IS THROWN.

GUY: Oh, it doesn't matter.

HE GOES.

▸▸ HOSPITAL CHAPEL

THE CHAPLAIN IS READING A BIBLE STORY TO SOME SMALL CHILDREN. STATHAM IS SITTING AT THE FRONT, LISTENING.

CHAPLAIN: Long ago, the people of the Earth were being bad and this made God very sad. He wanted to wash his world clean again. He would make it rain.

STATHAM: Noah.

CHAPLAIN: Yes, that's right Alan, very good. Let's not shout out, it's not a test. Let's just listen and enjoy. But there was a good man and his name was Noah.

STATHAM LOOKS SMUGLY AT THE CHILDREN AROUND HIM.

▸▸ GENERAL MEDICAL RECEPTION

CAROLINE GIVES A FILE TO BOYCE.

BOYCE: Thanking you most kindly.

CAROLINE: No, thank you.

BOYCE: My, aren't we civilised, God save the Queen.

CAROLINE SPOTS GUY SIGNING TO A DEAF MAN.

CAROLINE: Now I have seen everything.

BOYCE: Oh — she's not here is she?

CAROLINE: No look, he's signing. Incredible, he's got hidden talents. He seems like such a wanker in public, in private he's practically a saint.

CAROLINE GOES. GUY COMES OVER TO BOYCE.

GUY: Greetings dogsbody.

BOYCE: I didn't know you could sign.

GUY: Yeah, well, you've got to make an effort, haven't you? It's not their fault.

BOYCE: So is he a deaf relative is he?

GUY: No, that is Dominic Carver, a guy I was at school with.

BOYCE: Wow, he must have been a really good friend.

GUY: No. Jesus, no! He used to pull these faces whenever he tried to say anything. You know, sort of... (HE TRIES TO DEMON-STRATE) ...He used to make this popping noise with his mouth, drove me mad, I couldn't bear him.

BOYCE: I don't understand — then why did you learn sign language?

GUY: I didn't, I can only do — (HE SIGNS) "I don't understand sign language", and "Fuck you deaf boy". (HE TRIES TO GET THE SIGNING RIGHT) "Deaf... boy."

BOYCE: Yeah, well...

DOMINIC CARVER COMES OVER TO THEM. HE SIGNS TO GUY "YOUR DICK SMELLS OF SWISS CHEESE". GUY LOOKS BLANK.

BOYCE: What?

DOMINIC REACHES INTO HIS POCKETS, AS IF SEARCHING FOR SOMETHING. HE FINDS WHAT HE'S BEEN LOOKING FOR — IT IS A MIDDLE FINGER GESTURE, WHICH HE BRANDISHES AT GUY. HE LEAVES.

GUY: Yeah, well, very funny, Stevie Wonder! No, he was blind, wasn't he? (TO BOYCE) He said he'd hurt his finger, he's come in for a... Did you see the spittle? Did you see the — and the popping, that's what he's like. Loser! He can't hear me.

▶▶ HOSPITAL CHAPEL

STATHAM IS STILL LISTENING TO
THE CHILDREN'S BIBLE STORY.

STATHAM: (TO A CHILD) Otherwise known as the Ark...

CHAPLAIN: Now Noah had three sons. Perhaps Alan can tell us their names?

STATHAM LOOKS LOST.

STATHAM: Hob? ...Path? ...Papheth? ...Meke?

CHAPLAIN: Their names were Ham...

STATHAM: (OF COURSE) Ham.

CHAPLAIN: Shem...

STATHAM: Yes, Shep.

CHAPLAIN: And Ja...?

STATHAM: Jab.

CHAPLAIN: Japheth.

▶▶ HOSPITAL GROUNDS

AGAINST A HOSPITAL WALL, A GROUP OF YOUNG DOCTORS ARE FORMING A HUMAN PYRAMID ON THE TOP OF WHICH SOMEONE IS HOLDING A JESUS FACE ON A STICK AND MAKING IT LOOK IN THROUGH THE WINDOW.

▶▶ GUY'S CAR

GUY IS TAKING CAROLINE OUT FOR A DRIVE,

GUY'S GAYS

<u>PROPER</u> HOMOSEXUALS I WOULDN'T FEEL ASHAMED TO BE CAUGHT HAVING A PINT WITH.

ALEXANDER THE GREEK

NOT THE ONE WHO WASHES UP IN THE CANTEEN, THE OTHER ONE. HE NEARLY RULED THE WORLD AT ONE POINT, WOULD HAVE HAD A PINT WITH HIM, BUT IF HE'D TOUCHED MY LEG, OR ANYTHING LIKE THAT, I'D STILL HAVE HIM. NOT SEXUALLY, OBVIOUSLY, THAT WASN'T HOW I MEANT IT.

ALAN TURING

WORLD WAR TWO CODEBREAKER. KNEW HIS MATHS. BIT QUIET THIS ONE, BIT OF A GEEK, SO WE COULD HAVE HAD QUITE A RESPECTFUL TALK ABOUT HISTORY AND WARS AND THAT, AND I DOUBT HE'D TRY TO TOUCH ME UP ACTUALLY, SO IT WOULD BE FINE.

OSCAR WILDE

TWO LEGENDARY WITS MEET   MIGHT HAVE ONE PINT WITH HIM (NOT ALONE OBVIOUSLY). LOOKS A BIT TOO MUCH LIKE JONATHAN ROSS (NOT QUITE AS CAMP), BUT HAD SOME TOP INSULTS FOR WOMEN.

KENNY EVERETT

QUITE FUNNY, BUT IF HE CAME TOO NEAR, I'D PUNCH HIM OUT WITH ONE OF HIS BIG FAKE HANDS, OH YES. ANYWAY, HE'S DEAD NOW.

BUT THEY'RE STUCK IN A TRAFFIC JAM IN THE TOWN. HE IS SINGING ALONG TO A QUEEN CD.

GUY: (SINGS 'WE ARE THE CHAMPIONS' BY QUEEN. HE CAN'T MAKE THE HIGH NOTES, SO MISSES THEM OUT)

CAROLINE: You've got four Queen CDs.

GUY: So?

CAROLINE: Four?

GUY: Yeah, what's wrong with that?

CAROLINE: It's too many.

GUY: They're really good.

CAROLINE: That's as may be.

GUY: Brian May caresses that guitar like a woman.

CAROLINE: Oh, do women make better guitarists then?

GUY: No no, like the guitar is a woman, not him, he's not a woman.

CAROLINE: He looks like one.

GUY: No no no, very much a hot-blooded male is Brian.

CAROLINE: What, like Freddie Mercury?

GUY: Yeah.

CAROLINE TURNS AND STARES AT GUY.

CAROLINE: What?

GUY: What?

CAROLINE: Freddie Mercury, you know, the one that was in Queen?

GUY: Yeah.

CAROLINE: Hot-blooded male — what, straight?

GUY: Probably, I don't know.

CAROLINE: You don't know?

GUY: Does it matter?

CAROLINE: Well not to me, no, but as a fan, I think you ought to know — he was gay.

GUY: Huh! Big deal.

THEY SAY NOTHING FOR A MOMENT OR TWO. FREDDIE MERCURY IS SINGING ON THE CD PLAYER.

GUY: Shall we have something else?

CAROLINE: Yeah.

GUY: Yeah, I mean it's not — you know, I'm not homophobic or anything.

CAROLINE: No no, I know.

GUY: No, it's just that, you know, you get certain things, images, pictures in your head and then, anyway... You've spoilt it for me now.

CAROLINE: Sorry.

GUY HAS PUT A NEW CD ON.

GUY: (SINGS 'YOUR SONG' BY ELTON JOHN) Now that's more like it!

CAROLINE LOOKS AT HIM.

▸▸ **PLAYGROUND**

GUY AND CAROLINE ARE SITTING AT A PICNIC TABLE BY A CHILDREN'S PLAYGROUND. THEY ARE EATING ICE-CREAMS.

MUM: Sorry about that.

GUY: It's all right, bye Josh. What a lovely-looking kid.

CAROLINE: Aww.

GUY: I know, isn't he?

THEY SIT THERE FOR A BIT.

CAROLINE: Well, this is nice.

GUY: Yeah.

THEY SIT QUIETLY.

GUY: (SUDDENLY SCREAMS) Oi!!!

CAROLINE: (DEAFENED) Oh!

GUY: (LOOKING OFF TO HIS RIGHT) Get out of there!

WE SEE THAT GUY IS SHOUTING AT A SMALL FAIR-HAIRED BOY IN THE SAND PIT. THERE IS A HUGE ELABORATE SAND CASTLE WITH A SWISS FLAG ON TOP.

GUY: That took me ages that did! I said get out of there! I'm talking to you, blondie! That is my — (HE BECOMES AWARE OF CAROLINE'S SHOCK) ...just sometimes... I love kids though, absolutely love them.

CAROLINE: Have you had operatic training?

GUY: I do sing actually, could you tell?

CAROLINE: Yeah.

GUY: Oh, you remembered. (GUY STARTS SINGING 'YOUR SONG' AGAIN)

CAROLINE: Don't start that again.

GUY: I know quite a few of his songs, actually.

CAROLINE: I know.

▶▶ HOSPITAL CHAPEL

STATHAM HAS GOT THE CHAPLAIN TRAPPED IN CONVER-SATION.

STATHAM: You — you spread love, like — like honey. Like butter and honey.

CHAPLAIN: *His* love.

STATHAM: Well, and *your* love.

CHAPLAIN: No, not so much actually.

STATHAM: Well, I can... I can feel it.

CHAPLAIN: Well, that's very interesting, um...

STATHAM: Yes, can you feel — can you feel mine?

CHAPLAIN: Yeah, I think you're confusing two different kinds of love...

STATHAM: Love is love isn't it?

CHAPLAIN: Well no, I don't think it is actually.

STATHAM: Well — well we must all love each other, surely?

CHAPLAIN: Yes...

STATHAM: So, I love you.

CHAPLAIN: Okay...

STATHAM: And you love me.

CHAPLAIN: Yes, I can see what you're getting at, and in many ways it's a very sound argument...

STATHAM: There we are, that's settled then, we love each other.

CHAPLAIN: No, you see...

STATHAM: I — I have to go now... duty calls. Got to sort out a few lymphocytes, but can I come back later and pick up where we left off?

CHAPLAIN: How much later?

STATHAM: Should be about twenty minutes.

CHAPLAIN: Are you sure you're getting enough work done?

STATHAM: Work, yes... but we — we have fatter fish to fry.

▶▶ COUNTRYSIDE

GUY AND CAROLINE ARE WALKING ALONG THE EDGE OF A FIELD. GUY HAS SOME BREAD WITH HIM.

CAROLINE: Was I supposed to bring sandwiches?

GUY: Oh, I thought we could feed the deer.

CAROLINE: On bread?

GUY: Yeah, I don't know — don't they eat bread?

CAROLINE: No, not usually. There's a shortage of good bakeries in the forest and they've had to adapt to eating bark, things like that.

GUY: It's wholemeal...?

CAROLINE SHAKES HER HEAD.

GUY: Right. Oh look, nettles. I bet you'd think these would sting me, wouldn't you?

"Yeah. You are — you are the **complete man.** I see that **now.**"

CAROLINE: Yeah, nettles will sting you.

GUY: Yeah, that's where you're wrong you see, because it's all about the way you hold them, all right? Okay. Watch this, all right? Are you ready?

HE RIPS UP A BUNCH OF NETTLES. CAROLINE WINCES.

CAROLINE: Oh, argh!

GUY: See? Look at that, it's all about the direction of the hairs on the leaves.

CAROLINE: Is it?

GUY: That is pretty impressive isn't it?

CAROLINE: Yeah. You are — you are the complete man. I see that now.

SHE WALKS AWAY AND BEHIND HER BACK GUY IS NOW CLEARLY IN AGONY; HE TRIES TO LICK SOME OF THE PAIN OUT OF HIS HAND. CAROLINE GOES THROUGH A GATE, GUY TRIES TO CLIMB OVER IT.

GUY: Sheep! Get down, get down!

▸▸ **STAFF LIAISON OFFICE**

SUE HAS A DESK FAN ON HER DESK AND IS SWISHING HER LOOSE HAIR ABOUT IN FRONT OF IT.

MAC: It is a ridiculous shift pattern, if it allows Secretan the arse and another key member of my team to go off — to go off at the same time. You know. Together.

SUE: Key member of the team? No. Scatterbrained floozy, yes.

MAC: Okay, right, I don't want to be without the scatterbrained floozy *and* without the arrogant knob-head *at the same time.*

SUE: Well, there is more than adequate cover.

MAC: I don't think there is.

SUE: Guy is far from irreplaceable. Now that is — that's something you've always said.

MAC: Yeah, yeah, yeah, I've always said that, yeah. Guy, very happy to have him out of my sight.

SUE: And you managed fine before the scatterbrained floozy arrived.

MAC: Did I?

SUE: Yeah.

MAC: Yeah, I suppose I did, yeah.

SUE: So what's the problem?

MAC: I don't want them to be off, both at the same time, I don't.

SUE: Why?

MAC: Just because.

SUE: Because why?

MAC: Because — because Guy is a wanker.

SUE: Yeah, well I actually — you know, I don't draw up the rosters.

MAC: Sorry, are you on my side here, or not?

SUE: Doctor MacCartney, yes, I am on your side. I'm always on your side. I'm — you know — I'm by your side, I'm — I'm up your side, I'm through your side, I'm, I'm under your side...

MAC: Thank you. Yes, it's time for me to go now, thank you.

SUE: I'm all over your side. I can do headstands. Now, would you like to see that?

MAC GOES.

SUE: Would you? The... Like to see that. Yeah.

SUE LIFTS HER SKIRT IN FRONT OF THE FAN TO TRY AND COOL DOWN.

SUE: Ooh!

▶▶ WOODS

GUY AND CAROLINE ARE WALKING ALONG A COUNTRY PATH. GUY POINTS AT SOMETHING IN A FIELD AHEAD OF THEM.

GUY: Oh look, a sheep. Love them.

CAROLINE: I think it's a car.

GUY: Oh.

CAROLINE: If you... if you had a son...

GUY: Yeah?

CAROLINE: Would you encourage him to go into medicine?

GUY: Um, no — I would encourage him to go into Formula One.

CAROLINE: No! He might get killed.

GUY: Yeah, but come on, buckets of dosh, loads of gash!

CAROLINE: I'm sorry? Gash?

GUY: Um... yeah, it's a motor racing term, it stands for... gearbox and... suspension... hiccup.

CAROLINE: Ah well, that would be irresistible to any young man, wouldn't it.

GUY: Oh yeah, yeah. It would.

CAROLINE: Oh no, it was a sheep.

GUY: It does look like a Mazda.

▶▶ RADIOLOGY

STATHAM IS GIVING A LECTURE TO SOME STUDENTS. HE IS DRESSED MUCH MORE CASUALLY THAN USUAL — A BEIGE POLO NECK REPLACING THE SHIRT AND TIE. HIS MANNER TOO IS MUCH MORE FRIENDLY AND RELAXED — MORE 'CHRISTIAN'.

STATHAM: Before we get started, um — guys — I'd just like to say a few words, if I may. (PRAYER MODE) Oh Lord, help us to understand more clearly the complexities of your creation, to see its beauty and comprehend the — the totality of all your works. Help us to humbly pay attention and not try to undermine the authority of those you have so rightly put in charge, with — with insolence and silliness. Amen.

BOYCE: That was for my benefit, wasn't it?

STATHAM: Pardon, Mr Boyce?

BOYCE: That last bit, the insolence and silliness, that was for my benefit?

STATHAM: Well, that's not for me to say Mr Boyce, or maybe for you to fathom, if that were to indeed be the case, or otherwise.

BOYCE: Come on, in fairness, it was just a dig at me wasn't it, because you find me infuriating?

STATHAM: So let he who is without sin cast the first stone. And if that indeed were to prove to be the case Mr Boyce, I do solemnly hereby forgive you.

BOYCE: And I forgive you.

STATHAM: Pardon?

BOYCE: I forgive you.

STATHAM: No no, I — I forgive you.

BOYCE: And I forgive you.

STATHAM: Mr — Mr Boyce, if anybody is going to do forgiving, it'll be me.

BOYCE: But in the Lord's Prayer it says...

STATHAM: Yes, Mr Boyce, forgive me but — no don't forgive me — but I think you probably know as much about our Lord the Jesus as you do about...

BOYCE: I'm Jewish.

STATHAM: No, no way are you Jewish.

BOYCE: No, I actually am Jewish, I'm a practising Jew Hebrew, I'm a — you know, Son of David.

STATHAM: Okay, prove it, lend me some money!

BOYCE: No.

STATHAM: No? No no. Are you circumcised?

BOYCE: I might be. Might not be. Could just be for hygiene reasons.

STATHAM: Right, come on, show us your foreskin.

BOYCE: No.

STATHAM: Mucky cock!

▸▸ COUNTRYSIDE

CAROLINE AND GUY WALK THROUGH A FIELD AND SIT DOWN ON SOME HAY BALES.

CAROLINE: Yeah, but you know — I mean how would you feel if you were a fox?

GUY: I'd love it. I'd relish the challenge, I'd look at the hounds and I'd go — yeah, bring it on!

CAROLINE: Yeah, well that's because you're quite sporty. I mean how would you feel if you were a non-sporty fox?

GUY: What, a sort of geeky intellectual fox?

CAROLINE: If you like, yeah.

GUY: Well, then I would accept that I was a pest and that I needed to be culled on quite a large scale.

CAROLINE: That's very selfless of you.

GUY: Yeah, well you know, you did say I was intellectual.

CAROLINE: Yeah, but I mean supposing you were chased into the next county and you had to abandon your poor little cubs...?

GUY: Well, then I would find me another super vixen and I'd... I'd start all over again.

CAROLINE: (MEANINGFULLY) Yes... Yes I think you would.

CAROLINE GETS UP TO GO.

CAROLINE: Shall we get back now?

GUY GETS UP TO FOLLOW HER.

GUY: Yeah, but that was only hypothetical, wasn't it?

CAROLINE: Well, yes, you're not actually a fox, Guy.

GUY: I mean that's just what I'd do if I was a fox and I'm not, I'm a human being.

CAROLINE: Are you?

GUY: Yeah, and I'm going back for them.

CAROLINE: What?

GUY: I'm going back for the cubs. I can't leave them there all alone.

CAROLINE: Oh, it's too late now.

GUY: No, it's not too late.

CAROLINE: Oh, it really is.

GUY: Why?

CAROLINE: The hounds tore them to shreds.

GUY COLLAPSES TO HIS KNEES.

GUY: (SCREAMS IN AGONY) No!!

CAROLINE: What are you doing? Get up.

GUY: Argh! My cubs! My cubs!

CAROLINE: Get up.

GUY GRABS HOLD OF CAROLINE.

GUY: Oh no, no!

CAROLINE: Don't, you're going to rip my top, get off.

GUY: My cubs! My cubs, dead! Why?? How could you let this happen?!

GUY SHRIEKS AND SHOUTS.

THE CHAPLAIN IS CONSOLING A WOMAN BY THE DOOR OF THE CHAPEL. STATHAM COMES UP AND LEANS VERY CLOSE TO THE CHAPLAIN.

CHAPLAIN: ...There are clearly times when you can't be with your husband, and I understand that you wouldn't want to go home, and waiting rooms can be depressing places at the best of times. You'd be surprised how many people prefer to spend time here, not for any particular religious reason, but because it's a very peaceful and relaxing place, at a very stressful time.

STATHAM: Yes, yes that's right...

CHAPLAIN: Yes, it's also nice to escape from the medical paraphernalia, the doctors everywhere. It's just nice to cut yourself off for a few moments.

STATHAM: Mmm, we feel it's important to — to escape.

CHAPLAIN: (TO STATHAM) Was there actually something that you wanted?

STATHAM: No, no. I'm... just you know — (TO THE WOMAN) *do* feel that we — we are here for you.

CHAPLAIN: No, *I'm* here.

STATHAM: Togetherness, as the Lord said himself...

CHAPLAIN: Right. (TO THE WOMAN) Would you like to come through...?

"So, you want your **ginger** friend placed in bin bags all over the city **do you?**

STATHAM: Yes.

THE CHAPLAIN TAKES THE WOMAN INTO THE CHAPEL AND CLOSES THE DOOR ON STATHAM.

▸▸ GUY'S CAR, NIGHT

A PENSIVE-LOOKING GUY IS DRIVING BACK FROM THE COUNTRY. 'YOUR SONG' BY ELTON JOHN IS PLAYING ON THE CD PLAYER.

▸▸ DAY WARD, NIGHT

MARTIN IS BUILDING A HOUSE OF CARDS OUT OF PATIENTS' NOTES. A WEARY CAROLINE COMES IN.

CAROLINE: I forgot my stupid house keys.

MARTIN: Are you all right?

CAROLINE: No. I'm exhausted, I've eaten my bodyweight in chocolate in the car, I'm all bloated and my feet hurt. And I haven't had sex in months.

MARTIN: Well, I know how you feel.

▸▸ PUB

GUY IS LINING UP A POOL SHOT. HE MOVES THE WHITE BALL. A SINISTER-LOOKING MAN APPEARS AND GRABS THE CUE BALL.

GUY: You're late.

▸▸ DAY WARD, NIGHT

CAROLINE: Look Martin, what I just said about not having had sex in a while...

MARTIN: Yes?

CAROLINE: Well I was wondering...

MARTIN: Yeah, yes I will.

CAROLINE: But I haven't told you what I want you to do yet.

MARTIN: Don't worry, because I'm a really adventurous man.

CAROLINE: Are you?

MARTIN: Yes.

CAROLINE: I just don't want you to go round telling everyone that I haven't had sex in ages.

MARTIN: (CRUSHED) Fine, okay. Well, my lips are sealed.

CAROLINE: Oh, thanks Martin.

SHE GIVES HIM A HUG. HE LONGS TO KISS HER.

▸▸ PUB

GUY AND THE SINISTER MAN ARE SITTING BACK TO BACK.

SCISSORS: So, you want your ginger friend placed in bin bags all over the city do you?

GUY: Jesus, no!

SCISSORS: It's all right, just kidding.

GUY: So, how much for what we discussed?

SCISSORS: What, for cutting his hair off?

GUY: Yeah.

SCISSORS: Two.

GUY: Two thousand pounds?!

SCISSORS: No! Two hundred. Jesus!

GUY: Oh, right.

▸▸ DAY WARD, NIGHT

CAROLINE: Oh, you're like a girl aren't you, I can say anything to you.

MARTIN: No, no, I'm not a girl, I'm a — I am a man, with a man's needs.

CAROLINE: Yeah, but to me you're just like a girlfriend.

MARTIN: Have you ever thought about having a sexy girlfriend who you sleep with?

CAROLINE: No.

▸▸ PUB

SCISSORS: If I'm going to do this thing, I need to know that you've thought it through. So tell me, have you thought it through?

GUY THINKS FOR A BIT.

GUY: No.

SCISSORS: People don't normally. Usually it's just a case of "Oh, there's a man with long hair who's irritating me, I'll call up Scissors Bentley to have him taken down a peg or two."

GUY: (TURNING ROUND) That's what I thought.

SCISSORS: Don't look at me or touch me.

GUY: (TURNS BACK) Right.

SCISSORS: And you still want me to do it?

GUY CONSIDERS HIS OPTIONS.

GUY: No.

SCISSORS: Really? Bugger.

GUY: What about a really tight perm? Or a — or an afro, you know, like early Jackson 5?

SCISSORS: (MENACING) What am I? A stylist?!

GUY: Oh, sorry.

▸▸ STAFF LIAISON OFFICE

STATHAM IS SITTING IN SUE'S OFFICE, LOOKING TOWARDS THE WINDOW.

▸▸ MAIN CORRIDOR

CAROLINE IS BEING PURSUED BY THE REMOTE CONTROL CAR DOWN THE CORRIDOR.

▸▸ PUB

GUY STEALS SCISSORS' WHISKY AFTER HE'S GONE. SCISSORS RETURNS LOOKING FOR SOMETHING.

SCISSORS: Did I leave my packet of Bonbons here?

GUY: Um... I don't think you did actually Julian, maybe by the table.

SCISSORS: Oh.

▸▸ MAIN CORRIDOR

THE CAR IS STILL FOLLOWING CAROLINE.

CAROLINE: Stop it Mac! I know it's you!

THE CAR CHASES HER AS SHE HEADS FOR THE EXIT.

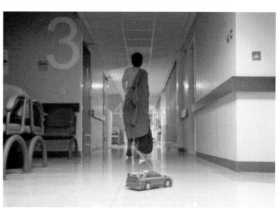

CAROLINE: Stop it at once!

SHE RUNS OUT OF THE BUILDING.

▸▸ STAFF LIAISON OFFICE

STATHAM IS STILL SITTING IN SUE'S OFFICE. THE CLEANER COMES IN.

CLEANER: Sorry love.

STATHAM: It's all right, I'm just waiting.

THE CLEANER CARRIES ON.

CLEANER: I think she's gone home, you know.

STATHAM: Yes, I'm just waiting for Jesus.

THE CLEANER LEAVES. STATHAM KEEPS LOOKING AT THE WINDOW.

EPISODE 8

BOYCE, WEARING A HAT AND SHADES, IS BUSKING FOR CHARITY — HE IS DOING 'TAINTED LOVE' BY SOFT CELL, ACCOMPANYING HIMSELF ON A STYLOPHONE. A BANNER TELLS US HE IS TRYING TO RAISE MONEY FOR THE FLUOROSCOPY SUITE.

GUY IS WALKING ALONG THE STREET, ASSESSING ANY YOUNG FEMALES HE SEES.

MARTIN IS WALKING ALONG, TRYING NOT TO STEP ON THE PAVEMENT CRACKS.

BOYCE: (SINGS 'TAINTED LOVE')

CAROLINE GETS OUT HER BANK CARD BY A CASH MACHINE.

GUY SMELLS A GIRL HE PASSES IN THE STREET.

AS CAROLINE USES THE MACHINE, IN THE BACKGROUND MARTIN IS HOPPING ALONG THE PAVEMENT, STILL AVOIDING THE CRACKS.

BOYCE AND THE OFFICE GIRLS ARE DANCING.

BOYCE: (SINGS 'TAINTED LOVE')

AN ATTRACTIVE YOUNG MAN EYES UP GUY. GUY DOESN'T LIKE IT.

MARTIN SEES CAROLINE AT THE CASH MACHINE.

BOYCE: (SINGS 'TAINTED LOVE')

WHILE CAROLINE'S AT THE CASH MACHINE, MARTIN STICKS A FINGER IN CAROLINE'S BACK, PRETENDING IT'S A GUN.

MARTIN: Give me all your cash.

SHE TURNS AND SPRAYS SOMETHING IN HIS EYES.

MARTIN: Ow! Ow, it's me, it's Martin!

CAROLINE: Oh shit, oh my God!

MARTIN: Argh, you've got me in the eyes!

CAROLINE: Oh God Martin, I'm so sorry!

BOYCE: (SINGS 'TAINTED LOVE')

GUY WALKS PAST A HOMELESS MAN, STILL LOOKING AT GIRLS.

HOMELESS MAN: Got any spare change mate?

GUY: No, I've got no change at all.

HOMELESS MAN: Yeah...

GUY: No, actually I don't have any change, and er — I resent being called a liar, okay? (THE MAN IS UNCONVINCED) No no, it's — look, see? See, I've actually, I've got no coins at all. I've only got notes...

IN AN ATTEMPT TO DEMONSTRATE THAT HIS TROUSER POCKETS ARE EMPTY, GUY HAS TO SLING HIS JACKET OVER HIS ARM — AT THIS POINT, LOADS OF COINS TUMBLE OUT OF HIS JACKET POCKETS, LANDING ALL OVER THE PLACE.

CAROLINE IS TRYING TO DAB MARTIN'S EYES.

CAROLINE: How's that?

MARTIN: Ow!

CAROLINE: Oh God!

MARTIN: Aargh! Argh!

GUY PICKS UP HIS COINS FROM ALL OVER THE PAVEMENT.

GUY: Apart from these, which are… an emergency supply for the parking meters. One went in there.

GUY POINTS TO THE HOMELESS MAN'S CUP OF COINS.

HOMELESS MAN: Er no — I don't think it did.

GUY: No, no, don't get cute, okay?

GUY TAKES A COIN OUT OF THE CUP.

HOMELESS MAN: Well…

GUY: No no, I saw one, when it fell, and it went in there. That one there, all right. So don't — don't pull that face. Don't make any sudden movements either, okay? Because I am a doctor, I have a knife as well…

CAROLINE IS LEADING MARTIN, WHO IS EFFECTIVELY BLIND.

CAROLINE: Good job we work in a hospital, eh?

MARTIN: Argh. God!

CAROLINE: You'll be fine, you'll be fine.

SHE LETS GO FOR A MOMENT AND HE COLLIDES WITH A TELE-PHONE BOX.

CAROLINE: Shit!

MAC AND EMMY GO PAST BOYCE AND THE GIRLS SINGING, AND INTO THE HOSPITAL.

KAREN WATCHES HARRIET SIT DOWN AT HER DESK WEARING RABBIT EARS.

MAC AND EMMY ARE MAKING THEIR WAY INTO THE HOSPITAL.

EMMY: So, will I be able to see you tonight?

MAC: Probably. Unless I've perfected my invisibility serum, yeah. I've nearly got it, my little toe disappeared last week.

GUY SEES THEM.

GUY: Morning.

MAC: Morning.

GUY: Hi. Oh, um — your wife rang.

MAC: Yeah...

GUY: She said the clinic called with the test results on your pussy penis.

MAC: Great.

GUY: And your bleeding anus.

MAC: Thanks.

GUY: So if you could give your *wife* a ring.

MAC: Will do. See ya.

GUY GOES.

EMMY: Your wife?

MAC: Ignore him, he's insanely jealous.

▸▸ OFFICE

HARRIET NOTICES KAREN LOOKING AT HER AND REALISES SHE'S STILL WEARING RABBIT EARS.

HARRIET: Oh. It's the only way I can get his breakfast down him. I thought everyone looked friendly this morning.

KAREN: Well, there you go. At least you've made people happy.

HARRIET: (ANOTHER REALISATION) I went to put flowers on Mum's grave!

▸▸ DAY WARD

CAROLINE IS BATHING MARTIN'S EYES.

MARTIN: Ow. Ow! Oh, ah!

CAROLINE: You're not blind, don't worry.

MARTIN: Look, I know you're more of a doctor than I am, okay — but actually, you're wrong, I am blind.

CAROLINE: Well, for now maybe, but it won't last.

GUY COMES IN.

GUY: What's going on here? Why are you crying?

MARTIN: I'm not crying.

GUY: Has one of the nurses been shouting at you again?

MARTIN: No.

CAROLINE: Stop it Guy, Martin's gone blind.

MARTIN: You said I wasn't blind!

GUY: Aaah. Oh, oh blind. Oh, of course.

MARTIN: What's that supposed to mean?

GUY: Well everybody knows, good for the prostate, bad for the eyesight. We've got to get you a girlfriend. What about Caroline here, she's single?

MARTIN: Oh don't listen to him Caroline! (TO GUY) Go away!

CAROLINE: You're distressing the patient.

GUY: *I'm* distressing the patient? Was it me who sprayed nasty peppermint in his face?

CAROLINE: Oh, you heard.

GUY: Yeah, oh I'm trying to think of somebody in the hospital who hasn't heard... Let me think, um — no I can't think of anybody.

> Karen,
>
> No, there was nothing missing from my e-mail. 'Karen — just a couple of tiny points' was a physical description.
>
> Joanna

CAROLINE DAUBS GUY.

GUY: Ow, that's blind man's swab! You'll be all right. (HE KISSES MARTIN) And so will you...

HE GOES TO KISS CAROLINE, WHO PULLS AWAY. GUY DOES 'WANKER' HAND GESTURES TO MARTIN WHILE HE HAS HIS EYES SHUT. GUY GOES.

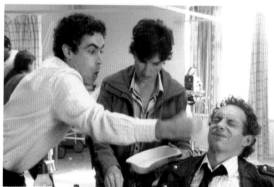

MARTIN: Caroline, are you here?

CAROLINE: I'm still here, Martin.

MARTIN: Maybe you should take my pulse again?

CAROLINE: Yep, sure.

CAROLINE HOLDS MARTIN'S ARM. HE SIGHS AND LEANS BACK MORE.

▶▶ MAIN CORRIDOR

JOANNA TALKS TO STATHAM IN THE CORRIDOR.

JOANNA: I haven't had you clinging to my ankles recently. What's the matter, are you ill?

STATHAM: Never been ruder — health-wise — thank you.

JOANNA: Not missing me then?

STATHAM: No, the gap of you has been amply filled, thank you.

JOANNA: Yeah, I bet you'd still like to fill my gap though?

STATHAM: No, thank you.

JOANNA: Come on, who is she, who is she? Oh — not the cleaner? For Christ's sake, she hasn't got a funny sexy smile, she's got a cleft lip!

STATHAM: Hah! Do I detect a note of jealousy?

JOANNA: God, you've changed your tune.

STATHAM: Yes, I march to a different tune. (HE SINGS 'ONWARD CHRISTIAN SOLDIERS') "La la la la, la la la la..."

JOANNA: What? What?

STATHAM: And by the way, it's not a she, it's a he.

JOANNA: I knew it.

STATHAM: Jesus.

JOANNA: Jesus? What the one up in the sky, or some South American gay boy you've picked up?

STATHAM WAVES A BIBLE AT JOANNA.

JOANNA: Stop it. Stop it. You're scaring me now.

▶▶ GENERAL MEDICAL RECEPTION

CAROLINE: I wish I had bigger bosoms.

ANGELA: Why?

CAROLINE: Well, you know, just to know what it's like to really fill a top.

ANGELA: Well, you've got perfectly decent breasts.

CAROLINE: Have I? Thanks Angela.

ANGELA: Not many people with a smaller cup size have such good shape and buoyancy, without a bra.

CAROLINE: Really? How do you know?

ANGELA: Because I've seen them, haven't I?

CAROLINE: You have? When?

ANGELA: Well you know...

CAROLINE: No, I don't.

ANGELA: We live together Caroline, of course I've seen them.

CAROLINE: When?

ANGELA: I don't know, just around.

CAROLINE: Around what?

ANGELA: I don't know, maybe the bath, maybe your room. Just around. Look, if you don't believe me, they look a bit like...

SHE DRAWS CAROLINE'S TITS.

CAROLINE: Oh God, you have seen them!

ANGELA: Yeah.

CAROLINE: Right.

▸▸ CORRIDOR

GUY: So, does she have, like, rosettes in the bedroom?

MAC: Who?

GUY: Emily Brandenburg Concerto Number One von Posh.

MAC: No, you can't have it both ways, you can't complain about my girlfriend being too posh and at the same time continue to be the biggest snob in the whole hospital.

GUY: Snob?!

MAC: You're not going to contest this one, surely?

GUY: I'm a man of the people, all things to all men. I can't be a snob.

MAC: Yeah, really? How do you make that out?

GUY: Well, I know lots of working class people.

MAC: Yeah, patients don't count.

GUY: No, not patients. I've got lots of working class chums... mates.

MAC: Really?

GUY: Yeah.

MAC: Have you?

GUY: Yeah.

MAC: Like who?

GUY: Like... some of the cleaners here.

MAC: Oh okay, yeah, what — you hang out with them do you?

GUY: Yeah, look, there's Steve. Steve!

GUY AND MAC GO UP TO A CLEANER.

GUY: Steve-o!

TERRY: Eh?

GUY: Steve, innit?

TERRY: No.

MAC: "Innit."

GUY: Um — well, where's Steve?

TERRY: I don't know any Steve, mate.

GUY: Really? Well you — you look a lot like him.

TERRY: Yeah?

MAC: They all look a bit the same do they Guy?

TERRY: Hey, Mac my man — how you doing?

MAC: Hey, Terry, good to see you man, how are you doing?

▸▸ LADIES' TOILETS

CAROLINE IS LOOKING IN THE MIRROR. SHE IS SEEING HOW SHE LOOKS WITH BLONDE HAIR.

CAROLINE: I like it. What do you think?

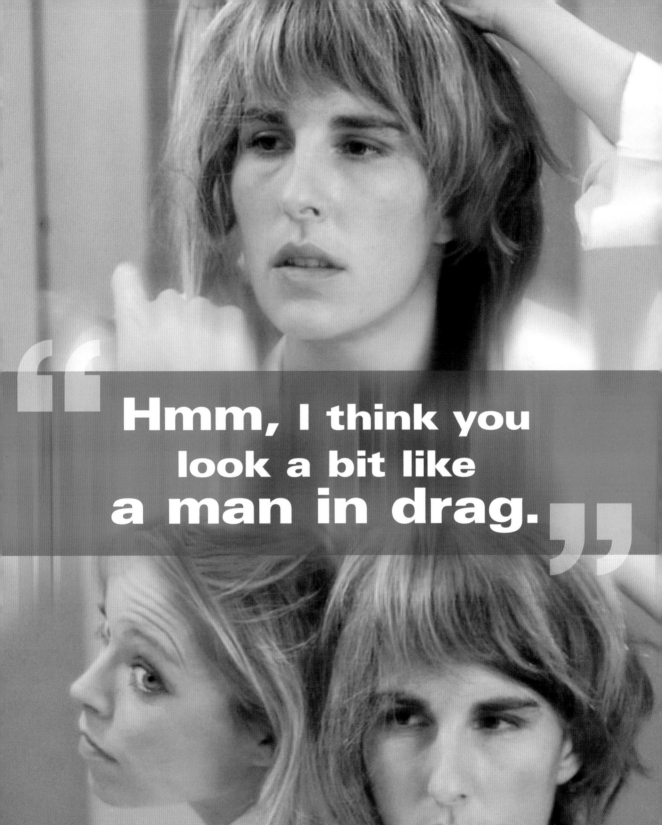

"Hmm, I think you look a bit like a man in drag."

ANGELA HAS BEEN LENDING CAROLINE HER HAIR FROM BEHIND, AND NOW LOOKS ROUND.

CAROLINE: Hmm?

ANGELA: Hmm, I think you look a bit like a man in drag.

CAROLINE PULLS ANGELA'S HAIR.

ANGELA: Oi! I said a man *in drag*! Coh!

CAROLINE GOES OUT OF THE LOOS, PULLING ANGELA'S HAIR ON THE WAY.

▸▸ CORRIDOR

MAC: Did you get your shift sorted out all right?

TERRY: Yeah, much better, much better, thanks for that.

MAC: Yeah, no worries mate, no worries.

GUY: I expect you're rushed off your plates, aren't you?

TERRY: What?

GUY: Your plates. You're rushed off your plates — your plates of meat, your feet?

TERRY: Right.

GUY: Yeah... Would you Adam and Eve it, eh...

TERRY: What?

GUY: I was only down the old... Hackney Stadium last night, blew a monkey on a dog.

MAC: Really? You'll have the RSPCA after you.

GUY: No, a monkey, it's fifty sheets.

TERRY: Five hundred.

GUY: Is it? What's — what's a pony then?

MAC: It's a kind of small horse?

TERRY: (TO MAC) Who's the ponce?

MAC: His name's Gay — 'Gee'. Short for... Guillaume.

GUY: Excuse me, did you call me a ponce?

TERRY: Have you got a problem?

GUY: No, I do not have a problem. Do you have a problem?

TERRY: I ain't got a problem.

GUY: Well I then neither have a problem either.

MAC: Well that's neither good isn't it, nor bad, because now we can all be chums together.

TERRY: See you Mac.

MAC: Yeah, take it easy man.

TERRY: Later.

MAC AND GUY HEAD OFF.

GUY: Ah — oi! Yeah, goodbye Terence. Go and do something menial.

TERRY: Twat.

GUY: Drone.

MAC SIGHS.

▶▶ DAY WARD/CORRIDOR

MARTIN PUTS PLASTERS OVER HIS EYES AND TRIES TO FIND HIS WAY AROUND USING A WHITE CANE. HE HAS TO LIFT ONE OF HIS EYELIDS TO GET THROUGH THE DOOR, BUT THEN CLOSES IT AGAIN WITH THE PLASTER. THE WHITE CANE COLLAPSES AT ITS MID-POINT BUT HE CARRIES ON REGARDLESS.

▶▶ BOARDROOM

CEO: Item six, tonight's charity event.

STATHAM: Ah ha, yes.

CEO: Oh yes, this is your thing, isn't it?

STATHAM: Er yes, if you like — charity is very much *my thing*. I personally have been working tirelessly on our latest fund-raising event.

JOANNA: I don't know how you find the time, what with all your praying.

STATHAM: Tonight's... fun-filled extravaganza — the grand slave auction.

CEO: I always thought this slave auction thing was a bit tacky...

JOANNA: Puerile.

CEO: A bit old hat.

STATHAM: Yes, yes, yes. No no no, that's exactly what I was saying to Martin Dear, er... whose idea the auction actually was.

LYNDON: I thought you personally worked tirelessly on this?

STATHAM: Sorry, is — is he here?

CEO: We've been through this.

STATHAM: He's Maintenance.

CEO: He is a head of department.

STATHAM: Not a proper department.

JOANNA: He's Head of IT.

CEO: Every week we get this.

JOANNA: I suppose radiology is proper medicine is it?

STATHAM: I'm not even going to dignify that with an answer. Yes, it bloody is!

▶▶ STAFF LIAISON OFFICE

CAROLINE: Sorry, I should have got you to sign them ages ago; I've just been a bit distracted recently.

SUE: Oh, right — is it something you'd like to talk about?

CAROLINE: No.

SUE: Well, if something's distracting you from your work Caroline, it might be best you get it off that lovely chest of yours.

CAROLINE: I'd rather not discuss it, thank you.

SUE: All right, fine then, bye.

CAROLINE: All right then. I'll start from the beginning. There's this doctor, right? And when I first arrived, I remember thinking...

SUE: No no no!

CAROLINE: What?

SUE: Is it a long story?

CAROLINE: Well, yes, I suppose...

SUE: Well it might be best if we don't start at the beginning.

CAROLINE: Oh, okay. Okay, what — halfway through?

SUE: No.

CAROLINE: Three quarters?

SUE: Oh, okay.

CAROLINE: Fine, well basically I didn't like him at all, in fact I hated him, although I thought he had kind eyes, but he was rude and offhand and clever, so I thought no, no. But now, well, now I think maybe I like him. I think I was right about the eyes... Yes, I do like him.

SUE: I see.

CAROLINE: In a non-professional way.

SUE: Ah.

CAROLINE: And I work with him every day, so...

SUE GASPS.

CAROLINE: What?

SUE: Nothing, it's er — you er... you work with him every day?

CAROLINE: Yeah.

SUE: (HOPEFULLY) Guy?

CAROLINE: No.

SUE: The other one?

CAROLINE: Yeah.

SUE: Yeah. The one with the lion's mane?

CAROLINE: I... well, yeah.

SUE: I see. Well, Doctor Trodd. Maybe you've had your chance with him. Maybe it's too late; maybe someone else deserves to take priority. Maybe you should just stay away or pay the price, hmm? Hmm? Now maybe you should think about that. You've been warned, lady!

▶▶ **BOARDROOM**

CEO: I will of course write you a cheque for a hundred pounds, to ensure that I don't have to attend.

STATHAM: Right. Anybody else coming?

JOANNA: Well, I don't see the point...

LYNDON: Yeah, sure. It's for charity, cool.

JOANNA: I don't see the point in ignoring it, yeah, yeah; I'll be there.

STATHAM: Can't you think up your own mind? (TO LYNDON) All right, why don't you put yourself up for auction then, if

it's for a good cause?

LYNDON: Yeah, sure. Are you going to put yourself up?

STATHAM LOOKS WORRIED.

STATHAM: Well I — I... I am the auctioneer...

THE CEO IS ENJOYING STATHAM'S OBVIOUS RELUCTANCE.

CEO: Well all right, I'll be the auctioneer.

JOANNA: Oh well done, Charles.

CEO: Yeah, go on.

LYNDON: I don't think we should force him, I'm sure he knows his own limitations.

STATHAM: All right, all right, I hereby put myself up for auction! It'll set the benchmark, as it were — you know, set a gold standard.

CEO: Hurrah!

STATHAM: Right.

JOANNA: Suddenly I can't wait!

JOANNA GETS UP TO GO. SHE ACCIDENTALLY ON PURPOSE CATCHES STATHAM OVER THE HEAD WITH HER HANDBAG AS SHE PASSES BEHIND HIM.

CEO: Item seven...

JOANNA: Oh, I'm sorry, I thought you'd finished.

STATHAM: Don't — don't you think...

JOANNA COMES BACK. AWARE THAT SHE IS LIKELY TO GET HIM WITH THE HANDBAG AGAIN, STATHAM DUCKS, BUT DUCKS SO VIOLENTLY THAT HE SLAMS HIS HEAD HARD INTO THE TABLE.

LYNDON: Oh mate...

STATHAM FALLS ON THE FLOOR.

▶▶ **THEATRE**

MAC AND CAROLINE ARE ABOUT TO PERFORM AN OPERATION. GUY IS THERE.

MAC: Are you ready Doctor Todd?

CAROLINE: I am, Doctor Mac.

THEY DO A PAT-A-CAKE HAND CLAPPING ROUTINE AS THEY SING:

MAC/CAROLINE/GUY: (SINGING) "Ging gang gooly gooly gooly gooly watcha, ging gang goo, ging gang goo... Ging gang gooly gooly gooly gooly watcha, ging gang goo, ging gang goo... Ging gang gooly gooly gooly gooly watcha, ging gang goo, ging gang goo."

THEIR HANDS GO TOO FAST TO CLAP IN SEQUENCE. CAROLINE

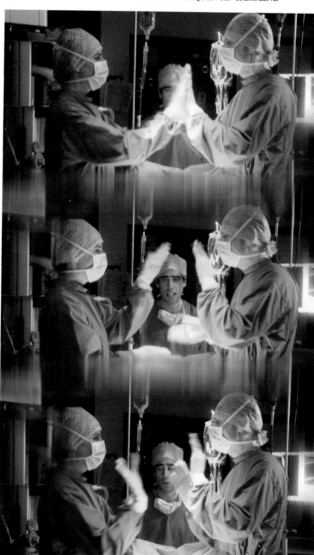

HOLDS SWABS UP TO HER EARS TO LOOK LIKE CARRIE FISHER IN *STAR WARS*.

CAROLINE: Princess Leia.

▸▸ **OFFICE**

LYNDON IS SORTING OUT HARRIET'S COMPUTER.

LYNDON: I think, Harriet... I've got most of it out. So if you just keep the liquids away from the keyboard, it should help.

HARRIET: Yes. Sorry about that.

LYNDON: No, it's all right.

JOANNA SEES LYNDON AND COMES OUT OF HER OFFICE.

JOANNA: Hi, hi hi hi, can I...? Can I help you at all?

LYNDON: No, it's all under control.

JOANNA: Fine, fine, well I'm just in my office if you need me.

LYNDON: (TO HARRIET) So what was it anyway?

HARRIET: Sea Monkeys.

LYNDON: Sorry?

HARRIET: Well I dropped a Malteser in the tank and then I tried to hoik it out with a nail file and it went whoosh... no more Sea Monkeys. Shame.

RACHEL: Psst! Lyndon, could you help us over here a minute please?

RACHEL, KIM AND KAREN ARE LINED UP TO TALK TO LYNDON.

RACHEL: Lyndon, you're a man. In your opinion, who would you say has the best arse?

LYNDON: Well, I haven't had a look at them.

KIM: Well here's your chance.

LYNDON: I'd rather not see flesh.

RACHEL: No, these.

THERE ARE FOUR PHOTOCOPIES OF BUMS ON THE WALL.

LYNDON: Oh.

KIM: Which bottom do you think is the sexiest?

LYNDON: Um... well it's just a personal preference, but I'd say number three.

RACHEL: What — big pants?!

LYNDON: Told you, it's a personal preference.

HARRIET IS JUMPING TRIUMPHANTLY UP AND DOWN THE OFFICE WITH HER ARMS IN THE AIR.

LYNDON: I like big pants and those were the biggest.

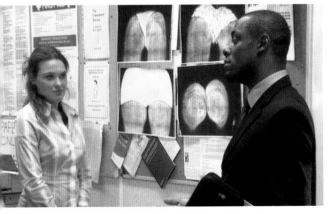

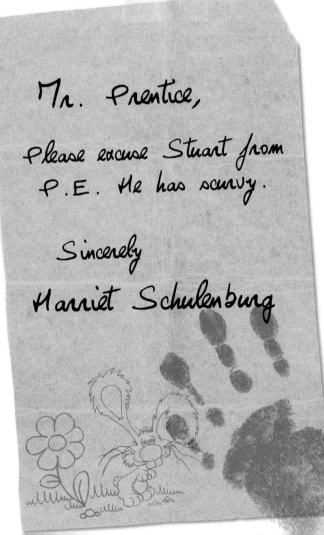

Mr. Prentice,

Please excuse Stuart from P.E. He has scurvy.

Sincerely

Harriet Schulenburg

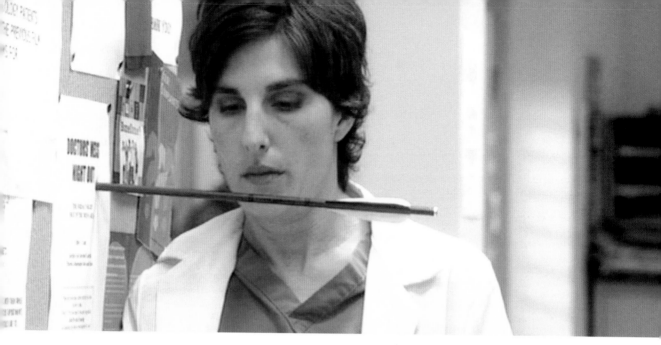

▸▸ OUTPATIENTS, WAITING AREA

CAROLINE IS PUTTING SOMETHING ON THE NOTICE BOARD. SHE DROPS IT AND BENDS DOWN TO PICK IT UP.

CAROLINE: Oh bloody...

A CROSSBOW ARROW SLAMS INTO THE NOTICE BOARD EXACTLY WHERE CAROLINE HAD BEEN STANDING. WHEN CAROLINE STANDS UP AGAIN, SHE SEES THE ARROW AND ANXIOUSLY LOOKS AROUND TO SEE WHERE IT HAS COME FROM. WHEN SHE'S GONE, SUE, WEARING A FAKE BEARD, GOES TO RETRIEVE HER ARROW.

▸▸ MAIN CORRIDOR

MARTIN IS WITH MAC.

MAC: Have you got anyone in mind?

MARTIN: I'm thinking about putting in a bid for Caroline, maybe.

MAC: Really?

MARTIN: Yeah.

MAC: Who would have thought it, eh?

MARTIN: Yeah.

MAC: Mind you, you might have a bit of competition. Our donkey-faced friend. He might try and outbid you.

GUY IS FLIRTING WITH A NURSE.

MARTIN: Yeah, yeah, but not if I get him to put his name down for the auction, because slaves can't buy slaves.

MAC: Clever. Go on then. Go on.

MARTIN GOES TENTATIVELY OVER TO GUY.

MARTIN: Hi, Guy... do you want to put your name down...?

GUY: No.

MARTIN WALKS BACK TOWARDS MAC. MAC MAKES HIM GO AND TRY AGAIN.

MARTIN: Please...?

GUY: I'm not a fucking whore!

MARTIN TURNS BACK TO MAC, WHO WHISPERS TO HIM. MARTIN GOES BACK AND TRIES AGAIN.

MARTIN: It is for a good cause.

GUY: I don't do good causes. Okay, a charity shag maybe, but certainly not to raise fucking money for medical equipment!

MAC: Well no, you won't *make* him Martin, he'd be up against me, probably be too embarrassing for him.

GUY: Er — hah! I'd sell for more than you.

MAC: Yeah? I guess we'll never know.

GUY: (TO MARTIN) Put my name down, put it down. Go on. Yeah, these things need to be quantified, right. He'll learn.

THE NURSE GUY WAS TALKING TO HAS GONE.

GUY: Where did she go?

MARTIN: Cheers Mac.

MAC: Hmm, wasn't too hard was it?

MARTIN: No.

▸▸ STAFF LIAISON OFFICE

STATHAM IS IN SUE'S OFFICE. SUE HAS VERY LONG ARMS.

SUE: Ah, you see, I always thought of God as more of a huge shapeless entity. Massive. Very lumpy. Resounding with shapes and colours and smells, you know, there's no face or legs or body, just all these arms. Many many arms, that just scoop up people from this world and set them down on a balcony up there somewhere beyond the clouds, where they can look down on those they've left behind. I found it very comforting, to me, when my mother died, yeah.

STATHAM: Yes, well that's — that's just wrong, isn't it? And if you stuck to what it actually says in the Bible, you might have been *more* comforted. And perhaps your mother wouldn't have died.

SUE: Well thanks very much for coming in Doctor Statham.

SUE PUTS ONE OF HER LONG ARMS OUT TO SHAKE HANDS, BUT STATHAM JUST GOES. SHE POKES HIS BOTTOM AND FLICKS A 'V' AFTER HIM.

SUE: Fuck off!

SHE DANCES AROUND WITH HER NEW LONG ARMS AND LEAVES HER OFFICE.

▸▸ A&E, WAITING

CAROLINE TALKS TO MAC.

CAROLINE: You are a very very lucky man, Doctor MacCartney.

MAC: Am I?

CAROLINE: Yes you are. I've decided to take you up on your offer.

MAC: Yeah? What offer is that?

CAROLINE: You asked me if I wanted to try the new Armenian restaurant.

MAC: That was ages ago. And you said, and I quote, "I would rather eat poo."

CAROLINE: Yeah, but that was when I thought you were conceited and mean.

MAC: I see.

CAROLINE: Which is why you're so very very lucky...

MAC: Uh-huh?

CAROLINE: Because I've had a change of heart. I believe we're both free nine o'clock on Friday.

MAC: I don't think I am.

CAROLINE: (SARCASTICALLY) Oh, are you — washing your hair?

MAC: No. ...I'm going to go and see La Traviata, with um — yeah, with this lady here, in fact.

EMMY COMES OVER.

EMMY: Hello, I'm Emily.

CAROLINE IS STUNNED. SHE NEEDS A MOMENT TO TAKE THIS IN.

CAROLINE: April fool!

EMMY: In what sense?

CAROLINE: September fool! Everyone's always on the look-out in April, so I like to do it seven months early, catch people off guard.

MAC: So you still don't like me, do you?

CAROLINE: (LAUGHING) Can't stand you!

EMMY: Well nice to meet you.

CAROLINE: Nice to meet you too, Emilily.

EMMY: Emily.

CAROLINE: I'm Caroline Todd.

EMMY: Hi.

CAROLINE: That's Doctor Todd. Are you a doctor? Oh no, oh no — you're not are you? Are you anything?

MAC: Emily is a Lady.

CAROLINE: Yeah, well so am I.

MAC: No, Emily is a Lady.

CAROLINE: So am I.

EMMY: Really? You're Lady Caroline? What an amazing coincidence.

CAROLINE DOESN'T FLINCH.

CAROLINE: Yeah, I just don't like to use the title.

EMMY: Absolutely, me neither.

MAC: Anything else you'd like to know? Emmy's in physiotherapy.

CAROLINE: Oh, how lovely.

EMMY: Shall I tell her about Mr Chips?

MAC: Yes, why not, yes. Emmy has a horse.

CAROLINE: Oh dear, couldn't afford a car?

EMMY: No no, it's a hobby.

CAROLINE: A hobby horse?

MAC: Okay, you know what? I think you two are going to have a lot to talk about, but right now, right now, I think surgery beckons.

CAROLINE: And where do you keep your palace? How many counties do you own?

MAC PICKS CAROLINE UP. HE SLINGS HER OVER HIS SHOULDER AND WALKS OFF.

MAC: (TO EMMY) You take care yeah? And I'll see you later. Bye.

CAROLINE: Yeah, bye, Lady Emily, Your Highness.

MAC CARRIES CAROLINE OFF TO SURGERY.

MAC: Stop it.

CAROLINE: What?!

▶▶ **RADIOLOGY**

STATHAM IS GIVING A LECTURE TO SOME STUDENTS.

STATHAM: Sorry to have left you all so abruptly, panic over, I am now all yours once again. Now then, where were we? The third upper metatarsal in...

STATHAM'S POINTER HAS A STAR ON THE TOP.

BOYCE: Is there something wrong Doctor Statham?

STATHAM: No, no, nothing at all.

BOYCE: Are you going to grant us three wishes?

THE STUDENTS LAUGH.

STATHAM: No.

BOYCE: Well, it's just you've got a star on the end of your pointer.

STATHAM: Yes, yes, so there is. Little, little Star of Bethlehem. Never mind, not to worry.

BOYCE: That's really frustrating, because you know, you can't see exactly what's being pointed at, can you?

STATHAM: Yes, lighten up Mr Boyce, I think you'll find a sense of humour will help us overcome this little problem.

BOYCE: No, I don't think you understand, that's soldered on. I mean, that's never going to come off, it's not going anywhere.

STATHAM: Yes, quite remarkable, and all achieved in apparently under five minutes, quite amazing.

HE VIOLENTLY WHACKS BOYCE IN THE FACE WITH THE POINTER. BOYCE DOUBLES UP IN AGONY.

STATHAM: Right, moving on to the third upper metatarsal...

BOYCE: Arrrgh!

▸▸ STAFF LIAISON OFFICE

GUY IS SITTING IN SUE'S OFFICE, PRETENDING TO USE HER COMPUTER.

GUY: Piece of piss this job. (DOING AN OTT SUE WHITE IMPRESSION) "Have I got any meetings this afternoon? I said, have I got any meetings this afternoon?"

HE USES A GLUE-STICK TO STICK HIS FOREHEAD TO THE DESK.

▸▸ STATIONERY ROOM

RACHEL IS ADJUSTING HER BREASTS. MARTIN LEANS ON THE STABLE DOOR AND WATCHES. THE DOOR SWINGS BACK AND HE BANGS HIS HEAD.

RACHEL: Oi, peeper!

MARTIN: What, me?

RACHEL: Yeah, you. Lurking and watching.

MARTIN: I wasn't lurking, I'm moving about, I'm in motion in the hospital, just you know...

RACHEL: All right, well, seeing as you're here, I've just put a new bra on and I think it makes my boobs look uneven. What do you think?

MARTIN: Well... um... maybe the... the right one is a tiny teenth higher than the — the left.

RACHEL ADJUSTS HER BRA.

▸▸ CORRIDOR

CAROLINE: So, Emilily.

Mr. Prentice,

Please excuse Stuart from the cross country run. He is allergic to grass pollen, cows, training shoes and his own sweat.

Sincerely
Harriet Schulenburg

MAC: Emmy, Emmy. Yeah, what about her?

CAROLINE: No disrespect, but she is a bit posh.

MAC: Yeah, maybe she is, but you know what? There's nothing wrong with being a bit posh.

CAROLINE: I'm not saying there is. I suppose I'm just thinking about my own experience with posh girls at college.

MAC: Oh yeah.

CAROLINE: She doesn't march about a bit too much? You know, with quite big strides and swinging her arms? "Rah rah rah", for instance?

MAC: For instance no, she doesn't do that, no.

CAROLINE: That's good.

▸▸ STATIONERY ROOM

RACHEL IS JUMPING UP AND DOWN IN FRONT OF MARTIN.

RACHEL: Well? Well?

MARTIN: Um... rocks, they're like — yeah, solid, absolutely...

RACHEL: Great. Cheers. Go on then, go back to your moving around thing you do.

MARTIN: Um...

MARTIN GOES.

▸▸ X-RAY WAITING AREA

CAROLINE: So she doesn't have a big snorty laugh, but no sense of humour? Or have unresolved sexual tensions with her father or a brother who works in the City? Or a friend called Poppy who's an interior designer and always seems to be squeezing out babies, and she doesn't covet an Aga or have a great aunt who agreed with Hitler? Or have friends in Wiltshire and she's never stopped the car to have a wee in a bush...

MAC: No, she hasn't, she has not and she doesn't, and she, and she, no. No.

CAROLINE: Good.

MAC: Fine.

CAROLINE: She sounds great then.

MAC: Yes.

▸▸ OFFICE

JOANNA COMES OUT OF HER OFFICE TO TALK TO KIM, WHO IS SITTING AT HER DESK, BUT IS RELUCTANT TO MOVE AND LOOKING A BIT DISTRACTED.

JOANNA: Kimmy, where are the F25s?

KIM: Hmm?

JOANNA: The F25s?

KIM: Um... top drawer.

JOANNA: Get them myself, shall I?!

KIM: Yeah.

JOANNA GETS THE FORMS.

JOANNA: Are you all right?

KIM: Uh?

JOANNA: Are you all right?

KIM: Yeah.

JOANNA: Are you going to this auction thingie tonight?

KIM: Er — er — probably.

JOANNA: Hmm. Got your eye on anyone in particular?

KIM: No.

JOANNA: Hmm, well thanks for the scintillating conversation.

JOANNA GOES BACK INTO HER OFFICE. BOYCE'S HEAD APPEARS FROM UNDER KIM'S DESK. HE GETS SOME AIR AND THEN GOES BACK UNDER AGAIN.

▸▸ CORRIDOR BY LIFT

CAROLINE IS WAITING FOR THE LIFT. SUE COMES UP TO HER.

CAROLINE: What?

SUE: Lovely day.

CAROLINE: I thought it was cloudy and chilly.

SUE: Yeah.

A LIFT ARRIVES.

SUE: In you go.

CAROLINE: Don't you want it?

SUE: No no. No no, just wanted to see you safely into the metal womb.

CAROLINE SUDDENLY CHANGES HER MIND ABOUT USING THE LIFT.

CAROLINE: I'll take the stairs.

SUE: Sure?

CAROLINE: Yeah.

SUE: Can't tempt you?

CAROLINE: No. And don't follow me.

CAROLINE GOES DOWN THE STAIRWELL. SUE LISTENS. MARTIN COMES UP AND SEES SUE.

MARTIN: (IN AMAZEMENT) Someone tied this bloody wire across the stairs, that's really dangerous!

SUE SLAPS MARTIN.

MARTIN: Ow!

SUE: Give me that!

MARTIN: What was that for?

SUE: Nothing, nothing at all.

SUE STORMS OFF.

▸▸ OFFICE

RACHEL IS PRETENDING TO BE STEVIE WONDER AT HER DESK, SWAYING FROM SIDE TO SIDE, WITH A PAIR OF SUNGLASSES ON. JOANNA COMES OUT OF HER OFFICE AND BREAKS THE LENSES OUT OF THE GLASSES. SHE PUTS THEM BACK ON RACHEL'S FACE AND GOES BACK INTO HER OFFICE.

RACHEL: Thanks for the glasses mate.

RACHEL GIVES THE FRAMES BACK TO KAREN. IN THE INTERIOR OFFICE, JOANNA IS DROOLING OVER PICTURES OF LYNDON IN THE HOSPITAL MAGAZINE.

▸▸ STAFF LIAISON OFFICE

SUE: Oh God, do you know I am sorry to drag you in here again Mac, I know this is boring. Bloody computer virus has wiped off half your records. So... (SHE REFERS TO HIS RECORDS) still single I see, and no one can understand it, why you haven't been snapped up is a mystery to me.

MAC: Ah ha.

SUE: God I want you. But not just sexually, in every way. I want

"No no, just wanted to see you safely into the metal womb."

to wake up next to you, watch you sleep, run my hand over your back and edge forward into regions knowing that in my hand I could make you feel like no other could. Mobile phone number?

MAC: 07956 — actually I'm between networks.

SUE: Right, okay. And, oh my God, I want to feel you in my mouth. House number?

MAC: Twenty-one.

SUE: That's it, that's all we were missing. All righty. Well, you know, you're free to go. See you at the slave auction.

MAC: Oh yes.

SUE: I have an unlimited budget.

MAC LEAVES.

▸▸ NOTICE BOARD, CORRIDOR

MAC RUNS DOWN THE CORRIDOR AND FINDS MARTIN AT THE NOTICE BOARD.

MAC: Martin! Martin, I'm in grave danger.

MARTIN: From what?

MAC: White Mischief, The Madness of Queen Sue, she said she wants to reach into my regions and feel me in her mouth.

MARTIN: No one ever says that to me.

MAC: I want to be withdrawn from the auction.

MARTIN: No, no, you can't do that, because you're the star attraction.

MAC: Mate, I'm sorry, okay, I'll write a big cheque out towards the Fluoroscopy Suite...

MAC SEES SUE LURKING ROUND THE CORNER.

MAC: Fuck it, fuck it, I'll buy the whole thing, all right? A 150 grand? Bargain.

HE RUNS OFF. SUE CHASES HIM, HOLDING ONTO HER CROTCH. MARTIN WATCHES.

▸▸ BAR

GUY, CAROLINE AND MAC ENTER.

GUY: No, no, she's not in here... Look, I know what's cheating and what isn't, because I know the rules. (TO BARMAID) Hello Barbara, I'd like a pint of Guinness and two bitter lemons for the ladies, please. (TO MAC AND CAROLINE) The match is null and void and Mac is a cheat.

MAC: No, you won't have to put up with me cheating much

longer. Unless you come and visit me in Sheffield.

CAROLINE: What?

GUY: Sheffield?

MAC: Yes, in South Yorkshire.

CAROLINE: What would you want — what's the point of Sheffield?

MAC: What's the point of Sheffield?

CAROLINE: Hmm.

MAC: I think originally it was an easily defended site, because there was a river to the north and the east. They built a castle, then there was a church, a market, they made wool. Er — then they became famous for cutlery and then there was the invention of crucible steel...

CAROLINE: I know, I know, I know, but what's the point of you going to Sheffield?

MAC: Because that's where my new job is. And I thought, hey, if that's where my new job is, I should go there. I know a lot of people work from home these days, but it's really hard for surgeons.

GUY: They sacked you at last, did they? They saw through the ginger bluff and the boyish charm. I can't say I'm surprised.

MAC: No I resigned, because Sheffield offered me a consultancy.

CAROLINE: A consultant? Wow! Congratulations.

MAC: Thank you.

GUY: Yeah, well I mean, Sheffield.

CAROLINE: When do you leave?

MAC: Next week.

GUY: Oh God! Couldn't they make it any sooner?

CAROLINE: Guy.

GUY: Well, come on, I know technically he's a good surgeon, so in that case I suppose he'll be missed, but I'm sure we'll cope.

CAROLINE: He is your friend.

GUY: Dah, he's a wanker!

CAROLINE: And I'm sure he'll miss you as well.

MAC: Dah, he's a wanker. Jesus, here she comes. Cover me. Cover me.

MAC GOES, AS SUE COMES OVER TO GUY AND CAROLINE.

SUE: Hi, has anyone seen Mac?

GUY: Yeah, he's in Sheffield apparently.

▶▶ SCHOOL

IT IS PARENTS' EVENING. HARRIET IS WAITING TO SEE ROBBIE'S TEACHER. ANOTHER MUM SITS NEXT TO HER.

MUM: Hello.

HARRIET: Hi.

MUM: I'm Josh's mum.

HARRIET: Hi, I'm Robbie's mum.

MUM: Oh right. Wow!

HARRIET GETS ON WITH HER KNITTING.

SCHOOL TEACHER: Mrs Schulenburg.

HARRIET: Hello.

TEACHER: Hello.

HARRIET: Hi.

TEACHER: Would you like to come through?

HARRIET: Yeah. Sorry.

Mr. Prentice,

Please excuse Stuart from rugby practice. He has a tremendous fear of anything ovoid.

Sincerely
Harriet Schulenburg

▶▶ BAR

PREPARATIONS ARE UNDERWAY FOR THE STAFF SLAVE AUCTION.

TECHNICIAN: (TESTING MIKE) One two. One two.

CEO: ...Slave auction...

▶▶ SCHOOL

TEACHER: Now. Robbie... Is there any history of mental illness in the family?

HARRIET: No.

TEACHER: Are you sure?

HARRIET: Yeah, I think so.

TEACHER: You know about the penguin with the chainsaw?

HARRIET: Yes... but every child has an imaginary friend.

TEACHER: Robbie twitches quite a lot facially, except when he's pretending to be dead, which can last for several hours in a day.

HARRIET: I — I imagine that's less disruptive.

TEACHER: He licks people's legs and he's told us that you and his father don't bleed.

HARRIET: Hmm...

TEACHER: It's best to nip it in the bud. Are there any major problems at home?

HARRIET: He does... he does like to eat bread straight from the freezer — bread lollies he calls them — but we thought that was kind of sweet.

THE AUCTION HAS BEGUN.

CEO: He can slip off your cover and tamper with your circuits, he's our very own IT man, it's Lyndon Jones.

THE GIRLS ALL CHEER FOR LYNDON.

CEO: Certainly a popular lad. We have twenty pounds from the lady in pink. Thirty. All right, thirty... forty... and seventy from the lady in the spots. Okay. Seventy pounds...

WOMAN: One hundred pounds.

CEO: One hundred pounds from the lady down here on the right, thank you very much madam.

WOMAN: Two hundred!

CEO: All right, I have two hundred pounds from the lady on my left. Any advance on two hundred pounds?

JOANNA: (COOL AND DELIBERATE) Five hundred pounds.

THERE IS A BIG REACTION FROM THE AUDIENCE.

CEO: Well! We have five hundred pounds from Joanna Clore. Any — any advance on five hundred pounds? ...No, it doesn't look like we're going to get anything else there. Sold to the Head of Human Resources — Joanna Clore.

APPLAUSE AND CHEERS FROM THE AUDIENCE, AS JOANNA AND LYNDON MAKE THEIR WAY TOWARDS THE DOOR.

CEO: If you'd just like to collect your restaurant voucher on the way out from Maria... and be gentle with him. All right, now we have a new member of staff on offer, it's none other than... Doctor Todd.

SOME APPLAUSE AS CAROLINE WALKS ONTO THE STAGE.

CEO: Right. Who's going to open the bidding for Doctor Todd?

GIRL: Five pounds.

GUY: Oh, a snatch terrier! You do know that's a woman, don't you? Don't let the manly features fool you.

MARTIN RUSHES IN, PANTING WITH EXHAUSTION.

MARTIN: Hang on, wait, wait. Three thousand pounds!

THE AUDIENCE GASP.

CEO: Three *thousand?*

MARTIN: It's a banker's draft.

CEO: (BAFFLED) Right. Sold to the gentleman down here for — three thousand pounds.

APPLAUSE ALL ROUND AS MARTIN STRUGGLES TO CARRY CAROLINE OFF.

CEO: Love lift us 'Up Where We Belong'…

» SCHOOL

THE TEACHER IS SHOWING HARRIET AN EXERCISE BOOK.

TEACHER: …And here he's been making sentences using words beginning with SM.

HARRIET: I see.

TEACHER: (READS) "My mummy smokes", "My mummy smacks me"…

HARRIET: Oh no, I don't actually.

TEACHER: Oh no no, it's just a — it's just an exercise.

HARRIET: No, we don't believe in smacking.

TEACHER: Mm, I'm sure.

HARRIET: And… this one actually is wrong — this one…

TEACHER: "My mummy's bottom smells."

HARRIET: Yes, that one's obviously made up.

TEACHER: Oh yeah, I'm sure it is.

HARRIET: Yes, but you've ticked it, you've given it a tick?

TEACHER: Yes, yes well that's because it is correct within the confines of the exercise.

HARRIET: Hmm. You see, I don't think you should have ticked it, because it looks like you're agreeing with the statement.

TEACHER: Oh no no, I wasn't in any way condoning the accusation, or…

HARRIET: Right. Because I mean that's obviously a crazy imagination running riot.

TEACHER: All right.

Mr. Prentice,

Please stop referring to Stuart as Spazzo. it is not his fault he's physiologically flimsy. A ten month pregnancy and toxic umbilical chord have left him in a weakened state. Your derogatory comments and name calling set a poor example for the other children and unlike Stuart, you have no excuse.

Harriet Schulenburg

▶ TAXI

JOANNA AND LYNDON ARE ON THE WAY TO THEIR REST-AURANT DATE. LYNDON LOOKS FAR FROM EXCITED.

JOANNA: So, Lyndon. What fascinates you, hmm?

LYNDON: Binary code.

JOANNA: Does it? Yeah, yeah, it does me too, all those ones and zeros.

LYNDON: Indeed.

JOANNA: Hmm, hard little rods and tight little holes just waiting to meet up and make something very very special.

LYNDON: You should teach.

JOANNA: You don't give much away do you, Lyndie? You're like an iceberg.

LYNDON: White?

JOANNA: No, no, we just don't ever get to see more than one tenth of you.

LYNDON: So what are you — the Titanic?

JOANNA: Yeah, yeah — I'm the Titanic and you can rip into my hull and flood my front lower chambers...

JOANNA LAUGHS. LYNDON IS A PICTURE OF UTTER DISDAIN.

▶ DAY WARD, NIGHT

MARTIN, BREATHLESS WITH JOY, RUSHES UP TO MAC.

MARTIN: I did it! I did it! Caroline's going home, she's getting ready — we're going to meet in the restaurant!

MAC: No!

MARTIN: Yeah!

MAC: Nice one. Congratulations.

HE SHAKES MARTIN'S HAND.

MARTIN: Thanks!

MAC: Yeah.

SHEER PANIC SETS IN.

MARTIN: I can't do it.

MAC: What?

MARTIN: I'm not going to be able to do it.

MAC: Of course you can.

MARTIN: I can't.

MAC: Just let go, let go. That's it. Of course you can.

MARTIN: I feel like I'm doing something wrong. I just, we — me and Caroline, we talk, blah blah blah, you know...

MAC: Is it always those three things, or...?

MARTIN: That — well that was this morning — but what I'm saying is, I want to get onto the next level.

MAC: Okay. Maybe... she sees you as too much of a friend.

MARTIN: God, yes.

MAC: Have you tried being — have you tried being nastier?

MARTIN: No.

MAC: Okay, well you know, look at Guy, right? Complete bastard — doesn't seem to stop him getting to the next level, does it? In fact, it seems to help.

MARTIN: Right, yeah! Like — treat 'em keen, keep 'em mean?

MAC: Yeah. Well, other way round, but yeah.

▶ BAR

GUY IS 'ON STAGE'. THE CEO CHECKS HIS NOTES FOR THE NEXT INTRODUCTION.

CEO: He's Swiss...

GUY: Yes.

CEO: He's Gay Secretan.

LAUGHTER ALL ROUND.

GUY: Yeah, that's — that's *Guy* Secretan.

CEO: Sorry, sorry. He's gay Guy Secretan.

GUY: No, no. There's no gay, it's just Guy.

CEO: Right, yes, he's — he's just — he's plain old Guy Secretan.

GUY: That's right, girls.

CEO: So. Who'll er... who'll start the bidding? Who would like to try this fine figure of a man?

RACHEL: Yeah, we've all tried him.

KIM: He's easy.

RACHEL: Slag.

SUE: Right, this is shite!! Can we just have Doctor MacCartney on now please?

CEO: Er, sorry... (CONSULTING NOTES) Doctor MacCartney has had to withdraw from the auction because his cat is ill.

SUE: (A HORRIBLE, UNEARTHLY SCREAM) No-o-o-o-o-o-o-o-o-o-o-o-o-o!!!!!!

THE WHOLE ROOM HAS FALLEN SILENT IN ASTONISHMENT.

GUY: Well, the old sick cat excuse comes out again, some people just can't stand the heat, can they?

CEO: Right... could we have your bids please?

GUY: Come on.

KAREN: Four pounds.

GUY: Yeah, see? There we go.

WOMAN: Oh yes, ten pounds.

GUY: Yeah, all right — no wrinklies, thank you.

SUE: Okay, thirty quid for donkey boy.

CEO: Sold over there.

SUE MAKES DONKEY NOISES.

GUY: (LOOKING WORRIED) There might be some other bids...

CEO: No, I don't think so.

APPLAUSE FROM THE CROWD AND MORE DONKEY NOISES FROM SUE.

MAC: I tell you what, a bit of shadow boxing, okay?

MARTIN: Shadow boxing?

MAC: Right, okay. Right, hit these babies, lay on me, okay? Come on, lay on me.

MARTIN: I don't want to hurt you.

MAC: Come on. Come on...

MARTIN PUNCHES MAC'S HANDS.

MAC: Woah, that's it. Yeah, not too hard. Yeah, that's it, lovely, right.

MARTIN: Yes!

MAC: It's the end of the evening...

MARTIN: Right.

MAC: Right, you've been out...

MARTIN: Yeah.

MAC: Great time — but be assertive, don't be so nice. Assertive.

MARTIN: Okay.

MAC: Right. I'll be Caroline.

MARTIN: Okay, right.

MAC: Oh, you know — thank you, thank you for a lovely meal. What shall we do now?

MARTIN: Um... right, well, let's — let's go upstairs, get into bed and have some bloomin' sex.

MARTIN HITS MAC QUITE HARD.

MAC: Argh!

MARTIN: Sorry, sorry.

MAC: Jesus fucking Christ!

MARTIN: I'm just — I can be a bit dangerous sometimes.

MAC: No, better, better. Better. Right, okay...

MARTIN: Right. Yes.

MAC: All right?

MARTIN: Yeah! Come on, let's have sex, you bitch! Grrr!

MAC: Yeah.

CEO: Next up we have... a senior consultant. Yes, it's your ever-popular Director of Radiology — it's Doctor Alan Statham.

STATHAM MAKES A DRAMATIC ENTRANCE, WEARING A GLADIATOR COSTUME WHICH IS NOT QUITE LONG ENOUGH TO HIDE HIS RATHER UNSETTLING GREY UNDERPANTS. HE IS HOLDING A CASSETTE PLAYER, WHICH IS PLAYING A FANFARE.

CEO: (UNDER HIS BREATH) Holy fuck... (TO THE AUDIENCE) Sorry. Well I... I thought it was Alan Statham, but it appears we've got Russell Crowe instead. Um... who's going to open the bids? Do I hear fifty pounds?

BOYCE: I'll give you 50p.

STATHAM: No, a man can't buy a man. It's against the law.

CEO: Oh? And what law is that then?

STATHAM: It's... Julius Caesar's... quad hominis lex.

CEO: Right. Okay... any advance on 50p?

BOYCE: 30p!

CEO: 30p...

STATHAM: Stop it! That's enough.

CEO: Come along now... The sword alone must be worth more than 30p...

CAROLINE JOINS MARTIN IN A RESTAURANT. MARTIN IS SLOUCHED IN HIS CHAIR IN WHAT HE CONSIDERS A VERY COOL FASHION.

CAROLINE: Hi.

MARTIN: (VERY OFFHAND) Whatever.

CAROLINE: Oh. Can you pour some wine?

MARTIN: Get it yourself.

CAROLINE: What?

MARTIN: Get the bloody wine yourself!

CAROLINE: Martin? Is that you?

MARTIN: Well yeah. I mean, of course it's me, fuzz head.

CAROLINE: Hello? It's me — Caroline...? You've been to my house, remember?

MARTIN: It's not *your* house, it's your brother's house. Bloody women.

CAROLINE: I'm not sure I like your tone tonight, Martin.

MARTIN: Fuck off.

▶▶ MEXICAN RESTAURANT

LYNDON IS LOOKING VERY UNCOMFORTABLE AND FORMAL. JOANNA IS GETTING INCREASINGLY HYSTERICAL.

JOANNA: (LAUGHING) Naughty! You are so funny, Lyndon!

LYNDON: I didn't say anything.

JOANNA: GSOH. Good Sense Of Humour. Crucial. "Cruc-i-al."

JOANNA DRINKS SHOTS.

JOANNA: Oh! Ole! Andale! Ariba!

▶▶ LOUNGE BAR

GUY AND SUE ARE SITTING HAVING A DRINK.

SUE: Right, now you are my slave and I can make you do anything I want you to, Doctor Secretan.

GUY: Yeah, within reason, okay?

SUE: Well not necessarily, you know. Right, for instance, pop this on.

SHE GIVES GUY A GINGER WIG.

Subject: Racism Initiative
From: guy.secretan@ehtrust.gov.uk
To: charles.robertson.CEO@ehtrustboard.gov.uk

Whilst I applaud the ANTI-RACIST INITIATIVE being proposed by the Trust, can I suggest that a certain degree of discrimination should surely be allowed for the following obvious exemptions?

French (big noses, shrugging)
Chinese (spitting, wrong colour)
Italians (wavy-about hands, general smell)
Dutch (that throat noise when they 'talk')
Germans (shorts, thick necks)
Australians (look keen but dim, like wrong dogs)
New Zealanders (as above, but dimmer)
Americans (obvious)
Belgians (Poirot)
Irish (sausage fingers, ruddy faces)
Greeks (look like they wank in bushes)
Welsh (whine, whine, whine, whine, whine)
Scots (pale, too much nylon)
Russians (the men look like murderers, the women like prostitutes)
Swedes (beards, Abba)
Mexicans (childish food)
Spaniards (women all look like lesbian tennis players)
Turks (moustaches, tiny cups of sweet tea)
Indians (thin legs, shit cars)

Totally unacceptable! Report sender to H.R.

GUY: What?

SUE: Come on, slave. Pop that on. Pop it on, pop it on, pop it on.

GUY PUTS THE WIG ON.

SUE: Oh, that's pretty good, yeah. It's... ooh, just — you know, suck your cheeks in.

GUY: Why?

SUE: Just do it.

GUY: Right. Okay.

SUE: Just, you know — pretend you've got cheekbones, that's it, and say — say — "Hello Sue."

GUY: Hello Sue.

SUE: "I'm, I'm — I'm Doctor MacCartney."

GUY: I'm Doctor — oh I'm not saying that, oh for God's sake!

SUE: Yeah, touch my bottom. Touch. Touch.

RELUCTANTLY, GUY DOES INDEED TOUCH SUE'S BOTTOM.

▶▶ CHIC RESTAURANT

BOYCE AND STATHAM ARE SITTING IN A RATHER CAMP RESTAURANT, SAYING NOTHING.

WAITER: Shall I light the candles now?

STATHAM: No thank you.

BOYCE: Yes please.

THE WAITER LIGHTS THE VERY CAMP CANDLE LAMP.

BOYCE: Thank you.

WAITRESS: Who would like to taste the wine?

STATHAM: Er yes — yes *I* would.

BOYCE: Actually, that'll be me.

STATHAM: I — I rather think, with my years of experience...

BOYCE: Yes, well I rather think...

STATHAM: No no, I rather...

BOYCE: I bought you for 30p!

STATHAM: Would you sssh, speak in...

▶▶ OUTSIDE BRASSERIE

MARTIN IS ON THE PAVEMENT, USING HIS MOBILE PHONE. CAROLINE IS TRYING TO HAIL A CAB.

MARTIN: Hello Mac? It's Martin. Um... well, on the whole, I'd say it's not really working.

CAROLINE: Taxi!

MARTIN: No, Mac, Mac, Mac. Mac, Mac, Mac, no, she's not actually speaking to me any more.

▶▶ MEXICAN RESTAURANT

JOANNA IS EROTICALLY LICKING SOME SOUR CREAM.

LYNDON: No. I'm allergic to sour cream.

JOANNA: Have some.

LYNDON: No.

JOANNA WIPES SOME CREAM ONTO LYNDON'S MOUTH.

LYNDON: That's lovely, thanks.

JOANNA WIPES LYNDON'S MOUTH. HE PUSHES HER AWAY.

JOANNA: Sorry.

▶▶ OUTSIDE BRASSERIE

MARTIN IS STILL ON HIS MOBILE. CAROLINE IS STILL DESPERATELY TRYING TO HAIL A CAB.

MARTIN: Right. Oh that is — that is brilliant! Thank you Mac, thank you, oh I love you! In a manly man kind of a way. Thank you. Okay, yes, goodbye.

CAROLINE: Stop!!

▶▶ CHIC RESTAURANT

BOYCE AND STATHAM ARE SITTING TOGETHER AT THEIR TABLE.

STATHAM DOESN'T SAY ANYTHING.

BOYCE: Well this is nice, isn't it? Civilised. Two men alone. (SILENCE) So. Er... any interest in football? No, me neither. (SILENCE) So, top ten favourite films...

THE WAITRESS COMES WITH FOOD AND OVERHEARS STATHAM.

STATHAM: Joanna brought me here once... to discuss hospital employment policy. Um... surreptitiously, however, I was bringing her to climax with a breadstick.

▶▶ LOUNGE BAR

GUY IS SUFFERING, STILL WEARING THE 'MAC' WIG.

SUE: Let's — let's buy a sofa together Mac, shall we? It's nice, isn't it?

GUY: Oh it's great.

SUE: Nice showroom this, isn't it? Not too — not too busy for a Saturday. Like this one... shall we?

GUY: Yeah, oh yeah, yeah.

SUE: Yeah, shall we, shall we...? Shall we buy it?

GUY: Yes, let's buy it, darling. Yes.

SUE: Okay.

GUY: I can see my white puny body draped across it.

SUE: Can you?

GUY: Yes, I can see... I can see my ginger pubes.

SUE: (LOVING IT) Oh stop it!

GUY: You know, collecting in the cracks.

SUE: Oh in my crack, you can collect it in my crack, yeah, yeah. Ooh, you're lovely. Eh? Oooh, you lovely thing.

▸▸ MEXICAN RESTAURANT

LYNDON IS STANDING STILL. JOANNA IS SALSA DANCING ALL OVER HIM.

JOANNA: You are a wonderful dancer.

LYNDON: Thanks. That's lovely, thanks.

▸▸ CHIC RESTAURANT

STATHAM AND BOYCE ARE DRINKING A LOT OF WINE.

STATHAM: This is super.

▸▸ BRASSERIE

MARTIN AND CAROLINE ARE BACK SITTING AT THE TABLE.

CAROLINE: (LOOKING A BIT PUZZLED) So, when Mac suggested

this nightclub, did he know there was going to be a hypnotist?

MARTIN: Well, um... no, you see — sorry, sorry about all that, because that's — what I meant is that we went for a drink and there happened to be a cabaret there and muggins here gets picked on and, you know, pulled up on stage, and hey presto — I'm turned into a complete bastard. And so — bummer. Sorry.

CAROLINE: And the... the trigger word is er...

SHE PICKS UP A WINE BOTTLE.

MARTIN: Exactly, yeah, the word beginning with W, rhymes with nine. Yeah. And Mac knew to snap me out of it he had to say "milk", and that's why...

CAROLINE: Hmm. Good old Mac...

MARTIN: Yeah. So, I was thinking that, that maybe, you know, it's time for you and me to get to know each other properly?

CAROLINE: (BUT HER MIND HAS DRIFTED) Good old Mac... He'll be gone soon.

MARTIN: Yeah. Yeah. Anyway, coming back to the us getting to know each other properly thing for a moment...

CAROLINE: I love Mac.

MARTIN: Hmm...

▸▸ STREET

JOANNA IS STILL DANCING AROUND LYNDON.

LYNDON: Right, well I'd better get a cab.

JOANNA: What, to mine?

LYNDON: Home.

JOANNA: Mi casa es su casa.

LYNDON: No thanks.

JOANNA: Oh come on, we've had a fantastic night. We don't want to stop the fun now.

LYNDON: It's for charity.

JOANNA: Yeah, well you know, charity begins at home.

▸▸ CHIC RESTAURANT

STATHAM: You are a very clever man.

BOYCE: No, *you* are a very clever man.

STATHAM: No. No, no, you are a very clever clever man.

BOYCE: No, no you are.

STATHAM: No, no you are...

BOYCE: No you, you...

STATHAM: No no, don't be stupid.

BOYCE: I'm not stupid.

STATHAM: No no, I never said you were.

BOYCE: I think you did, I think you said I was stupid.

STATHAM: You crazy bitch!

BOYCE: Interesting, but put the breadstick down.

STATHAM: Ah — ah.

▸▸ STREET

JOANNA: Look, there's no point beating about the bush Lyndon, I'm going to let you into a little secret. I find you immensely physically attractive.

LYNDON: I'm sure you're just saying that to be kind.

JOANNA: Join with me and pleasure your physical body as well as your mind, you poor poor lovely man.

LYNDON: I'd rather not.

JOANNA: Why?!

LYNDON: Because you're disturbing, tedious and desperate. That's why.

JOANNA: Me?

LYNDON: Yes, sorry, that's how it is. Look, why, why don't we just go back and forget this ever happened?

JOANNA: Yeah. Yeah, you're right, yeah, let's do that.

LYNDON: Right, well bye.

LYNDON GETS IN A TAXI. JOANNA RUNS ROUND TO GET IN AS WELL.

JOANNA: I don't mind swallowing!

SHE GETS IN THE CAB WHICH PULLS AWAY. LYNDON HAS GOT OUT OF THE OTHER SIDE AND IS LEFT STANDING ON THE PAVEMENT — A RELIEVED MAN. HE RUNS OFF.

▸▸ BRASSERIE

THE WAITER BRINGS THEIR FOOD.

WAITER: Spaghetti carbonara?

MARTIN: Oh I think um...

CAROLINE: That's me, thank you.

WAITER: "Oeuf a la coq mouillette." Boiled egg and soldiers?

MARTIN: Oh yeah, that's me, thank you.

WAITER: Would you like to drink some more wine?

MARTIN: I don't think, do we — ?

MARTIN REALISES THAT THE WAITER HAS SAID "WINE" — THE TRIGGER WORD — AND THAT CAROLINE IS LOOKING AT HIM FOR A REACTION.

MARTIN: ...no, piss off, you Spanish bastard!

CAROLINE: French.

MARTIN: I don't speak French, you stupid bitch!

CAROLINE: Milk, milk, milk...!

WAITER: Is that two milks?

MARTIN: (SUDDENLY MILD-MANNERED AGAIN) Yes, thank you very much. Thanks.

CAROLINE: Phew.

JOANNA IS BACK AT HOME. SHE TAKES A POLAROID PHOTO OF HERSELF AND GLUES IT INTO AN ALBUM. SHE WRITES IN SOME DETAILS.

JOANNA: Right. Day four, week twenty-five.

SHE FLIPS THROUGH THE ALBUM OF POLAROIDS, LIKE A FLIP-BOOK, FORWARDS...

JOANNA: Younger... older. (...AND THEN BACKWARDS) Older... younger. (FORWARDS) Siren... hag.

SHE CARRIES ON FLIPPING THROUGH THE PHOTOS OF HERSELF.

▸▸ STATHAM'S BEDROOM

STATHAM IS ASLEEP IN BED WITH A THUMB IN HIS MOUTH. HIS ALARM CLOCK GOES OFF. WE REALISE THE THUMB BELONGS TO SOMEONE ELSE. STATHAM DISCOVERS THAT THE OTHER PERSON IS BOYCE.

STATHAM: Just — silence!

BOYCE: No, but...

STATHAM: Get out! Get out!

BOYCE: I can't.

STATHAM: Just get out of my inner sanctum this minute!

BOYCE: But I've got no pants on.

STATHAM IS PANICKING. HE WARNS BOYCE TO KEEP HIS EYES SHUT.

STATHAM: Closed.

BOYCE: Closed.

BOYCE KEEPS HIS EYES CLOSED WHILE STATHAM GETS OUT OF BED, CLUTCHING HIS ROMAN OUTFIT.

BOYCE: (EYES STILL SHUT) Ooh, you look lovely.

STATHAM: Sssh! No no! If you, if anything — you...

STATHAM SIDLES OUT OF THE BEDROOM.

STATHAM: It's not — !

EPISODE 9

▸▸ STREET

TO THE SOUND OF THE BEE GEES' 'STAYING ALIVE', GUY IS STRUTTING TOWARDS WORK, LIKE JOHN TRAVOLTA IN *SATURDAY NIGHT FEVER*.

▸▸ HOSPITAL CAR PARK

MARTIN ARRIVES IN THE HOSPITAL CAR PARK ON HIS SCOOTER.

▸▸ RADIOLOGY CORRIDOR

STATHAM SWIRLS HIS WHITE COAT AS HE WALKS DOWN THE CORRIDOR.

▸▸ CORRIDOR

BOYCE IS PEDDLING A KID'S TRICYCLE DOWN THE HOSPITAL CORRIDOR.

▸▸ STREET

GUY DELIBERATELY OBSTRUCTS A NURSE AS HE BOOGIES DOWN THE STREET.

▸▸ HOSPITAL CAR PARK

MARTIN PULLS HIS SCOOTER UP NEXT TO JOANNA'S CAR.

▸▸ HOSPITAL CHAPEL

STATHAM GOES INTO THE HOSPITAL CHAPEL.

▸▸ OUTSIDE THE HOSPITAL

GUY'S ARMS NEARLY DECAPITATE TWO NURSES AS HIS TRAVOLTA ROUTINE CONTINUES.

▸▸ HOSPITAL CAR PARK

MARTIN PARKS NEXT TO JOANNA'S CAR. SHE IS CHECKING HERSELF IN THE REAR-VIEW MIRROR.

▸▸ OUTSIDE HOSPITAL

GUY STRUTS HIS STUFF TOWARDS THE ENTRANCE.

▸▸ HOSPITAL CAR PARK

MARTIN TAPS ON JOANNA'S CAR WINDOW. SHE KNOCKS MARTIN WITH HER DOOR AS SHE OPENS IT.

JOANNA: What are you doing here?

MARTIN: Well, I'm not allowed to come to your home, we can't speak at the hospital, so...

JOANNA: Well that includes the car park, you cretin!

▸▸ CORRIDOR

EMMY LINKS ARMS WITH MAC AND GIVES HIM A HUGE SMILE.

▸▸ HOSPITAL CAR PARK

MARTIN: I've been to see a therapist.

JOANNA: Oh, how fascinating. Did he agree with everyone else? Did he say hopeless case? Freak of nature?

MARTIN: No, she said that I've got a lot of anger inside me and I should let it out, express my inner feelings, all the things that have upset me. So do you have a minute?

JOANNA: No!

▸▸ WAITING AREA

SUE WHITE IS RIDING ON A CAMEL THROUGH THE HOSPITAL.

▸▸ HOSPITAL CAR PARK

MARTIN: You've let me down; you weren't there for me Mum.

JOANNA: Shut up! Not here.

MARTIN: Look, I needed you to make my packed lunches, I needed you to pick me up from swimming and I needed you to make that Incredible Hulk costume for Halloween.

JOANNA: Yes, and I need you to shut up right now, or you'll be looking for another job.

SHE SLAPS HIS CRASH HELMIT.

▶▶ **OUTSIDE HOSPITAL ENTRANCE**

GUY JUMPS ON A GURNEY WITH A PATIENT ON IT, WHICH A PARAMEDIC IS PUSHING ALONG.

▶▶ **HOSPITAL CAR PARK**

MARTIN: I've got an angry penis!

SOMEONE WALKS PAST AS HE SAYS THIS. MARTIN THROWS HIS GLOVE ONTO THE BONNET OF JOANNA'S CAR. THE ALARM GOES OFF.

▶▶ **HOSPITAL ENTRANCE**

GUY TURNS HIS BACK, LIFTS HIS JACKET AND USES HIS ARSE TO BUMP A WHEELCHAIR WITH AN OLD MAN IN IT INTO THE CAR PARK. GUY GOES THROUGH THE HOSPITAL DOORS, GRABBING A PASSING NURSE IN A ROMANTIC 'DANCE' MOVE. HE DROPS HER AND SHE FALLS TO THE GROUND.

▶▶ **WARD AREA**

ANGELA: You can't not go to his leaving drinks. It's his last day. You won't see him again.

ANGELA IS PUTTING COINS INTO AN OLD LADY'S CHARITY TIN.

CAROLINE: I know, it's just that Emily's going to be there, I'm not sure I can take that, that's the worst thing, I think. I can handle just Mac going to Sheffield, it's the fact the little slut bitch daughter of Satan has arranged to go there with him! (TO THE CHARITY COLLECTOR) Sorry, sorry. Er, no thank you.

ANGELA: Oh this is stupid; you've got to tell him how you feel.

CAROLINE: What's the point? They're practically married.

ANGELA: Well what have you got to lose? You're never going to see him again. Look, the worst that can happen is that he rejects you, totally humiliates you.

CAROLINE: Good point.

▶▶ **MAIN CORRIDOR**

GUY IS HOLDING MARTIN AGAINST THE WALL ABOUT TWO FEET OFF THE GROUND.

GUY: Yes. You see, it's all about upper arm strength.

MAC: Yeah.

GUY RELEASES MARTIN AND CARRIES ON TALKING TO MAC.

GUY: Yeah, and that's why you will never be able to sail around the world. At least, not single-handedly.

MAC: Right, but you would, would you?

GUY: Yeah, if I had the backing, if I had the time, you know. Oh shit! Um — Martin, in my car, brown leather briefcase, quick as your little pixie legs can carry you. Go on, run along, I'll be in HQ.

MARTIN: I'm not your slave.

GUY: You've been misinformed.

MAC: (TO GUY) Nice trousers.

GUY: Yeah.

GUY WALKS OFF. MARTIN TURNS TO GO OUT TO THE CAR PARK.

MAC: You're not going to go are you?

MARTIN: Well yeah, I'd better.

MAC: Why? What's he going to do? He's not going to attach electrodes to your nipples is he?

MARTIN: Well no. He'll probably do something different this time, but you know — don't worry, because I'm going to get him back, in some sort of subtle way.

MAC: Right, what — some sort of subtle way that he never finds out about?

MARTIN: Yeah, right.

MAC: Oh.

▶ OFFICE

JOANNA IS ON A CROSS-TRAINING EXERCISE MACHINE IN HER OFFICE. HARRIET SITS DOWN AT HER DESK IN FRONT OF KAREN.

HARRIET: Ten minutes late, that doesn't count does it?

KAREN: I like your cardigan.

HARRIET: Do you?

KAREN: Yeah, the pattern.

HARRIET: It's plain green isn't it?

KAREN: No, the pigs and cows on the back.

HARRIET LOOKS AT THE BACK OF HER CARDIGAN. IT HAS FUZZY FELT ANIMALS ON IT.

HARRIET: Oh, it's fuzzy felt. Aw! Little lamb.

Harriet,
i found this by the photocopier. Is it your womb?
Joanna

▶ GENERAL MEDICAL RECEPTION

THE WARD SISTER BUMPS INTO MAC.

WARD SISTER: Ah, Doctor MacCartney.

MAC: Hello. Yes?

WARD SISTER: Sorry to screw the schedule — you know, on your last day — but Doctor Secretan's had to pop out, said he'd be about twenty minutes.

MAC: (SARCASTICALLY) Fantastic. Yes. I don't expect he bothered with an excuse or an apology?

WARD SISTER: Yeah, he said he'd come to work wearing linen trousers and you could see his cock.

MAC: Fair enough.

MARTIN COMES IN CARRYING GUY'S BRIEFCASE.

MARTIN: Right, where is he?

MAC: He's gone off to change; his cock was visible.

MARTIN: I've got his thing, what shall I do with it?

MAC: Look, I'll take it with me to theatre. You haven't wanked in it have you?

MARTIN: No.

MAC: No.

MARTIN: Do you think I should?

MAC: No. What about his car, is that unscathed?

MARTIN: Well, let's just say there's more saliva in it than usual.

MAC: Can we be a little bit more original; you're a doctor, not a waiter.

MARTIN: Well okay, um — let's put an appendix in his bag, can you get me an appendix?

MAC: What?

MARTIN: What about a heart?

MAC: A heart? For fuck's sake, you're not in the Mafia! Hearts don't just grow on trees, do they?

MARTIN: Right. I am going to rifle through his bag and mess up his things a bit.

MAC: My God, you are evil.

MARTIN: Unopened letters, brilliant! Get him back for opening my exam results.

MAC: You've gone power mad.

MARTIN OPENS AND READS ONE OF GUY'S LETTERS. HE'S VERY SHOCKED BY WHAT'S IN IT.

MAC: Well?

MARTIN: Oh my God. Oh my God!

MAC: What? Are you all right?

MARTIN IS GASPING WITH SHOCK.

MARTIN: Yeah.

MAC: Hey, what is it?

MARTIN: Nothing.

MAC: What is it?

MARTIN: Nothing.

MAC: Come on. Hey...

MARTIN: I'm dizzy. I'm going... I'm going to find a place to lie down...

MARTIN STAGGERS OUT.

MAC: Martin...? Martin...!

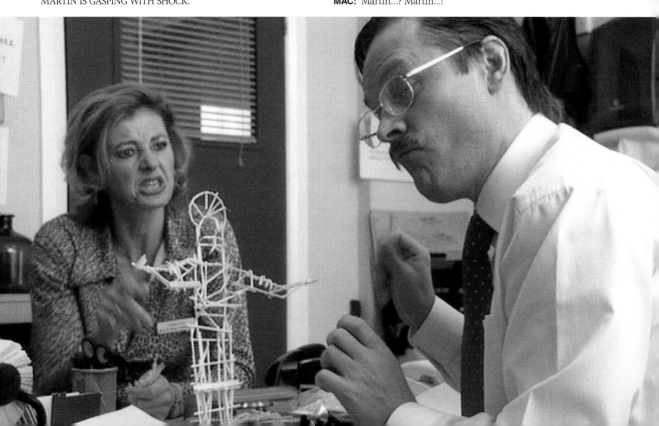

STATHAM IS BUILDING A MATCHSTICK MODEL OF JESUS.

JOANNA: So when you've finished building Jesus, maybe you could stop by my office.

STATHAM: I'm afraid I have other duties to attend to.

JOANNA: What, like looking up cathedrals on the internet?

STATHAM: Writing letters to Christian children in Africa, probably.

JOANNA: Please! Do you really think some starving kid in Upper Zululand is going to be cheered up by a humourless letter from a foreign radiologist with a shitty haircut, who's only found God because no one else will have him?!

STATHAM: I hear your words, but I turn the other cheek.

JOANNA: Alan, I'm just — I'm just trying to make you understand. I just — I just want you to listen to me. I just want — I just want to...

SHE SNAPS THE ARM OFF THE MODEL.

JOANNA: I've got Jesus's arm.

SHE WALKS OUT OF THE OFFICE WITH IT. HE PUTS A SINGLE MATCH IN ITS PLACE AT A RATHER JAUNTY BUT UNCONVENTIONAL ANGLE.

GUY HAS SKI-POLES AND IS PRETEND SKIING. BOYCE IS SUCKING DIRECTLY FROM A WATER COOLER.

BOYCE: Much better trousers by the way.

GUY: Thank you.

CAROLINE COMES PAST.

CAROLINE: Some people are so insensitive...

GUY: What's up? Can I help?

CAROLINE: Not really, no, I had a fight with Angela, that's all.

GUY: Were you wearing bikinis?

CAROLINE: What?

GUY: Bikinis — were you wearing bikinis when you fought? It would help if I could visualise the situation.

CAROLINE KICKS HIS SKI-POLE, GIVES HIM A THREATENING LOOK AND THEN HEADS OFF.

GUY: Yeah, they were wearing bikinis.

BOYCE: Of course.

MARTIN: Um... what would you do if say, hypothetically, okay, you accidentally opened someone's very personal letter, okay? And... this someone was a work colleague, maybe... an anaesthetist maybe, and — and you er... you discovered that he was keeping a secret, and that secret was that he was actually adopted? And... and you accidentally read in the letter that his adopted father had told him who — who — who his biological parents are, okay? What would you do? Would you — would you own up to it and risk being killed? Or — or would you cover all your tracks and just deny all knowledge of the letter?

SUE: Yeah, yeah, yeah, yeah, I can see, yeah.

SUE TAKES HEADPHONES OUT OF HER EARS.

MARTIN: Were you listening to me?

SUE: Yes.

MARTIN: Promise?

SUE: Yes.

MARTIN: Well what would you do then?

SUE: Well... you know, it's — it's obvious, I'd... I'd just, I'd just sit them again next year.

MARTIN: You bloody Nora! You —

SUE HANDS HIM A LOLLY.

SUE: Take this with you.

MARTIN: Yes, thank you.

MARTIN IS FURIOUS — HE LEAVES SUE'S OFFICE.

SUE: (SINGS) "Play that funky music white boy..."

▶▶ X-RAY AREA

MAC IS LOOKING AT SOME X-RAYS. CAROLINE PICKS UP A NEWS-PAPER.

CAROLINE: Hmm, that's interesting.

MAC: What's that?

CAROLINE: It says here, that natural levels of background radiation in Sheffield are ten times the national average...

MAC: I'm still going.

CAROLINE: Good, good, I'm glad. It says here that there are many varieties of flesh-eating spiders in the Sheffield area, some of them up to six feet in diameter.

MAC: No it doesn't.

CAROLINE: Well no, not in so many words, I'm just reading between the lines.

MAC: Ah ha.

CAROLINE: What would happen if you didn't go to Sheffield?

MAC: The earth would spin off its axis and we would all plunge screaming into the heart of the sun.

CAROLINE: No seriously — don't you like it here?

MAC: Specifically here? It's okay, yeah. But you know, I still yearn sometimes for the days when I was over there, close to the skirting, but you should never go back, never go back...

CAROLINE: Why do you have to turn everything into a joke?

MAC: Generally it's to avoid confronting the very real and difficult issues that most proper adults have to deal with.

CAROLINE: Can't you try to be serious for just one minute?

MAC: Yeah, go on then, I'll give it a go.

CAROLINE: We didn't really get on before, did we?

MAC: I wouldn't say that.

CAROLINE: Yes you would. You thought I was some sort of incompetent neurotic who went to a boys' barber, and I thought you were a rude off-hand bloke with ladies' hair.

MAC: Okay, being serious, maybe I would have said that, but I wouldn't say that any more. We... seem to get on okay now, don't we?

CAROLINE: I hope so. I think we do.

MAC: Hmm. Better late than never.

MAC GOES.

▶▶ STATHAM'S OFFICE

JOANNA STORMS IN.

JOANNA: Oh just snap out of it Alan!

STATHAM: You make my faith sound less than genuine. I cannot simply snap out of the love of our Lord.

JOANNA: Just stop it! Just stop pretending to be calm.

STATHAM: This is no pretence.

JOANNA RUFFLES STATHAM'S HAIR, REMOVES HIS GLASSES AND THROWS HIS MATCHES ALL OVER THE DESK. SHE GRABS HIS SEED TRAY OFF THE WINDOWSILL.

STATHAM: Please return those seedlings.

JOANNA: Hmm... shan't.

STATHAM: I want you to — please, put them back where you found them.

JOANNA: No, no, I'm going to eat them.

STATHAM: Don't eat my seedlings.

JOANNA: I'm going to eat your seedlings.

STATHAM: You bloody — you bloody leave them alone, you bastard!

JOANNA EATS A COUPLE OF PLANTS. STATHAM TRIES TO GRAB THEM BACK.

STATHAM: Give them, give them here! You! You dirty, dirty woman!!

THEY WRESTLE AND STATHAM ENDS UP ON TOP OF JOANNA, ACROSS THE DESK, EATING SEEDLINGS AS WELL.

JOANNA: I am, I am, I'm a dirty seedling eating tart!

STATHAM: Feed me, feed me. I love it — talk toilet, talk toilet.

▸▸ CANTEEN

MARTIN IS WITH THE CHAPLAIN, WHO IS READING GUY'S LETTER.

CHAPLAIN: Mon cher Guillaume...

MARTIN: Dear Guy...

CHAPLAIN: Yes, thank you Martin. You really shouldn't have opened this Martin.

MARTIN: Yeah, I know. He's not just a bastard, he's a bastard bastard! Sorry, is it all right to swear in the canteen?

CHAPLAIN: I'd rather you didn't. Right, now... (SHE LOOKS AT THE LETTER) So his real father is Fabien Leclerq, ski instructor. And his mother is a Joanna Pearson, student.

MARTIN: Yeah, but that's her maiden name, okay? And she kept the name that she took from her second marriage, which was Clore — Joanna Clore.

CHAPLAIN: You're fucking joking!

MARTIN: No. She spent a year in Switzerland as an exchange student.

CHAPLAIN: Oh! Can you imagine having that for your mother?!

MARTIN: Yeah, yeah I can actually, in a funny kind of way. But look, I'm sure if you were her son, you would be able to think of some good points.

CHAPLAIN: Does she know? Well she must, I mean otherwise why would they be working in the same hospital?

MARTIN: No, no, she doesn't know.

CHAPLAIN: How do you know?

MARTIN: I — I just know.

CHAPLAIN: Right, you're going to have to give it back to him.

MARTIN: I can't, I can't, he can't know. And look, the envelope's all torn.

CHAPLAIN: Well, you're just going to have to put it in a new envelope and post it to him.

MARTIN: Yeah, but the postmark's from Switzerland, it's from Lausanne.

CHAPLAIN: Ah.

MARTIN: But, right, I've been thinking. If I can type his name and address on a new envelope, go to Switzerland and post it back from there...

CHAPLAIN: Or — or you could say you just opened the envelope but you didn't actually read the letter. Hmm?

MARTIN: Yeah. I'm going to go to Switzerland.

▸▸ LOCKER AREA/MESS

MAC: We can keep in touch you know, if you want.

GUY: Keep in touch? Er — why?

MAC: Or not, if you're not bothered.

GUY: No, let's keep in touch if it'll make you happy.

MAC: Aren't you going to miss me?

GUY: Fuck off!

MAC: Yeah, I'm going to miss you too. Hey...

MAC HUGS GUY.

GUY: Yeah, well, whatever.

MAC: I tell you what, I'll give you a photo, stick it in your locker, of me. We can be like Goose and Maverick in *Top Gun*.

GUY: Yeah, well I'm Maverick.

MAC: Yeah, right! You're Goose.

GUY: No way! What? No way!

MAC: You're Goose.

GUY: No, you're Goose, with the gay pointing and the no chin and the silly moustache.

MAC: Okay, I'll be Ice Man, the best and hardest.

GUY: No actually, you're right, okay, I want to be Ice Man.

MAC: You can't be Ice Man and Maverick.

GUY: All right, I'll be Ice Man, you can be Maverick.

MAC: Fine. Basically you hate me, believing you're the best, but then you develop a respect for me and realise that I am truly the best.

GUY: Oh hang on.

MAC: You develop a kind of gay love type of thing.

GUY: Okay, it's a crap film anyway. I tell you what, I'll be Butch Cassidy, and you can — that's *Butch* Cassidy — and you can be the Sundance Kid. Okay? "Oh, look at me, I'm dancing in the sun like a big kid."

MAC: Great, so I'm better with a gun than you.

GUY: Not necessarily.

MAC: Well not necessarily so, because Sundance was the best gun fighter in the world.

GUY: No, Butch was the best, he just didn't like to talk about it.

MAC: Yeah, not in the film he didn't.

GUY: Yeah, that's because it was sub-text, you know, it's there if you're looking for it.

MAC: Are you ready?

GUY: Yeah. Are you ready?

MAC: Uh-huh.

THEY BURST THROUGH THE DOORS OUT INTO THE CORRIDOR — AS IN THE ENDING OF *BUTCH CASSIDY AND THE SUNDANCE KID.*

▸▸ RADIOLOGY

STATHAM IS GIVING A LECTURE TO SOME STUDENTS.

STATHAM: And of course the pelvis is an immensely complex structure. Some areas are denser than others. Clearly, the denser the area, the less prone to trauma.

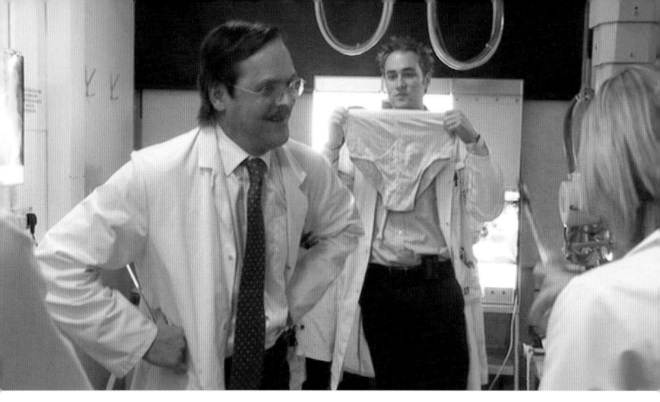

BOYCE JOINS THEM.

STATHAM: Er... good — good evening Mr Boyce.

BOYCE: It's morning actually you toss-bag.

STATHAM: Get out!

BOYCE: No no, you see you're a Christian, so you have to forgive me, that's the whole point.

STATHAM: Not any more. I've decided to take a more agnostic approach, it's less morally demanding.

BOYCE: Oh.

STATHAM: Yes, "oh".

BOYCE: Well I just wish you'd keep me informed.

STATHAM: Right, I hereby inform you to report to my office at nine o'clock tomorrow morning, not ten past nine, not five minutes past nine, nine o'clock precisely, please. You see that device over there Mr Boyce?

BOYCE: What, the clock?

STATHAM: Yes, it's a cunning piece of devilry which allows us to tell the time and thereby be prompt! Hmm?

BOYCE: Yeah. Actually it's remarkably like the one in your bedroom...

STATHAM IS SUDDENLY ON THE BACK FOOT.

STATHAM: If we could leave it there.

BOYCE: Well you know, if you think it's for the best.

STATHAM: (PANICKING) Yes, I do think it's best, if we do... and next you'll — you'll be spinning some bizarre yarn about how you know where everything in my bedroom is because of some cock and bull nonsense about drinking too much wine after a slave auction and — and being in my bed and one of us not wearing any pants, and having — having to, to borrow a pair of pants! Which is...

BOYCE: What, like these?

BOYCE PRODUCES A PAIR OF STATHAM'S PANTS.

BOYCE: Sorry, I haven't had time to wash them yet.

STATHAM IS SPEECHLESS AND JUST WHIMPERS.

▸▸ SQUASH COURT

MAC AND GUY ARE PLAYING SQUASH — GUY IN FULL KIT, MAC JUST PLAYING WITH A PING-PONG BAT. MARTIN LOOKS ON.

MAC: Siobhan?

GUY: Had. Yes. (SPOTTING TWO WOMEN) Hi. Hi ladies.

MAC: Okay.

GUY: Yeah, had both of them as well.

MAC: Receptionist in the path lab.

GUY: Could have. (SERVING) Match point. (HE WINS THE POINT) Nine nil! Oh ho ho. Yeah, oh yeah, oh yeah, oh aaah! That is game, set and match.

MAC: I'd like to say congratulations, well played.

GUY: I think the better man won on the day.

MAC: No.

GUY: Yes.

MAC: Do you know what? I've just got a feeling, maybe it was you who had the hunger.

GUY: Is that right?

MAC: Yep.

GUY: You should look after yourself, my son.

MAC: Yeah.

GUY: You know, I keep myself in peak physical condition.

MAC: Of course you do, ready for that immediate call-up to the Swiss Olympic Association, yeah.

GUY: Yeah, well it could happen. (TO MARTIN) Janet Street Porter, would you please collect the balls? And I think you missed one. Off you go, and the towel.

AS HE LEAVES THE COURT, GUY THROWS THINGS DOWN FOR MARTIN TO PICK UP. MARTIN TRAILS BEHIND MAC AND GUY AS THEY MAKE THEIR WAY DOWN THE CORRIDOR. GUY CHECKS OFF EACH FEMALE THEY PASS ON THEIR WAY.

GUY: Yeah, had... Had front and back.

NURSE: Hi Guy.

GUY: Hi... Oh I wish I hadn't had... Had, twice, while you were going out with her...

MAC: Yeah, right. This is all very well; they're not very great conquests are they?

GUYBALL SCORES

Many of you will be interested to know the latest international Guyball result, from the Secretanstadt, Lausanne:

Guy Secretan 12: 3 Marcus Geissler
(sent off; illegal use of the 'hefty fondue')

Cuckoo Clock Geneva   7: 2   Nazi Gold Rovers

Number of People   3?: 0   Number of People
Who Play   Who Care

Doomed attempt   0: 9   Actually makes you
to appear successful   look sad and
      desperate, Guy

GINGERGIRL   0 : 20   MR BIG BALLS

Dr. Not   1000000000000001 : 0   A Donkey
really bothered

GUY: What do you mean?

MAC: Well, for a start, they're all impressionable young innocents. In mountaineering terms, you've kind of got as far as the foothills. It's not exactly scaling Everest is it?

GUY: What would be Everest?

MAC: Everest would be a woman who is a little bit more mature, who has had some real experience, and who is a woman as opposed to a girl.

QUIZ NIGHT
BIG PRIZES
THURS 8PM

MAC:
Of course you
do, ready for that
immediate call-up
to the Swiss
Olympic
Association,
yeah.

GUY: Like who?

JOANNA: Morning doctors.

GUY: Hi.

MAC: Morning. Morning... (A THOUGHT HAS OCCURRED AND HE LOOKS AT GUY) Morning...

GUY: Oh fuck off!

MAC: Fuck off says you can't.

GUY: Of course I — her?! Easy.

MAC: Can't.

GUY: With my dick tied behind my back.

MAC: You can't.

GUY: Do you want to bet?

MAC: Yeah. My first month's consultant's salary says you can't.

GUY: Well your first month's consultant's salary has got a very big mouth.

MAC: Yeah? Yeah?

GUY: Yeah.

MAC: Are you going to make it shut up are you?!

GUY: Yeah, you're damn right I am.

MAC: Yeah?

GUY: Yeah. We are talking about Joanna here, not Martin?

MAC: Do you know, I think we are, yeah.

GUY: You've got a deal.

MAC: Put it there baby.

GUY: You're going to regret it.

MAC: Yeah?

GUY: Oh yeah. Right.

MAC: Thanks very much.

GUY: You're on.

MAC: Proof required.

GUY: You'll just need to look at her — have you ever seen a completely and utterly satisfied woman?

MAC: Yes, yes, I have, I have. The young dental student that kicked you in the bollocks and made you cry. Do you remember that?

GUY: I was laughing actually.

MAC: Of course you were, of course you were.

MAC GOES. MARTIN COMES UP TO GUY WITH THE SQUASH BALLS.

MARTIN: I think that's it.

GUY: There were seven, there's one missing.

GUY KNOCKS ALL THE BALLS ONTO THE FLOOR FOR MARTIN TO PICK UP AGAIN.

▶▶ **STAFF LIAISON OFFICE**

SUE IS SITTING ASTRIDE HER OFFICE CHAIR, COMPLETELY NAKED. THERE IS A KNOCK ON THE DOOR.

SUE: Enter.

STATHAM COMES IN. HE DOESN'T KNOW WHERE TO LOOK.

SUE: Oh, God, it's you! I was expecting somebody else.

STATHAM STARES AT THE CEILING.

STATHAM: I — I can see that. You do realise you're naked?

SUE: Yes, I know that, you fool! Now what do you want?

STATHAM: I — I don't know.

SUE: Well, get out then!

STATHAM GOES. SUE PICKS UP THE PHONE.

SUE: Yeah, could you page Doctor MacCartney again? Thank you.

SHE LIGHTS A CIGARETTE AND WAITS.

▶▶ **GENERAL MEDICAL RECEPTION**

CAROLINE IS LOOKING AT THE COMPUTER SCREEN. MARTIN COMES UP TO HER.

MARTIN: Can I ask your advice about something?

CAROLINE: Your shirt tucked into your pants doesn't really work for you Martin.

MARTIN: Shit... (HE ADJUSTS HIS SHIRT) No look, it's not about clothes, it's about something more serious.

CAROLINE: More serious than clothes? I don't understand.

MARTIN: It's about relationships. Inter-relationships.

CAROLINE: Not now Martin, I'm trying to find fault with Sheffield...

MARTIN: Well that's going to be easy enough, isn't it?

CAROLINE: Yeah, you'd think, wouldn't you?

MARTIN: You really like Mac don't you?

CAROLINE: Oh... he's all right I suppose.

MARTIN: Yeah, well good luck. Right. I'm going to go and find my brother.

CAROLINE: Okay. (PUZZLED) I thought you were an only child?

MARTIN: Yeah... well I thought so too.

MARTIN GOES. CAROLINE IS CONCENTRATING ON THE COMPUTER.

▶▶ STAFF LIAISON OFFICE

SUE IS FINISHING DRESSING. MAC IS THERE.

SUE: So, you prefer me like this?

MAC: I like clothes, generally.

SUE: Oh all right, have it your way. Okay Doctor Mac, now that you're leaving...

MAC: Yes.

SUE: It falls to me to give you your exit interview.

MAC: Right.

SUE: So, how have you enjoyed working here generally?

MAC: Generally... I've enjoyed it.

SUE: So don't go!

MAC: Excuse me?

SUE: Don't go. Stay.

MAC: I can't stay.

SUE: Why, why, why?

MAC: Well, I can't stay because I've already accepted the post and I don't think Doctor Mancoo is going to retire for a few years, so there's no chance of me getting a similar post here.

SUE: Well, why don't I kill him? Just give me the nod.

MAC: (SMILES) Yeah, okay then, kill him.

SUE: Fine. So, you were saying, generally you found the post here...?

MAC: Yeah, it's been very fulfilling, I've enjoyed it. There've been one or two... Sorry, excuse me, you're not *actually* going to kill him, are you?

SUE: No, of course not. If something were to happen to him, we never had this little chat.

MAC: So you're not going to kill him? See, I don't think you quite understood: I don't want you to kill Doctor Mancoo.

SUE: Of course you don't!

MAC: No. So you really are not going to kill him?

SUE: No.

MAC: Was that a yes or a no?

SUE: It was a no.

MAC: Yeah.

SUE: A big fat no.

MAC: Good. This is my leaving questionnaire, that's probably it, isn't it? Sort of — bye for now?

SUE: Yeah, bye.

MAC: Yep.

SUE: Bye, bye, yeah, okay. And don't worry about that little matter, I'll take care of it.

MAC: What — what matter?

SUE: Exactly.

Rachel,
Do not yodel whilst
i'm in my office.
Joanna

KAREN IS TIMING RACHEL AND KIM AS THEY STRUGGLE TO GET THEIR BRAS OFF UNDER THEIR CLOTHES. RACHEL WINS.

RACHEL: Yes! How long?

KAREN: Ten seconds.

RACHEL: Ten seconds! Champion! Are you going to take me on Karen?

KAREN: No. It's a stupid game.

KAREN LOOKS AT HER BREASTS. SHE PUTS SOME FRUIT DOWN HER BRA TO MAKE THEM BIGGER.

MAC: Backing out, are you?

GUY: No, I — bring it on, I can't wait.

ANGELA AND CAROLINE COME OVER.

GUY: It's Ken and Barbie.

ANGELA & CAROLINE: Hi.

GUY: Oh bloody hell, cheer up!

ANGELA: We would if we could, but it's Mac's last day.

MAC: Aww.

CAROLINE: We're allowed to be miserable.

MAC: They've got a point.

GUY: No! So it's Mac's last day — big deal, cheer up! Lighten up, come on, there'll be other Macs.

CAROLINE: Will there?

GUY: Right, I'm picking you up and I'm spinning you round, like they do in the movies.

CAROLINE: No, no, no, Guy, I don't think this is a good idea.

GUY: Yes.

GUY PICKS CAROLINE UP AND SPINS HER ROUND.

CAROLINE: No really, I don't think this is a good idea! Stop! Oh!

CAROLINE LAUGHS.

GUY: Yes!

CAROLINE: Have you stopped?

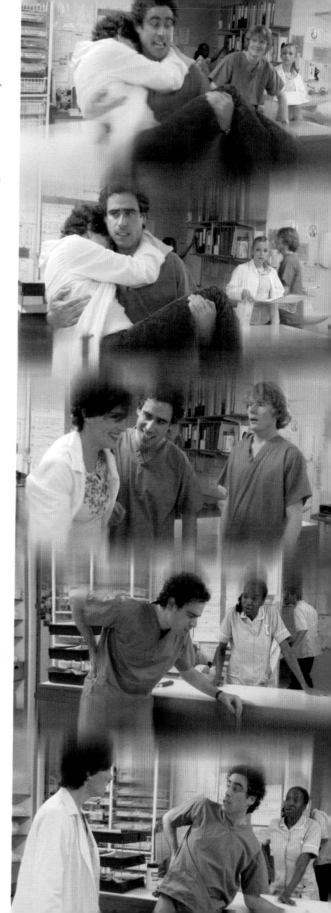

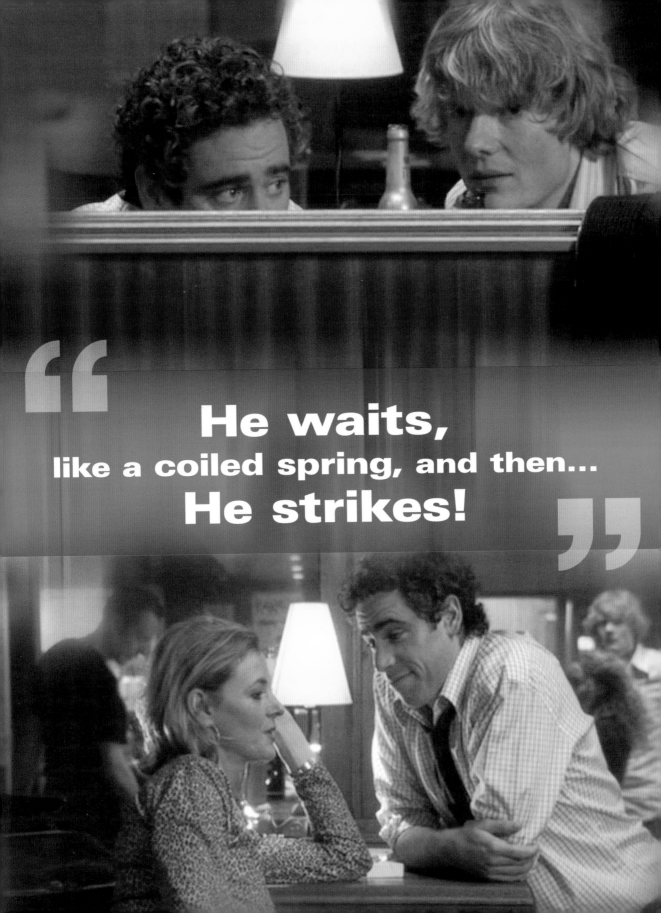

"
He waits,
like a coiled spring, and then...
He strikes!
"

GUY: Yeah. Feel better?

CAROLINE: Um, yeah, I kind of do.

GUY: Yeah.

CAROLINE: Thanks Guy.

GUY: Any time, lovely Caroline.

CAROLINE LAUGHS.

MAC: I'm continuing my final day in this direction...

MAC WALKS OFF.

GUY: Okay.

MAC: Yeah, good luck.

ANGELA: Oh no, wait for me, final day man.

MAC: Woah. See ya!

THEY ALL LEAVE GUY NEXT TO THE COUNTER, WHERE A NURSE IS WORKING. GUY DOUBLES UP IN PAIN.

GUY: Oh! God, she's heavier than she looks.

NURSE: And amazingly, you're slimier than you look.

GUY: Ow, get a doctor.

NURSE: I thought you were one?

GUY: I am! Get another doctor!

NURSE: Er... a proper doctor, hang on... ah, Doctor Todd...?

CAROLINE HAS COME BACK.

GUY: No, no, no not her! Not her!

NURSE: He's hurt his back.

GUY: No! (TO CAROLINE) Hello.

CAROLINE: Have you?

GUY: No.

CAROLINE: Was it from lifting me?

GUY: No, no. You are as light as a feather. Watch, look. I'll lift you up. (HE TRIES TO DO SO) Oh!

NURSE: He said you were heavier than you looked.

GUY: Ow!

CAROLINE: Did he?

SHE PUSHES GUY DOWN AND WALKS OFF.

GUY: God damn! Aargh!

▶▶ **BAR**

MAC AND GUY ARE TOGETHER. JOANNA COMES IN WITH A GROUP OF PEOPLE.

GUY: Oh God, here she is!

MAC: (A DAVID ATTENBOROUGH WHISPER) The hunter spots his prey. But there is a problem; the herd of totty is sticking together, making it hard to target any one individual. He's in luck — the herd has split, leaving one creature alone and vulnerable...

JOANNA: (TO BARMAN) Double vodka.

MAC: ...She's old and weaker than the rest. This surely is his best chance...

GUY: Fuck off.

MAC: ...The hunter will tolerate no interruption to his meticulous preparations. He waits, like a coiled spring, and then... He strikes!

GUY LEAPS OVER THE CHAIR, HURTING HIS BACK.

GUY: Ow! Ow.

GUY DOWNS TWO DRINKS AND GOES OVER TO JOANNA AT THE BAR. HE PRETENDS TO BE FINISHING A PHONE CALL.

GUY: Ow! Help me Jesus! (INTO PHONE) Yeah, I'll see you in Zurich. (HE PUTS THE PHONE AWAY) Joanna!

JOANNA: What?

GUY: Hi.

JOANNA: (WARY) Hello.

GUY: Haven't seen much of you lately.

JOANNA: No, we don't have much call for anaesthetists in the admin block.

GUY: Ha ha! No, I suppose not.

JOANNA: Half the admin girls are doped up to the eyeballs as it is, the last thing we need is you peddling your wares.

GUY: Yeah. Hey, is that — have you got — is that cress in your hair?

JOANNA: No, it's a seedling.

GUY: Hmm. Good God, what extraordinary ear lobes you have.

JOANNA: Are you making a pass at me?

GUY: Is there a law against it?

JOANNA: I heard that you had one.

GUY: What's that?

JOANNA: No one over twenty-five and everyone under.

GUY: Er yeah, well I was a fool. I was... I was shallow. I've realised there are women like you, so I've doubled my upper age limit.

JOANNA: There's no need to double it!

GUY: Let me finish — I doubled it, and then took away ten.

JOANNA: Hmm... complicated.

GUY: Yeah, a bit. Poison...

JOANNA: What?

GUY: You're wearing Poison by Christian Dior.

JOANNA: So?

GUY: The smell is so evocative, it's fifteen years...

JOANNA: I'm sure this conversation was booked in English.

GUY: Sorry, sorry, you see there was this, there was this girl — Angelique. I first saw her on the steps of the Musée des Beaux Arts, in Nice, Avenue des Baumettes, and I don't know why, but I followed her. And well, actually, I followed that scent, Poison, by Christian Dior, as it wafted through the streets, just tantalising me. And you know how it is when you feel you've just known someone...

IN ANOTHER PART OF THE BAR, KAREN GOES UP TO MARTIN.

KAREN: Hello again.

MARTIN: Hello.

KAREN: How are you?

MARTIN: Very well. Yeah.

THEY DON'T KNOW WHAT TO SAY TO EACH OTHER.

MARTIN: You've got nice hair.

KAREN: Have I?

MARTIN: Yeah, sort of, you know, weird kind of candyfloss hair.

KAREN: Thanks.

MARTIN: Would you like to maybe go out for a drink with me sometime? Just us alone, one night — or day, I mean it doesn't have to be a night, in case you think I'm, you know — I'm a murderer, which I'm not. So?

KAREN: Okay then.

MARTIN: Really?

KAREN: Would you like some of my hair? I could cut a bit off for you.

MARTIN: No thanks.

THEY DOWN THEIR DRINKS RATHER FAST. MARTIN BURPS.

MARTIN: Pardon me.

BACK AT THE BAR, GUY CONTINUES HIS 'POISON' STORY.

GUY: ...Do you know what they found at the hospital, clutched in her hand? A copy of *Tess of the D'Ubervilles*, inscribed to me. They actually had to break her fingers to release it. That's what Poison by Christian Dior means to me.

JOANNA: Look, if you fancy a fuck, just say so.

GUY: Do you want to?

JOANNA: Yeah, okay. New balls please.

GUY: Not bad though, eh?

JOANNA: They had to break her fingers?!

JOANNA PINCHES GUY'S ARSE.

GUY: Yeah... ow!

THEY LEAVE IN THE CAR.

▶▶ OUTSIDE HOSPITAL ENTRANCE, NIGHT

DR MANCOO IS LEAVING WORK FOR THE DAY.

STAFF MEMBER: Goodnight Doctor Mancoo.

DR MANCOO: Yes, goodnight, goodnight.

STAFF MEMBER: Goodnight.

DR MANCOO GETS IN HIS CAR AND DRIVES OFF, REVEALING SUE ON A TROLLEY UNDERNEATH THE CAR WEARING A HEAD TORCH AND HOLDING A PAIR OF CABLE CUTTERS.

SUE: Goodbye Doctor Mancoo. Bye bye.

▸▸ **BAR**

CAROLINE GOES UP TO MAC AND EMMY.

CAROLINE: Stop right there.

MAC: Hi.

EMMY: Hi.

CAROLINE: Stop right there!

MAC: We are, we're stopped; we're not moving, look.

EMMY: We're not moving.

EMMY LAUGHS. CAROLINE LOOKS ANGRY.

CAROLINE: Can I have a word?

MAC: Yeah, course you can.

EMMY: Course you can.

CAROLINE: Without the parrot.

MAC: Anything you want to say, you can say in front of Polly.

EMMY: It's Emmy!

MAC: Shit, I know, yeah...

CAROLINE: Okay, okay. Shall we just say that I've been doing a little bit of surfing.

MAC: Radical, dude!

CAROLINE: No, on the internet. Let's talk about your career so far, shall we, Emily Lewis Westbrook?

EMMY: Oh, okay.

MAC: Shouldn't you have like a big red book?

CAROLINE: Right. Emily Lewis Westbrook, at the age of twenty-two, was thrown out of medical school for inappropriate behaviour and financial irregularities. In '96, she founded the Holistic Power Clinic, the HPC, in Dublin. Her co-director at the HPC is currently serving four years, whilst Emily herself served six months for malpractice and forging physiotherapy qualifications. Shall I continue?

EMMY: No.

CAROLINE: Do these events ring a bell? Emily?

EMMY: Yes they do.

MAC: Good God!

CAROLINE: I just bet they do.

MAC: That is ridiculous, I am such a fantastic judge of character...

EMMY: Can I just say one thing in my defence?

CAROLINE: Go on then, you fraudulent little tart!

EMMY: I'm not that Emily Lewis Westbrook. I'm a different Emily Lewis Westbrook. It's a small point I know, but I just thought I'd mention it. In fact Emily Lewis Westbrook isn't her real name at all, and I have in the past had to take out a private action against her, as obviously it's particularly inconvenient when we both claim to be physiotherapists.

THERE IS SILENCE FOR A BIT.

CAROLINE: I will... I will of course take that into consideration.

CAROLINE WALKS OFF, VERY EMBARRASSED.

▶▶ **GUY'S CAR**

GUY IS DRIVING JOANNA BACK TO HIS FLAT.

GUY: It's not a stupid name.

JOANNA: What, Secretan? It sounds a bit like secretion, and that's not entirely pleasant is it?

GUY: Well it depends on what's being secreted.

JOANNA: True.

GUY: Yeah, it's Swiss.

JOANNA: Yeah, so I believe.

GUY: Would you like me to tell you a little bit about Switzerland? You probably only know about Toblerones and the tragic shortage of beaches.

JOANNA: No, I know plenty about Switzerland, thanks. I went to school there for a year when I was fifteen. You know, exchange student. I used to go skiing in Gstaad.

GUY: Ah, I've been to Gstaad many times.

JOANNA: Oh, well maybe we've bumped into each other without knowing.

GUY: I shouldn't think so; I wouldn't have been born.

JOANNA GIVES HIM A LOOK.

GUY: Let me finish — I wouldn't have been born there, in Gstaad, I mean — but actually, thinking about it, that's irrelevant, so yes, we could easily have bumped into each other, yeah. Yeah. Easily.

JOANNA: You don't sound very Swiss.

GUY: Yeah, well my dad moved to London when I was four. He was one of the Gnomes of Zurich.

JOANNA: What was that, a circus act?

GUY: What?!

JOANNA: Was he a dwarf?

GUY: Jesus! The Gnomes of Zurich, international financiers, bankers.

JOANNA: Oh, sorry.

GUY: I mean, the Gnomes of Zurich, everybody knows that!

JOANNA: Well I didn't, I'm very sorry.

GUY: I can't believe you thought my dad was a dwarf!

JOANNA: Let's just leave it, shall we?

GUY: Jesus!

▶▶ **BAR**

MARTIN GOES OVER TO MAC AT THE BAR.

MARTIN: Are you all right mate?

MAC: All right mate.

MARTIN: Where's Guy? You're wet.

MAC: Yeah I know, someone poured beer over my head here. It's fine; it's really good for your hair. Are you all right?

MARTIN: Yeah, I've just pulled!

MAC: You've pulled? Really?

MARTIN: Yeah, yeah, over there.

MAC: No?

MARTIN: Yeah.

MAC: Well done man, wow! Yeah! Who did you pull?

MARTIN: Um... some office totty.

MAC: Careful, careful, you're going to start sounding like Guy.

MARTIN: Guy, yeah, where is he?

MAC: I don't know, I think he went off with Joanna.

MARTIN: Went off?

MAC: Yeah.

MARTIN: Why would he want to go off with Joanna?

MAC: Oh, I don't know, maybe because he fancies her.

MARTIN: That is... disgusting!

MAC: Hey, hey, calm down. Calm down, all right, she's a tiny bit older than he is.

MARTIN: That is obscene!

MARTIN GRABS MAC'S PINT AND A CIGARETTE.

MAC: Just live and let live — you don't drink Guinness. You don't smoke fags.

MARTIN: Well — well did they go, you know, to have...?

MAC: What?

MARTIN: Are they going to do *things*?

MAC: Things? Yeah, I think that things are pretty much top of his agenda.

MARTIN: Over my dead body!

MAC: Well, that is obscene.

MARTIN: They can't, they mustn't.

MAC: Why not?

MARTIN: Well... because she's mine!

MARTIN RUSHES OUT.

MAC: Argh! Jesus, fuck!

▶▶ **GUY'S CAR**

GUY HAS 'SEX MACHINE' PLAYING IN HIS CAR. JOANNA PUTS HER TONGUE IN HIS EAR.

▶▶ **HOSPITAL CAR PARK**

STATHAM IS LEAVING THE HOSPITAL. HE SEES THAT ONE ENTIRE SIDE OF THE BUILDING IS COVERED BY A HUGE PROJECTION OF HIMSELF HAVING GAY ANAL SEX AND BRANDISHING A COWBOY HAT. HE GOES BERSERK.

STATHAM: Boyce! No! Boyce!!

HE JUMPS UP TO TRY AND COVER THE IMAGE.

▶▶ **GUY'S FLAT**

GUY AND JOANNA ARRIVE.

JOANNA: Hmm, nice pad.

GUY: Oh yes.

JOANNA: Bathroom?

GUY: Through there.

JOANNA: I'll just… slip into something…

GUY: More comfortable?

JOANNA: That isn't chaffing me quite so much. New thong, it makes me feel like a slice of Edam.

GUY: Ha ha! (TO HIMSELF, ONCE SHE'S GONE) Oh Jesus!

GUY DRINKS STRAIGHT FROM A WHISKY BOTTLE. HE TRIES TO PSYCH HIMSELF UP.

GUY: Argh! Come on!

GUY RIGS UP A HIDDEN VIDEO CAMERA IN A BAG.

JOANNA (OOV): Have you got any vodka?

GUY: Yeah. Yeah, coming up. Yeah.

HE GETS OUT THE BOTTLES, THEN TURNS THE VIDEO CAMERA ON.

GUY: (INTO THE LENS) Right, you ginger fucking freak! Welcome to the undersea world of Cock Cousteau. I'm going to be plumbing depths that only a few thousand men have ever been before.

JOANNA COMES OUT OF THE BATHROOM.

JOANNA: What's up, Doc?

GUY: Oh, look at the state of you.

SHE HOLDS A JAR.

JOANNA: Smashed mango and summer blush peach.

GUY: No thanks; I've already eaten.

JOANNA: Do you want to go first, or shall I?

GUY: No, you go, I'll… I'll rub it on you.

JOANNA: Can you flick it across me first in big stringy blobs…?

GUY: Right, of course.

JOANNA: I knew you'd like that.

GUY: Yeah. I'm just going to — just going to move you.

GUY POSITIONS JOANNA IN FRONT OF THE CAMERA.

GUY: Oh, trim bush…

JOANNA: What?

GUY: TrIm — end — ush.

▸▸ LECTURE THEATRE

CAROLINE IS DEPRESSED, SITTING ALONE. MAC COMES IN.

CAROLINE: Go away.

MAC: Shan't.

CAROLINE: I am such a tit.

MAC: Yeah… yeah.

CAROLINE: You don't have to agree with me.

MAC: I was just being polite.

CAROLINE: Thanks.

MAC: I was very impressed.

CAROLINE: By what? Me wrongly attacking your girlfriend?

MAC: These things happen.

CAROLINE: I called her a fraudulent little tart.

MAC: Yeah. Still, it was the thought that counts.

CAROLINE: What does that mean?

MAC: Well, I was impressed you… you felt you needed to run a check on her.

CAROLINE: Well, it's a fairly standard security procedure.

MAC: Oh I see, I see. Have you run checks on all 850 members of staff?

CAROLINE: No, not yet.

MAC: How many so far?

CAROLINE: Just her so far.

MAC: Oh.

CAROLINE: I guess it was just random testing.

MAC: I love that.

CAROLINE: What?

MAC: The way your random testing comes up with my ex-girl-friend.

CAROLINE: Well don't flatter yourself. (PAUSE AS CAROLINE REGISTERS THIS) Your *ex*-girlfriend?

MAC: Hmm, yeah. Well we had an exchange of words and I got quite a nice lager shampoo. She… you know, she said she thought that I ought to be angry with you.

CAROLINE: Yeah, yeah, you should have been.

MAC: I know, I know, yeah. Whereas in fact, strangely, I found myself a) impressed, b) amused, and c)…

CAROLINE: You already knew about the other Emily Lewis West-brook didn't you?

MAC: Well, she'd… she mentioned it.

CAROLINE: You bastard. What was c)?

MAC: c)? That was er…

MAC AND CAROLINE KISS.

▸▸ OUTSIDE GUY'S BLOCK OF FLATS

MARTIN IS FRANTICALLY LOOKING FOR GUY AND JOANNA. HE CAN'T GET INTO THE BUILDING.

▸▸ GUY'S BEDROOM

JOANNA IS IN BED, WAITING FOR GUY.

JOANNA: Where are you dream-boy?

GUY COMES IN FROM THE BATHROOM.

GUY: I'm right here, dream... woman.

JOANNA: Girl.

GUY: Whatever. Why have you got a hypodermic in your bag?

JOANNA: Yeah, don't touch that.

GUY: What's it for?

JOANNA: It's nothing, it's — oh, it's heroin.

GUY: No it's not; (READING FROM BOTTLE) it's botulinum toxin type A; it's Botox.

JOANNA: Yeah, all right, all right, there are some clinical trials going on, they needed a guinea pig, all right?

GUY: Guinea pig? You've got enough in there to smooth over a small herd of elephants.

JOANNA: Oh, yeah — just get back into bed, okay?

▶▶ GUY'S BLOCK OF FLATS

SOMEONE COMES OUT OF THE MAIN DOOR OF THE BUILDING, SO MARTIN MANAGES TO GET IN.

▶▶ GUY'S BEDROOM

GUY IS PLAYING TO THE HIDDEN CAMERA.

GUY: So... you were saying how — ow — how good I was? Perhaps you'd like to give me a score, on a scale of eight to ten?

JOANNA: Oh I don't know.

GUY: You can feel free to go to eleven if you want, and remember, I don't always call out my own name when I come.

JOANNA: Yeah, well that was just a bit of a warm-up really,

wasn't it? I mean I'll give you your score after the main action.

GUY: Right, that's it! You're getting my best moves.

JOANNA: Oh Christ.

GUY: You hussy!

JOANNA: Hang on, hang on.

GUY: Come here, you dirty... woman.

▶▶ STAIRWELL, BLOCK OF FLATS

MARTIN BANGS ON THE DOOR.

MARTIN: Let me in, let me in! Stop!

▶▶ GUY'S BEDROOM

GUY IS MANOEUVERING HIMSELF.

GUY: No, hold on. No...

▶▶ STAIRWELL, BLOCK OF FLATS

MARTIN SHOUTS THROUGH THE DOOR.

MARTIN: Do not sleep with that woman!

A MAN OPENS THE DOOR BRANDISHING A KITCHEN IMPLE-MENT. HIS WIFE STANDS BEHIIND HIM.

MAN: Who are you?

MARTIN: Sorry, I thought this was Guy Secretan's flat.

WOMAN: No, that wanker lives upstairs. Top floor.

▶▶ GUY'S BEDROOM

GUY: No, you're going to have to give me ten more minutes...

JOANNA LOOKS AT GUY'S BEDSIDE TABLE.

JOANNA: Why have you got a picture of men with skis by your bed?

GUY: Don't laugh, one of them's my biological father.

JOANNA: What?

GUY: Yeah, one of them's my real father. That's the only picture I've got of him. I was abandoned on the steps of the ski school when I was two days old.

JOANNA SITS BOLT UPRIGHT.

JOANNA: (IN HORROR) Oh my God!

GUY: It's all right babe; I'm over it.

JOANNA: (HARDLY DARING TO ASK) And your mother?

GUY: Never knew her, she just dumped me and ran, you know, she left me a note saying one of the instructors was my father, but she didn't know which one! My pretend father keeps threatening to, you know, release all the details to me, but frankly I couldn't be bothered... What's wrong with you? Are you all right?

JOANNA SUDDENLY LOOKS QUITE ILL.

JOANNA: Yeah, I'm fine. Um... Actually um, I think maybe I should go.

GUY: Do you know what baby? You shouldn't think; you should just feel.

HE FONDLES HER BREAST.

JOANNA: Oh my God, I think I'm going to be sick! Oh my God! God!

JOANNA RUNS INTO THE BATHROOM.

GUY: Why are they always sick?

THERE IS A LOUD BANGING ON THE DOOR.

MARTIN (OOV): Stop!

GUY: What the — ? Who the hell...?! Oi!

MARTIN (OOV): Let me in or I'll break the door down!

GUY OPENS THE DOOR AND MARTIN — WHO WAS TRYING TO BREAK IT DOWN — FALLS ON THE FLOOR.

GUY: Doctor Tit?

MARTIN: You didn't — ? You — ? Did you — ?

GUY SLAPS MARTIN.

MARTIN: Don't do it!

GUY: Do what?

MARTIN: Sleep with Joanna.

GUY: I can sleep with whoever I want.

MARTIN: No, no, you can't, there's reasons.

GUY: What reasons? It's not like either of us is married.

MARTIN: Bigger.

GUY: What?

MARTIN: Bigger reasons.

GUY: What, one of us has a disease?

MARTIN: No, bigger.

GUY: She's my long lost sister?!

MARTIN: Similar.

GUY: What's similar to that? She's my long lost brother?

MARTIN DOES THE CHARADES ACTION FOR 'SOUNDS LIKE'.

GUY: Why are you masturbating your ear?

MARTIN: No...

GUY: Oh *sounds like* brother. Smother?

MARTIN DOES THE FINGER ACTION THAT MEANS 'SHORTER'.

GUY: Shorter? She's my long lost smoo?

MARTIN TAPS TWO FINGERS ON HIS ARM.

GUY: Two...? Two arms? Two syllables. What?! One syllable, one syllable...

MARTIN CAN'T SAY THE WORD. HE DOES MORE ACTIONS.

GUY: Buzzy buzzy penis?

MARTIN: She's my smoo too!

GUY: She — she's your smoo? And my smoo?

THE AWFUL TRUTH HAS DAWNED ON GUY.

MARTIN: What are we going to do?

THEY WHACK EACH OTHER.

▸▸ **HOSPITAL ENTRANCE, NIGHT**

CAROLINE: Do you, do you want to come round my gaff tonight then?

MAC: Come round your gaff?

CAROLINE: It's not rude.

MAC: I never said it was.

CAROLINE: Well you implied it with the tone of your voice.

MAC: I'm not coming if it's not rude.

CAROLINE: Okay. It's quite rude then.

MAC: I'll be there. Okay.

SUE RUNS UP TO THEM IN A STATE OF BREATHLESS PANIC.

SUE: Stooopppp!!

MAC: Woah!

CAROLINE: What? What?!

SUE: There's — there's been a — a — a — some — there's been an incident at...

MAC: Sssh.

SUE: There's been an incident at Guy's flat!

MAC: Slowly, slowly. Guy's what?

SUE: (DOES STABBING ACTIONS) A stabbing, a stabbing! At Guy's flat!

MAC: Right, okay, okay, okay.

SUE: Yes, yes, yes. Yes, up, yes.

MAC: Come on, let's go, let's go.

MAC AND CAROLINE JUMP INTO THE BACK OF THE AMBULANCE THAT IS ABOUT TO SET OFF. SUE GETS LEFT OUT.

CAROLINE: No, not you, not you, not you!

MAC: Guy's flat. Come on, in we go, in we go, in we go. (TO SUE AS HE CLOSES THE BACK DOORS) No!

MAC AND CAROLINE DRIVE AWAY IN THE AMBULANCE.

SUE: (DISTRAUGHT) No, no, no, no! Hey, no, no, listen, listen! She's not good enough for you! She's never going to be good enough for you Mac! She doesn't have a fanny! No, stop!

▸▸ **OUTSIDE GUY'S FLAT**

MARTIN IS CRAWLING FULL-LENGTH DOWN THE STAIRS AND STAGGERING OUT. HIS LEGS APPEAR TO BE COMPLETELY STIFF. THE AMBULANCE PULLS UP, MAC AND CAROLINE GET OUT.

MARTIN: I had to warn them.

MAC: Warn who?

MARTIN: Guy and Joanna. Somebody had to tell them.

MAC: Tell them what?

MARTIN: That they're mother and son, we're half brothers. It didn't go down too well.

CAROLINE: Oh — what's wrong with you?

MAC: Apart from a tendency to talk bollocks?

MARTIN: Guy didn't believe me, so he stuck Botox in my legs. My legs are Botoxed.

MAC: Oh Christ! Go and lie down in the big white taxi, all right?

MARTIN: Okay.

JOANNA STAGGERS OUT OF THE APARTMENTS, IN A STATE OF COLLAPSE.

MARTIN: I'll be fine.

MARTIN FALLS OVER.

JOANNA: Taxi! Taxi!

SHE TRIES TO HAIL A CAB BUT COLLAPSES.

JOANNA: Hello Doctor MacCartney, Doctor Todd.

MAC: Oh dear. Okay, okay.

JOANNA: No, it's fine, it's fine, one too many vodkas I expect.

CAROLINE: You've got a hypodermic needle in your arm.

JOANNA: No, no, that's fine, it's fine, I'm a diabetic. It's fine. It's supposed to be like that. Will you all just fuck off!!

MAC: Nice and easy.

GUY COMES OUT, VERY DRUNK AND RANTING.

MAC: Nice and easy.

GUY: Where's my fucking car?!

MAC: Hello. Hello.

GUY: Morning.

MAC: Okay?

GUY: Yeah.

MAC: Where are you going?

GUY: I'm going for a little spin.

MAC: Yeah, not like that you're not.

GUY: (LOOKS DOWN AT HIS SHORT DRESSING GOWN) Um — what, a bit flashy? I think this is a bit smart-cajsh.

MAC: No, I think you look terrific, yeah. What I'm worried about is the units of alcohol in your bloodstream.

GUY: I know. I don't care.

MAC: You will care if you smash yourself to pieces.

GUY: No, no, I won't actually.

MAC: Okay, you will care if you smash your car to pieces.

CAROLINE, SUE WHITE, KAREN AND THE CHAPLAIN ARE GATHERED TOGETHER, WAITING ANXIOUSLY FOR NEWS OF THE RUNAWAY AMBULANCE.

KAREN: Just thinking about it makes me feel dirty, yucky.

CHAPLAIN: Yes, all right, they didn't know at the time.

CAROLINE: It's like a bad dream.

KAREN: They're quite alike really, mentally. And Martin's related to them, Martin's part of a family of mad people.

CAROLINE: Ironically, Martin's probably the sanest person in this hospital.

SUE: Yeah. Well apart from me, of course.

CHAPLAIN: I'm just worried about what he might do.

SUE: Well, he's not going to show his face around here, that's for certain. Not after that, no. He's going to have to move to America and live in a caravan with his mother, where they'll have big fore-headed children with very small hands. Very small.

GUY: That's a point. Shit!

MAC: Come on, I knew you'd see sense, come on.

GUY: Let me finish — I'm going to, I'm going to, and then I'm going to...

GUY SWINGS ROUND AND PUNCHES MAC IN THE FACE.

GUY: This is your fault! I'm going to take this big chap over here.

GUY GETS IN THE AMBULANCE AND STARTS TO DRIVE IT AWAY. WE SEE MARTIN LYING IN THE BACK — HE LOOKS UP IN SURPRISE AS THE VEHICLE MOVES OFF.

MAC: Fuck!

MAC RUNS AFTER THE AMBULANCE AND JUST MANAGES TO JUMP IN THROUGH THE BACK DOORS BEFORE IT DISAPPEARS.

CAROLINE: You don't think they're going to keep on sleeping together now they know?

SUE: Yes! Of course they will, he's a pervert. And she's just desperate.

ANGELA JOINS THEM.

ANGELA: Any news?

CAROLINE: Last we heard, they were on the B4778.

CHAPLAIN: Somewhere in Wales.

CAROLINE: And the police say Mac's going to try and get them to turn back.

SUE: Poor Mac, oh God...

CAROLINE: Yes, poor Mac. (TO SUE) I'll say that, actually.

CHAPLAIN: Look, I'm sure they're going to be fine.

SUE: Fine?! Well mummy's boy's driving and he's pissed out of his skull, I don't think it's going to be fine!

▸▸ IN THE AMBULANCE, COUNTRYSIDE

MARTIN IS IN THE BACK, MAC IS ON HIS MOBILE PHONE TO THE POLICE AND GUY IS DRIVING WILDLY.

MAC: No, he's definitely getting more rational... I think — I think I can get him to stop, yeah.

GUY: Who are you talking to?

MAC: The filth.

GUY: (SHOUTS) Come and get me porkie!

MAC: No, he's not... What? No, he's had a bit of a shock recently, and it's just left him a little bit unbalanced.

GUY: Look at me Ma, top of the world!

MAC: Yeah, well — no, he had sex with his mother.

GUY: Don't tell them that!

MAC: Why not?

GUY: Jesus! What's wrong with you?!

MAC: Why not? It's not a crime... (TO THE PHONE) Oh it is? Wow! (TO GUY) Apparently you can get up to seven years.

GUY: This is you trying to talk someone *out* of a suicidal depression is it?

MAC: Yeah, I'm just giving them mitigating circumstances for joy-riding.

GUY: Joy-riding? Do I look like I'm joyous?

MAC: Fine, fine, fine. I'll check out the penalties for misery-riding.

GUY: I can't believe you told them!

MAC: (TO THE PHONE) Hello? Yeah, it's me again, yeah. Yeah. No, forget the mother thing, that was a slip of the tongue, yeah, yeah. What I meant was, no, he's just discovered that one of his colleagues is in fact his brother.

MARTIN & GUY: Half brother!

MAC: Half brother, yeah. Can I get back to you...?

GUY SNATCHES THE MOBILE PHONE OFF MAC.

GUY: Fuck off Kojak!

HE THROWS THE PHONE OUT OF THE WINDOW.

MAC: That's my fucking mobile!

GUY: Fuck off!

MAC: Get your hands on the wheel.

GUY: Sod the wheel, fuck off!

THE AMBULANCE SWERVES THROUGH A GATE AND HEADS OFF ACROSS A FIELD. MAC PICKS UP THE RADIO HANDSET.

MAC: Hello? Mayday.

GUY: Give me that!

GUY RIPS IT OUT OF THE AMBULANCE AND THROWS IT OUT OF THE WINDOW.

GUY: Get off the fucking phone! Just go back to fucking fairyland!

THEY SEE SOME SHEEP IN FRONT OF THE AMBULANCE.

GUY & MAC: Sheeeeep!!

THE AMBULANCE SWERVES, MISSING THE SHEEP, BUT ENDS UP LODGED PRECARIOUSLY HANGING HALF OVER A CLIFF WITH

THE BACK DOORS OPEN FACING THE SEA.

CHAPEL GARDEN, EARLY MORNING

THE WOMEN ARE STILL WAITING NERVOUSLY.

KAREN: Could we have a quick huddle?

SUE: Well Doctor Todd will give you a cuddle; she's into that.

KAREN: A huddle, not a cuddle.

CAROLINE: What do you mean, "I'm into that"?

SUE: You know.

CAROLINE: I do not!

SUE WAGGLES HER TONGUE AT CAROLINE.

KAREN: (TO THE CHAPLAIN) A group huddle would be a good thing, wouldn't it — spiritually?

CHAPLAIN: Um, well I...

KAREN: (TO CAROLINE) Wouldn't it?

CAROLINE: Well it might be. As long as it's a group, not just you and me.

KAREN: Is that a yes?

CAROLINE: Yes, all right.

SUE: No surprises there then.

CAROLINE: Shut up!!

CHAPLAIN: Okay, okay, this is just the tension speaking. I think it's a great idea. Let's all have a huddle, a moment's contemplation in complete silence, in the hope that our friends will be returned to us safe and sound very soon.

THEY FORM A HUDDLE.

AMBULANCE, EDGE OF CLIFF

THE AMBULANCE IS TEETERING ON THE BRINK. THE OCCUPANTS DARE NOT MOVE.

MAC: Okay, okay, very calm. Very careful, no sudden moves.

MAC AND GUY ARE BALANCING THE FRONT END OF THE AMBULANCE. MARTIN IS IN THE BACK, UNABLE TO MOVE.

MARTIN: Jesus!

MAC: If Martin climbs forward, we'll be all right; we can all get out.

MARTIN: I can't move, my legs are like zeppelins.

MAC: Okay, all right, okay. Okay.

GUY: If Martin can't move, what are the options?

MAC: Okay. If we get out and leave him, Martin will go over the edge. If we go down and get him, we'll all go over the edge.

GUY: That's tricky. Okay, that's enough debate; let's move to a vote.

MARTIN: Don't worry about me, you get out. I'll take my chances.

MAC: Can't let you do that I'm afraid, Martin.

GUY: Well he has got a point...

MAC: Shut up.

GUY: What? What? I mean, you know, the way I see it, either three people die or one person dies.

MAC: Yeah, and why should it be Martin?

GUY: Isn't it obvious? Look at him!

MAC: No, it's not obvious.

GUY: Look at his face. He's all wrong.

MAC: He's your half brother.

GUY: Will you stop saying that!

MAC: He's your half brother.

THE AMBULANCE SWAYS AS THOUGH IT'S GOING TO FALL.

MARTIN: No, no!

GUY: No, no!

MAC: Martin! Okay, okay.

GUY: No! If, if he wants to go, who are we to stop him?

MARTIN: Guy's right. Well, I've never really done anything to make the world a better place. Not like you two proper doctors. So just save yourselves. This will be my one big gesture, last chance to prove myself.

GUY: That is right. Until — until you hit the ground anyway.

MAC: No, listen. All of us are going home. All of us or none of us.

GUY: What are we, The Three Musketeers?

MAC: Yeah, okay, yeah.

GUY: Can I be Porthos?

MAC: No, I'm Porthos, you can be Aramis.

GUY: Fuck off, that's a perfume, I don't want to be a perfume!

MAC: Why not?

GUY: Well, it's like being called Paco Rabanne or L'Air du Temps.

MAC: Okay, you can be d'Artagnan.

GUY: No, actually, because d'Artagnan wasn't one of the three, he was, you know, he was trying to become a musketeer. He was unqualified. So if anyone should be d'Artagnan, it's Martin.

MAC: Okay, if you're not d'Artagnan, you're not Porthos, you're not Aramis, that would make you...

GUY: The other one.

MAC: Yeah, whose name is...?

GUY: I know this, um...

CAROLINE, SUE, ANGELA, KAREN AND THE CHAPLAIN ARE IN A HUDDLE. SUE BREAKS AWAY FROM THE CIRCLE.

SUE: (POINTING AT CAROLINE) She just touched my jacksie! Yeah, the one without the fanny, touched my jacksie!

CAROLINE CHASES SUE ROUND AND ROUND THE BENCH.

CAROLINE: You bastard!

MARTIN: I still think you should just get out.

MAC: You've got too much to live for. What's her name — is it Karen?

GUY: Karen.

MAC: Karen would want you to live.

MARTIN: Well Caroline would want *you* to live.

MAC: Yeah, you know, we've all got nice reasons like that we can think of, but — (HE LOOKS AT GUY) ...well most of us have anyway.

GUY: I've got reasons, I've got — I've got reasons to be saved.

MAC: Yeah, have you? Like what?

GUY: I can't die until I...

MAC: Until what?

GUY: Until I... um... until I remember the name of the third Musketeer.

MAC AND GUY CONTEMPLATE THIS STATEMENT. THERE IS SILENCE.

MARTIN: Athos.

MAC: Yep.

GUY: Oh yeah. Athos.

THE AMBULANCE TILTS AND GROANS. THE CAMERA PANS UP TO A SHOT OF THE SEA AND DISTANT CLIFFS.